A People's Reformation

MCGILL-QUEEN'S STUDIES IN THE HISTORY OF RELIGION
Volumes in this series have been supported by the Jackman Foundation of Toronto.

SERIES ONE: G.A. RAWLYK, EDITOR

1 Small Differences
Irish Catholics and Irish Protestants, 1815–1922
An International Perspective
Donald Harman Akenson

2 Two Worlds
The Protestant Culture of Nineteenth-Century Ontario
William Westfall

3 An Evangelical Mind
Nathanael Burwash and the Methodist Tradition in Canada, 1839–1918
Marguerite Van Die

4 The Dévotes
Women and Church in Seventeenth-Century France
Elizabeth Rapley

5 The Evangelical Century
College and Creed in English Canada from the Great Revival to the Great Depression
Michael Gauvreau

6 The German Peasants' War and Anabaptist Community of Goods
James M. Stayer

7 A World Mission
Canadian Protestantism and the Quest for a New International Order, 1918–1939
Robert Wright

8 Serving the Present Age
Revivalism, Progressivism, and the Methodist Tradition in Canada
Phyllis D. Airhart

9 A Sensitive Independence
Canadian Methodist Women Missionaries in Canada and the Orient, 1881–1925
Rosemary R. Gagan

10 God's Peoples
Covenant and Land in South Africa, Israel, and Ulster
Donald Harman Akenson

11 Creed and Culture
The Place of English-Speaking Catholics in Canadian Society, 1750–1930
Edited by Terrence Murphy and Gerald Stortz

12 Piety and Nationalism
Lay Voluntary Associations and the Creation of an Irish-Catholic Community in Toronto, 1850–1895
Brian P. Clarke

13 Amazing Grace
Studies in Evangelicalism in Australia, Britain, Canada, and the United States
Edited by George Rawlyk and Mark A. Noll

14 Children of Peace
W. John McIntyre

15 A Solitary Pillar
Montreal's Anglican Church and the Quiet Revolution
Joan Marshall

16 Padres in No Man's Land
Canadian Chaplains and the Great War
Duff Crerar

17 Christian Ethics and Political Economy in North America
A Critical Analysis
P. Travis Kroeker

18 Pilgrims in Lotus Land
Conservative Protestantism in British Columbia, 1917–1981
Robert K. Burkinshaw

19 Through Sunshine and Shadow
The Woman's Christian Temperance Union, Evangelicalism, and Reform in Ontario, 1874–1930
Sharon Cook

20 Church, College, and Clergy
A History of Theological Education at Knox College, Toronto, 1844–1994
Brian J. Fraser

21 The Lord's Dominion
The History of Canadian Methodism
Neil Semple

22 A Full-Orbed Christianity
The Protestant Churches and Social Welfare in Canada, 1900–1940
Nancy Christie and Michael Gauvreau

23 Evangelism and Apostasy
The Evolution and Impact of Evangelicals in Modern Mexico
Kurt Bowen

24 The Chignecto Covenanters
A Regional History of Reformed Presbyterianism in New Brunswick and Nova Scotia, 1827–1905
Eldon Hay

25 Methodists and Women's Education in Ontario, 1836–1925
Johanne Selles

26 Puritanism and Historical Controversy
William Lamont

SERIES TWO IN MEMORY OF GEORGE RAWLYK
DONALD HARMAN AKENSON, EDITOR

1 Marguerite Bourgeoys and Montreal, 1640–1665
Patricia Simpson

2 Aspects of the Canadian Evangelical Experience
Edited by G.A. Rawlyk

3 Infinity, Faith, and Time
Christian Humanism and Renaissance Literature
John Spencer Hill

4 The Contribution of Presbyterianism to the Maritime Provinces of Canada
Edited by Charles H.H. Scobie and G.A. Rawlyk

5 Labour, Love, and Prayer
Female Piety in Ulster Religious Literature, 1850–1914
Andrea Ebel Brozyna

6 The Waning of the Green
Catholics, the Irish, and Identity in Toronto, 1887–1922
Mark G. McGowan

7 Religion and Nationality in Western Ukraine
The Greek Catholic Church and the Ruthenian National Movement in Galicia, 1867–1900
John-Paul Himka

8 Good Citizens
British Missionaries and Imperial States, 1870–1918
James G. Greenlee and Charles M. Johnston

9 The Theology of the Oral Torah
Revealing the Justice of God
Jacob Neusner

10 Gentle Eminence
A Life of Cardinal Flahiff
P. Wallace Platt

11 Culture, Religion, and Demographic Behaviour
Catholics and Lutherans in Alsace, 1750–1870
Kevin McQuillan

12 Between Damnation and Starvation
Priests and Merchants in Newfoundland Politics, 1745–1855
John P. Greene

13 Martin Luther, German Saviour
German Evangelical Theological Factions and the Interpretation of Luther, 1917–1933
James M. Stayer

14 Modernity and the Dilemma of North American Anglican Identities, 1880–1950
William H. Katerberg

15 The Methodist Church on the Prairies, 1896–1914
George Emery

16 Christian Attitudes towards the State of Israel
Paul Charles Merkley

17 A Social History of the Cloister
Daily Life in the Teaching Monasteries of the Old Regime
Elizabeth Rapley

18 Households of Faith
Family, Gender, and Community in Canada, 1760–1969
Edited by Nancy Christie

19 Blood Ground
Colonialism, Missions, and the Contest for Christianity in the Cape Colony and Britain, 1799–1853
Elizabeth Elbourne

20 A History of Canadian Catholics
Gallicanism, Romanism, and Canadianism
Terence J. Fay

21 The View from Rome
Archbishop Stagni's 1915 Reports on the Ontario Bilingual Schools Question
Edited and translated by John Zucchi

22 The Founding Moment
Church, Society, and the Construction of Trinity College
William Westfall

23 The Holocaust, Israel, and Canadian Protestant Churches
Haim Genizi

24 Governing Charities
Church and State in Toronto's Catholic Archdiocese, 1850–1950
Paula Maurutto

25 Anglicans and the Atlantic World
High Churchmen, Evangelicals, and the Quebec Connection
Richard W. Vaudry

26 Evangelicals and the Continental Divide
The Conservative Protestant Subculture in Canada and the United States
Sam Reimer

27 Christians in a Secular World
The Canadian Experience
Kurt Bowen

28 Anatomy of a Seance
A History of Spirit Communication in Central Canada
Stan McMullin

29 With Skilful Hand
The Story of King David
David T. Barnard

30 Faithful Intellect
Samuel S. Nelles and Victoria University
Neil Semple

31 W. Stanford Reid
An Evangelical Calvinist in the Academy
A. Donald MacLeod

32 A Long Eclipse
The Liberal Protestant Establishment and the Canadian University, 1920–1970
Catherine Gidney

33 Forkhill Protestants and Forkhill Catholics, 1787–1858
Kyla Madden

34 For Canada's Sake
Public Religion, Centennial Celebrations, and the Re-making of Canada in the 1960s
Gary R. Miedema

35 Revival in the City
The Impact of American Evangelists in Canada, 1884–1914
Eric R. Crouse

36 The Lord for the Body
Religion, Medicine, and Protestant Faith Healing in Canada, 1880–1930
James Opp

37 Six Hundred Years of Reform
Bishops and the French Church, 1190–1789
J. Michael Hayden and Malcolm R. Greenshields

38 The Missionary Oblate Sisters
Vision and Mission
Rosa Bruno-Jofré

39 Religion, Family, and Community in Victorian Canada
The Colbys of Carrollcroft
Marguerite Van Die

40 Michael Power
The Struggle to Build the Catholic Church on the Canadian Frontier
Mark G. McGowan

41 The Catholic Origins of Quebec's Quiet Revolution, 1931–1970
Michael Gauvreau

42 Marguerite Bourgeoys and the Congregation of Notre Dame, 1665–1700
Patricia Simpson

43 To Heal a Fractured World
The Ethics of Responsibility
Jonathan Sacks

44 Revivalists
Marketing the Gospel in English Canada, 1884–1957
Kevin Kee

45 The Churches and Social Order in Nineteenth- and Twentieth-Century Canada
Edited by Michael Gauvreau and Ollivier Hubert

46 Political Ecumenism
Catholics, Jews, and Protestants in De Gaulle's Free France, 1940–1945
Geoffrey Adams

47 From Quaker to Upper Canadian
Faith and Community among Yonge Street Friends, 1801–1850
Robynne Rogers Healey

48 The Congrégation de Notre-Dame, Superiors, and the Paradox of Power, 1693–1796
Colleen Gray

49 Canadian Pentecostalism
Transition and Transformation
Edited by Michael Wilkinson

50 A War with a Silver Lining
Canadian Protestant Churches and the South African War, 1899–1902
Gordon L. Heath

51 In the Aftermath of Catastrophe
Founding Judaism, 70 to 640
Jacob Neusner
52 Imagining Holiness
Classic Hasidic Tales in Modern Times
Justin Jaron Lewis
53 Shouting, Embracing, and Dancing with Ecstasy
The Growth of Methodism in Newfoundland, 1774–1874
Calvin Hollett
54 Into Deep Waters
Evangelical Spirituality and Maritime Calvinist Baptist Ministers, 1790–1855
Daniel C. Goodwin
55 Vanguard of the New Age
The Toronto Theosophical Society, 1891–1945
Gillian McCann
56 A Commerce of Taste
Church Architecture in Canada, 1867–1914
Barry Magrill
57 The Big Picture
The Antigonish Movement of Eastern Nova Scotia
Santo Dodaro and Leonard Pluta
58 My Heart's Best Wishes for You
A Biography of Archbishop John Walsh
John P. Comiskey
59 The Covenanters in Canada
Reformed Presbyterianism from 1820 to 2012
Eldon Hay
60 The Guardianship of Best Interests
Institutional Care for the Children of the Poor in Halifax, 1850–1960
Renée N. Lafferty
61 In Defence of the Faith
Joaquim Marques de Araújo, a Comissário in the Age of Inquisitional Decline
James E. Wadsworth
62 Contesting the Moral High Ground
Popular Moralists in Mid-Twentieth-Century Britain
Paul T. Phillips
63 The Catholicisms of Coutances
Varieties of Religion in Early Modern France, 1350–1789
J. Michael Hayden
64 After Evangelicalism
The Sixties and the United Church of Canada
Kevin N. Flatt
65 The Return of Ancestral Gods
Modern Ukrainian Paganism as an Alternative Vision for a Nation
Mariya Lesiv
66 Transatlantic Methodists
British Wesleyanism and the Formation of an Evangelical Culture in Nineteenth-Century Ontario and Quebec
Todd Webb
67 A Church with the Soul of a Nation
Making and Remaking the United Church of Canada
Phyllis D. Airhart
68 Fighting over God
A Legal and Political History of Religious Freedom in Canada
Janet Epp Buckingham
69 From India to Israel
Identity, Immigration, and the Struggle for Religious Equality
Joseph Hodes
70 Becoming Holy in Early Canada
Timothy Pearson
71 The Cistercian Arts
From the 12th to the 21st Century
Edited by Terryl N. Kinder and Roberto Cassanelli
72 The Canny Scot
Archbishop James Morrison of Antigonish
Peter Ludlow
73 Religion and Greater Ireland
Christianity and Irish Global Networks, 1750–1950
Edited by Colin Barr and Hilary M. Carey
74 The Invisible Irish
Finding Protestants in the Nineteenth-Century Migrations to America
Rankin Sherling
75 Beating against the Wind
Popular Opposition to Bishop Feild and Tractarianism in Newfoundland wand Labrador, 1844–1876
Calvin Hollett
76 The Body or the Soul?
Religion and Culture in a Quebec Parish, 1736–1901
Frank A. Abbott
77 Saving Germany
North American Protestants and Christian Mission to West Germany, 1945–1974
James C. Enns

78 The Imperial Irish
Canada's Irish Catholics Fight the Great War, 1914–1918
Mark G. McGowan

79 Into Silence and Servitude
How American Girls Became Nuns, 1945–1965
Brian Titley

80 Boundless Dominion
Providence, Politics, and the Early Canadian Presbyterian Worldview
Denis McKim

81 Faithful Encounters
Authorities and American Missionaries in the Ottoman Empire
Emrah Şahin

82 Beyond the Noise of Solemn Assemblies
The Protestant Ethic and the Quest for Social Justice in Canada
Richard Allen

83 Not Quite Us
Anti-Catholic Thought in English Canada since 1900
Kevin P. Anderson

84 Scandal in the Parish
Priests and Parishioners Behaving Badly in Eighteenth-Century France
Karen E. Carter

85 Ordinary Saints
Women, Work, and Faith in Newfoundland
Bonnie Morgan

86 Patriot and Priest
Jean-Baptiste Volfius and the Constitutional Church in the Côte-d'Or
Annette Chapman-Adisho

87 A.B. Simpson and the Making of Modern Evangelicalism
Daryn Henry

88 The Uncomfortable Pew
Christianity and the New Left in Toronto
Bruce Douville

89 Berruyer's Bible
Public Opinion and the Politics of Enlightenment Catholicism in France
Daniel J. Watkins

90 Communities of the Soul
A Short History of Religion in Puerto Rico
José E. Igartua

91 Callings and Consequences
The Making of Catholic Vocational Culture in Early Modern France
Christopher J. Lane

92 Religion, Ethnonationalism, and Antisemitism in the Era of the Two World Wars
Edited by Kevin P. Spicer and Rebecca Carter-Chand

93 Water from Dragon's Well
The History of a Korean-Canadian Church Relationship
David Kim-Cragg

94 Protestant Liberty
Religion and the Making of Canadian Liberalism, 1828–78
James M. Forbes

95 To Make a Village Soviet
Jehovah's Witnesses and the Transformation of a Postwar Ukrainian Borderland
Emily B. Baran

96 Disciples of Antigonish
Catholics in Nova Scotia, 1880–1960
Peter Ludlow

97 A Black American Missionary in Canada
The Life and Letters of Lewis Champion Chambers
Edited by Hilary Bates Neary

98 A People's Reformation
Building the English Church in the Elizabethan Parish
Lucy Moffat Kaufman

A People's Reformation

Building the English Church in the Elizabethan Parish

LUCY MOFFAT KAUFMAN

McGill-Queen's University Press
Montreal & Kingston • London • Chicago

ISBN 978-0-2280-1679-3 (cloth)
ISBN 978-0-2280-1680-9 (paper)
ISBN 978-0-2280-1774-5 (ePDF)
ISBN 978-0-2280-1775-2 (ePUB)

Legal deposit second quarter 2023
Bibliothèque nationale du Québec

Printed in Canada on acid-free paper that is 100% ancient forest free (100% post-consumer recycled), processed chlorine free

---

Library and Archives Canada Cataloguing in Publication

Title: A people's reformation : building the English church in the Elizabethan parish / Lucy Moffat Kaufman.

Names: Kaufman, Lucy Moffat, author.

Series: McGill-Queen's studies in the history of religion. Series two ; 98.

Description: Series statement: McGill-Queen's studies in the history of religion. Series two ; 98 | Includes bibliographical references and index.

Identifiers: Canadiana (print) 20220465630 | Canadiana (ebook) 20220465916 | ISBN 9780228016793 (cloth) | ISBN 9780228016809 (paper) | ISBN 9780228017745 (ePDF) | ISBN 9780228017752 (ePUB)

Subjects: LCSH: Reformation – England. | LCSH: Church of England – History – 16th century. | LCSH: Church and state – England – History – 16th century. | LCSH: England – Church history – 16th century.

Classification: LCC BR375 .K38 2023 | DDC 274.206 – dc23

This book was designed and typeset by Peggy & Co. Design in 11.5/14 Adobe Garamond Pro.

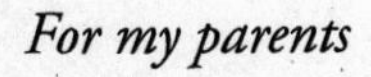

For my parents

Contents

Figures xiii

Preface xv

Acknowledgments xvii

Note xxi

Introduction 3

1 Bounding the Parish 24

2 Policing the Parish 53

3 Funding the Parish 89

4 Taxing the Parish 134

5 Receiving in the Parish 181

Conclusion 245

Notes 249

Bibliography 295

Index 333

Figures

I.1 A cope, made in England in the early sixteenth century. The Cloisters Collection, 1953 5
1.1 The parish church of All Saints, Cawood. Aisle / Alamy Stock Photo 25
1.2 A sketch from a book of legal forms and opinions from the Durham church courts. Reproduced by the kind permission of Durham Cathedral 34
3.1 A sample of churchwardens' accounts taken from St Mary's, Reading. Reading Room 2020 / Alamy Stock Photo 90
3.2 Elizabethan Royal Arms, Ludlow, Norfolk. Angelo Hornak / Alamy Stock Photo 99
3.3 The interior of Langley Chapel, built in 1601. Wyrdlight / Alamy Stock Photo 102
3.4 The frontispiece of the 1569 Bishop's Bible. ART Collection / Alamy Stock Photo 107
4.1 A Victorian copy of a portrait of Sir Ralph Ellerker. Sir Ralph Ellerker of Risby (b.1548/9) by Rebecca Dulcibella Orpen Ferrers, later Mrs Edward Henege Dering (1830–1923), CMS_PCF_343133, Collections – Public. © National Trust 136
4.2 "February" from Edmund Spenser's *The Shepherd's Calendar*. World History Archive / Alamy Stock Photo 141
4.3 Tithe prices and prosecutions in the Courts of York, 1590s 151
5.1 Elizabethan communion cup, c. 1580s. Metropolitan Museum of Art, Gift of Irwin Untermyer, 1968 197

Preface

The Elizabethan Reformation transformed England.

When Elizabeth came to the throne in 1558, she inherited thirty-odd years of religious turmoil. In those decades, real conformity was impossible. The country had seen a new definition of orthodoxy, in doctrine or in practice, every four or five years for three decades. What was permissible was soon prohibited; what was forbidden was soon required. Religion, society, and the state were unmoored.

When Elizabeth died in 1603, she left behind over forty years of relative stability. The religious settlement of the first five years of her reign set the tone and shape for what was to come. Though dissent and resistance were rife, the English church held firm. Indeed, if anything the commitment to conformity had only intensified in the face of opposition. Religion, society, and the state were tied together more closely than ever before.

A People's Reformation tells a new story of this change.

It is a story that focuses not on the radicals or the recusants, not on the bishops or the members of parliament, not on the crown or the council. These people all shaped the English church, challenged it, directed it. But they did not build it.

Instead, the English church was built in the Elizabethan parish, by everyday people making everyday choices. These decisions were charged with new power and urgency by a church that relied on its lay parishioners to enact its Reformation.

Throughout, the book explores these choices: their constraints, their contexts, and their consequences. Though largely a story of conformity, it is not a story of consensus. The annealing of the Elizabethan Reformation profoundly shaped the social, economic, political, and religious realities of English parishioners. For some it was a longed-for process, providing stability or even truth. For others, it was a painful, coercive process. The Elizabethan church was, after all, hierarchical, involuntary, and constantly monitored. Nevertheless, across the parishes of England, it offered new avenues for participation in the church, profoundly shaping its character and its contours.

This story is thus neither dirge nor paean. It is, instead, an exploration of the strategies, the decisions, and the priorities of English men and women in the face of massive change.

It is, in the end, the story of a people's Reformation, and the church they built, together.

Acknowledgments

I finish this book far from where I began it. It has travelled with me to four different institutions, two continents, and through a pandemic. My thanks are many and widespread.

My experience with McGill-Queen's University Press has been exceptional. My editor, Richard Baggaley, and the entire editorial and production team (particularly Pat Kennedy) have made this process far easier than I could have hoped. I would also like to thank the three anonymous readers for their comments that so helpfully shaped the book.

This book has been the product of conversations that have advanced my thinking in new and often unexpected ways. My first foray into this project was as a student at Yale, and I remain enormously grateful for the generosity of those I encountered there. Keith Wrightson let me grow into myself as an academic and historian, encouraging me with unstinting kindness, wry humour, and intellectual rigour. I owe him more than I can say. Bruce Gordon and Carlos Eire offered thoughtful advice and penetrating editorial eyes. Julia Adams, John Demos, Rona Johnston Gordon, Steve Pincus, Jim Scott, and Francesca Trivellato opened my eyes to new questions and helped me articulate my answers in ways I never could have expected.

Since that time, I have been lucky enough to work at three different institutions, each of which treated me with kindness and supported my work. My colleagues and mentors at Clark University, at the University of Oxford (and particularly Keble College), and now at the University of Alabama have made my academic journey a joy. Special acknowledgment is due to Ian Archer, John Beeler, Julia Brock, Lawrence Cappello, Michelle Dowd, Alex Gajda, Holly Grout, Steve

Gunn, Martin Ingram, Diarmaid MacCulloch, Tricia McElroy, Jimmy Mixson, Margaret Peacock, Erik Peterson, Juanjo Ponce Vázquez, Dan Riches, Jenny Shaw, and Sarah Steinbock-Pratt, each of whom has talked with me extensively about my research or writing and given me invaluable feedback. Particular thanks are due to Wim Klooster, Paul Monod, Ali Rogers, Jonathan Phillips, and Josh Rothman, who have been outstanding directors of the various departments, colleges, and centres to which I have been attached while writing the book.

Beyond these institutions, conversations with scholars, collaborators, and friends have pushed my work in new directions. I would especially like to thank Amanda Behm, Bill Bullman, Megan Lindsay Cherry, Leslie Theibert Cooles, Justin duRivage, Elizabeth Evenden, Elizabeth Herman, Steve Hindle, Richard Huzzey, Brendan Kane, Krista Kesselring, Irene Middleton, Sarah Kinkel Miller, Ted Pulcini, Alec Ryrie, Ethan Shagan, Tim Stretton, Bob Tittler, James Vaughn, Jennifer Wellington, Andy Wood, and Jeff Wood. Some of them do not know the impact they have had on my work and the way I see the past; each of them has been kind and generous to me at a critical moment. Particular thanks are due to Richard and Irene for their kindness in housing me during my final research trip for the book.

Findings from the book have been presented at conferences and seminars, including the North American Conference on British Studies, the Sixteenth Century Society and Conference, the European Reformation Research Group Symposium, the Institute for Historical Research, the Southern Conference on British Studies, the Northeastern Conference on British Studies, the Mid-Atlantic Conference on British Studies, the Early Modern Britain and the Religion in the British Isles, 1400–1700, Seminars at Oxford, and the Montreal British History Seminar, amongst others. I thank the many convenors, fellow panelists, commenters, and audience members for their unstinting thoughts and feedback.

Generous financial support has been provided by the Durham Residential Research Library Fellowship; the Department of History and the Dean's Office at the University of Alabama; the Warden and Fellows of Keble College, Oxford; the Folger Library; the Beinecke Library; the Henry Hart Rice Fellowship; the MacMillan Center for International and Area Studies; the Foundation Scholarship of Jesus College, Cambridge. The archivists and librarians at every institution listed in my bibliography have been invaluable. Particular thanks are due to the staff of the Durham Research Libraries, the Norfolk Record Office, the London Metropolitan Archives, the Borthwick Institute for Archives, the Beinecke Library, and the Southwest Heritage Trust, all of whom dealt with me for far longer than they might have expected, as well as those archivists and researchers who helped me to digitize images.

This work would not have been possible without the tireless work of records societies, archivists, antiquarians, researchers, and others who have preserved and publicized the historical record. Writing in a global pandemic, trapped far away from the archives for over two years, I realized my debt to them – living and dead – was greater than I imagined.

My family has been my strength and support. My in-laws, the Heid-Lockwood-Macqueen-Yi clan, have loved me like one of their own (which I am, with gratitude). Barbara and Tracy Cate, Nancy Dalva, James Kuhn, Gwen Arner and Donald Moffat, Anne Murray, and the rest of my family have been supportive in every way possible. I have lost some of them along the way, but their memories live with me every day. Bob and Deb Fulham Winston have been my family in everything but name. Emma Kaufman, Eric Gardiner, Henry Gardiner, and Nina Kaufman understand me. I find that I cannot write about my husband, Matt Lockwood, without falling into cliché. He has read every word of this book, many times over, and heard about it even more. His is the opinion I trust most in the world. I could not have done this, any of this, without him.

I dedicate this book to my parents, Wendy Moffat and Donald Kaufman: to my father, who taught me to love history, and my mother, who taught me how to write it.

Note

The quotations from archival sources have been partly modernized for readability. Though you lose some of the rhythms and lyricism of the language, the regionalism of the accents, the sense of time past, it also renders complex and sometimes abstruse, technical, or archaic language more legible.

The dates have, as far as possible, also been partly modernized to the current calendar, with the New Year set at 1 January (rather than in March).

I have, however, preserved the old currency and its abbreviations: pound (£), shilling (s.), pence (d.), and half-penny (ob.). For those unfamiliar with the currency, there were twelve pence to a shilling and twenty shillings (or 240 d.) to a pound.

A People's Reformation

Introduction

Jeffrey Whitaker was breaking the law. It was 1578 in the parish of Edington, Wiltshire. On a hill nearby, exactly seven centuries earlier, King Alfred had won the famous battle against the "Great Heathen Army" of the Danes. Now, Edington was a sleepy parish, deep in the heart of the North Wessex Downs, rich from the profits of the woollen trade. Jeffrey was one of the richest of them all: the owner of a fulling mill that had been in the Whitaker family since at least 1519 and at least three other mills besides, with thousands of pounds of liquid assets and debts owed to him.[1] He was as respectable as they came, the employer of dozens of parishioners, from a long-established family, later to be a major donor to the church, a leading man of the parish, with his name blazoned atop lists and rates kept by the churchwardens.[2] But he had in his possession something outlawed and illicit.

Jeffrey and his family had hidden the item for decades. The archives hid his secret for centuries, the only evidence a throwaway line buried in the parochial accounts. These accounts are, on the surface, quite unextraordinary records, neither particularly voluminous nor particularly elegant. Begun in 1577, they are far less detailed than those of Mere, just twenty miles away; in contrast to the beautifully illustrated presentation copy of St Botolph's Aldgate in London, replete with dragons and beasts and patriotic messages, they were workaday documents.[3] Their main function was a routine, relatively cursory list of names of local officeholders and the sums brought in by the church flock. But on page three, amidst the usual line-item receipts, they reveal Jeffrey's secret. Buried between a note about the transfer of the parish funds and another about the purchase of building material, the entry reads: "Also there is received of Jeffrey Whitaker for A cope which his grandfather had in keeping."[4]

Jeffrey's hidden cope was one of the pre-Reformation vestments of the Catholic clergy, often elaborately embroidered with images of the saints or the seven sacraments. Certainly the cope that Jeffrey turned over to his churchwardens was precious, valued at 53s. 4d., roughly eighty days' wages for an average labourer. It was a relict of a time gone by: a vestige of a pre-Reformation material culture undone and destroyed by the decades of change that had followed. It was also illegal. At the most generous interpretation – that it had been purchased in the brief years of Mary Tudor's reign – it was an item that had been illicit to own for nearly twenty years. More likely it had been hidden by his grandfather in the first rounds of the Reformation thirty or forty years previously, saved from the destruction of Henrician or Edwardian authorities, only now surrendered to the churchwardens of Edington, sold to fund parish life.

If Edington's accounts are not elegant, they are revelatory. In the seemingly anodyne lines of elections, inventories, debts, and receipts lies the story of the Elizabethan Reformation. It is a story of continuities with the past, where parishes like Edington in Wiltshire could fund expenses with communal shepherding of a church flock whose wool was sold to profit the parish, just as had been done for centuries. It is a story of increasing governance, with churchwardens and sidemen and swornmen and auditors and vestries who managed and enforced the laws passed by the state church. And it is a story of change: of Jeffrey Whitaker, coming to the churchwardens, illicit cope in hand, no longer preserved or cherished in the family but turned over to church officials to be sold to provision a new, Protestant church. Indeed, the sale of this Catholic vestment may have funded some of the purchases of the books listed in the inventory just a few years later: two vernacular bibles; two copies of the Book of Common Prayer; four psalters with their English verses; Erasmus's *Paraphrases*; eight singing books; and a Book of Homilies.[5] It was the Elizabethan Reformation manifested.

The religious upheavals of the English Reformation shook and shattered everyday life in sixteenth-century England. It seemed to many as if everything had changed: property-owning, politics and power; taxes, communal life, education; even the rituals of birth, marriage, and death

Figure I.1 A cope, made in England in the early-sixteenth century. This was the kind of vestment, heavily decorated and devotional – and outlawed by the Elizabethan church – that Jeffrey Whitaker (also Whitacre) surrendered to his churchwardens.

that marked the passage of life. This book examines the ways in which English society both changed and was changed by the Reformation. It clarifies the intensified relationship between the state and its people during periods of enforced upheaval. And, finally, it considers both the power and limitations of agency and negotiation in the face of this great change. Whether wanted or not, such changes were rigorously enforced by a state insistent on compliance and orthodoxy to preserve a fragile political stability. And yet, despite the strict conformity demanded by the church and crown, the lived experiences and choices of the English people fundamentally shaped the English Reformation.

It is impossible to divorce religion from the life of early modern England. Communities were built around parishes, church courts regulated social order, church councils collected taxes and distributed poor relief, and religion shaped patronage, politics, and protest. The reformations of Henry VIII, Edward VI, and Mary in the mid-sixteenth century had left the patterns and the structures of everyday life uncertain. When Elizabeth I came to the throne in 1558, she began a process of Protestant religious change that left great scope for private personal belief, but little room for public disobedience or nonconformity. In the relative doctrinal and institutional stability of the forty years that followed the Elizabethan settlement, Englishmen and women had to create new understandings of authority, subordination, and power.

This book provides new perspectives on the English Reformation and the roots of the Church of England. Drawing on archival material from across the United States and Great Britain, it examines the growing influence of state authority and the slow building of a robust state church in the parishes of Elizabethan England. The Church of England was a fragile endeavour launched in a fractured country, where political and religious loyalties were often at odds. In the face of such dissent, the Elizabethan state relied on the co-operation of everyday Englishmen and women to implement its reforms; in doing so, it also sought new powers to monitor and control their behaviour and beliefs. The foundations of the reformed English church and the newly empowered modern English state were thus twinned, and they were profoundly shaped by the participation of the commons. *A People's Reformation* explores this world not from parliament or the pulpit, but from the pews, reimagining the lived experience and fierce negotiation of both church and state in the parishes of Elizabethan England. It places the people of England at the heart of not just the local or cultural but the *political* story of the Reformation and its remarkable, transformative effect on the world.

The Elizabethan Settlement in Historical Context

This book is organized thematically rather than as a chronological narrative. While developments over time loom large in the thematic analyses, this is not a decade-by-decade assessment of the Reformation as a whole, or of the Elizabethan church in particular. Many thorough works on these topics have already been written and serve as excellent, often-provocative narratives of this century of religious change.[6] In contrast, this book investigates its contours and its causes through specific lenses and centres the lived experiences at an immediate and local level. Nevertheless, for those less familiar with the details of religious change in the sixteenth century, a very brief review of the seventy-odd years following Henry's break from Rome may serve as a useful contextual frame for the close parochial studies throughout the book. The survey also distills a vital point for understanding the Elizabethan Reformation: the sheer number of official policies over the course of the first three decades following the establishment of the English church – and the dizzying uncertainty they caused.

When Elizabeth came to the throne in 1558, she inherited a country weary from thirty years of seemingly constant religious upheaval. Since Henry VIII's split from Rome in 1534, a dizzying series of new orthodoxies had been commanded by the state. The five years following the Act of Supremacy in 1534, which declared Henry the Supreme Head of the church, were a whirlwind of structural and doctrinal change. Thomas Cromwell led the push for dissolution of the monasteries and iconoclasm in the parishes. Thomas Cranmer, meanwhile, rewrote church doctrine to introduce hints of Lutheranism and encouraged the laity to read the vernacular scripture. In 1538, all parishes were required to have an English Bible, and the following year the crown-approved Great Bible was officially authorized. Some portions of the country embraced these initial changes with fervour; others rose up in open rebellion.[7] The thoroughly conservative Henry, who despised popular fervour he could not harness, froze the Reformation in its footsteps. In 1539, parliament passed the Six Articles, which reinforced the doctrines of transubstantiation, communion in one kind (with eucharistic wine still reserved for the clergy), clerical celibacy, masses for the dead, and auricular confession. The following year, Cromwell was beheaded. By 1543, reading of the Bible had been confined to the social elite, with even the "better sort" in a smaller village (a modest yeoman, a skilled craftsperson) banned from reading the vernacular scripture.[8] As time passed, though, the sharp swing towards counter-reform began in turn to decelerate or, at least, to hesitate. If the period of 1539 to 1543 was one of high conservatism, then the period of 1544 to 1547 was befuddled. Henry approved of and even mandated vernacular texts that minimized the importance of the saints, but he executed evangelicals; in the last year of his life, he both seized chantries and left £600 for perpetual masses for his soul.[9] Even within Henry's reign, then, everyday Englishmen and women were confronted with a series of contradictory religious dictates. Entrenched conformity was impossible.

Upon the accession of nine-year-old Edward VI in 1547, the pendulum swung very much toward the reformers. Though not without internal dispute, the five years that followed were a program of evangelical modelling. Under the direction of Thomas Cranmer, English Books of Common Prayer were issued in 1549 and 1552 with a doctrine increasingly in line with that of Continental reformers.[10] Iconoclasm was reinvigorated, with churches stripped of icons and images.[11] Clergy were encouraged to marry and to preach, and an ambitious program of canon-law reform was attempted (though never officially adopted).[12] Edward's early death in 1553 set the course of the Reformation barrelling back toward Rome. Mary I, Edward's elder sister and the daughter of the devoutly Catholic Catherine of Aragon, immediately attempted to return the church to its traditional roots.[13] In an abrupt about-face, Protestant texts were forbidden and Catholic ornament restored; vernacular services were suspended and the mass reinstated. Public opinion about these changes was decidedly mixed and was coloured irreversibly by the well-publicized program of burning Protestants as heretics, which began in earnest in 1555. Chief among these casualties was Cranmer himself, who had survived the vicious personal politics of the Henrician court to become the architect of English Protestantism just five years before his death.[14] The parish church slowly began to be restored to its Catholic roots.[15] In many cases, these changes were greeted with a degree of enthusiasm, but two decades of doctrinal and ceremonial fluctuation left a sizable portion of the population uncomfortable with the traditional worship of the late-medieval church. Whether Mary's restoration would have been successful must remain a matter of speculation, as her death in 1558 effectively cut short any attempt to bring England back into the Catholic fold.[16] But perhaps more to the point, it represented yet another wearying change. What had been legal one year was illegal the next; what was sold under Edward had to be repurchased under Mary; what had been compulsory could, just a few years later, lead to execution. The old joke about the Vicar of Bray – who claimed that he was no hypocrite for conforming to contradictory religious orders, as he had always followed a simple policy: survival – was not actually particularly funny. It was gallows humour, quite literally.

Elizabeth was thus met with a peculiar conundrum upon her accession. The English church was very much a state church: its doctrine and character were largely determined by the monarch; its doctrine was passed into statutory law by the parliament. It should have been easy to define: one would merely have to look at statute law. And yet the religious vicissitudes of the 1530s, 1540s, and 1550s had largely prevented any sustainable religious program from truly taking root. By 1558, the

English church was defined far more by its negatives than its positives. It was decidedly not the church of the pre-Reformation years, with its organic worship of saints and heavy investment in good works. It was not monastic, nor was it particularly loyal to the papacy; however, it was also not uniformly enthused with Continental evangelical models. Its defining feature was confusion, tinged with more than a hint of exhaustion. This is not to say that Elizabeth was met with a religious tabula rasa upon her accession. Powerful ideologies had developed over the previous thirty years. It would be too simplistic to divide these groups into "Protestant" and "Catholic," as there was a profusion of competing interests at play; as Elizabeth would soon discover, many who supported the initial Protestant settlement would soon become hostile to its orthodoxies.[17] Instead, it is better to say that she had inherited chaos.

In the face of this disorder, Elizabeth took an early stand with the Acts of Supremacy and of Uniformity. The Act of Supremacy was the very first piece of Elizabethan legislation, a telling priority. It proclaimed Elizabeth as Supreme Governor of the church, and it compelled an oath of allegiance of all clerics, from archbishops to parish ministers, and of all magistrates.[18] The Act of Uniformity placed Cranmer's 1552 Book of Common Prayer at the centre of ceremonial and doctrinal orthodoxy.[19] This statutory law was reinforced by the Convocation of 1563's adoption of the Thirty-Nine Articles, which became the central tenets of faith for the Church of England. The Articles were clearly reformed: justification was by faith alone; good works had no redemptive power; preaching was to be in the vernacular; purgatory was abolished; sacraments were restricted to baptism and communion; communion was to be given in two kinds and the real presence was denied; and priests were permitted to marry.[20] Affirmed by parliament in 1571, the Articles defined the theological and doctrinal understanding of the Elizabethan church.

The 1563 Articles were also the final major innovations permitted in the Elizabethan church, despite forty more years of her reign. As Diarmaid MacCulloch puts it, "the Queen was determined not to move with the continental times."[21] The attempts by godly clergy to change her mind is a well-documented struggle, with clerical and magisterial reformers alike trying to wrest the English church closer to continental developments. In the first decade, influenced by their personal experiences of persecution under Mary, the reformers attempted to rid the church of any ceremonial vestiges of Catholicism, focusing on clerical vestments; their efforts were summarily rebuffed. In the 1570s and early 1580s, reformist energies were turned toward church structure, with presbyterian challenges issued to the episcopal system. This movement came closest to success in the mid 1580s, following an angry reaction to Elizabeth's hardline new archbishop, John Whitgift. A series of presbyterian bills put forward to parliament were summarily dismissed and their proponents thrown in the Tower. Elizabeth made her feelings clear: "I see many over-bold with God Almighty, making too many subtle scannings of his blessed will, as Lawyers do with humane Testaments. The presumption is so great as I may not suffer it (yet mind I not hereby to animate Romanists, which what Adversaries they be to mine Estate, is sufficiently known) nor tolerate new fangledness. I mean to guide them both by Gods holy true Rule."[22]

As Supreme Governor of the church, she had the power to appoint bishops and guide church doctrine; as Queen, she had the power to abrogate parliamentary session. Elizabeth's watchwords were conformity, orthodoxy, and uniformity, and they became the defining tenets of the Elizabethan church. In other words, Elizabeth provided, for the first time, the stability under which real change could take place. Instead of the constant topsy-turvy world of the first three decades of the Reformation, the Reformation could actually take root in a parish. By Elizabeth's death in 1603, the population had experienced forty-odd years of general continuity. Babies born in the year of the Elizabethan settlement could have watched their grandchildren baptized under the very same legislation. It was something that had never before been experienced: the building of an English church.

One more piece of the contextual puzzle must be sketched out before we move on: the continuing influence of the recusant – the fugitive Catholic – faction in the country. Again, this story has been well told by historians, but a few points are worth highlighting.[23] Though the first decade following the settlement saw the episcopal hierarchy largely purged of its Catholic supporters, parishes experienced a relatively gentler push toward conformity. Attendance at church was required, but fines were limited to a shilling a week. Christopher Haigh argues that many Catholics initially behaved toward Elizabeth's settlement as they had toward Edward's: lightly conforming in the hope that the pendulum of official Reformation would soon swing back toward the traditional church.[24] Such hopes were irretrievably dashed by 1570, a result of twin disasters of Catholic political policy. The first was the Northern Rebellion of 1569 (known alternately as the Rising of the North or the Revolt of the Northern Earls), in which nobles attempted to overthrow Elizabeth, to bring the church back to Rome, and to put Mary, Queen of Scots, on the throne. Poorly planned and even more badly executed, the rebellion was quickly routed and the earls fled to Scotland. The reprisals were harsh and fell largely on the shoulders of the common people, whose popular Catholicism had fuelled their allegiance to the earls. The ill-timed attempt by Pope Pius V to drum up support for the rebellion by declaring Elizabeth a heretic only made matters worse. With a papal decree, *Regnans in Excelsis*, absolving English subjects of their oaths to the queen and the wreckage of the rebellion still smouldering, English Catholicism became indelibly stained with treason.[25]

By the 1580s, Elizabeth's position on Catholicism had hardened. Waves of Jesuit-trained priests sent to England raised alarm amongst both church and crown, and commissions to hunt these seminary priests became more common. In 1581, new anti-recusancy laws raised fines for church nonattendance by a hundred-fold, to £20 a month.[26] The spectre of "papism" and "popery" became an effective and near-ubiquitous rhetorical tool for both conformists and reformers to throw at one another. John Whitgift, Elizabeth's last and longest-lasting archbishop, likened the presbyterians to papists in their willingness to challenge orthodoxy, while Thomas Cartwright (a noted presbyterian) argued that the conformists refused church discipline just like the papists.[27]

The overall shift from 1559, at Elizabeth's accession, to 1603, at her death, was deep and complex. The hopeful energies of reformers, both Catholic and evangelical alike, were frustrated. There were, of course, still powerful Catholic families and at least some degree of church papistry; influential evangelicals continued to hope to push England toward greater godliness and to grumble about Whitgift's policies. But by the later 1580s, few thought seriously that any change would come in Elizabeth's reign. A tiny, though loud, minority turned to separatism, openly defying the English church and living either in exile or in fear of discovery. Meanwhile, the religious legislation created by crown, parliament and convocation some forty years previously still stood, little changed. As a guide to ecclesiastical doctrine, that legislation could prove frustratingly ambiguous: clearly Protestant, but girded by a conservative, high-church position on ceremonies and an occasionally equivocal sacramental structure. But as a guide to national stability, it was extraordinary, providing a constant (though by no means universally beloved) presence in English lives. By the end of the reign, generations had lived under the rubric of the Elizabethan church, had been baptized or married or buried with its rites. It was a nation transformed. Just how this transformative shift unfolded, and why it was possible, are the core questions this book sets out to answer.

Transforming a Nation

How had this happened, and why? It was far from inevitable. The political tensions were deep, and the ideological ones still deeper. But perhaps the most profound ruptures had happened at the very local level. The first few decades of the Reformation had changed so much in the lives of everyday people: of course doctrinally, with the entire structures of sacrament, the afterlife, the saints, redemption, and salvation all upended – but also in ways that were less expected, from agricultural economics to courting opportunities to the rhythms of the year and of life. If we take seriously the scholarship of the past half-century, which this book certainly does, it is clear that the changes of the first few decades of the Reformation tested, and in many places shredded, the tight-knit bonds between religion and society.[28] Brilliant, vital histories like those by Ethan Shagan and Eamon Duffy have clarified the ways in which the old world was destroyed – and challenged our understanding of why this destruction occurred. But the story did not stop there. To transform the nation, those bonds had to be rewoven, into a cloth neither entirely new nor a replica of the old.

This book investigates that reknitting of religion and society in the Elizabethan years. It asks, at its core, how a society was able to rebuild after an episode of massive, even violent, change. In doing so, its approach is to examine external behaviour rather than internal belief, parochial action rather than parliamentary act. The seeming mechanistic nature of this approach belies the very real dynamics and tensions that it can uncover. Actions were fraught and contested, and more than that, they were legible – both to us now and to the Elizabethan authorities. For us, this means that we can analyze religious change far down the social scale, beyond the elite or even just the literate to those whose lives were equally caught up in these transformations. For the Elizabethan authorities, it meant that some semblance of order could be maintained. Dissent could hide behind conformity, to be sure. But in terms both of promoting the general stability of the country and of creating the space for the new doctrines of the church to be taught, the emphasis was on base conformity of action. It was a resolutely practical decision. Action was legible, quantifiable, and recordable. It was also controllable, correctible, and easily punishable.

The book thus takes the Elizabethan Reformation on its own terms. Its focus, from the very start of Elizabeth's reign, was not on belief but on behaviour – and this book follows suit. As intrusive as they might have been, the mechanisms for scrutinizing the population were, as we shall see in chapter 1, visitation not inquisition, an examination of public action not private faith. Behaviour could reveal belief – or, reformers hoped, inculcate it – but the primary goal was a uniformity of practice. The refusal to "make windows into men's souls" was shared not just by the queen. At various times, parliamentarians on quite different sides of arguments insisted on focusing on policing outward action rather than investigating inward conscience. When the 1571 parliament considered a bill to make it a civil crime to avoid communion (rather than an ecclesiastical penalty), MP Edward Aglionby protested "that there should be no humane, positive law to enforce conscience, which is not discernable in this world." He argued that legally enforcing church attendance was acceptable, as "for that it is public and tendeth but to prove a man a Christian," but that conscience was "internal, invisible, and not in the power of the greatest monarch in the world" to constrain.[29] (The bill was nevertheless passed with the support of the godly contingent, only to be firmly vetoed by the queen, who refused to open the Pandora's box of religious reform.)[30] A decade later, the godly were themselves protesting a measure that would compel belief rather than behaviour. In petitions, speeches, and an avalanche of correspondence, they vociferously protested Archbishop Whitgift's attempts to require all ministers to swear an oath that there was nothing in the Book of Common Prayer contrary to God's word. Their argument rang with a similar argument: they would certainly *use* the Book of Common Prayer. They agreed – or at least purported to agree – that it promoted good order and encouraged the masses toward better practice. Nevertheless, they could not swear that they *believed* it to be perfect, as they knew it was not.[31] The government could compel their conformity, but they could not compel their conscience. In sum, the measure of conformity was, time and again, asserted to be action not ideology. Orthopraxy, not orthodoxy, ruled the day.

What this means is that in order to really understand how England was transformed, we must understand that the Elizabethan Reformation was experienced holistically. By this I mean that the people who lived through the Elizabethan settlement *also* lived through the demographic crunch of the late sixteenth century, with its climbing prices, stagnating wages, increased mobility, fears of enclosure, grain riots, and the rise of the middling sort. They lived through the experimentations with poor laws; the vituperative court cases; the magnificent literature; the increase in nationalism; the foundation of the merchant companies; the English circumnavigation of the globe; the informal economies of credit; the redefinition of masculinity and household authority; the transformation of London; the educational revolution; the decrease in marriages; the expansion of the power of the justice of the peace, the coroner, the constable.[32]

They did not merely experience these things in parallel to religious change, as some sort of siloed area of their lives. Instead, these epistemic shifts *influenced religious change*, and religious change in turn influenced these epistemic shifts. This book will thus touch on broadly different historiographical approaches, bridging the divide between the religious and the secular. To take a few examples that we will see throughout the book, our understanding of local state formation in England cannot start with poor laws or policing; these changes were predicated on a highly functioning bureaucratic parish with entrenched conceptions of power and office-holding, and as such need to be understood as rooted in the religious reforms of the mid-century. Our studies of conformity often consider catechizing and prayer books, but they miss ideas like reputation, credit, popular patronage, or family finances. Conflict over tithe payment for ministers had far more to do with crop prices and legal court policies than with anticlericalism. Choice over searchers for the sick in a time of pandemic was intimately tied to parochial politics and religious conformity. Those who feared paying extra taxes to support children born out of wedlock could and did levy deep-seated fears of the power of excommunication to root out undisclosed paternity; anxieties about social reputation helped to enforce church attendance. Just as we cannot understand early modern religious change without considering the Elizabethan parish, we also cannot understand early modern social and economic changes without a real understanding of the building of the Elizabethan church.

And we must understand this period as one of change, sharp-edged, high-stakes, and essential. The Elizabethan church may have had comparative stability in its official policy, but stability should be confused neither with consensus nor with stasis. Though the essential core of doctrine and ceremony remained consistent throughout the Elizabethan period, the settlement was faced by sharp contestations from both the conservative and radical wings of the church – not to mention the recusant and separatist populations, which grew their own strong identities during the period. Such conflict has, perhaps unsurprisingly, drawn the most attention from historians. Two tiny minorities of the population, the openly Catholic[33] and the vocally Puritan,[34] have been the subject of countless studies. There is, in fact, good reason for such a focus: both groups had politically powerful allies and remained constant sources of worry and frustration for the crown and the church. Nevertheless, despite the oversized influence of these groups upon the religious tenor of the later sixteenth century, they did remain a minority of the population. And while many studies have been made of the parliamentary and ecclesiastical elite, such works often ignore the experience of the masses of the population.[35]

The focus on these figures can lead us into a tendency to depict conforming parishioners – the vast majority of the population – as passive or tractable. Political agency can almost seem reserved for the minority, be it an ideological or socio-economic one. Such an impression is reinforced by the fact that the Reformation historiography that we do have, with notable exceptions, too often ignores the granular work on social history that has been so influential over the past thirty years – and social history in turn quite often sidelines religion.[36] This creates an artificial division between the sphere of religion and the sphere of popular politics, power, and authority. Though resistance and negotiation are key to understanding the politics of both the parish and the polity, historians can sometimes depoliticize the study of popular religion – especially in the relatively stable years of the late sixteenth century – with the sense of happy accommodation in the name of harmony.[37] And yet, emphasizing consensus (rather than conformity) when analyzing a change that had profound political catalysts and consequences undermines the real stakes at play; as Ethan Shagan puts it, "there is a great danger in a decontextualized notion of 'popular piety' in which religious beliefs and practices are disassociated from notions of authority, legitimacy, and power."[38] This is no less true for the more conformist years of the 1590s than for the heady years of change of the early Reformation.

Indeed, Elizabethan parishes were a prime site for the evolution of such notions, a sort of crucible of political negotiation. This book emphasizes the need to engage with a wider concept of the political nation based on an understanding of politics as "any attempt to extend, reassert or challenge the distribution of power."[39] Conflicts over orthodoxy and conformity, peace and righteousness, continuity and change – conflicts that permeated parish relations – were essentially and inherently political. This study of parish religion will thus call upon the insights and theory of popular protest and politics. Only by joining together these two disparate historiographies can we begin to approach an understanding of this fundamental shift in English society. Such an approach has been used to excellent effect in the past; however, these books almost exclusively focus on the late-medieval church and the years of the early Reformation.[40] The end result is that Elizabethan popular religion – and thus the understanding of how fundamental change happened – has remained peculiarly depoliticized. By reconceptualizing the everyday religious world of the later sixteenth century as a matter not simply theological or ideological but also specifically *political*, this book reintegrates questions of power and authority into the narrative of the Elizabethan Reformation as it was experienced by the people who lived it.

Themes and Arguments

This book approaches the building of the church from five distinct angles, each laid out in a chapter. The first chapter investigates new efforts by the state church to make the parishes legible, from increasing the frequency and efficiency of visitations to more closely bounding the parish. The second explores the policing and governing of the parish, particularly the growth in both power and authority wielded by the churchwardens and the vestry. The third chapter dives into the transformation of the material culture of the parish, looking particularly at its financial implications. The fourth returns to questions of economics, analyzing the methods and means by which parochial tithes were reshaped and administered in the Elizabethan parish. And the final chapter examines the role of sacramental conformity in the English church, looking at both rates of reception and the mechanisms by which conformity was enforced. It is, by no stretch of the imagination, the sum of everything to be explored. Indeed, one of the main *cris de cœur* of the book is that the Elizabethan Reformation demands *more* study of this nature. But even in these chapters alone, themes begin to ring out, again and again. Startling commonalities begin to rise to the surface, in topics as different as visitation returns, altar repairs, tithe litigation, churchwardens' elections, and communion reception. They weave in and out of the book, but they appear in some guise in every chapter.

The first main theme is the increasing involvement of the laity in the Elizabethan parish. The painstaking work of revisionist historians long ago put paid to the idea that the late-medieval church was unpopular and unloved; we know that the laity were involved with the rich devotional life of the parish on the eve of the split from Rome. But while this corrective was vital, it does often leave the wider popular impression of a population begrudgingly conforming to a hollow parish. Simply put, this could not be more untrue. Community and religion reknit in the Elizabethan period. In some places, they continued long-standing practices of church ales and communal ownership of a church flock long after the traditional lights and stores had been abolished. In others, this devotion was reconfigured, with status marked not by leadership in confraternities but by the pews placed closest to the pulpit or generous donations made toward the recasting of the bells. Indeed, the most significant change came not in popular lay devotion, but in the relationship between the laity and the institutional church. As we will see throughout the book, the machinery of the state church rested in large part upon the labour of the laity. Unwilling or unable to reform English religious practice through the clergy or the ecclesiastical officials, the church turned to the parish laypeople. It was they who most often policed, governed, financed, managed, administered, and implemented the Reformation. The laity were invested with more formal parochial power than they had ever possessed before. They became an integral part of ecclesiastical machinery, the state agents of a reforming church, investing everyday decisions with new political urgency. All decisions, at every level, became political.

In order to enforce conformity – in order to reform the people – the Elizabethan state expanded its bureaucratic and administrative capabilities. In doing so, however, it relied on the active participation of the parish laity. The process of state formation that emerged, then, was a religious iteration of the early modern blend of centralization and localization. In this space, the laity found their choices more constricted; however, in the increased political and ideological power devolved on them by the state church, they also found new avenues for agency and empowerment. But these choices served to bind Englishmen to their state church as much as any injunction or visitation could ever have done. This was another legacy of the Elizabethan Reformation: the unexpected consequences of major state religious change, particularly in an early modern England that relied on the local and the lay to implement it on a day-to-day level.

This kind of transformation is often linked to the theory of *Konfessionsbildung*, or confessionalization, which described the creation and consolidation of religious identities in the later sixteenth century, most often imposed by central authorities.[41] Some of what follows in the book maps quite closely onto these theories, especially in the exploration of ecclesiastical visitations. And yet, in the English context, the reliance on the localities, the influence of the laity, and the continued contestation of religious ideology in both print and in politics undermines the neater top-down typologies of these theories.[42] What we see in the English case is a new church being built from both the top down *and* the bottom up, quite often in consultation with one another. Those making policies within the English church, from crown to assembly to episcopate, were hyper-aware of the limitations of their power, at the exact time that they were seeking to enforce it. As we will see throughout the book, concessions were often made for local needs or local politics; energetic reformers, at least the most effective ones, could and did temper their enthusiasms with an understanding that they had to meet the English people where they were. The machinery of governance became well-oiled and efficient, but at all times it relied on local labour and participation. Ethan Shagan famously argued that the undoing of the pre-Reformation church was "not done to people, but with them."[43] This book argues that this must be taken one step further:

that the Elizabethan church was built not just *with* the English people, but *through* them. Participation was not optional (nor, of course, was it in Shagan's analysis, but the coercive potential of the state took on a new tenor in the long Elizabethan reign, when parishioners could no longer hide in or prevaricate in the face of chaotic religious change). It was compulsory, and it was state-defined. And yet, it was not merely a will imposed. Instead, the settlement was modulated, mutated, shifted, and changed by the very people who carried it out. This was not confessionalization, it was reciprocal state formation.

Second, the Elizabethan Reformation emphasized results, not process. It was far more important to ecclesiastical officials *what* was done, rather than how it was accomplished. Conformity was vital. But just how that conformity was to be enacted varied enormously across England. That Bibles were to be bought and church walls repaired was non-negotiable, but the strategies that the parish would employ to raise those funds were largely unregulated. Churchwardens had to be elected, but how they were elected and who chose their churchwardens was left almost entirely up to the parishes. Parishes could employ sidemen to help surveil the congregation, but they were not required; annual communion was to be provided, but whether it was given at once or over several services, or what the quality of wine would be, or from whom it was to be purchased, or how the records of sacramental reception were to be kept – each parish decided these matters. The Elizabethan Reformation was a profound moment of state centralization and expansion of state bureaucracy. But it was one that cared far more about result than about intention or strategy.

What this meant was that the Reformation could be, and was, subtly adapted for the needs of each of the thousands of parishes across the country. What worked in the giant borderland parishes of Northumberland might not work for a tight-knit agricultural parish in Oxfordshire; what worked in the wool parishes of Devon might not work in the inner-city parishes of Norwich; what worked in the wealthy and well-established parishes at the heart of London's walled city might not work for the teeming suburbs just a few miles away in the East End. For each example in this book, an expert historian might give a counter-example. While presenting my research, I have come across excellent scholars who point out that their city or county experienced things slightly differently than the narrative I was telling – that the altars came down a little slower, or that regular communions happened earlier, or that the parish church they were studying had decayed. This book is richer for their comments and their interventions. But at its core, this kind of flexibility was a *feature*, not a bug, of the Elizabethan settlement. While put in place by a combination of a practical understanding of the limits of ecclesiastical power to mandate everything to a granular level and a monarchical distaste for precisionism, its consequence was an exquisitely adaptable program of reform. A narrative of confessionalization rather misses the point: it cannot and does not account for the remarkable variations of experience in Carlisle and Kent, Newcastle and Ninfield, Oxford and Osgathorpe. As a result, the Reformation could respond to local problems, local customs, local hot spots of recalcitrance or enthusiasm. To be sure, the Elizabethan Reformation had national standards, and those baseline standards were clear and non-negotiable. This was not a weak Reformation. Refusal to comply could have serious penalties: shaming, loss of status and privileges, fines, branding, whipping, imprisonment, execution. But alongside this iron fist was a general policy of allowing parishes to operate with some independence and discretion. The Elizabethan Reformation thus became more easily interwoven into people's lives, in part because it played into long-standing systems, institutions, customs, and structures. This was not a *via media*, it was a *via sola*. Only one road was acceptable in the Elizabethan church. But it was a broad road, easily travelled by those who wished to do so.

The third main theme is the legacy of history and memory of the Reformation. Time and time again, early compromises to preserve administrative and structural stability created surprising, long-lasting continuities between the pre-Reformation church and its Elizabethan iteration. This does not mean, again, that the Elizabethan church is best understood as a coda to the reforms of the 1530s and 1540s. But it *does* mean that the Elizabethan church had to grapple with old problems in new ways – or perhaps it is better to say that old problems had to be truly confronted for the first time. With the remarkable stability provided by forty-odd years of official continuity of policy, cracks that had been ignored in the heady early years of reform and the high political battles that followed now became unavoidable chasms. To take but one example, we can look to the economic policies of the church, discussed in chapter 4. In the see-sawing of the earlier Reformation, it was easy enough to ignore the ossification of tithe policy by the new state church when both commons and clergy were distracted by Edwardian iconoclasm or Marian restoration. (When martyrs are being made, questions of whether tithes should be collected in kind or coin tend to fade into the background.) When tithe laws were made in the 1540s, they prioritized short-term stability over long-term prosperity, declaring that tithes would be run by customary agreements made three decades earlier. This stranded the ecclesiastical funding model of the church in the economic realities of the 1510s. In the turmoil that followed, no substantive changes were made to these laws. Thus, by the late sixteenth century, the Elizabethan church was left to cope with a reformed institution funded by a nearly century-old economic model – and its courts were suddenly filled with tithe disputes brought on by earlier equivocation. This is but one example: throughout the book, decisions made in the 1530s, 1540s, and 1550s had long, reverberating effects half a century later. Just how to address these consequences was a deeply charged political decision. To move to a post-Reformation world, the English church first had to decide how to comprehend, litigate, and negotiate its own history.

Fourth and finally, emerging from this book is the theme of compulsory community. The Reformation tends to be conceived of as a triumph of individualism, at least in the broader imagination. Instead, this book argues that the defining feature of the Elizabethan church was compulsory communalism and performative conformist lay piety. Its spiritual life may have been intensely personal, but its *religious* life was intensely collective. The community was explicitly bound to the edges of the parish, with local belonging mattering more than ever before. Participation in the community was not voluntary, it was compulsory. This did not mean that it was unwelcome or begrudged; school attendance is mandatory today, but many children love (or at least value) school. But it does mean that new publics were constructed and that old ideas of communalism infused the church as never before. The congregation became fixed in new church seating; it became counted with parochial censuses; it became monitored over anxieties about obligations to provide for its own poor; it became defined by those with whom the Lord's Supper was shared. It was the audience for penitential confession, it was the site for marriages and baptisms, it was the entire expression of the community, joined together, week in and week out, year after year. The Elizabethan reforms centred the community, not the individual.

Conclusion

In the end, this is a story about decisions made in the face of constraints: the demands of the state, the shifts in economy and demography, the doctrine of the church, and above all, the long legacy of the Reformation. The English church at the dawn of the seventeenth century had been shaped by these choices, and by the strategies, priorities, and practices of the parishes and their parishioners. In short, this book argues that the Reformation was mandated by the state but built by its people. England became a Protestant nation not in spite of its people, but through their active participation in creating a new church in England, an England where social, political, and religious conformities were tied ever closer.

When Elizabeth I came to the throne in 1558, the country balanced on a knife edge between Catholicism and Protestantism. It takes little imagination to picture the situation in England devolving into wars of religion that would echo the experience of France or the German lands. When she died in 1603, only the most hopeful thought that England could revert back to Rome. Something had changed in those forty-five years: England had become, at its core, a Protestant nation. The answer to why this happened can't, and doesn't, lie solely with scholars and courtiers, bishops, ambassadors, and queens. Nor does it rest solely with the slim minority of religious radicals who were willing to fight, to risk, and to die for their convictions. Instead, it lies with the anodyne, daily choices of parishioners across the parishes of Elizabethan England. For early modern Englishmen and women, there was not a strict line between the sacred and the profane. Some decisions that might at first glance seem purely practical – say, agrarian development of wasteland – had profound impacts on the ability of a parish to hire and sustain a learned minister. And some decisions that could seem purely devotional – sitting close to the minister during his sermon, for example – were rooted more in notions of social hierarchy than in unalloyed faith. By exploring and unpacking these choices, *A People's*

Reformation uncovers a world in which being a good neighbour and being a good English subject increasingly became tied to being a conforming member of the parish community.

The Elizabethan reformation, and the church of England that emerged from it, was in part a theological reformation, an institutional reformation, a high political reformation. It was a reformation that changed history, that birthed an Anglican communion, that would eventually launch new wars, new language, even a new national identity. But it was, above all, a *people's* reformation, that not only shaped everyday lives but was profoundly shaped by them in turn. It is their stories I seek to understand, and it is their stories I tell here.

1

Bounding the Parish

On the morning of 21 February 1591, Elizabeth Watson stood before the congregation of her parish church. All Saints Cawood sat on the low bank of the river Ouse, so close that the winter floods would create "great danger off ye water" that rose just a few yards from the church door.[1] Cawood was a small town on the borders of the West Riding, most famous for its castle, the country palace of the archbishops of York and the site of Wolsey's arrest just sixty years earlier. This, though, was a typical winter Sunday in the modest, damp church. The entire parish community was assembled: Elizabeth's family, perhaps, or at least her neighbours; probably her employers; possibly her friends. Standing in front of them, Elizabeth began her confession:

> Whereas I, good people, forgetting my duty to almighty god have committed the detestable sin of fornication and whoredom with Walter Webster. I am heartily sorry for the same, and do much humbly beseech almighty god to forgive me this and all other my sins and offences, and now I do likewise desire all you that be now present whom I have offended or given any evil example unto by my evil behaviour also to forgive me, and to beware by this my punishment that none of you do offend in the like. And to aid me also with your hearty and earnest prayers unto almighty god to give me grace to lead a new life, and never to offend in the like fault again, unto whom let us pray as we are taught in the Gospel, Our father, which art in heaven …[2]

And the congregation joined her in the familiar prayer.

Figure 1.1 The parish church of All Saints Cawood, on the bank of the Ouse, where Elizabeth Watson made her confession in 1591.

It must have been excruciatingly mortifying. And it grips the historical imagination – it is easy to envision the setting, the sound, the looks on the faces of those witnessing her penance. (Perhaps they looked on with sympathy; perhaps with disgust.) But this was not merely a moment of high personal drama, nor was it an organic communal confession. Elizabeth's penance was the culmination of a politically charged process orchestrated by a state church whose nerve centre lay hundreds of miles away and enacted by everyday Englishmen who lived and worked alongside her. It was a scripted shame, quite literally, with the words dictated by the senior church officials who occasionally came to stay in the grandeur of the archbishop's castle, just around the river bend; they had mandated it in the church courts, part of their regular business, as unremarkable to them as it must have been cataclysmic to Elizabeth. Her confession had a compulsory audience, with everyone living in Cawood gathered by law to worship together, to pray together, to listen to Elizabeth speak. It would be – and was – confirmed to the church authorities, with a printed certificate signed off by the wardens and the minister, then filed away by a court official. It was a moment of power, of politics, of community, of the complicated ties between local and national. It was, in short, the Elizabethan Reformation, enacted.

To understand how Elizabeth Watson came to be standing there on that February morning is to understand the process by which the state church's reforms were enacted in the parishes of Elizabethan England. It started with the visitations, a system of surveillance and control far greater than any that had come before it. These visitations required the active participation of both the localities and the laity; through them, the local became enmeshed in the national and the laity became enmeshed in the ecclesiastical. Visitations – and the English Reformation more generally – also required a locality that was fixed, legible, and controllable. As such, they emphasized local borders in ways that had never been done before.

The story of the transformation of England, then, has to begin with these borders. Which is to say, it has to begin with the parish. This chapter will explore the new efforts by the Elizabethan state church to define and enforce the boundaries of parochial life. The emphasis on lay conformity of action, including attendance at weekly services and compulsory communion, meant the state had a vested interest in fixing Englishmen and women in specific locations, where they could be more easily supervised and regulated. This interest was only reinforced by the visitation system, which relied on compulsory but amateur surveillance and reporting, again requiring boundaries of authority and control. That such a push for definition happened at a moment when internal migration was increasing was neither ironic nor coincidental: as we will see, such movement engendered fear of losing that control. Authorities doubled down, requiring tighter adherence to parochial boundaries. Other changes further increased the newly intensified focus on defining community. Chief amongst these innovations was widespread pew construction, which materially and physically fixed the congregation in large part to generate new income streams for a church that had lost its traditional devotional revenues. With all of these pressures – political, religious, demographic, economic – the idea of belonging had never before been more important, nor more precarious.

Beginning with the parish is easier said than done. The Elizabethan parochial system was complex, bewildering, irrational – and the backbone of the church in England. Parishes were born in the deep roots of the Anglo-Saxon church, evolving organically as the country did: growing, shrinking, being carved up and amalgamated as populations ebbed and flowed.[3] The Black Death had meant parishes merged or even vanished, while the dissolution of the monasteries had resulted in another wave of organizational upheaval. By the mid-sixteenth century, there were roughly 9,500 parishes in England, part of a kaleidoscopic jurisdictional system that was not only to provide the population with services and rituals, but also to enforce the new state Reformation.

It was a daunting task. The size and character of parishes differed enormously. Our imagination most often springs to the compact arable parishes of about a thousand acres, centred around a village, with fifty or sixty families gathering together in their church. This was certainly the norm for much of England, particularly in the southeast and Midlands, but it was by no means ubiquitous. In the tight urban warrens of the major cities, parishes could be only a few streets wide, serving the broad thoroughfares and packed alleys of a space not much bigger than a modern city block. In the teeming suburbs of London, reeling from the demographic expansion and redistribution that saw waves of migration, a single parish could serve several thousand people, with cramped services-by-rota during the most important festivals of the year. Parishes in pasture lands or moorlands were often the inverse: small populations spread over many miles. On the Cumbrian coast, three parishes alone covered almost three hundred square miles between them; the parish of Whalley in Lancashire extended for 106,000 acres; in central Northumberland, a single parish stretched from Hadrian's Wall to the Scottish border; the parish of Lydford, in Devon, covered fifty-six thousand acres over Dartmoor and beyond.[4]

This landscape was overlaid with other geographies of devotion. Large parishes were frequently dotted with chapels-of-ease. These ranged from small way stations to private chapels in manor houses to places like St Nicholas in King's Lynn, larger than most parish churches in the country.[5] Some had been built as chantry chapels and were now abandoned or poorly staffed; others functioned almost like parishes, although without holding the official cure of souls. The most wrenching change to the devotional landscape had been the dissolution of the monasteries just a generation earlier. Religious buildings, whether abandoned or reappropriated, still anchored the topography. Sites of pilgrimage still left their footprint on the landscape. The paths, roads, even highways created to funnel pilgrims' traffic framed the infrastructure long after these spaces had officially been desacralized. And even older religious areas remained: holy wells and holy springs, tors, caves, hills, and barrows.[6]

The parish was the easiest way to make chaos legible. Administering such a vast territory, let alone promulgating and enforcing religious change, required a strong ecclesiastical structure, one based on the principles of clear hierarchy and authority. The parochial and episcopal system gave the church precisely that. Each parish was grouped together in a deanery, each deanery in an archdeaconry, each archdeaconry in a diocese, each diocese in a province.[7] At every level there were (or should be) church officials who supervised their divisions. Dioceses were not only governed by bishops, but also managed by archdeacons, rural deans, ordinaries, visitors, sub-deans, and others. Such a practice meant stability, even in the face of personnel turnover and temporary absence. Even in extreme cases, like the newly formed diocese of Oxford, which remained without an incumbent bishop for almost the entire reign of Elizabeth, the bureaucratic stability of this system kept things ticking along with relative efficiency.[8]

The hierarchical system created, at least in the ideal, a clear chain of command from the archbishop to the pew and the pulpit. At its best, this structure could be an incredibly effective means of communicating messages of orthodoxy and control from the centre to the periphery, both geographically and socially. Questions, concerns, and demands for information could radiate from London to any parish in England in a matter of days, with the answers returning equally quickly. In 1579, the newly installed bishop of Exeter, John Woolton, received orders from the privy council to investigate the dissemination of an illicit book. It was most likely John Stubbs's *Gaping Gulf*, a condemnation of the queen's marriage negotiations with the Duke of Anjou, which had been popular amongst some of the godly clergy of the countryside. The privy council wrote a circular to the bishops, telling them to remind their clergy "to contain themselves within the limit and bands of their Calling … [not] intermedling in such matters inpertinent to their calling … by which unorderly dealings there can not but grow great prejudice to the cause of religion."[9] Woolton, no fan of the godly activist wing of his clergy, leapt into action, immediately writing to his archdeacon of Cornwall: "the privy Council have lately sent me their letters charging me within this diocese to call in and suppress a certain seditious book … which is thought to be spread abroad in this country … I am now therefore most earnestly to will and require you Mr Archdeacon or your official that you do with all convenient speed call before you all the preachers within your Archdeaconry and communicate to them … that in their sermons and other public exercises they deal no way with any such matter."[10]

The message spread from the highest authorities in the land to the minister of every far-flung parish in Cornwall, in just a few short steps. Information also rebounded up the ladder, with the privy council requiring bishops to compile registers, reports, and returns gleaned from their parishes on various matters of interest.[11] Similar requests could, of course, also come from the archbishop. John Whitgift, Archbishop of Canterbury from 1583 to the end of Elizabeth's reign, and a man who prized conformity above nearly all else, was particularly fond of such orders, but they were not unique to him.[12] In the fight for religious conformity, the episcopal system's ability to transmit and enforce directives from central authorities made it an invaluable tool. The ecclesiastical structure of Elizabethan England was thus a perfect architecture of centralization – and of state power.

The most potent weapon of episcopal authority, however, was not the direct missive but the visitation. Visitations were the primary method of enforcing orthodoxy in the parishes of Elizabethan England. Regular, extensive ecclesiastical reviews, they allowed church officials to examine every parish under their jurisdiction to reveal cases of disorder, heresy, immorality, and unorthodoxy. Like so much of the English Reformation, visitations were medieval systems remade to new purposes. The medieval church had used visitations primarily, though not exclusively, to monitor the state of religious houses. By the sixteenth century, visitation machinery had turned increasingly toward the inspection of parishes and of parishioners' behaviour, a trend that took on new urgency in the Elizabethan church.[13] The regularity of these visitations varied, based both on local custom and the zeal of particular ecclesiastical officials, but the general mandate saw visits by the archdeacons twice a year; visits by episcopal officials at least once every three years; and general visitations of the archbishops' provinces on their accession, at their discretion, or by order of the queen and privy council.[14]

Just how closely these requirements were followed – and to what extent they were continuations of previous Tudor practice or were innovations – is difficult to parse. A comparative account of the numbers of visitations held before and after the break from Rome is, unfortunately, impossible. Fragments of records have allowed us to find a long history of monastic and episcopal visitation, but their archival survival is extremely limited.[15] In many cases, any sort of comprehensive schedule for visitations appears only in the Elizabethan records.[16] There are hints, though, of previous large-scale visitations. For example, in the diocese of Norwich, the first full extant diocesan visitation in the archives dates from 1555, though the records do preserve a visitation from one of its archdeaconries from more than twenty years earlier, and evidence of an Edwardian visitation also survives. In the West Country, visitations survive from the early sixteenth century, though the most substantial records exist from the 1550s onward.[17]

What *is* clear, however, is that by the mid-Elizabethan period at the very least the prescribed calendar of visitations was largely followed and that the process became regularized. The diocese of Chichester held episcopal visitations near to clockwork every three years from 1558 onward.[18] The diocese of York saw primary or ordinary visitations at least once every four years from 1567.[19] While archidiaconal records survive less fully than episcopal ones, these too seem to have been regularly held. In West Sussex, the call books record the archdeacon's visitations every single year of the 1560s; in the archdeaconry of Norwich, surviving records indicate an almost-unbroken streak of annual visitations beginning in the late 1580s.[20] Church officials became adept at the process. Early, slightly chaotic visitation books, with parishes hastily added in the order they appeared, gave way to orderly, even elegant volumes, with parishes listed in alphabetical order for ease of reference.[21] The Elizabethan ecclesiastical officials had learned how to monitor, and they could do it with brutal competence.

In other words, across much – if not all – of England, parishioners regularly and routinely were examined by ecclesiastical authorities. In some cases, particularly by the end of Elizabeth's reign, this could mean parishes saw two, three, even four visitations per year. The churchwardens of Tintinhull in Somerset recorded travel expenses for their biannual trips to the visitation in Somerton, some nine miles away, or the closer one in Ilchester, as well as a January 1596 "extraordinary visitation …

for the recusants."[22] The fragmented accounts of Shobrooke, Devon, record two visitations as early as 1588.[23] Pittington, just outside the city of Durham, was the subject of frequent regular visitations and special summonses from ecclesiastical authorities. In 1593 alone, the wardens appeared twice before the archbishop, who held two separate visitations in July and September, and at least once before Robert Prentice, their local ecclesiastical official.[24] Far-flung areas were nevertheless visited with regularity; the borderlands of Northumbria saw visitations at least twelve times in the last five years of the sixteenth century.[25] The most extreme examples of the system can be found in the records of the London parishes, whose proximity to England's bureaucratic centre left them subject to the strictest scrutiny. In St Martin-in-the-Fields, visitations were part of the annual parochial calendar from the first years of Elizabeth's reign. Beginning in the early 1580s, biannual archdeacons' visitations began to be explicitly mentioned, as did "quarter bills" of presentment. Neither political nor epidemiological emergency halted the bureaucratic grind. During the horrific outbreak of plague in 1593, the wardens and sidemen attended the archdeacon's visitation in the spring and another visitation held by Dr Creake of the Court of Arches in July, presented a quarter bill in the end of summer, and appeared at the bishop's visitation in mid-October.[26] It was an exhausting level of oversight. But the result was a system in which parishes, from the capital to far-flung Devon or Durham, were brought ever closer into engagement with the state church.

This engagement was, on the surface in any case, fairly straightforward. In the weeks leading up to the visitation, a set of questions was delivered to the parishes for the consideration of the ministers, churchwardens, and sidemen. These queries, many of which survive today in their original printed format, were known as the visitation articles. Parish officials were expected to examine the state of affairs in the parish with a mind to these questions, and to report to the site of the visitation with a full presentment of parochial faults (or the lack thereof). The visitations themselves were held over the course of several weeks in a succession of market towns or ecclesiastical seats. There, church officials would hold a religious session that mixed the most mundane administrative work with the high drama of a local inquisition.

The visitation was a pageant of obedience. The audience arrived well in time for the beginning of proceedings; those from farther afield often came to town the night before, treating themselves to meat and drink on the parish's dime before appearing at the appointed place to give their reports. There, they heard opening sermons rendered with great fervour and pomp, touching on issues of conformity and church discipline. These were also moments to entrench and defend the ecclesiastical system itself. Particularly in the mid-Elizabethan period, there was a push amongst the godly to refashion visitations as presbyterian synods, which is to say a gathering of learned church elders instead of a model driven by a bishop or his authorities; this was sharply rejected in both personal meeting and public preaching.[27] In the face of critique, the conformists doubled down. John Beatniffe, a protégé of Richard Bancroft, castigated critics of the episcopal system in his 1588 visitation sermon. "We live under a Christian Magistrate," he proclaimed, "without whose authority (in my judgment) it is not lawful for any man to execute any office in Church or commonwealth."[28] Such sermons were coupled with the power of the process in action, with the very presence of the ministers – however reluctant or disgruntled – legitimating the authority of the episcopate and its oversight. In the case of episcopal visitations, ministers were next enjoined to present their licences to preach and evidence of fitness: again, a ritual of episcopal authority and validity of that authority. The laymen's obeisance came next. Churchwardens and sidemen presented their reports of the parochial defaults, which visitation officials translated into their own records. These records created a master index of individuals charged with offences, from which citations to appear in an ecclesiastical court were formed.[29]

The process continued in the weeks that followed. Church courts compiled the lists of presentments, then issued citations to parishes, calling upon those at fault to appear before them. The summoner, sometimes called the apparitor, often transported these missives; one can imagine the opinion of these officers bearing such writs varied little from that of Chaucer's some two hundred years earlier. ("But wel I woot he lyed right in dede; Of cursing oghte ech gilty man him drede."[30]) In general, such citations have not survived, though there is some evidence that they would have been posted on parish doors if not handed directly to the accused party.[31] Once a parishioner had received a citation, he or she was compelled to attend the court or be excommunicated. Here, location mattered. Citations were issued geographically, so parishioners attending the court could expect to be in the company of others presented from their deanery, if not their parish.[32] The gathered co-defendants were known, not just to the courts but to each other. It was nearly impossible to stay anonymous: both the accusation and the testimony was recorded by the clerks and overheard by one's neighbours.

Surviving court books reveal the pace and quality of such appearances. The clerk or registrar first recorded the name of the parish, accompanied by a short description of the accused and the offence. Testimony regarding the offence followed, usually begun in Latin but with verbatim testimony inscribed in English, with details of the court's findings or sentence ending the entry. The detail present in both the testimony and the findings varied considerably, with some immediately confessing and others attempting to explain their behaviour. Those who did not appear were noted as excommunicate, while others either had their charges dismissed or were required to produce evidence of penance for their transgression.[33] Notably, the court books remained live documents, active long after the visitation itself had disbanded. Charges could be resolved months, even years, after the visitation process had begun. For example, when Gabriel Anderson visited the court in York in 1591 to answer the charge that he was a recusant, the court's registrar detailed evidence that Gabriel had not taken the required communion the previous Easter. The court ordered Gabriel to make immediate correction and conform to the sacramental requirements of the church. Eighteen months later, the same registrar recorded a confirmation by Gabriel's minister that he "hath received the communion twice since he was presented and is dutiful in coming to the church." As such, all Gabriel's charges were dismissed, and he was absolved – nearly two years after the accusation had first been made.[34]

In other words, the visitation was very much a *process*, rather than a one-off event. From the first issuance of the citations to the conclusion of the last closed case, a visitation could take upward of three years to complete, with the larger and more complex metropolitan and episcopal visitations particularly expansive. Context is important here: with archdeacons' visitations occurring anywhere from two to four times per year, episcopal visitations at least every three years, and metropolitan visitations held at will, the parish would be under near-constant investigation.[35] These visitations often overlapped, both in chronology and in content.

Figure 1.2 A sketch from a book of legal forms and opinions from the Durham church courts. The figure in the middle exhorts the petitioners, *Dic mihi veritatum*, "Speak the truth to me!"

The demands of such a complex and constant system of investigation and assessment were heavy. Indeed, by the end of Elizabeth's reign, even the convocation of bishops began to wonder whether such visitations were too onerous for parochial officials. Archbishop Whitgift, in 1601, circulated a letter to the bishops in which he claimed "that by reason of the often keeping of courts by commissaries, and by the archdeacon's officials, and by the multitude of several Apparitors serving under them, the subject was almost the next weekly with attendance on their several courts, to their infinite charge and daily vexation. And further, that by a disorder … of making quarter bills of presentments … the poor men, who were chosen churchwardens, by their continual attendance on those courts, were, in their estates, hindered greatly in leaving their day labour for attendance there."[36] If annoying for the wardens, the over-investigation of parishes created a tight net to catch both the socially and religiously unorthodox. It brought them from the parishes across England into the church courts, there to receive sentence and to return to the parishes to make their penances and their apologies.

Such processes, of course, were only effective if taken seriously by the population. Traditionally, historians described such visitations as impotent and incompetent. Mid-twentieth-century historians were particularly acerbic in their assessment of the inadequacies of visitations, arguing that offenders routinely ignored citations and that neither the process nor the punishments of the church courts were taken particularly seriously.[37] In doing so, they leaned heavily on the Elizabethan critics of the visitation, particularly the godly anti-episcopals who critiqued the process, and particularly the sentence of excommunication, as weak and inadequate. These historians never really grappled, though, with the contradiction at the heart of the puritan critique: the godly argued on one hand that visitations and ecclesiastical justice were toothless or ignorable and, on the other, that they were draconian and despotic.[38] (What these critics wanted, of course, was a system of disciplining that was exactly as invasive as the visitations, but managed by synods or even individual clerics rather than bishops.[39]) Nor, on the whole, did they examine the records of the church courts themselves, instead more often taking written complaints at face value.

When Martin Ingram began to look at the courts in the 1980s, however, he found something startling: Elizabethan men and women *did* take these visitations and their court processes seriously. Indeed, his analyses of ecclesiastical records indicated that anywhere from 60 to 90 per cent of those cited in the visitations did appear at some point before the ecclesiastical courts – roughly on par with those cited to appear in civil courts.[40] The numbers are similar in other visitations. In the diocese of Bath and Wells, for instance, a 1597 visitation saw over fourteen hundred laymen presented for offences as parishioners (rather than in any official role, such as wardens). Of these, just 250 refused to come to court and were excommunicated.[41] To some, that number might seem evidence of the weakness of the court, but that is only true if one is seeking perfection. In fact, 82 per cent of those presented for misdemeanours appeared at the church courts, a number in line with Ingram's findings in Norfolk. By and large, people called to the church courts took the proceedings and punishments seriously enough to attend to be sentenced.

Such figures are even more remarkable when one thinks about just who was being hauled before the church courts. These were not an unbiased cross-section of the parish community: they were, by definition, those who had been accused of violating serious social and religious norms. Some of these accusations were minor, like tangled probate business or not helping to keep parish paths clean. But those presented also included accused adulterers, drunks, scolds, swearers, brawlers, gamblers, and witches – as well a scattering of avowed recusants or radical separatists.[42] These were not usually model citizens. And yet, even among those so accused, there was a remarkable obedience to the ecclesiastical courts. Some may have come eagerly, to clear their name or plead their case, but the sheer coercive power of the ecclesiastical courts should not be underestimated. While some describe them as toothless, they had potent tools at their disposal. As we will see in the final chapter of the book, the penalty of excommunication – one often scoffed at by godly critics of the church – was taken seriously by most of the population. It had significant spiritual, material, and social consequences, and many attended the courts despite the difficulties or costs in order to forestall or resolve threats of becoming an excommunicate. There was financial coercion, too, with fines levied against those who refused to come to court. And while the Elizabethan ecclesiastical courts themselves had limited powers of physical coercion, they could and did work with secular courts to punish the most stubborn offenders. Thus, for instance, Elizabeth Maunswell of North

Petherton, Somerset, was presented to the justices of the peace in 1593 "for remaining excommunicated for the last four months for absence from the church and not receiving communion."[43] But such cases were rare. In most, the accused came to clear their names, to avoid or to lift the sentence of excommunication, or to avoid further fines and costs.

It was not a system of perfect justice. Resolute nonconformists (whether godly or recusant), the transient, those living in borderlands or very remote parishes, and noted criminals were less susceptible to ecclesiastical pressures to attend court once cited.[44] Indeed, the minority of people who failed to appear did so for a host of reasons. In some cases, it was contempt or apathy. But in others, it was incapacity rather than recalcitrance. The aged, the pregnant, the infirm, the dipsomaniac, or the destitute might avoid court for reasons that had nothing to do with their opinions about its legitimacy or about religious orthodoxy more generally. The long process of justice did not help: much could happen in the three, twelve, even eighteen months after the visitation. In the most extreme examples, the accused died before the case could be resolved. And yet, if the system was not perfect, it was extraordinary and, on the whole, effective.

Though lacking the extensive capacity for physical coercion enjoyed by the secular courts, the ecclesiastical system had distinct advantages in the monitoring and control of misbehaviour. By and large, the secular courts relied on the passive response of local officials in the implementation of justice, while the spiritual courts had an active program of investigation.[45] That is to say, for example, if men engaged in a brawl, they would be arrested by a constable and brought before the quarter sessions; the imperative for action lay with the local official reacting to the crime. In contrast, the ecclesiastical courts themselves compelled the presentation of crimes and misdemeanours through the mechanisms of the visitations (and on more rare cases, the summoners themselves). Rather than waiting for the report of a crime to reach the courts, the visitations actively delineated offences and pursued offenders.[46]

Thus, through the visitations, the ecclesiastical justice system fundamentally defined the terms of its own inquiry. Presentable offences were what the visitations deemed them to be. Unlike statutory law, which was subject to legislative oversight, visitation articles did not have to pass parliamentary muster, nor were they always subject to Convocation's approval. Though these articles and injunctions often drew from the

Acts of Uniformity and Supremacy, they were not limited to matters included therein. Issues deemed particularly dangerous or important could be added or stressed in the visitation articles, resulting in an investigative survey tailored to suit the most pressing current needs of the diocese, the archdeaconry, or the church writ large. Thus, in addition to their broad scope of inquiry, visitations allowed the kind of specificity necessary to cope with evolving challenges to religious orthodoxy. It was flexibility, not rigidity, that made the visitations so effective.

An early example of such responsiveness can be found in the very first visitation articles from Elizabeth's reign. These visitations privileged the restoration of basic reformed principles and the suppression of the most obvious Catholicism in the parishes. The first three articles of the 1559 visitation inquired whether ministers were resident and performing sacraments; whether churches had been stripped of their Catholic fabric; and whether the ministers recited "the Lords prayer, the belief, and the ten Commandments in English."[47] Similar queries were made in the first of the 1561 Injunctions of the Bishop of Norwich.[48] In 1563, however, the newest concerns about nonconformity centred not on Catholicism but on reformed ministers who refused to wear the surplice.[49] The "vestarian controversy" of the mid-1560s preoccupied Archbishop Parker and, to a lesser extent, the queen, who had no patience for lack of uniformity amongst those who had heretofore been general champions of the settlement. Immediately, questions regarding the clerical vestments entered the purview of the visitation. Parker's 1563 visitation began as before, asking about the performance of service and sacrament and the implementation of church fabric reform. The third question, however, now inquired whether clergy "do use in the time of the celebration of divine service to wear a surplice."[50] Preoccupation with clerical dress continued in the visitation articles and injunctions in the 1560s; as late as 1567, the metropolitan visitation of the diocese of Norwich still placed questions about the wearing of the surplice in the first three articles of inquiry.[51] However, the Catholic fears engendered by the Northern Rebellion of 1569 refocused investigatory attention, and the emphasis of the articles shifted quickly to an emphasis on prayer-book conformity within the parishes.[52] The responsiveness of the visitation articles permitted episcopal authorities to react swiftly and decisively in probing English parishes for the most pressing forms of misbehaviour.

The visitation articles themselves, then, give a glimpse into the anxieties of the church at any given time. Though some articles repeated in every visitation, others appeared or vanished as matters came to the fore or faded into the background. Some of these changes will be outlined in more detail later in the book: church fabric in chapter 3, rectorial responsibility in chapter 4, and church attendance and participation in the eucharist in chapter 5. In brief, however, the articles reveal a church deeply concerned about matters both doctrinal and social. Visitations always sought to find those outside of conformity to the church, whether they be Catholic recusants or Protestant radicals. The material life of the church was scrutinized to make sure it was in order, both in terms of provision and upkeep. Clerical fitness was interrogated, as was the rectitude of churchwardens and other lay officials. Some fears were perennial. Chief amongst these constant concerns was the moral and social regulation of the country. Much of the best work in social history over the past half-century has been devoted to understanding the reasons behind such panic.[53] The growing demographic and economic pressures of the late sixteenth century, combined with a reformed emphasis on regulation of social ills and sin, resulted in an increased emphasis on moral probity. While there may not have been a full-fledged "crisis of order," there was certainly a growing obsession with monitoring potential lapses in morality.

Ecclesiastical courts, especially the archidiaconal courts, began to prosecute these matters in record numbers by the early 1580s, a trend that continued well into the seventeenth century.[54] "Bawdy courts," as they came to be known, were the places where the offences raised in the visitation articles were adjudicated. As the process of visitations became a well-oiled machine, and authorities became increasingly panicked about moral decline, the level of ecclesiastical inquiry deepened ever further. Sexual immorality, including fornication, illegitimate childbirth, and adultery, was a target from the earliest Elizabethan articles. The 1559 visitation inquired simply if "there be any incontinent persons," in the parish.[55] By the later Elizabethan period, the description of such offenders had multiplied, as in this 1592 visitation of the diocese of Hereford: "whether any be known or suspected to be adulterers, fornicators, incestuous persons, bawds, or receivers of incontinent persons into their houses, or which convey or suffer them to goe away before they doe make satisfaction to the congregation offended."[56]

Other moral offenders included "blasphemers of the name of God, great or often swearers";[57] "all sowers of discord between neighbour and neighbour within your Parish";[58] "drunkards … railers, scolds";[59] "or any persons that by common fame and speech of people, are noted, as vehemently suspected of any of these or such like faults, or either wise act scandalous or offensive."[60] Importantly, little evidence was required to present an offender on moral grounds. Rumour, or "common fame," was enough to yield a presentment to the church courts. The visitation records became littered, even dominated, by such accusations.[61]

From swearing to churchyard fence repair, illegitimate birth to recusancy, drunkenness to missing tablecloths, the church targeted anything that it felt undermined the religious and moral stability of the country. By the last decades of the century, visitations had grown far longer and more comprehensive than anything imagined during the early years of the Elizabethan Reformation. The first visitation, meant to enforce the Injunctions, had fifty-five points of inquiry, but the majority of visitations in that first decade were far less detailed. Elizabeth's first archbishop of Canterbury, Matthew Parker, in his initial metropolitan visitation of Canterbury had just twenty-five interrogatories; Bishop John Parkhurst's 1569 visitation of Norwich had only thirty.[62] But as the visitations became more regular and less experimental, and as the church became more stable, the scope of inquiry often expanded. While some stayed within the general remit of the early visitations, others grew granular and even baroque. Bishop John Aylmer's 1586 visitation of London had seventy-five articles, divided up into six different subsets of inquiry.[63] The Lincoln visitation of 1588 included a kind of subject tag in the margins ("schoolmasters," "superstitious books defaced," "visiting the sick," "tellers of destinies," "forgers of wills"), presumably to allow wardens to easily find the offences without wading through the dense text.[64] The 1600 visitation of the bishop of Chichester had a full eighty-four questions, from the first, asking if the church was kept in good repair, to the last, examining whether the minister let anyone else hold his benefice, tithes, or glebe land.[65] Visitations had become massive undertakings.

So how was all of this to be regulated, to be monitored, and to be policed? The obvious answer would be a turn to the ministers as the agents of Reformation. And yet, the clergy, not the laity, were in many ways the prime targets of visitations. Visitation after visitation asked first and foremost for churchwardens to report on clerical orthodoxy and doctrinal adherence. Archbishop Parker began his 1563 visitation articles by asking "whether Divine service be said or sung by your Minister … duly and reverently, as it is set forth by the laws of this realm, without any kind of variation. And whether the holy Sacraments be likewise ministered reverently, in such manner as by the laws of this Realm is appointed."[66] Similar wording or concerns can be found in the first question of metropolitan and episcopal visitation articles throughout Elizabeth's reign; almost forty years later, in 1601, Richard Bancroft's London visitation began by asking "Whether is common prayer read by your minister … distinctly and reverently upon all Sundays and holidays, and in such order as is set forth by the laws of this Realm in the book of common prayer, without any kind of alteration, omitting or adding anything, and at due and convenient hours."[67] The echoes of language through the decades reminds us of the remarkable continuities of Elizabeth's reign – continuities neither unchallenged nor unquestioned, but still present.

This question was invariably followed by at least a dozen – sometimes closer to thirty – more questions about clerical behaviour.[68] These articles inquired whether ministers were resident in their parishes; whether they were licensed; whether they were learned in the Scripture; whether they were charitable to the poor and strict to the immoral; whether, in addition to reading the service of the Book of Common Prayer, they had sermons preached at least four times a year; whether they instructed the youth; and whether they preached obedience to Queen Elizabeth.[69] The motivation for this concern was clear and obvious: especially in the early years, the Elizabethan church did not trust its ministry. How could it? The religious turmoil of the first thirty years of the Reformation had produced zealots of all stripes – as well as thousands more clerics who had learned to conform for reasons both personal and pastoral. Some, especially the most prominent, had publicly declared their disapproval of the Elizabethan settlement, but most quietly adapted to yet another religious change.[70] Pre-Elizabethan clergy generally served well into her reign; one study of Lincoln shows that almost 40 per cent of clergy in 1576 had been ordained before Elizabeth's accession some seventeen years earlier.[71]

These were not the spiritual leaders that a Reformation needed. While the quietly skeptical-yet-conforming ministers bothered the queen very little, they deeply troubled the more militantly Protestant of her bishops. Still more insidious, in the minds of the new church hierarchy, of Elizabeth, and of her privy council alike, were clerics they feared were secretly promulgating Catholic practices in their parishes. As the bishop of Carlisle wrote to Elizabeth's chief councillor in 1561, "The priests are wicked imps of Antichrist, and for the most part very ignorant and stubborn; past measure false and subtle. Only fear makes them obedient."[72] The bishop of Hereford reported to the privy council in 1564 that many of his ministers were "but dissemblers and rank papists," making the church "very darkness and an example of contempt of true, religion."[73] Immediately after the settlement, tight regulation of the clergy was recommended to the bishops, including quarter-annual public perusal of the licences of ministers and schoolteachers, restricting the clergy to those graduated from the universities of Cambridge and Oxford, and the proof of ministers' good reputation at the time of licensing.[74] Such plans never came to fruition, largely because of the enormous clerical shortage facing the church in the early 1560s.[75] In the diocese of Ely, for example, only a third of parishes had a resident clergyman, while only half of those – or a mere two dozen – were learned preachers.[76] While the clergy gradually became more learned and more sympathetic to Protestantism, these concerns continued well into Elizabeth's reign.

What this meant, at its base, was that the state church could not trust its own agents. The process of enacting and enforcing religious reform, then, could not be left solely in the hands of the clergy. Instead, the church had to turn to lay parishioners to regulate orthodoxy in the parishes – including the orthodoxy of the minister. Though churchwardens had long been responsible for parish finances and administration, such regulation of behaviour was new, a product of the later English Reformation.[77]

To some extent, this worked. Visitation records are littered with presentations of parishioners and clergy alike for irreligion and misconduct. The churchwardens of Haverland in Norfolk, for example, reported their vicar "for that we had no Sermon for the space of three years, and for that we had no [officially-promulgated] homily except one for the space of five quarters of a year, and no communion never since Easter last."[78] And yet, such a reliance on lay members had the unintended consequence of putting much of the control of the Reformation outside the hands of the church. Unlike ministers, churchwardens were both elected and unlicensed; in their responsibilities and importance to the state, they were perhaps most akin to constables and other local office-holders.[79] The course and pace of the English Reformation, then, was built on twinned but very different structures of power and authority: the top-down bureaucracy of the episcopal system, and the participation of amateur local laymen.

The reliance on churchwardens thus gave the parishes a new centre of power and authority. Officially, a check was placed on dissenting ministers; churchwardens were, as we shall see in the next chapter, empowered to report their ministers for moral, personal, or religious faults. Visitations asked churchwardens to report their ministers for everything from poor preaching to sexual immorality to suspicious doctrine.[80] These new powers were, in theory, meant only to bring the parish in line with church conformity. But in practice, the religious, political, and personal proclivities of the churchwardens could deeply colour the course of the Reformation. Conservative churchwardens could protect ministers who leaned toward Catholicism; radical churchwardens could protect those who shied away from the ceremonial compromises of the Elizabethan Reformation.[81]

Of course, the converse was also true: zealous churchwardens of all stripes could and did promote their own interests in the parishes. Ministers who expressed themselves contrary to the opinions of the churchwardens could find themselves, at the very least, deeply embarrassed. Mr Fisher of Horstead, Norfolk, was reported by the wardens for refusing to wear his surplice (a garment much despised by evangelical preachers for its similarity to Catholic vestments) – as was his reply when questioned by them: "what dost thou make such an account of it; it is but a shitten Rag."[82] And when hostilities between churchwardens and ministers boiled over, churchwardens had a powerful tool at their disposal: they could, and did, report ministers for dereliction of duty – a charge far more serious in the eyes of a wary church than the minister's counter-claims of lay misbehaviour or unneighbourliness.[83] Ministers found themselves brought before Church courts, deprived of their livings, and even imprisoned, based largely on the evidence of lay churchwardens; conversely, unorthodox ministerial activity could be hidden from the eyes of the authorities for years with the connivance of sympathetic churchwardens.[84]

This is not to say, of course, that ministers were without power or that churchwardens were always trusted by the authorities – far from it. There was suspicion that churchwardens were reporting dishonestly, and some went so far as to accuse them of being corrupt. Bishop Horn of Winchester, a Marian exile, actively accused wardens of taking bribes for covering up misbehaviour, writing bitterly that "such is the fear of the purse more than of God's curse."[85] Visitation records reading *omnia bene* are looked on with skepticism by contemporary historians, and no doubt much was hidden from church authorities, whether because of friendship, sympathy, fear, or kickback. The authorities dealt with this by creating an elaborate set of checks and balances, not dissimilar to how they dealt with other potentially corruptible officials like coroners.[86] First was the check on their own conscience, with churchwardens forced to swear an oath that they would "not present any person for malice, hatred, or evil will, nor spare any for favour, for fear, or any corrupt affection, but … shall faithfully discharge [their] consciences, as men having the fear of God before [their] eyes."[87] By the later Elizabethan period, articles often added a new check, requiring churchwardens to report on previous holders of the office. Wardens were asked not only if they had failed in their duties, but whether "the Churchwardens in the years before you" had permitted any misdoings and whether they "have of any private corrupt affection concealed any crime or other disorder in their time done in your parish, and have not presented the same to the Bishop, Chauncelor, Archdeacon, Commissary, or such other as had authority to reform the same."[88] As a last constraint, visitations brought in the clergy, routinely asking ministers to report on their parishioners and even the wardens themselves.[89] Churchwardens and other lay officers who had failed to inform on their neighbours' faults could find themselves in the crosshairs of the church courts. To take but one example, Henry Roome of Bathford was excommunicated for "not presenting John Tyler and Edith Longe, being to his knowledge suspected of [sexual] incontinence," his charges only dismissed by evidence that he "had been for a long time released from [formal] office."[90] Little wonder, perhaps, that churchwardens frequently presented even their own defaults, often for minor offences like a dilapidated churchyard fence.[91] It was an effective system, but it was not perfect. Perjury, whether pious or no, was a subtle undercurrent in the visitation process. The argument is thus not to suggest that the laity became the sole reliable or religious authority in the parish. However, what *is* clear is that a new power base had opened in the parish, one that could hasten or hide the discovery of religious misbehaviour. The course of the Reformation in the parishes was directed as much by the behaviour and beliefs of the laity as that of the ministry.

This was the world in which Elizabeth Watson gave her penance. Her transgression with Walter Webster had reached the ears of the churchwardens, who duly reported it to the ecclesiastical authorities in one of their regular visitations. She had travelled from Cawood to York, where in front of the church court she was duly examined and confessed. In doing so, she avoided the burdens of excommunication, but she brought upon herself the shame of penance. She returned to Cawood, stood in front of her congregation, recited the penance as written by the church authorities (routine for them, so much so that they had preprinted forms with instructions; intensely personal and humiliating for her). She had the congregation pray together, uniting in concert as a communal voice of both sanction and reparation. And all this was then certified and recorded by parochial authorities, who sent notice back to the church courts, where it was again sorted, recorded, and preserved.

It was state formation in action. The levels and layers of bureaucracy that grew up around the mill of ecclesiastical justice were unlike anything that had been seen before, touching far more of the population and invading far more deeply into people's personal lives. And yet, it was a central bureaucracy that was built on a seemingly paradoxical reliance on the parish: the professional, rigidly hierarchical, and increasingly powerful ecclesiastical centre at York relied on the local, communal structure of the parish, supervised largely by semi-elected, unpaid laymen. Crucially, the Elizabethan church did not see this as a paradox. The reliance on the parish and its laymen was deliberate and generally effective, just as it was for the system of secular justice. Indeed, in its capacity to create, maintain, and regulate change, the parish community was ideal. It knew its participants.

The Elizabethan church relied so heavily upon the parishes because its goal, ultimately, was conformity – and in the parish, conformity was legible in ways that it never could be to the centralized church. As one of her very first proclamations, in December 1558, made clear, Elizabeth found religious dissent an "occasion to break common quiet" and interrupt "the quiet governance of all manner [of] her subjects."[92] This is not to say that the concept of orthodoxy itself was not contested. In fact, as we shall see throughout the book, such contestations were at the heart of religious debate in the period.[93] But the harder reformers or radicals or recusants pushed against state-mandated conformity, the more Elizabeth doubled down on it: resistance became evidence of the need for firmer rules and laws. Though primarily intended to regulate what was seen as dangerous religious nonconformity en masse, measures adopted to regulate religious behaviour compelled the construction of strict parish communities in which such authority could be maintained.

Take, for instance, the question of church attendance, which was made mandatory from 1559. From the first, the Elizabethan church used visitations to ensure that parishioners came to their church. In order to do so, they created a new emphasis on borders, one that delineated and essentialized the bounds of the public community. The limits of the parish – who belonged and who didn't, who was local and who was foreign – began to be emphasized in new and intensified ways. While the Act of Uniformity, passed in 1559, had allowed parishioners, "to endeavour themselves to resort to their parish church … or upon reasonable let thereof, to some usual place where common prayer and such service of God shall be used," church authorities were suspicious of those who regularly worshipped outside of their home parish.[94] The first Elizabethan visitation, made only a few months after the passing of this act, asked wardens to report "whether you know any that in contempt of their own parish Church, do resort to any other Church."[95] Still, a number of early Elizabethan visitations were more flexible – or at least more vague – in this regard. Archbishop Parker's metropolitan visitation of 1563, for example, merely asked "whether the lay people be diligent in coming to the church on the holy days," a formula used throughout the 1560s.[96] The events of 1569–71, however, which saw the Northern Rebellion and the issuance of *Regnans in Excelsis* (the papal bull that formally excommunicated Elizabeth and declared that her subjects owed her no duty), prompted a far stricter approach to root out recusant resistance.

New emphasis was placed on church attendance and, more specifically, attendance in one's *own* parish church. Such a fixed notion of legitimate worship had a twofold effect: first, it ensured that parishioners could not give a false excuse of attending a fabricated service somewhere else; second, it created a licit, legible community. The London episcopal visitation of 1571 queried "whether the people of your parish … do faithfully and diligently resort with their family to their parish church or chapel," continuing, "whether your … minister hath at any time received any that is not of his own parish to the holy Communion, and for what cause or consideration he has done so.[97] The Canons of 1571 similarly instructed churchwardens to report "any strangers from other parishes, [who] come more often and commonly to their church."[98] Despite being a national church, the question of *belonging* was very much defined in the local, particularly from the 1570s.

As time went on, new visitation articles often contained specific innovations meant to fix the boundless within boundaries. The parliament of 1581 had raised the fine for non-attendance from a shilling to £20 a month, and anxiety over nonconformists only grew, prompting new ways of delineating a congregation.[99] The metropolitan visitation of Canterbury in 1582 explicitly tied together those who avoided sermons and those who moved outside the bounds of the parish, ending in a series of questions focusing on those who slipped out mid-service – or otherwise "disturbeth the Minister" – by asking "whether in contempt of their parish Church or Minister, doe resort to any other Church."[100] Just two years later, the bishop of Coventry and Litchfield attempted to control wealthy recusants by asking "whether any having divers houses of remove, doe shift from place to place, in colours to defeat the performance of the Christian duties in those behalfs."[101] And as there was anxiety about those leaving the parish, so too was there concern over strangers entering a parish. Wykeham's 1594 episcopal visitation of Lincoln demanded to know "whether there be any strangers that sojourn in your parish, especially about Easter, and doo absent themselves from Church" – an obvious reference to fears of Jesuit missionaries, but also one that touched on fears of local recusants leaving their home parishes to falsely claim communion in another.[102] Children were to be fixed in the parish, with baptism made "in their own Parish church," not "baptized in any other place."[103] (These baptisms, of course, would then be recorded in the parish registers, which were shared with ecclesiastical authorities on a regular basis.)

Delineation of belonging was only one side of the coin: these laws and the questions they prompted in the visitation articles demanded an extension of local bureaucracy to maintain accurate counts of the congregation. In order to regulate church attendance in the bishopric of Exeter, for example, churchwardens were instructed to make a list of all servants in the parish, to keep this list in writing, and to cross-check it against church attendance every month.[104] Such controls were clear and were to be made public. In 1598, one set of visitation articles insisted that the "Minister or Reader, do openly every Sunday, after he have read the second lesson at morning and evening prayer, monish and warn the churchwardens and sworn men … to observe who contrary to the said Statute offend in absenting themselfs negligently or willfully from the parish church or chapel."[105] Such lists could and did make their ways to the highest echelons of church and state; surveys of non-attendance were compelled not only by the bishops but also by the central organs of state, as we will see in chapter 5. These small, weekly, local reports could make their way into the hands of men like Burghley or Walsingham, and they shifted policy: from the parish to the privy council in a few short steps.

All of this required a clear understanding of local communities: who should be attending services, who was officially part of the parish, who *belonged*. It relied on a firm understanding of boundaries and borders, only encouraged by the mandated ceremony of "beating the bounds," a Rogationtide perambulation in which the community, as Steve Hindle puts it, was "in the act of defining themselves."[106] It also required an understanding of the parochial population. While the main targets of attendance requirements were, of course, recusancy and radicalism, the end product was a population that was far more intelligible to the state. It was an iterative cycle. Real terror over religious nonconformity created intensifying laws about church attendance; these laws created a new emphasis on borders and belonging; this emphasis required new oversight; and this increased oversight revealed new evidence of nonconformity, which provoked the sequence again. As the cycle continued, there was a growing ecclesiastical and legislative effort to locate and to fix people within their parishes, an effort that was only strengthened by the regularity and vigour of the visitation process. The growing confidence and scope of the visitations was the product of this cycle: the state crystallizing on the page.

Such regulation seems at odds with our sense of the vitality and vibrancy of migration patterns and geographical mobility in late-sixteenth-century England. The early modern English identified not only with their parish, but also with their county and, increasingly, with their country and the wider world.[107] Seasonal, economic, and life-cycle mobility resulted in a continual influx of new people into the parish. And yet it was this very vibrancy that seemed so threatening and that provoked a debate about residency. We have seen this in studies on poverty in early modern England, where economic stakes of residency were magnified as the proliferation of civic poor relief put the onus for providing support for the poor on the inhabitants of the parish. An increasingly loud and heated national and parochial conversation ensued about the definition of just who was worthy to receive this local support – a definition that often included long residency in an area.[108] Thus, in a time of increased geographical mobility, there was also an increased emphasis on defining and controlling that mobility – just as, in a time of high-stakes debate over religious identities and allegiances, there was an increased emphasis on controlling church attendance and behaviour. And, as in debates about poor relief, this attempt at control was focused around a stricter and clearer definition of community and its boundaries.

It was, in essence, the codification of a particular conception of the public – one with very clear outlines. The efficacy of penance like that of Elizabeth Watson and thousands of others relied on these changes. It was part of a larger project of sharpening the boundaries and definition of community in early modern England, a project embraced by an Elizabethan church and state deeply concerned by questions of order, orthodoxy, and conformity.[109]

Penance had, of course, been part of the church in England for centuries. Indeed, penance was at the heart of late-medieval Catholic ecclesiology: a sacrament, central to both cosmology and soteriology. Penance was bound closely to one's afterlife, reducing time spent in painful purgatory; as one late-medieval poet put it, "But in purgatory, the souls dwelleth still, till they be cleansed of all manner ill … every day of penance, that is done here, shall stand there in stead, of a whole year."[110] Pre-Reformation penance took two forms, generally: that ordered by the parish priest and that ordered by the ecclesiastical courts. The former was tied to the practice of auricular confession and was a sacrament; this penance was meant to be private, and recent evidence has pointed to the relative seclusion afforded to those confessing, even in an age before the confessional had made its way into church architecture.[111] The latter, the penance mandated by ecclesiastical courts, tended to be far more public. By the early sixteenth century, such penance quite often involved localized pilgrimages to holy sites and large donations to charities and chantries.[112]

The Reformation saw an end to both these forms of penance. No longer a sacrament, penance was divorced from the relationship with the parish clergy. Auricular confession was attacked by English Protestant theologians as part of the elevation of the priesthood. The early evangelical Clement Armstrong wrote dismissively, "What then hath man to show sin to the priest, that cannot forgive him?"[113] In order to separate it from its priestly roots, and to better control its implementation, penance became the province of the ecclesiastical courts alone – yet another example of the centralizing forces at play within the Elizabethan church. Bancroft's first visitation of London made this point perhaps the most clearly, asking whether any minister "without the consent or privity of the Ordinary, caused any to do penance, or be punished either openly or otherwise for any crime punishable by the Ecclesiastical laws only."[114] It was a complete monopoly of punishment. But here too was change. Unlike the peripatetic penance of late-medieval pilgrimage, Elizabethan penance was almost always sited very specifically in the home parish of the offender.[115] Even in cases when an offender was allowed to contribute charitable funds rather than make a confession and apology to the congregation, many parishes still insisted that such payment be proclaimed publicly by the minister in time of service.[116] By the last decades of the sixteenth century, penance, as the punitive arm of the ecclesiastical courts, had become both specifically public and particularly sited within the parish.

Penance was tied as closely to place as was church attendance. The people who assembled to hear Elizabeth Watson's penance, or any similar penance, were her neighbours, her community – assembled at *their* church by rule of law, a captive audience. They were, in essence, a *mandated public*. It was this fixity and this publicity that made the stakes of penance so much sharper by the late sixteenth century. The shame of the moment was relived not with strangers at a pilgrimage site, but in front of neighbours, family, employers, friends, and enemies. This could have devastating consequences, both personally and practically. As we know from the work of historians like Craig Muldrew, Keith Wrightson, and Steve Hindle, social standing, credit, reputation – the "common fame" – were not psychological or ephemeral, but real, hard considerations of personal economy and stability.[117] The consequences of losing one's credit were immediate, damaging, and often indelible. As an angry Margaret Cotton testified to Cambridge's Commissary Court in 1603, "he that taketh away his neighbour's good name is a robber and he that robbeth his neighbour of his goods may restore them again, but he that taketh away his neighbours good name can never restore it again, he is a robber that so doethe."[118] The desire to control religious orthodoxy in the Elizabethan church, and the resulting compulsory assembly of one's neighbours and community in the parish church on a weekly basis, created a potent site of social control, a place where public, localized penance would have its largest and most powerful impact.

Moreover, the doctrine and legislation of penance in the Elizabethan church underlined and emphasized the question of community. English protestant theologians of many stripes agreed that restitution for sin had to be made as much, if not more, to *man* as to God.[119] And in cases of moral or religious failings, the crime was as much a communal as a personal one – that is to say, that those who had been offended, those who required restitution, were members of the community: the penitant had provided an "evil example," encouraging others' misbehaviour by their own. A particularly helpful example of this rhetoric can be found in the records of Wistow, where the church courts ordered John Maycock to apologize to his congregation for his lack of church attendance by using the following words: for "being absent from prayer and … abroad in the streets and other places whereby diverse concourses and assemblies of people were occasioned or allured to be present with me … and were also absent from divine service, to the dishonour of god, the grief of the godly, and the most pernicious example to others."[120] As the subject of restitution, the community was both the wronged and the means to right the wrong. Penance was about admitting fault, but it was also about asking for the spiritual assistance of one's community. Maycock was ordered to end his penance by asking the congregation, "to strengthen me that here after I do not offend in the like, I shall desire you to assist me with your prayers to almighty God."[121]

Communal shame was thus coupled with communal rehabilitation, and religious offences were cast as social offences. One's moral and religious behaviour and belief was adjudged to be of social concern, and one's reputation was tied to religious belief and behaviour. Disobedience to the church – a rejection of church authority or of the broad definitions of orthodoxy prescribed in the Thirty-Nine Articles, the Homilies, and the Book of Common Prayer – was not merely private sin but a matter of public interest. The penitential system in

Elizabethan England thus increasingly intertwined conformity and community, enforcing and reinforcing the power of the state church.

In the process of restricting and regulating attendance in the Elizabethan church, a new emphasis on parish boundaries and residency arose. This was not merely a matter of self-determined cultural identity. It was, instead, a method of controlling state-imposed behavioural practices. By enforcing strict notions of residency and by mandating compulsory attendance within these boundaries, the Elizabethan church defined the parish community – and a localized sense of the public – far more sharply than in the past. And by mandating a *public* confession, with a *public* act of penance, in which the offender both apologized to the congregation and *publicly* admitted behaviour that could ruin his or her credit or reputation, the Elizabethan state church had a profound impact on the construction of public opinion and common fame.

When Elizabeth Watson rose to her feet in 1591, she was thus enacting the Elizabethan Reformation. She spoke in front of an audience deeply seated in the parish. Watched and surveyed for their conformist attendance, the congregation was fixed to the place in new ways. To be sure, people moved in and moved away, but their residence in the parish would be noted, authorized, even reported. The entire community – or at least those physically capable of attending – were compulsory witnesses to her apology. Her misdeed had been judged and reported by men who were simultaneously agents of the state Reformation and her neighbours, her employers, maybe even family friends. The report had been official, made to the increasingly and shockingly expansive machinery of ecclesiastical oversight and justice – carried with these men as they wined and dined in the market town. Her words were formulaic, quite literally, echoing hundreds of women and men (but mostly women) across England in any given year. She spoke of her offence, of its contagious effect on public morality, begging forgiveness, asking her audience to pray for grace to be bestowed on her. A woman, alone and humiliated and vulnerable, her actions were a parable and a warning. Their potency lay in a parish more tightly bounded, a penance more clearly sited, and a church more centralized than ever before. The local was bound to the centre, and the local was bounded by borders. The new geographies of power in the Elizabethan world had built Elizabeth Watson's contrition, and as she spoke its words in that damp parish church on the banks of the Ouse, she made manifest an England transformed.

2

Policing the Parish

It was election season in the parish of All Hallows Staining. Just off Fenchurch Street – right around the corner from today's Fenchurch Street Station – the parish's stone tower was a solid, stolid landmark in the city.[1] Relatively but not extravagantly poor, it was tucked away from the busy thoroughfare, with little else to distinguish it from the constellation of other parish churches in the eastern end of the city.[2] On this day in 1568, though, it was the site of fierce contestation and sharp politicking. Four different men were vying to be elected the next churchwarden of the parish, and each had his supporters. Perhaps the richest man in the parish, Godfrey Marshall, lived on Mark Lane, just opposite the church, and was gunning for the office. But like his neighbour, John Wary, he had fallen far short: only two votes tallied, to John's single one. The real competition was between two men from the "High Street," John Montgomery on the north, and Robert Bemond on the south. If their assessments for the clerk's wages were anything to go by, they were equally matched in wealth, solvent but not rich. Robert had lived in the parish for over a decade; Montgomery for at least five years. Respectable, reputable, well-established, these two substantial men of the parish were running neck and neck. In the end, of the twenty-one votes cast, Robert secured eleven. The next year's collections bear his name at the top, his official duties recorded.[3]

The office that these men fought so fiercely to attain was a cornerstone of the Elizabethan Reformation. The machinery of the new state church ran on the energy and activity of these men (and, on some occasions, women). Everything – the gathering and distributing of church funds; the surveillance of church attendance and personal behaviour; the reports at visitations and the fulfillment of their sentences; the inventory of church goods; the selection of the clerk; the provision of poor relief – relied on their work. And yet, while the figures of churchwardens are found scattered throughout the historiography of the Reformation, comparatively little work has been focused on the office of the warden and, where it exists, tends to focus on its long history, emphasizing either its late-medieval origins or its seventeenth-century articulation. What we miss is the hinge: how and why we move from stalwart of the late-medieval gildsman to the "village snooper" of the Jacobean church.[4] Without the churchwarden, we have a Reformation by fiat, enacted by an invisible hand of change. In other words, to understand religious change in England, we need a real understanding of its churchwardens, the agents of the state church, and the rise of lay power within the parish.

The new English church was faced with a conundrum of its own making: how, exactly, was it to police its reforms? The clergy were few, and often recalcitrant or problematic. The state had neither the capability nor the interest to create, train, and deploy its own inquisition that could reach all parishes of England. Nor was a kind of Genevan consistory model plausible over such a broad area or palatable to episcopal interests. Instead, Tudor church reforms shied away from institutional innovation and toward the institutional familiar, turning to an old, familiar figure, the churchwarden. But this was a new model of a churchwarden, dynamic, influential, and deeply integrated into church machinery. Building on long-standing tradition, the Tudor reforms gave wardens powers, responsibilities, and authority far beyond anything that had come before. These lay local officers became the backbone of the English Reformation: its administrators, its executors, and its policemen.

By the time of the Henrician Reformation, churchwardens had been overseeing the parish for 275 years. Their origins in the parish are murky and organic, appearing first not in ecclesiastical statute or canon law, but rather in wills and records of gifts, part of the developing economics of medieval devotional life. Accounts from Shrewsbury Abbey's parish church make note of a group of laity known as the "Guardians of the light of the altar of the holy cross" by 1260.[5] It was a phrasing that would stick, well after altar lights were extinguished: the *guardiani ecclesiæ* of the English parishes, or as they would become known in the vernacular by the sixteenth century, the wardens of the church. The late thirteenth century found these unofficial caretakers of parochial funds springing up across England. The first known testamentary bequest came in 1261, when Alice Halye of All Saints, Bristol, left a bequest for an altar light to be managed in perpetuity by laymen drawn from across the parish. Crucially, this was not to be handled by a gild or a group of laity attached but partitioned from the parish itself, but from the parishioners writ large.[6] By 1287, the practice had become common enough that the church decided to step in; at the Synod of Exeter, the first duties of the *parochianis fide dignis* – worthy and faithful parishioners – were fully outlined.[7] In these earliest incarnations, churchwardens were above all custodians of property, responsible for the upkeep of the church goods and gradually that of the nave and the church fence. This marked a major shift in the responsibility of church finance, from the clergy to the laity.[8] Nevertheless, the authority of the thirteenth-century churchwarden was essentially (and statutorily) limited in scope, usually involving responsibility for independent and ad hoc funds, and overseen by the clergy. In most parishes, it took until the fourteenth century for any sort of real lay administration of the parish to develop.[9] This slow process of expansion meant that the churchwarden's role was very much defined by local custom and local need, varying in power, independence, and organization.[10]

By the late fourteenth century, the office of the churchwarden had grown into one of serious administrative responsibility in most English parishes. In addition to maintaining church property, churchwardens became responsible for raising funds, collecting alms, and providing the complicated accounting necessary to sustain the rich flow of late-medieval lay piety.[11] This in turn required new methods of record keeping, ones that involved literacy and numeracy in new ways. They began to write everything down: what they bought, what it cost, who sold it to them, when it was purchased, and how they paid for it. These churchwardens' accounts proliferated across this period. The very earliest extant accounts are found largely in the southwest and the northeast: Devon, Somerset, and Yorkshire.[12] Perhaps the earliest surviving account comes from the parish of St Mary, Bridgwater, a market town about thirty-five miles southwest of Bristol, where a flyleaf has been preserved noting a lease of land in 1311.[13] Those of Bath (1349), Glastonbury St John (1366), St James Yorkshire (1350), and Ripon (1354) followed close behind.[14]

On the eve of the split from Rome, the office of the churchwarden was absolutely central to the maintenance of the late-medieval parish.

The thick architecture of popular piety – church ales and summer fairs; painted walls and stained-glass windows; saints' icons, dressed and decorated and dusted; parish gilds, their dinners, and their fundraisers; bell-ringing and tapered candles; vestments, ornaments, and church plate; festal seasons adorned with holly or harvest – was supervised by the churchwardens. So too was the mundane work of roof retiling and church-fence fixing. Above all, churchwardens were the money men of the parish, collecting, managing, and distributing the accounts.

In all of this, the churchwarden stood surety, both in custody and in kind. There was prestige and honour attached to the position, as might be expected. But there was also expense and burden. Churchwardens were responsible for keeping safe the church ornament, stores, and funds, and they were personally liable for discrepancies or debts. In 1474, the four churchwardens of St Edmund's, Salisbury, oversaw the extraordinary expenses of rebuilding the church steeple and the reconstruction of the rood loft. The new marble stones, hundreds of feet of elm wood, dozens of pounds of lead, and countless lathes, nails, and pints of beer for the workers saw the payment of over £26 9s., nearly eight times as much as the previous extant accounts. Though there were good takings from gifts, collections, funeral expenses, gild lights, and church ales, the wardens still found themselves in the red and were rescued only by the indulgence of the parish: "And so the aforesaid Accountants owing clearly to the church 4s. 7d. the which been forgiven them for their good labours and so they been quiet."[15] In this case, the churchwardens of St Edmund's had been lucky – or perhaps persistent. Though the debt was not large, particularly when spread among the four wardens, the "been quiet" seems to suggest that they also forcefully laid out the case for their lack of liability. Such debts to the church were not an uncommon outcome of holding parochial office in this period. Despite the attendant prominence of such a position, some late-medieval parishioners actively tried to avoid the office, and parishes went so far as to fine those who did not serve when selected. St Michael, Oxford, for instance, fined William Minnell 8d. in 1475 "quia ipse negat esse procurator dicte ecclesie" ("because he refuses to be a manager of the church").[16] The complex rules of St Michael, Cornhill, required that "if any be elect and chosen to be Churchwardens of any of the Brotherhoods of the said Church and will not take it upon them forfeit as oft 10s."[17] Though full negligence seem to have been rare, it is clear that there was not untrammelled enthusiasm for office-holding despite general lay interest in the church.

If the responsibility of the late-medieval office was universal, its configuration was specific and idiosyncratic. As the office evolved across these disparate parishes in the fifteenth century, it responded to local customs, needs, and structures social and political. With relatively little direction from canon law and light oversight by the dioceses, the office of the warden proved to be remarkably flexible: an evolution rather than a prescription. Urban parishes often had a corporate and managerial structure, necessitated by their complex finances and informed at least in part by the institutional models of civic administration. In St Margaret Southwark, the year 1452 alone saw four paid weddings, three burials, the selling of church goods, six large-scale gatherings in the church on feast days, and money received for rent. This was spent, in turn, on church memorials, upkeep, organ playing, processions, plays, bell ringing, and the maintenance of the rood light.[18] Such a parish required four churchwardens to manage its intricacies. There were other ways of managing complex finances of particularly wealthy or populated parishes, particularly those with urban complexities; the late-medieval boroughs in the diocese of Bath and Wells, for instance, operated on a strict senior-junior wardenship rota that provided institutional stability and clear hierarchies, while the wardens of St Mary the Great, Cambridge, divided the custody of their overwhelming inventories of church ornaments between wardens past and present. Meanwhile, more rural parishes could implement a preplanned rota of wardens drawn from across the community, including widows, creating a more communal structure.[19] With little central oversight, the office of the warden was able to respond locally to the specific needs of the parish, its economics, and its population.

In the very first years following the break from Rome, perhaps surprisingly, the practical role of the churchwarden changed very little. Imprints of doctrinal or institutional change sometimes wend their way into the accounts – "to the glassier for taking down off the Bishop of Rooms head," reads one account from St Mary's Cambridge in 1541 – but the structure of the office itself was not altered at the parochial level.[20] Wardens were still primarily custodians and accountants, gathering, distributing, and tallying funds for the parish. Even the newly emboldened and centralizing state church did not wish to revise the office. On the contrary, every effort was put into stabilizing local infrastructure by promoting continuity rather than change. The commission appointed in 1534–35 to reform the system of canon law mentioned churchwardens only once: "that wardens and treasurers of churches shall be obliged and compelled … to render faithful account, according to the habit and custom of their parishes."[21] This formulation retrenched the patchwork parochial formulation, strategy, and tactics of the churchwarden.

Continuity, though, had its limits. The onslaught of the Edwardian Reformation's injunctions and legislation, which reshaped both the practical and doctrinal lives of the English parish, soon ruptured the stability of the office. In some ways, and on a purely instrumental level, this made the churchwarden's job simpler. The Edwardian reforms firmly eradicated the chantries, church lights, gilds, and much of the church ornament, vestment, and festal life (all of which had been under attack at some point during Henry's reforms). As a result, wardens no longer had to manage quite as many separate funds or expenditures. In other ways, though, the office of the churchwarden became more difficult and more fraught. Practically, while wardens no longer had to maintain the ornaments, they lost crucial revenue streams that had been used to fund the church for more than two centuries. With no attendant universal taxation put in place, many wardens were left without the fundraising mechanisms needed to run the parish. They also had to contend with the dismantling and distribution of the Catholic architecture and ornament, an additional administrative burden. As we will see in the next chapter, the transformation of the church posed both problem and possibility for the warden. But it also plunged these local officers into the heart of the battles over the pace and politics of religious change. While the churchwarden had long been a power player within the parish, and thus in some sense political, the Reformation forced – or perhaps allowed – them to make newly charged choices.

By the 1550s, the relationship between the state church and the local office of churchwarden had changed abruptly. Policies that heretofore had prioritized and encouraged an emphasis on fiduciary and material responsibilities suddenly swerved. Wardens were no longer to be mere administrators, but also arbiters of discipline. The Edwardian attempts to reform canon law in 1552 delineated these new responsibilities. As outlined by the *Reformatio Legum Ecclesiasticarum*, the text that laid out these proposed reforms, wardens were to focus less on accounts and fabric and far more on the regulation of parishioners' behaviour. In addition to keeping accounts and maintaining a Protestant church fabric, churchwardens were now expected to report licentiousness, absence from church, brawling in the churchyard, disruption to services, slander, fortune-telling, and heresy.[22] To be sure, the pre-Reformation model of churchwardenship had included some degree of moral regulation. But in the *Reformatio,* the office was fully and formally invested with both the power and the requirement to report moral disorder.

The *Reformatio* never passed into law, at least in part due to Edward's death soon after its drafting.[23] It is tempting to play a counterfactual game, to imagine an Edwardian regime in its maturity. In doing so, the most startling outcome is not really the concept of a Reformation of manners – an oft-debated and sometimes-derided concept in early modern historiography – but the ways in which churchwardens were to regulate *religious*, not just moral, behaviour. That churchwardens, with their attendant duties and dignity, would be drawn on to regulate moral incontinence is perhaps not surprising; these were local matters with local, social consequences. But the *Reformatio* also imagined a role for churchwardens as monitors of spiritual probity and personal religious conformity. Avoidance of services on Sundays or holidays, refusal to take communion, disturbances in church, any attempt to "hinder any order whatsoever, instituted by us in the church" – all of this required immediate action by the churchwarden.[24]

What the new Edwardian proposals insisted on, at their core, was that the churchwardens were to be agents of the reformed and state church. Their offices became inherently political on a day-to-day basis, not just in the moments of extreme iconoclastic change. The choices they made were not limited to dismantling rood screens or buying English texts, but expanded to a perpetual scrutiny of their fellow parishioners' piety and conformity. The authors of the *Reformatio* realized the enormous temptation this could create for churchwardens to hide their faults behind a report of *omnia bene*, and they attempted to ensure probity through further surveillance. In addition to voluntary reporting, churchwardens were to participate in all visitations, in person. As we have seen, a complicated system of checks and balances attempted to ensure that all wardens performed their duties entirely. If the bishop should hear of uncorrected, unreported behaviour, "by evidence of the fact, public rumor, or the report of some trustworthy person," he could levy fines against recalcitrant churchwardens.[25] The office of the churchwarden was thus drawn into the machinery of a centralizing state. The bureaucratic creep, the monitoring and reporting, the direction made by a national church, all played out within the sphere of local governance.

Despite Edward's death and the hiatus of the *Reformatio*, the new, activist model of churchwardenship continued. The statutes of the Marian Reformation never formally articulated the duties of the churchwarden, leaving the matter unsettled. It was not until the Elizabethan church that the next detailed description of the office and its duties was fully outlined, and here the Edwardian design was, if anything, expanded. In 1571, the Canterbury Convocation passed a major clarification and revision of canon law, one that focused on the practical implementation of the Reformation.[26] Churchwardens were prime amongst their targets. The Canons that prescribed the duties of the churchwarden begin with their age-old material and financial responsibilities. Here too, churchwardens were to collect funds and maintain the parish, making sure that "the churches be diligently and well repaired, with lead, tyle, lime, and glass," that they be "kept clean," that the accounts be presented annually to the parishioners, and that all surpluses should be "redelivered by them to the next churchwardens."[27] But while the duties remained the same, their motivation changed entirely. Rather than stating the responsibilities simply, the Canons gave justifications for their inclusion – justifications that reflected an explicitly reformed rationale. Thus, the roof was to be repaired so that bad weather would not interrupt "the holy ministry and worshipping of God," and books were to be free from tears or stains "lest it breed irksomeness or contempt amongst the people."[28] In this iteration, the practical, everyday duties of the churchwarden were explicitly linked to divine purpose, and ordinary action was filled with devotional intent.

This kind of language requires us to think differently about ideas of continuity and change. On its face, this seems like a radical reinterpretation of the role of the laity in the church, one connecting lay managerialism and bureaucracy to the evangelical thrust of the new Protestant church. And yet, in some ways this followed on naturally from the world of the pre-Reformation, where lay devotion was often expressed as practical action. Historians of the past half-century have detailed the many ways in which these actions had significant religious motives and repercussions.[29] The maintenance of the "church flock" – sheep owned collectively and raised communally – to fund altar lights, for instance, is described as an act of communal lay piety. In the Elizabethan Canons, churchwardens are to express piety by repairing roofs and mending windows. Thus, as in the pre-Reformation period, routine activity was to represent not only practical deed but also ideological purpose.

But the Canons' prescriptions were not, of course, pure analogues of the past. Though they explicitly nodded to custom (elections were to be made "according to the custom of every parish"), and though they reimagined a new model for practical piety, there were crucial innovations.[30] Most obviously, the piety was to be expressed along clearly reformed lines and with reformed priorities. The Canons detail the destruction of any remaining Catholic ornament and compel a new painting of the walls with lines of Scripture, "that by the reading and warning thereof, the people may be moved to godliness."[31] But, more subtly, the Canons enforce a kind of hierarchy and watchfulness that may have been inherent but was rarely made explicit in the pre-Reformation church. These were rules less for the congregation and more for the officers of the parish, and they were state-mandated rather than merely socially enforced. What the justifications of the 1571 Canons represent, then, is some degree of structural continuity under a changed ideology, a new iteration of the relationship between the lay community and religious services along distinctly reformed and regulated lines.

Like the *Reformatio*, the 1571 Canons moved beyond the purely material to require an activist model of churchwardenship. Here too, wardens were asked to regulate both the morality and the religious conformity of their parishioners. Wardens were to report any who did not come to church or take communion, as well as all "adulterers, whoremongers, incestuous, drunkards, swearers, bawdes, and usurers."[32] But while the *Reformatio* was both an idealized and slightly immature document, representing a push for Reformation that had barely begun, the Canons embodied over a decade of practical experience with regulating reformed religion in the parishes. As a result, they included detailed and careful descriptions of the multitude of troubles and dangers to conformity and orthodoxy that the Elizabethan parishes had experienced since the settlement – dangers that the churchwardens were to regulate.

The clearest example of this newfound caution can be found in the Canons' sabbatarian impulses. From the start, Elizabethan visitations had been keen to discover those who "idly or lewdly prophaneth the Sabbath day."[33] The 1571 strictures echoed this, placing particular emphasis on calm and quiet within the church: "but especially they shall look unto, that in every meeting of the congregation peace be well kept … and name all those, which rudely behave themselves in the church, or which by untimely ringing of bells, by walking, by talking, or noise, shall let the minister or preacher."[34] They also went further, quite literally. The new conception of the churchwarden brought him out of the church and into the Sunday streets. Thus, churchwardens were to "warn vintners and victualers … that they receive none into their tavern or alehouse, all that time wherein either is preaching, or common service." Other areas of sabbatarian regulation included "fayres and common markets," "light wanderers in markets and pelting merchants … whom they call peddlers," "beggars or vagabonds, which have no certain dwelling," and both corporal and capital punishment for criminals.[35] In the Elizabethan parish, the bleeding together of the civil and the sacred meant that churchwardens were to enforce a godly order far outside the bounds of the churchyard.

The 1571 Canons were a peculiar blend of control and autonomy. On one hand, they contained the kind of meticulous proscriptions and prescriptions detailed above. But on the other hand, the Elizabethan conception of the churchwarden both allowed and indeed required a remarkable degree of independent self-government. Here again we can see the complicated interaction of structural continuity and ideological change. The office of the warden had long allowed the laity significant latitude over the funding and provision of church fabric and liturgical equipment, and the organic, bottom-up evolution of the office had resulted in almost complete agency over electoral practices. But in the Elizabethan definition, this self-government was extended beyond the administrative to questions of moral and religious conformity. In cases of lay misbehaviour, the Canons required churchwardens first to discipline and correct *without* clerical supervision. For instance, in cases of moral lapse, the Canons proclaimed, "let the churchwardens warn them brotherly and friendly, to amend. Which except they do, they shall personally shew them to the parson, vicar, or curate, that they may be warned more sharply and vehemently of them."[36] Not only was the detection of fault to be made by churchwardens, the initial correction was also to be left in their hands. In this definition, churchwardens did not function merely as passive agents of the state church. Instead, wardens were expected to play an active role in not just surveillance but also discipline. To be sure, the Canons also required such offences to be reported to the episcopal and archidiaconal authorities at the visitations, where official note could be made of recidivism or dangerous patterns of disruption and disorder. But instead of leaving the issue in the hands of the centralized church, government and governing was instead to be done by the parish itself, led by the churchwarden. Internal control over lay behaviour, not recourse to the clergy, was the first step toward conformity. Parishioners were to be subject to one another.

The most radical shift in the Canons, however, related not to the laity but to the clergy. In a serious shift from earlier articulations of churchwardens' spheres of influence, the 1571 Canons required churchwardens to regulate the clergy. In the Edwardian formulation, the line demarcating the authority of the clergy and the laity was kept intact; the *Reformatio* had ministers being monitored only by their fellow clerics, and nowhere in the description of wardens' duties did its articles suggest correction or discipline of the clergy by laymen. The new Elizabethan model, in contrast, relied on churchwardens to govern their ministers' actions. In part, these new responsibilities were articulated as checks on the episcopal bureaucracy. So, wardens were to "receive no parson, nor vicar, to the ministry of their church, but whom the Bishop shall allow by his institution," and any outside preacher giving sermons was to be required to sign the churchwardens' book and write "the name of the Bishop, of whom he had licence to preach."[37]

But the Canons asked churchwardens to go still further. Rather than simply inspecting for episcopal licence, Elizabethan wardens were to monitor and report clerical behaviour: "if the Parson, Vicar, or Curate, behave himself otherwise in his ministry, or that he read ill, darkly, and confusedly, or that he live more loosely, and licentiously than is fit for a man of that calling, and thereby great offence be taken: the churchwardens shall speedily present him to the Bishop, that by and by he may be punished, and amendment of his fault may follow." This was an extraordinary charge. It asked churchwardens to survey and to assess clerical behaviour on a heretofore unseen level. The scrutiny of moral matters is perhaps not unexpected, with tales of a debauched ministry a centuries-old anticlerical complaint. The Canons, though, pushed beyond these bounds to compel laymen to render judgment on the clergy's professional performance. This was a fundamental shift in parochial power relations. While not extending churchwardens the same powers of governorship as when dealing with lay parishioners, the Canons still required the lay officials both to inspect and to evaluate the clergy. The church was, of course, reacting to that long-standing suspicion toward Marian holdovers in the clergy that we saw in the last chapter. But the Canons were also reacting to the growing strains of recusancy and radicalism that had ripened by the late 1560s. The 1569 Northern Rebellion, which did so much to accelerate anti-Catholic sentiment in the capital, was directly addressed by the required provision of "the holy Homilies, which lately were written against rebellion."[38] And only months before the publication of the Canons, Thomas Cartwright was preaching about presbyterian answers to the problems of the English church. What the Canons offered in the face of these challenges – indeed, what the Elizabethan construction of the office of the churchwarden as a whole provided – was a way to discipline the parish through an explicitly episcopal model. This definition of the churchwarden was not a holdover from an earlier, pre-Reformation understanding, nor was it a cautious vehicle for a *via media*. Instead, it was an articulation of a new power relationship that played out along old structural lines. It entrenched a profoundly episcopal model for centralized church governance that relied in large part on the active participation of local officeholders.

The 1571 Canons were never rendered legally binding. Elizabeth, while supporting the push "to have a perfect Reformation of all abuses," nevertheless demurred from giving her full imprimatur to the archbishops' reforms.[39] Nevertheless, the Canons were signed by all bishops in the province of Canterbury, as well as the archbishop of York and the bishops of Durham and Chester, and printed in English by John Day.[40] What this meant in practice was that the new, activist model of churchwardenship was enforced at the episcopal level by the visitation articles. With the 1571 Canons, and the subsequent inclusion of the canonical language in the visitation articles and injunctions of the next few decades, the Elizabethan church modelled the churchwarden into an essential cog in the machinery of parochial and clerical discipline. In doing so, they conceived of an office whose very power lay in a paradox: wardens were at once independent and subordinate, empowered yet heavily circumscribed. Authorized as autonomous agents of moral and religious discipline, they nevertheless reported directly to church hierarchy. Through this office, the laity were thus invested with significant power, in an almost radical Continental model of surveillance and discipline. But this power was sanctioned and harnessed by an episcopal model that stood directly opposed to the implementation of a radical ecclesiastical structure.

Attempts by the English church to redefine the duties and capacities of the wardens fundamentally changed their role within both a parochial and a national framework by the mid-Elizabethan era. Wardens were given a deepening and growing autonomy in disciplining the parish, but it was to be along reformed lines prescribed by the church; the state church made the rules, but it also depended in large part on the judgment of local office-holders. Such agency carried over into the long-standing duties of churchwardens, which were articulated as active support for reformed ideas. Of course, there were many across English who disagreed with these reformed lines, and not every warden paying for church roof repairs did so in order to improve gospel preaching. Nevertheless, the formulation of the 1571 Canons equated church maintenance and community building as actions of reformed piety: there could be, and certainly was supposed to be, a continuity between praxis and principle, between wardens' actions and doctrinal intent. Thus, continuities of care were leveraged as legitimization of protestant reform – and derelictions of practical duties were painted as undermining both spiritual and conformist ideals. And finally, the redefinition of churchwarden as a monitor of both lay *and* clerical behaviour created a new power structure within the parish. With visitations increasing throughout the Elizabethan era, some areas were seeing a visitation as often as every six months, each of which offered an opportunity for the wardens to report on lay and clerical behaviour they judged to be lacking. The new model of the activist warden had a direct, regular conduit to a centralizing system of oversight and regulation.

These new definitions, then, reshaped parochial power structures and invested the office of the churchwarden with new political powers.

Churchwardens had, since the thirteenth century, held significant social and economic influence within the parish. Indeed, the reformers counted on the continuity of this influence, both trusting and relying upon their prominence in local communities. But the efforts of the state church to reform the parishes at a grassroots level and to control the pace and tenor of this reform through a bureaucratic system that relied on the participation of local office-holders meant that the role of churchwardens was fundamentally reimagined. In Elizabethan England, they were parochial power players with regular connection to the machinery of the state church. How they chose to *use* that machinery varied enormously, as we shall see.

It is not enough, however, to focus merely on the religious or moral spheres of churchwardens' authority and responsibilities. Like so much else in English parish life, the dividing line between the temporal and the spiritual was blurred – or, perhaps better put, immaterial. Time and time again, the Elizabethan state turned to the wardens to keep the parish running, with a series of statutory laws extending the wardens' administrative duties beyond the ecclesiastical and well into the civil sphere. By 1600, in addition to collecting and distributing and accounting for money, to maintaining the church and churchyard, and to the regulation and reporting of conformity, churchwardens were responsible for a host of secular concerns. It is an exhausting and near-exhaustive list. Wardens were to administer highway maintenance; provide arms for a parish muster and report on defences; provide support for local gaols, prisons, and hospitals; control the vermin population; raise emergency funds following disasters or battles; design and implement public-health policy and provide relief for wounded veterans; and periodically help to co-ordinate celebrations for visiting notables.[41] It seems almost inevitable (though of course it was not) that the most extraordinary expansion of state power, the Elizabethan Poor Laws of 1597/1601, would put the responsibility for the poor squarely in the lap of the churchwarden: to nominate overseers, control funds, decide whether parents could properly care for their children, and meet monthly to review conditions.[42]

In doing so, the Elizabethan parliaments were following a path set by earlier Tudor regimes, in which matters traditionally belonging to the jurisdiction of the manor or the manorial courts were moved onto new administrative shoulders. This shift was thus of particular interest to twentieth-century constitutional and institutional historians, who saw changes to the churchwarden's office as just "another instance of the Tudor tendency to replace medieval institutions with new organs of government."[43] This description, though, rather misses the point. The expansion of the civil duties of the churchwarden was no mere iteration of an Eltonian revolution in local government. Instead, its implementation mirrored the expanded duties, power, and greater accountability found in the *religious* obligations of the churchwarden. Indeed, it is plausible that the relative success of the churchwardens in enacting the changes of the early Reformation had taught the state the potential of the office. Reformation had grown the capacity of the state to regulate the local and of local officers to enact state change.

Even the most mundane of the churchwardens' new tasks point to their newly authoritative role. Responsibility of highway upkeep, for example, invested wardens with a strikingly strong and independent authority. Road repair was first placed in the hands of the parish by Marian statutory law, which required churchwardens and constables to join together annually to elect surveyors who would maintain all roads leading to market towns. Badly preserved roads were to be investigated by the court leet (one type of manorial court) in the first instance, with any fines it collected distributed to the wardens, who had the sole authority to bring recalcitrant bailiffs to the justices of the peace.[44] The Elizabethan parliament of 1563 expanded this power, making two crucial changes. First, "forasmuch as the said Statute … serveth not to so good Purpose and Effect as it may be made," the surveyors appointed by the wardens were granted the right to confiscate gravel, stones, or other repair materials from private property without asking permission.[45] These surveyors, liable to the wardens, could seize private property nearly at will: an extraordinary power at a local level. Second, while the Marian law had placed local manorial courts as the enforcers of repairs, the Elizabethan statute placed oversight in the hands of the justices of the peace.

The result of these changes was simultaneously to increase the power of the churchwarden within the parish and to shift the oversight of parochial behaviour away from hyper-local courts and toward a county-wide judicial branch. This seemingly incidental change in road administration is thus strikingly similar to changes in the office that were more religious in nature. Wardens were given broad latitude within the bounds of the parish, permitted to seize private property as they were allowed to chastise the morally incontinent. But they were, at the same time, drawn into a centralizing state: not visitations and the episcopacy here, but instead the increasingly dominant justices of the peace. At the same time as the redefinition of churchwardenship was investing the office with unprecedented power to define and enforce religious conformity, they were also being given intensified civil power.

It was this version of the office of the churchwarden – one that combined prestige and authority, one that could significantly shape the fate of a parish and the lives of its inhabitants – that John Montgomery and Robert Bemond were so fiercely contesting in All Hallows Staining. But if we know much about the prescribed scope of the wardens' office, we know far less about how the wardens themselves were chosen. This vacuum has profound implications for how we conceive of authority and agency in a time of religious upheaval. It pulls the focus away from the warden and toward the central state, and it undermines the very real political power that the wardens had within their parishes. Indeed, for most Englishmen and women living in 1600, the churchwarden was perhaps the most visible, constant contact they would have had with the state. Moreover, particularly in rural parishes that lacked corporate elections, choosing a churchwarden – and the chance to participate in shaping these choices – was the closest thing many would have to any formal political agency. For the vast majority who would never reach the voting threshold of a forty-shilling freeholder or the freedom of a city, the churchwardens' elections could be the extent of their political franchise.

The reason for this obscurity about the wardens' electoral process is, in part, due to a maddening silence from the churchwardens' accounts themselves. As intrinsic documents, they most often simply state the names of the wardens rather than describing the method by which they had been chosen: they were statements of account and accountability, not of process. For the parish of Winterslow, Wiltshire, the record of transition came only at the moment when the money changed hands: "agreed that William More & John Webb hath given a true accompt of all the church goods of Winterslow the xxiiij day of october & hath delivered unto the hands [of] John Webb & William Best new church wardens the day & month above written."[46] The recording of names at this moment of transition, without any real detail about their selection, was entirely commonplace. Similar scripts run through parishes like St Michael-le-Querne and St Olave Jewry in London. And some ignored process even further. The granular, meticulous, and extensive records of London's St Stephen Walbrook simply listed the name of the churchwardens in the beginning of each account, as did St Martin, Salisbury; North Newton, Wiltshire; and Woodbury, Devon.[47]

Those accounts that did explicitly mention election tended to speak in vague terms. So, the receipts of the parish of Oswestry, Shropshire, merely stated that its officers were "chosen and elected church wardens of the parish … for this year."[48] The accounts of St Mary's, Reading, were entirely typical in their 1576 record of a parochial surplus "delivered to the said Will'm Twytt & Richard Aldwourth, the younger, churchwardens chosen by the parish."[49] The formulation of the parish of St Peters Marlborough is almost mysterious in its nebulous and passive construction: goods are "delivered to him John Baylie elder churchwarden for this next yere, and to him is chosen William Franklyn younger churchwarden."[50] So too the junior warden of St Mary Exeter "was chosen," and the wardens of South Newington alternately chosen or elected.[51] Just who was doing this choosing is rendered as implicit procedure. Some of this omission can be laid at the function of the accounts – a record of receipts, not rationales – but it was also grounded in the customary nature of these elections. As with so much of the archive, change rings loud; continuity persists in silence.

None of this is to say, though, that the election and selection of churchwardens was casual. A few parishes did render election processes explicitly, often officially codifying long-standing traditions. Elections were usually made at the rendering of accounts, with church goods passed directly into the hands of the new wardens. In Mere, Wiltshire, for instance, the new wardens were "elected and chosen … by such number of the parishioners as shall happen to be present and assembled at the making of the Accompt for the church goods, or by the most part of them."[52] Just what was meant by "the most part" is unclear. It is possible that "most" refers to a select few of those assembled whose votes were counted, a "principal inhabitants" approach to the franchise; if so, this would suggest that Mere was operating as a kind of village oligarchy. But it is also possible that the "most part" refers simply to a majority of those assembled, indicating both a more contentious and a more open process.

In fact, as in the election of All Hallows Staining, the process could become one of fierce competition. While the office of churchwarden imposed burdens upon its holders, its privileges were also attractive to those seeking authority in the parishes. Elections could be, and often were, contested. In some cases, this was a reflection of local factionalism. In the parish of St Mary's, Beverley, the appointment of John Jackson as churchwarden in 1594 provoked a lawsuit by those who claimed his election was invalid and had been held without the participation of the majority of the parish, including the mayor; a reflection of long-standing political tensions, the case worked its way through the courts before ending up at the Court of High Commission, the "Star Chamber" of ecclesiastical justice.[53] The evolution of Tudor churchwardenship made the political in multiple senses of the word: bureaucratic, empowered, competitive, and factional.

It was this sort of contest we see in All Hallows Staining. And Robert's 1568 election was no anomaly for the parish. The parish, across the Elizabethan decades, kept remarkably detailed memoranda of their annual elections. Scattered haphazardly across the back of the clerk's assessment book are a series of day-of-election returns: a list of names, followed by a hash mark for individual votes. A stunning early record of politics in action, these returns reveal a dynamic and fluid electoral system. Each year, All Hallows held a contest for junior churchwarden, who would become senior the following year. And each year, at least three and as many as five candidates stood for office. In many cases, the election was a landslide. The year after he lost to Robert, John Montgomery faced off against two of his fellow parishioners and won all the votes; in 1577, Thomas Townson was the unanimous victor over his four fellow competitors.[54] But in other years, the same candidates faced intense competition. Just three years before Townson's runaway victory, he had been pipped at the post by Thomas Bury, who won the office by just a single vote.[55]

This was not democracy, in All Hallows or anywhere else. The question over who would be part of the electorate was a charged one, and in the All Hallows records, it seems that no more than half of male householders were voting. But the election returns do indicate a robust interest in the role of churchwarden, one that belies an impression of the office as a begrudged burden.[56] For some, of course, it may have been so – akin to their late-medieval counterparts preferring fines to taking up the office, or a parish councillor today furiously avoiding eye contact when nominations for treasurer are called. But for others, it represented opportunity: to establish social position, to exercise authority, to shape religious or moral life in the parish, to fulfill a sense of service. Once we understand the office of the warden to be one of significant political and social power, rather than as a passive bottom rung of church machinery, the contestation makes sense.

Indeed, in some parishes the lure of official prestige and the potential power of the office was so great that elaborate systems were put in place to check corruption, cronyism, and concentration of influence. St Mary the Great, the university church of Cambridge, selected their wardens through a baroque regulatory process, perhaps as a nod to the strong personalities of so many of its parishioners. Serving churchwardens would select two men from the parish to serve as official nominators; the two nominators would each choose three different men to form a committee of selection; and the committee and nominators together would choose the next years' churchwardens from amongst the parishioners. To take but one example, in 1600 churchwardens Warren and King chose nominators Dr Ward and Mr Nicholson. Ward chose three committee members (Dr Grimeson, Mr Wolfe, and Mr Porter), as did Nicholson (Mr Medcalfe, Mr Pottall, and Mr Cobb). The six committee members joined with the two nominators to choose the next year's wardens: Mr Gibbs and Luke Curtis.[57] Each following year, the process repeated with a new cast of characters.

St Mary's convoluted system was not unique to the Elizabethan church. Indeed, while the Elizabethan church saw innovations in the responsibilities of the churchwarden, the processes of their selection tended to be grounded in long-standing tradition. Many of the accounts that did discuss processes were keen to stress their deep-rooted precedents. The accounts of St Mary the Great, for example, routinely noted that their arrangements were "according to the Ancient Custom of great St Mary's parish."[58] Appeals to custom were often, of course, rhetorical. The phrases "time out of mind" or "time out of memory of man" very often meant merely a generation.[59] And yet, at least in this case, the Elizabethan rhetoric is proved by the pre-Reformation records, which elaborate this rococo selection process at least from 1515.[60] Elizabethan continuities with pre-Reformation practices can be found across the country, from the market town of Bishop's Stortford, Hertfordshire, to the urban streets of St Mary Woolnoth, London, to the wool town of Chudleigh in Devon. The preservation of customary elections provided another anchor of stability for an office that was rapidly changing.

Continuities were important not only on the macrolevel of institutional constancy across a century of change but also on the more microscopic level of annual turnover within a parish. With the growing responsibility of the churchwarden, training office-holders became increasingly complex and important. Indeed, by the mid-Elizabethan period these duties had become so manifold and so central to the running of a parish that William Lambarde appended to his famous guide for constables and other local office-holders a section on "the duty of the churchwardens" precisely because the office was so laden with both ecclesiastical and civil responsibilities: "Whilst I passed through some of the Statutes before, concerning the Offices of Constable & Borsholder, I found them mingled with diverse duties pertaining to the churchwardens of parishes: the Surveyors of the highways: the Distributors of the provision for the destruction of vermin: the Collectors and Overseers for the poor: and the Wardens and Collectors for the houses of Correction: whereby I was also moved to add somewhat of these Offices, the rather because I was persuaded that with a little more of labour, I might do a great deal more of good."[61]

Manuals like Lambarde's are often described as the first step toward the professionalization of petty offices and a sign of growing standardization, centralization, and even modernization.[62] But methods for training churchwardens often continued to rely on pre-Reformation models and customs that provided a supervised, direct experience of office-holding. In many cases, Elizabethan parishes elected a junior churchwarden, who would serve a two-year term, becoming senior warden the following year.[63] This senior-junior structure provided institutional stability for the parish, giving new wardens time to become accustomed to the office. The best way to train amateurs for such an important role in the expanding state, it seemed, was simply practical experience guided by a seasoned partner.

What all this reliance on custom meant was that there was no national uniformity of either election process or official training of the churchwardens upon which the state relied. And this was intentional: the Elizabethan statutes explicitly required that custom was the foremost criterion for the choosing of the new wardens, rejecting any centralized or uniform model.[64] As long as the duties and responsibilities were carried out, the parishes were largely left to their own devices to figure out just who the wardens would be and how they would order themselves. The actions, not the personnel, were controlled by the state. This meant that exceptions to the standard election processes described above were common and generally unproblematic to ecclesiastical authorities. This was particularly true in parishes that were isolated, remote, or either so large or so small that they required special considerations. The tiny parish of Aisholt in Somerset, tucked amongst the Quantock Hills, chose their wardens not by election but by rota ordered by household geography.[65] Conversely, the immense, rambling parishes of the far north often elected up to a dozen wardens at a time.[66]

The Elizabethan churchwarden was thus, again, a creature both of the state and of his locality. The system embraced by church authorities lacked the intense oversight and control of a Genevan model of surveillance and governance. But in many ways, it was more sensitive to local needs and far more fit for a country divided not just by religious allegiance and temperature but also by prodigious geographic, economic, and social differences. The Elizabethan reliance on traditional forms and customs of office, combined with rapidly changing duties and responsibilities, placed churchwardens at the nexus of Elizabethan state formation. An odd combination of conservative and progressive, these offices were simultaneously flexible and constrained. The church was entirely clear about just *what* churchwardens should be doing: accounting, managing, monitoring, reporting. But *how* they went about these duties was, by and large, left up to each parish. Like constables or jurors, these parochial office-holders found themselves in the heart of the Elizabethan paradox: expanded agency at a local level combined with the intense scrutiny of the central authorities.

In fulfilling their duties, the churchwarden did not always stand alone. Though wardens were the only parochial office-holders formally required by the Canons or the visitation articles, they were often aided or even supervised by other ancillary positions. The most common of these were sidemen, who served as assistants for the wardens. Common too were auditors, particularly in those parishes with complicated revenue streams. More interesting were those officers whose presence suggests the messy reality of religious change in Tudor England. Some parishes preserved remarkable continuities with past structures. The parish of Chudleigh in Devon, for instance, retained vestiges of pre-Reformation accounting practices throughout the entire reign of Elizabeth. Their account books list not only the funds of the churchwardens, but also separate income streams managed by the Store Wardens. In their original incarnations, these wardens would have managed incomes for parochial gilds, most often used to pay for candles or perpetual lights before various shrines. Indeed, the earliest Elizabethan accounts from Chudleigh continued to list the income of the "wardens to the store of our Lady," a phrase that was used as late as 1567.[67] By the late 1560s, however, the parish had turned to the more anodyne and acceptable division of High Store and Young Men Wardens without any of the more overt trappings of Marian or other saintly devotion. At first glance, this seems like a traditional story of the twilight of Merry England, a gradual fading of pre-Reformation institutions in the long years of Elizabeth. But in Chudleigh, these institutions persisted: renamed, sheared of their devotional intent, but still very much in operation. Seeing their routine inclusion in a set of 1599 accounts is at first startling, an unexpected jolt of late-medieval popular piety in a world expected to have fundamentally changed.[68]

The preservation of these pre-Reformation offices is a reminder of the complicated process of religious change in the Elizabethan church. Rather than the sharp rupture of Edwardian reform, Elizabethan reform was often more gradual in its transformation, more akin to the parochial experience of the Henrician church: change, state-enforced, came to each of the parishes, but it was not accompanied by the fervour or rapidity of Edwardian reforms. It was also varied and, to a remarkable degree, flexible, responding to local custom and local tradition in a bid to preserve the continuities necessary for building, rather than breaking, a stable church. But this is not to say that the Elizabethan church was the cautious *via media* of so many textbooks. While the other parochial stores continued, the one explicitly devoted to the Virgin was not. It was the devotional intent of parochial institutions, not their administrative structure, that mattered to Elizabethan church authorities. The perpetuation of these medieval offices may have raised godly eyebrows and even generated jeremiads about the persistence of a church "half-reformed." In the eyes of Elizabethan authorities, though, wardens for a young men's store were acceptable, perhaps even welcome, as methods to provide crucial funding for infrastructure. Wardens to the "store of our Lady" were not. The account books stopped their separate entries for these wardens in 1565, and the store of our Lady disappeared from the entries entirely in 1567, never to be recorded again.[69]

Even in that first decade, though, it was clear that these store wardens had a very different purpose than they had in the pre-Reformation (or indeed the Marian) church. The wardens of our Lady's store preserved their traditional fundraising methods: church ales and "hoggenays," parochial gatherings where critical sums were collected. In the early 1560s, these events regularly raised well over £5 annually. But wardens of our Lady had no real expenses, other than payments for malt and brewing. The fundraising had stayed, but the devotion had died. By the mid-1560s, the money was flowing into the hands of the central wardens, who used it for purposes not just alien to the pre-Reformation church, but actively antipathetic. The ales ostensibly in the name of our Lady were used to pay for expenses at visitations that enforced the Prayer Book, for the purchase of reformed books, for the Protestant communion (with payment made for the laity's bread and wine), and for the destruction of the last vestiges of Catholic architecture and the erection of a pulpit.[70]

Thus, the continuation of pre-Reformation forms of parochial office cannot be conflated with a roadblock to Elizabethan reforms. Indeed, in some cases, they may have hastened them. The complicated parochial wardenship of Chudleigh was simultaneously preserved and transfigured. Those traditional offices that fit in neatly, or at least straightforwardly, with the new regime were continued, raising vital funds and providing the kind of socioreligious lay involvement of the old church. Those that smacked too loudly of forbidden "superstition" might be phased out slowly, but their devotional functions were almost immediately suspended. In both cases, the purpose and activities of the wardens were turned toward the building of a uniform church. At first glance it might seem paradoxical that funds raised by the wardens of "our blessed Lady" were used to pull down rood screens or attend visitations meant to ensure protestant conformity in the parishes. And yet this was the heart of the strength, not the weakness, of the Elizabethan church: continuity of form, transformation of substance.

Not all effects of reform were about continuity. In the wealthy, more godly parishes of Elizabethan London, they frequently led to innovation in official structures. Parish accounts from these urban centres record a bureaucratic machine slowly escalating in both personnel and authority. Some of this was a result of the rapid demographic growth in the metropolis. But much of it was a function of the accelerating demands placed on the wardens by the Elizabethan church and state. The increase in both secular and religious oversight meant not only a growth in control exercised over the parish, but also a need for new offices to manage the sheer work of the parish. By the 1580s, one small London parish alone annually elected two collectors for the poor; two constables; two members of the wardmote inquest; two sidemen; a scavenger; four visitors for the sick; two provisioners for the sick, all under the supervision of two churchwardens, who in turn were scrutinized by four auditors – nearly twenty separate office-holders in a parish of about ninety households.[71] The increased intensity of local governance in the Tudor era, and particularly under Elizabeth, led to a massive expansion in official personnel.

Perhaps the most discussed structural change was the development of the vestry, a committee that supervised the administrative matters of the parish. On its face, the vestry seems innocuous, merely a means to manage the complicated needs of the Tudor parish. But to historiography, the vestry has served as a signal, or even a strawman, of an increasingly elitist rule in Tudor England. The great Fabian sociologists Beatrice and Sidney Webb decried the "uncontrollable parish oligarchy" of parish government that wielded powers "which we should now deem inconsistent with civil liberty," and historians since have tended to follow in their footsteps.[72] In many ways, of course, the Webbs were right. Elizabethan society was increasingly becoming bifurcated, with the distance between the "better" and "lower" sorts of people both growing and deepening. Social historians of the past fifty years have painted a traumatic, even violent, picture of a society where the wealth gap was turning into a wealth chasm. This was a matter of both demography and policy. England was finally recovering from the population devastation of the Black Death, and the demographic surge of the mid- to late sixteenth century squeezed both land tenure and wages. This economic pressure was further compounded by policy decisions that saw the privatization of public land and, perhaps more devastatingly to the Elizabethan rural workforce, the shift from labour-intensive arable land to more manageable pastureland. These dual forms of enclosure, each of which contributed to a growth of the owner's capital profit at the expense of the rural labour force, only increased the disparity between the haves and the have-nots.[73]

Here too the Reformation played its role. The sale of former monastic land by successive Tudor regimes saw the creation of new landed fortunes. In some cases, these merely created new gentry families happy to become lords of the manor and run their farms in line with local custom. But in other cases, it devastated traditional forms of lordship and patronage, with an unfamiliar host of absentee landlords primarily concerned with maximizing the capital profit potential of their new properties. As John Walter described in his seminal study of the Oxfordshire Uprising of 1596, these nouveau landlords were frequently the target of local agrarian discontent, arising in part from their willingness to adopt enclosure and in part from a general feeling of disconnect between tenant and landlord.[74] The rippling consequences of the early years of post-Dissolution land tenure only exacerbated the growing wealth gap.

Structurally, then, vestries would seem to fit within the general trend of increasing oligarchy in the later Tudor era: another example of a society in which the "better sort" gained increasing control over local politics. But the story is not as simple or straightforward as that. The narrative of medieval collectivity and early modern oligarchy has some truth to it, but it needs to be heavily qualified. For one, vestries were not alone in developing parish oligarchy: they were, instead, only one of the ways in which powerful and influential medieval Englishmen and women could exert their influence on the parish. Second, vestries existed in the parish long before the Reformation, let alone before its Elizabethan incarnation. And third, Elizabethan vestries varied in their openness, with some actually *promoting*, rather than restricting, broad participation in the parish.

Social inequality was baked into the parish long before Elizabethan changes. From dedicated masses bequeathed by the rich of the parish to domination of the parish gilds, social differentiation was omnipresent in the pre-Reformation church. The parish church – and broader participation in chantries and extra-parish gilds – had long been the site for displays of wealth and power. It is perhaps unsurprising, then, to see vestries appearing in the records of English parishes well before the break from Rome. The excellent and well-preserved records of central London parishes record numerous parishes with a vestry system by 1510.

Perhaps the most remarkable example of these records can be found in the *The Book of Records* from St Christopher le Stocks, a parish on Threadneedle Street later demolished during the building of the Bank of England. At "A vestry the vj day of January in anno 1507," its priest, alderman, and some of its parishioners gathered to create rules and expectations for the wardens, parishioners, clerks, and even the chantry priests. The vestry composed these orders with a bracing confidence in their power. The Lady Mass was to be held every Saturday except during Lent, and "each and every one of our priests chaplains and our parish clerk or parish clerks shalbe attendant and helping unto the same duly and without failing & at the beginning thereof except a Reasonable cause."[75] Particular attention was due to the chaplains, chantry priests, and clerks, who were perhaps less diligent in their attentions than either the parish priest or the parishioners would have liked. They were in turn admonished not to allow strangers to sleep in the house donated to the chantry priests by a parishioner, John Wateler, in exchange for perpetual masses; reminded to attend not only Lady Masses but also High Mass, anthems, and morning masses; and required always to maintain the requisite material for mass, including vestments, mass books, and chalices. In turn, the parishioners were enjoined to provide a good fence for the churchyard, to lock it according to a finely detailed schedule, and to distribute keys to various inhabitants.[76]

The aim here was stability and control: or, as they put it, "to that intent and for that these foresaid Articles shalbe firm and stable hold & continue from henceforth without any variance or contradiction of any of the said persons or other hereafter."[77] Posterity was constantly on their mind, making rules to bind the church after those who had written them were gone. There is poignancy in this goal, the historic irony of the Reformation on the horizon. But the drive for stability and control continued – perhaps even intensified – as religious changes crashed down upon them. A new set of rules was established by the next generation of St Christopher's vestry just seventeen years later, when twenty-two "of the most substantial and honest persons of the parish" came together to institute a "perpetual quietness to be had among all the parishioners."[78] The matter was less about reform and more about taxation: parishioners were to be assigned pews and pay assessments based on their seating, with any who refused to be noted by the churchwardens and sent to the vestry to answer for his

"Rebellion."[79] Almost a decade before Henry's break from Rome – and nearly a half-century before the Elizabethan reforms took hold, St Christopher's office-holding was formally ruled by its lay elite.

And St Christopher's was not alone. London's St Michael, Cornhill, had a vestry from as early as 1504, while St Mary-at-Hill presented its accounts to "xij persons of the parish" by 1526. The parish of Morebath in Devon instituted a "small council" called "the Courte of the V men" by 1538. For a good half-century before the Elizabethan settlement, then, parishes were experimenting with and formalizing structures of authority and bureaucracy. These were layered on top of a long tradition of independent lay organization within the parish. In some ways, the destruction of the lights and the chantries and the gilds undermined lay power within the parish, cutting them off from positions that had both personal and political meaning. But the Reformation did not destroy all avenues for lay engagement and agency. Indeed, the development of the vestry gave the laity control over aspects of the church – the tenor of reform, the policing of its congregation, even the appointment of its personnel – that they did not have before. The laity remained deeply involved in the life of their parish long after the Reformation had stripped them of their gilds.

The structure of the vestry was thus more of an evolution than an imposition. In its Elizabethan incarnation, it was neither mandated by central authority nor implemented in the same way in every parish. Like so much of the Elizabethan reforms, local variation – as long as it did not violate basic principles of uniformity – was rife, even encouraged, as the "customs" of the parish.[80] Vestries differed widely across the Elizabethan church. Some, particularly in the larger urban parishes, produced a sharply oligarchic lay government, with enormous power held in the hands of a very few men. In others, the proliferation of local office-holding and of lay responsibility within the church meant that power was actually broader and more equally distributed than what had come before. As with so many changes in the Elizabethan church, the development of the vestries and the iterations of office-holding responded to local needs, local power struggles, and local demographics.

While vestries may have had long roots, change began to creep into some parishes under the guise of the formal select vestry. Here, the vestry was restricted to the "principal" or the "chief" inhabitants of the parish, rather than open to all parishioners with interest in parochial affairs.

As such, select vestries have for more than a century often been taken by scholars as the hallmark of Elizabethan oligarchical amplification. When Sidney and Beatrice Webb were looking for the villains of English local government, they singled out the select vestry as "a fragment of the parish, which conceived itself to be endowed with all the legal powers of the parish as a whole."[81] Just how much these select vestries were real innovations or merely formalizations of de facto oligarchies, however, is unclear. The medieval administration of the parish was, as we have seen, quite often run by the wealthiest or more substantial members of the parish. And the earliest incarnations of the vestry, like the handfuls of men running the parishes of St Mary, Cambridge, Morebath in Devon, or St Mary-at-Hill, London, bear more than a passing resemblance to a select vestry. Nevertheless, the formal distinction of the select vestry, with an explicit emphasis placed on control of parish affairs in the hands of the principal inhabitants, marked an evolution in the formal distribution of local power and politics.

Whether formalizations or innovations, Elizabethan select vestries were certainly undergoing a proliferation. By the 1580s, select vestries were increasingly recorded in the parish minutes. Perhaps the most explicit description of an Elizabethan select vestry came in the accounts of Pittington, a parish about ten miles northeast of Durham that had served as one of the retreats of the prior of Durham before the Dissolution.[82] In 1584, the accounts record a special meeting to establish this new political order: "Item it is agreed by the consent of the whole parish to elect and choose out of the same xij men to order and define all common causes pertaining to the church, as shall appertain to the profit & commodity of the same, without molestation or troubling of the common people (whose names hereafter followeth).[83] With that, the business of the parish was limited to the hands of a dozen men, who would go on to control parish financing, administration, and personnel, without "molestation or troubling of the common people."

To what extent this was the onset of oligarchic rule depends in part on how one reads the narrative of the vestry establishment. Most cynically, the account, created by the very people whom it empowers, could very well be a politic veil over a consolidation of control by the parish elite – a power grab cloaked with language of solicitude. It could, alternatively, reflect a patronizing, anti-democratic – yet sincerely held – belief that parochial interests were too complicated for the majority of the parish to understand or to perform effectively. Still more broadly, it can be read as an organic, even grassroots, eagerness on the part of the parish population to choose a committee to deal with the vital-but-tedious work of committees and bureaucracy, the genuine aggravation and trouble of parochial affairs. The answer most probably lies between these ideas, or at least incorporates elements of each. To be sure, the twelve men of the vestry almost immediately exercised exceptional power: they assigned the pews, they fixed a rota of church contributions, and they chose the churchwardens for the subsequent years.[84] And yet, they were also responsible for balancing the accounts, for making up shortfalls when the parish was in debt or needed a coin advance, and for wrangling with the episcopal bureaucracy on a regular basis. Like all office-holding positions in Tudor England, then, it was one of both power and obligation, authority and duty.

The proliferation of parochial responsibilities following the Elizabethan settlement amplified both the benefits and the burdens of running a parish such as Pittington. This was not the natural by-product of the growing oligarchic trends of Elizabethan social history. Instead, this was a construct, and a purposeful one: the growing needs of the central state – in this case, the desire of the state church to administer, monitor, and control its parishioners – created bureaucratic burdens that were most easily satisfied by those who already had parochial standing. Elizabethan church policy contributed to the growing stratification of the haves and the have-nots, just as secular economic policy did. And it was a self-reinforcing process, with those who had gained power being given additional responsibilities, which in turn produced more power in the parishes. By the late Elizabethan years, vestries like those of St Martin-in-the-Fields and others scattered throughout London were being formally licensed as select or closed organizations.[85]

This is not to say, though, that the development of parish oligarchies was unidirectional or uncomplicated. The small parish of Northill in Bedfordshire saw churchwardens elected by the "chief of [the] parish" in 1585, seemingly in line with a larger shift toward oligarchy. It did not last. In 1601, the accounts record that the wardens were chosen "by the consent general of the whole parish."[86] Whole consent is of course at some level a fiction. It certainly did not include children, nor almost certainly *femes covert* or servants, and quite possibly did not even include any women who were the heads of their own households. And yet, it speaks to a far more nuanced process than the model of Elizabethan oligarchy suggests. What the Elizabethan period saw, more than anything else, was experimentation. In some parishes, innovations worked well – at least in the eyes of those in power – and were continued. In others, new approaches were tried and rejected. The Elizabethan parish was a laboratory for governance.

The relative flexibility of the Elizabethan system allowed this process of trial and error to play out. With their reliance on custom and a system based on post-facto oversight rather than pre-emptive intervention, ecclesiastical officials made space for local government to emerge from the parish. This may have created the flexibility necessary for enacting a Reformation across a country of parochial diversity, but it also could produce very different results in different parishes. Indeed, while the growing bureaucracy of the Elizabethan church – combined with larger social and economic pressures – contributed to growing stratification and consolidation of power in some parishes, in others it opened new avenues for agency, action, and political involvement. These increasing demands and powers produced oligarchy in some places, but a broader politics in others.

Such a divergence of paths can be seen most clearly in the records of urban parochial life, which tend to be more substantial, extant, and granular than rural accounts. In a close study, and indeed only through microhistory, we can see the implication of this variance play out. Separated by only two miles, the parishes of St Dunstan, Stepney, and St Bartholomew by the Exchange were in different social worlds. St Dunstan was poor and sprawling, St Bartholomew, rich and compact. Though both were ancient parishes, St Dustan had been remade in the urban boom of late-Tudor England, growing from a sleepy agricultural parish of seventeen hundred to a teeming dockside parish of nearly thirteen thousand people; St Bartholomew, in contrast, looked much as it had a century or more earlier, with under a hundred houses along a few blocks of central London.[87] But both were part of the London diocese, and, crucially, both were subject to the same expansion of parochial responsibilities as all London parishes. They were, in short, demographically and socio-economically divergent, but institutionally quite similar. And they had entirely different responses to the bureaucratic surge of late-Tudor England.

In St Dunstan, there was a strict, oligarchic vestry. Its members were drawn from the elite of the parish, men like those of the Burrell family, who were appointed surveyors general of the East India Company and master shipwrights of the Royal Navy.[88] These men, facing a skyrocketing, itinerant population of immigrants and sailors, closed ranks. In 1589, they created a select vestry. Noting that "certain of the Worst disposed of this parishes Inhabitants" were avoiding taxes and obligations, the "Chief Parishioners being now assembled together for that purpose" created a new institutional order. These principal inhabitants chose a few dozen of their equals to join them in the vestry.[89] It was a profoundly anti-democratic institution. At a very rough estimate, by the close of the seventeenth century, less than 2 per cent of adult men – and .3 per cent of the total parish population – were represented on the vestry.[90] It was a self-consciously elitist institution, put in place to govern what it saw as an unruly population, "for reformation of disorders, and for ordaining and maintenance of good orders therein." Their notion of a responsible community was both limited and a radical appropriation of political power. "We the Parishioners presently assembled both for ourselves, and in the name of all the rest of the Parishioners," they wrote, "doe bind our selves, and them by mutual assents, To hold, observe and maintain."[91] This was unambiguous Elizabethan oligarchy at its most explicit: a select group of leading men, gathered together to create a new governing order "in the name of all the rest of the Parishioners." They claimed parochial rule for their own. There was continuity here, to be sure. Just as leading members of the parish had done for decades, if not centuries, they proclaimed that they would govern financial matters and the maintenance of the church fabric. But there was also change. The funds were to be raised from a compulsory church tax, assessed and collected by the same body. And the parish was far more explicitly involved in the secular lives of the laity than ever before explicitly expressed, tending to the poor and disciplining the immoral. This new, select vestry had extraordinary powers, ones they jealously guarded. The lived experience of the later Reformation in the parish, then, was thus an experience defined not by the population writ large but by an elite group whose perspective and needs could, and often did, differ from the larger parochial population.

Moreover, concentration of ecclesiastical political power in Stepney was in the hands of the same people who controlled so much of the secular power within the parish. Vestrymen were landlords, large-scale employers, and magistrates. They wielded enormous economic, social, and legal influence in a system that prized hierarchy and obedience. This did not mean instant compliance, of course. The increasingly heavy-handed approach of the vestry in financial affairs suggests that at least a portion of the populace remained stubbornly non-compliant. And yet, the impetus to obey was reinforced not merely by the vestry's power within the church but also outside of it. The "full power and authority to examine, here, order and determine" any disorder, including "the reforming of evil disposed contentious and disorderous people in the parish" was to be done by those who controlled the employment of nearly the entire parish. And poor relief, employment, justice, and taxation all lay in the hands of the same men who could use their discretion to order the parish. This meant that socio-economic, legal, political, and moral power were layered on top of each other, inflecting each other. The needs, perspective, and beliefs of the parochial elite dominated the parish.

As powerful a picture of Elizabethan oligarchy as Stepney paints, select vestries remained the exception rather than the rule. Even in London, which had perhaps the most advanced bureaucratic hierarchy in the country, relatively few parishes adopted the full Stepney model. While all of London's large suburban parishes had select vestries by the end of Elizabeth's reign, many fewer than half of its total parishes did. Indeed, even by Laud's 1638 survey of London, only 59 of 109 parishes had formally adopted a select vestry. Instead, most London parishes had an open vestry, if indeed they had any at all.

These smaller, inner-city parishes, though remaining hierarchical and elitist, became *more* participatory, not less, over the Elizabethan years. Here, the increasing demands of Elizabethan church and state upon local administration produced a widening, rather than a narrowing, of political power. Proliferation of bureaucratic responsibilities led to a multiplication of parish offices, which in turn were filled by an increasingly broad swathe of the adult male population. Unlike Stepney, these lower office-holders soon became part of the political sphere within the parish, often rising through its ranks to hold positions of ultimate authority in parochial affairs. In the case of

St Bartholomew by the Exchange, by 1598 over three-quarters of all male householders, at any rank, had held some form of parochial office over the previous two decades.[92] This included churchwardens, a full third of whom were drawn from the poorer half of householders. Despite having more power and authority to regulate the parish – moral, religious, and secular behaviour alike – and despite being drawn ever closer into the machine of the state church, the churchwardens of Elizabethan St Bartholomew's were becoming more, not less, representative of the parochial population writ large. Such broadening of representation did not occur in spite of the enhanced duties of churchwardens in the parish – it occurred *because* of it. The massive growth in administrative, fiduciary, and surveillance responsibilities was met with the proliferation of other offices: auditors, surveyors, overseers, and assessors, as well as more civil offices like constables, scavengers, and wardmote inquisitors. Unlike Stepney, which reserved high office and vestry participation to a few men, St Bartholomew's responded to the increasing responsibilities and authority placed on the parish by multiplying the rungs of the *cursus honorum*. That is to say, they increased lower-level positions that could, in turn, lead to much more powerful official roles in government.

Participation in the vestry was dominated by those who had served in some sort of formal office within the parish – and, in turn, they chose the men to serve in higher office from amongst themselves. In parishes like St Bartholomew's, access to office, even the lower or secular offices like street cleaners (known as scavengers), meant the ability to lay claim to legitimate participation within the vestry itself. And as the parish began to rely on a growing number of the middling, and then the lower-middling, sorts to fulfill the extensive needs of the Elizabethan state, the vestry actually became more accessible. In 1593, the vestry minutes record the attendance of thirty-three laymen, nearly half of rated male householders in the parish. Of these, nearly two-thirds were rated at or below the parochial average.[93] The poorest were almost always excluded, to be sure. But this structure stands in marked contrast to the explicit oligarchic construction of Stepney, where the vestry was fully monopolized by the parochial elite. In short, not all parishes responded equally to the requirements of the Elizabethan church and state upon the parish. In some cases, their demands actually opened up new avenues for political participation.

Important matters were decided in the vestry. Some were more secular in nature, like raising money "towards the charges of the ditches cleaning & new Casting abouts this City." Some were retrenchments of the socio-economic hierarchy, drives for order that scald in their coldness; in 1595, one of the poorest men of the parish was appointed to scare off "Common Rouges & beggars & masterless men." And much of it touched upon the growing provision for the poor who had been wrecked by the new Elizabethan economy.[94] But more than this, these men were helping both to administer and to define the pace and shape of religious change in Elizabethan London. They served in offices like wardens that reported directly to diocesan authorities, judging both their fellow parishioners and their own ministers. Supervision of the latter was particularly important in determining the religious experience of the parish, and the vestry exercised increasing powers over religious provision in the Elizabethan church. While few parishes held their own advowson (the right to appoint the clergy in the parish), they frequently controlled funding for lectureships that would supplement Prayer Book services. Much of this funding came from bequests, which were administered by the vestry as part of the general church funds, and selection of these ministers was often communal. In 1595, St Bartholomew's vestry delayed the discussion of Thomas Caters's £50 legacy for a weekly lectureship "to be further considered of in an ample vestry."[95] St Michael, Cornhill, went still further. By 1583, their vestry decided that they wanted to choose "an honest godly man" to give a regular "divinity lecture" in the parish; rather than waiting for a legacy, this activist vestry took up a general collection. They chose a "Mr Anderson," most likely the David Anderson who had recently been licensed as a preacher, who would hold the job "from this time forwards during the good liking of ye parish."[96] The power dynamics were clear: Anderson preached at the pleasure of the vestry. As vestries grew, then, more and more people had not just an interest in questions of religious change, but actually held agency in shaping that change.

The story of the vestry also asks us to look more closely at questions of continuity and change. Here, as with visitations and churchwardens, the lines between innovation and tradition remain muddied. Parochial elites had long run parishes, dominating key offices in confraternities and gilds from at least the thirteenth century. Oligarchy was not a Tudor invention. Nor was lay activity new: if we have learned one thing from the past half-century of Reformation scholarship, it is that the late-medieval parish hummed with the energy of the laity. What differed in the Elizabethan parish is that this energy had been harnessed and directed by the state. The vestry was in many ways a new articulation of an old idea employed to the new purposes of the Elizabethan regime. Indeed, what is perhaps most striking about these divergent paths is that both were allowed – and indeed encouraged – to be followed. As Michael Braddick has noted, the increasingly centralized English state relied on a system of local agents to expand, maintain, and deepen its power.[97] The vestry was a formal articulation of this dependence, and it yoked the vestry to the strength of the state machine. But this was in no way a unidirectional political exchange. The creation of the vestry through formal petitioning simultaneously legitimized state interference in local matters *and* the vestry's authority within its parish. The relationship between central and peripheral power was thus symbiotic and very frequently mutualistic. The vestries relied on state sanction to increase their local power; the state relied on the vestries to maintain their Reformation.

In many ways, this power exchange replicated that of the relationship between visitations and churchwardens. Wardens, however, were far better understood and controlled by the state. The office of the warden was relatively clearly defined, with its functions and its responsibilities outlined by statute and observed through regular review. While visitations consistently evaluated the performance and suitability of the wardens, the vestry was by and large ignored by archidiaconal or episcopal reviews until the closing years of Elizabeth's reign. The first set of visitation articles to take the power of the vestry seriously was Richard Bancroft's visitation in 1598, more than two decades after vestries began to proliferate in the parishes.[98] In these years of official neglect, the state church had sanctioned a new, lay-driven institution that operated with little oversight and significant authority. With little episcopal control, the vestries found themselves in unprecedented positions of power within their parishes. They selected office-holders; they oversaw decisions over selling church ornaments or buying new property; they hired preachers; they policed their neighbours. And in doing so, they expanded formal lay agency within the English church to a level never before seen.

ᔕ

Just why John Montgomery and Robert Bemond lined up with the other two contenders to become churchwardens of All Hallows is lost in time. Maybe they wanted the social status for personal reasons, moved by ego or ambition. Maybe they were attempting to bolster their position more practically, building up the reputation needed to increase their credit, be respected in their livery company and guild circles, bring in new clients or customers. Perhaps they cared deeply about their neighbourhood and had ideas to improve the parish and ameliorate the lives of the poor; perhaps they wished to punish disorder and curb crime. They may have had firmly held religious beliefs, godly men, working to secure the provision of the Word for their families and their city. But whatever their motivation, they were vying to become not just local notables or city men, but the real agents of the English Reformation

The Elizabethan Reformation was policed by its own people. Building on long-standing continuities with pre-Reformation structures, particularly the figure of the churchwarden, the state church vested a new authority in the laymen of the parish. Allowed a flexibility of constitution, depending on local needs and local customs, these wardens nevertheless enforced an inflexible conception of conformity: moral, personal, material, faithful. Like so much of Elizabethan England, the evolution of the warden, and the vestries they sometimes led, was organic rather than intentional. There was no clear, overarching plan that dictated the warden would become responsible for everything from rats in the rafters to sexual probity to wall repair to land confiscation for highways to feeding the poor to checking schoolmasters' licences to hiring searchers for the sick to monitoring the minister for radicalism or recusancy. It was a position loaded with unintentional consequences. But what emerged out of this office of sedimentary responsibility was a new position of massive power and influence. The English church relied on them every visitation, every accounting, every single Sunday. And in doing so, the Reformation created a new politics of the parish.

3

Funding the Parish

Tilney All Saints was a quiet, marshy parish, part of the great, yet-undrained Fenlands, just across the Ouse from King's Lynn. Charles Parkin recorded some two centuries later a tale told to James I, that the nearby common land of Tilney Smeeth was so rich that "if over night a wand, or rod, was laid on the ground, by the morning it would be covered with grass of that night's growth, so as not to be discerned."[1] The parish church, with its massive square tower and sharply pointed spire, must have loomed across those marshes. It was, and is, a solid, substantial building, with fat stone pillars supporting thick, ambitious Norman arches. A huge east window let in light over the chancel, while the nave was lit by windows in the walls and in the clerestory, all capped with a heavy hammerbeam roof. Even its fables were outsized: buried in the churchyard was Tom Hickathrift, the legendary fenland strongman who fought – depending on the story – either a giant ravaging the nearby marshes or landlords trying to oppress the commons.[2] And yet, for all its sturdiness and size, it housed a modest congregation, gathered from the nearby fens and farms.

The 1566 churchwardens' accounts from Tilney read prosaically. Paid for bread and wine: four shillings, eleven pence. For "a rope for the second bell," two shillings. For washing of the surplice, four pence; for "making clen of the bell loft," eight pence; for "two hundreds of reed for the porch," four shillings; for six bunches of rope, nine-pence. By far the greatest expense was the casting of the great bell, a large job that cost four pounds, six shillings, and eight pence, making a grand total of expenses some six pounds, nine shillings, and six pence.[3] Though a not-inconsiderable sum for a quiet Fenland parish, it seems at first glance to reveal little about the machinations of ecclesiastical life in

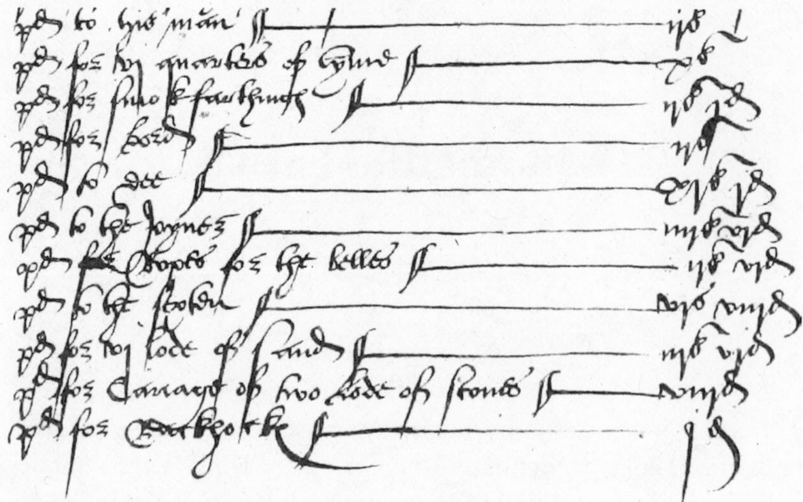

Figure 3.1 A sample of churchwardens' accounts taken from St Mary's, Reading. These accounts are far clearer and better preserved than most.

the Elizabethan church. And yet, here too we see the Reformation in action, and enacted. A closer look at the accounts, and indeed parish finances as a whole, from across England reveals the complex logistics of cultivating a Reformation in the late sixteenth century. It is in the anodyne records of the churchwardens – laundry bills here, payments for masonry there, purchases of ivy and incense, rent receipts from smallholdings or pews, fees for burials and wedding communions – that we find the lifeblood of the Elizabethan Reformation.

In short, no church can run without money. However pure a mission, the missionaries must eat; however noble an edifice, the windows must be repaired; however true the Word, the text must be printed. Nevertheless, the methods through which the institution chooses to raise and to spend this money are deeply revealing, underscoring priorities, power, and politics. To understand the financing of a church is, in a sense, to understand the church itself. From massive land sales to ha'penny tithe on eggs, the Elizabethan church raised enormous sums to power twin undertakings of doctrinal ministry and socio-political stability. To do so, it made compromises and concessions that fundamentally shaped the church in England and the country more broadly. This chapter will explore the contours of some of these compromises, looking at the expenses and income of the parish church. First, and relatively briefly, it covers the material life of the parish, and then, in more granular detail, the ways in which these changes – and indeed the regular expenses of the parish – were funded. In doing so, it will explore fundamental conflicts engendered by a quintessentially Elizabethan confluence of past and present, which so coloured the late sixteenth century. By examining the ways in which the fissures of economic and social stability caused by the Reformation were re-fused and remade, what soon becomes clear is just how deeply the administration of the parishes involved and invested the laity in the preservation of the Elizabethan church – and how much of that was revealed in the expenses and income of the parishes.

At first it seems a bit strange to talk about the robust material life of the Elizabethan parish. Historians were, for many years, skeptical about its material culture. With notable exceptions, the historical imagination tends to be captured by creation in the medieval church and destruction in the Reformation church. Of course, iconoclasm and dissolution were central to Reformation debates and fundamentally reshaped the English landscape, both literally and figuratively. Historians of all stripes have found rich soil in studying these questions, and in academic works, the material life of the Elizabethan church has been sometimes placed in contrast to the richness of the late-medieval church or the flowering of the Jacobean church.[4] Notable recent works by historians like Margaret Aston and Robert Whiting have refocused our attention on the nuances and potential of Elizabethan material culture.[5] Still, it can be tempting to listen too carefully to the louder voices of the past, which tend to come from godly jeremiads of the lamentable state of the parish fabric. As pamphleteer Philip Stubbes put it, at his dramatic best, "For where I have traveled (as I have travailed the whole realm over) I have found in most places, (nay almost in all) the Churches to lie like barns … worser than I have known many swine to lie in … far worser than either barns, or stables, God be merciful to us."[6] It is a depiction that has wended its way into the historiography.[7]

And yet, in light of such dire claims, the archival evidence is quite startling. Where we might expect vast swathes of crumbling churches, church walls, and steeples, contemporary accounts paint a far more vibrant and robust picture. Even areas far from the bureaucratic centres of Tudor England – and far from general enthusiasms for reform – saw a relatively hardy church fabric. The churchwardens' reports from the North Riding in the late sixteenth century, for instance, routinely presented fewer than 10 per cent of churches or chapels for default.[8] While some of the parishes were genuinely dilapidated, like the chapel of Bilsdale in the moorland parish of Helmsley, where the churchwardens confessed that the "body of the chapel is in decay," many of the defects presented were relatively minor.[9] Here, churchyard fences were the main culprits, with various parishes presented "for not fencing there parts of the church yard wall" or because "the church yard not well fenced."[10] Similar numbers can be found in Bishop Stills's 1594 visitation of Bath and Wells, where, of 305 parishes, only twenty were reported in need of repair, and much of it light.[11] Nor was this a matter of under-reporting by recalcitrant wardens wary of incurring the wrath of the ecclesiastical courts; a royal commission's 1602 survey of Lincoln's church fabric pronounced nearly 90 per cent of churches as "well repaired and decently kept."[12]

This is not the portrait of a crumbling infrastructure that one might expect from reading Stubbs or the historians who took him at his word. Instead, the evidence presents an imperfect but viable sound infrastructure showing signs of the sort of continued attention that required substantial financial outlays. Uncovering how the parish was transformed – and how the parish funded this transformation – shines a startling light onto the ways in which the church in England continued and evolved in the decades following the Reformation.

The Elizabethan settlement's hallmark of conformity was quickly brought to bear on the material life of the parish church. From the earliest years of Elizabeth's reign, the church placed a keen emphasis on the transformation of the English parochial architecture into a new Protestant ideal.[13] If the priority of the settlement was the establishment of clear standards of uniformity and conformity, parochial architecture and ornament was a natural target for scrutiny: patterns of misbehaviour were difficult to police or to prove, but the material life of communal liturgical spaces was discernable and conspicuous. This was in part a matter of sheer visibility, of the plausibility of enacting change. It was quite difficult to ensure that every child in every parish was receiving a sound Protestant education; it was quite easy to detect the presence of a communion table. But the material life of the church mattered on deeper levels too. Symbolically, it represented both the advent of a new religious order and the power of the state, through the Act of Supremacy, to determine that order. Practically, material life was intimately linked to the patterns and meanings of worship and the afterlife. The transformation of the parish church, then, became a battleground for much larger issues. In the early modern religious context, form did not follow function: it was coterminous.

In its policies of material Reformation, the Elizabethan church was no kinder, gentler world: with echoes of the destructive iconoclasm of the Edwardian reforms some fifteen years earlier, rood screens and altars were removed, giving way to new communion tables.[14] It was the *via sola* enacted. The texts, ornaments, and images of Marian England were yet again banned, replaced by the material life of a Protestant church. In some areas, particularly in the more radical southeast of England, the destruction was undertaken with heady enthusiasm. As Diarmaid MacCulloch points out, such destruction was generally done with the sanction of local ecclesiastical authorities and after extensive deliberation – "not manslaughter, but murder."[15] In many cases, indeed, it was less murder than it was state-ordered execution. In other words, to use Carlos Eire's typography, this kind of iconoclasm was both legal and collective.[16] In other areas, including much of the north and southwest, such legality and collectivism was matched by recalcitrance, subversion, and outright anger at yet another wave of destruction in the name of building a uniform Protestant church in England.

From the beginning of the settlement, then, eradicating Catholic ornament from the parish church was a priority. The Royal Injunctions of 1559 compelled the destruction of "all shrines, coverings of shrines, all tables, candlesticks, trindals, and rolls of wax, pictures, paintings, and all other monuments of feigned miracles, pilgrimages, idolatry, and superstition."[17] This language was echoed in the visitation articles of the first decade following the settlement. The interrogatory of the 1561 visitation of Norwich was remarkably specific, forbidding not only "any Images, beads, bokes of service, or vestments not allowed by law," but also "altars, images, holywaters stones, pictures, paintings, as of Thassumption of the blessed virgin, of the descending of Christ into the virgin in the form of a little boy at Thanunciacion of the Angel, and all other superstitious and dangerous monuments especially paintings & Images in wall, boke, cope, Banner or else where, of the blessed trinity or of the father (of whom there can be no Image made)."[18]

Similar, though less specific, iconoclastic language can be found in other visitations from the 1560s. The 1563 metropolitan visitation inquired "whether images and all other monuments of idolatry and superstition be destroyed and abolished in your several parishes," while the 1569 Norwich articles asked whether "all … monuments of Idolatry be pulled down and defaced."[19] These injunctions, followed by some of the most comprehensive metropolitan visitations of Elizabeth's reign, made clear the radical transformative goals of the new settlement.

What followed was a generally effective dismantling of the material vestiges of Marian Catholicism. A chief target was the altar: the real and symbolic heart of the parish church. The Queen's Injunctions of 1559, issued only three months after the passing of the Act of Uniformity, outlined the new policy toward altars in a surprisingly conciliatory tone. According to the articles, the queen acknowledged the appearance of the altar to be a matter of *adiaphora* – practices permitted but not mandated in the church – but still required, "for observation of one uniformity through the whole Realm & for the better imitation of the law," that the altars be replaced by communion tables.[20] This removal, the injunctions hastened to add, should be done carefully by the curate and churchwardens, not through a "riotous or disordered" iconoclastic mob.[21] The mention of *adiaphora* was calculated here, meant to serve as a warning sign to those who sought to challenge the new conception of the sacrament on either conservative or radical grounds. Nevertheless, it could not hide the radical implications of the injunctions. The claim that the altar was *adiaphora* signalled a basic desacralization of traditional architecture and the return of a reformed Church interior. Moreover, that matters *adiaphora* should be enforced in a uniformity decided by the queen – rather, say, than left up to individual parishes, ministers, or bishops – marked a clear position on church power, one grounded very much in the monarchical supremacy enjoined by the Henrician church. If this was conciliation, the velvet glove clearly covered an iron fist.

The steel behind these words soon entered official policies of parochial enforcement. Interestingly, the first set of metropolitan visitation articles did not directly address the matter of the communion table or altar, instead referring more vaguely to items of superstition or idolatry.[22] However, the removal of the altar and the institution of the communion table quickly became a central feature in both episcopal and metropolitan visitations. The earliest extant appearance occurs in the 1561 visitation of Bishop Parkhurst of Norwich, which inquired "whether they have a fit and decent table to minister the communion on."[23] The 1563 metropolitan visitation of Archbishop Parker was even more explicit, asking if each parish had "a comely and decent table for the Holy communion … And whether your Alters be taken down."[24] Five years into Elizabeth's reign, the church was enforcing a reformed liturgy practised on a reformed fabric.

For the most part, parishes conformed quickly to these new requirements. The majority of surviving account books from the period record the destruction of the altar or the purchase of a communion table, a communion book, or a communion tablecloth by 1561. The sheer destruction, and the rapidity of construction, can be read through the anodyne lines of receipts and payments. The account books of great St Mary's church in Yatton, towering over the north-Somerset moors that surrounded its village, reveal the inexorable drumbeat of reform. In 1559, the wardens bought the Book of Common Prayer to guide communion services. Soon thereafter, they spent six shillings installing a new communion table. Within a few months, they were paying the clerk to write out their answers to the local visitation, which they attended. They bought an injunction book, paid for communion in two kinds in Easter of 1560. That year, they removed the altar, bought a "table cloth" of six yards' length, and finished the provisions with sixpence spent on a "glass bottle to keep wine for ye Communion."[25] They weren't alone. The altars were taken down with remarkable rapidity in many parishes. Similar expenditures can be found in the account books of Woodbury, Devon (1559); St Martin-in-the-Fields, London (1559); Oxford St Martin (1559); St Mary-on-the-Hill, Cheshire (1559); Steeple Ashton, Wiltshire (1559); Cratfield, Suffolk (1559); St Michael Cornhill, London (1559); Swaffham, Norfolk (1559); Ludlow, Shropshire (1559); Ashburton, Devon (1559); Shipdham, Norfolk (1559); Mere, Wiltshire (1559/60); St Martin's, Leicester (1559/60); St Stephen Walbrook (1560); St Mary's, Reading (1560); South Tawton, Devon (1560/61); St Mary the Great, Cambridge (1560/61); and Stanford-in-the-Vale, Norfolk (1561).[26] This list – indicative, but far from exhaustive – is striking in its diversity. Here we have parishes from the conservative north and west and the evangelical southeast; from university towns, market towns, great cities, and rural parishes alike, all conforming to the Elizabethan Injunctions.

Compliance, though, was neither simple nor direct. The timeline of Yatton's accounts, for instance, reveals traces of the tensions that must have swept through many an English parish. Here we see the heavy hand of the state, with at least two visitations in 1559 alone, as well as the purchase of the injunction book. The rapidity with which the wardens purchased a communion book and a communion table seems to reveal an eagerness to conform. And yet the altar stood for at least another year, newly revealed by the destruction of the rood screen.[27] Perhaps it remained shrouded with cloth and shadow at the far end of the church; perhaps it was bedecked and candlelit, looming over the bare communion table that sat alone in the chancel, a silent rebuke to the new order. We cannot know. But it is clear that the process of change was far from straightforward.

In some extreme cases, such as the remote area of Holderness in the East Riding of Yorkshire, altars persisted until almost a decade after the first injunctions were issued.[28] More common in these areas was probably what Eamon Duffy calls a "reluctant and partial conformity" – a slower, perhaps hesitant, adoption of Elizabethan orthodoxy.[29] Reasons for such hesitance are perforce speculative; Hutton suggests the lack of urgency compelled by the moderate tone of the injunctions and the tenuous hold Elizabeth had on the throne in the early days, while Duffy argues that it represents dislike of the new orthodoxy itself.[30] These analyses are no doubt true for the reaction of many of the parishes. Another reason can also be ventured: the sheer enormity of the expense of the churches' remodelling. The construction of a reformed communion table happened at the same time as expenditures on new linens, vestments, books, and ornaments, as well as the charges for pulling down rood lofts and other major repairs – and all in addition to the normal operating costs of the parish. Moreover, the change mandated by these injunctions was the third in less than ten years, following rapidly on the heels of the Edwardian and Marian instructions on church furniture.

What we can know, however, is this: whatever the motivation, by the mid-1560s all but the most recalcitrant parishes had reworked their eucharistic furniture to be in line with the 1559 injunctions. A survey of Lincolnshire parishes in 1566 provides the most comprehensive picture of the rate of compliance. The survey had sprung from then-archdeacon John Aylmer's visitation of Lincoln, which he found "hath as much a need of [Reformation] as any place in England."[31] After a sustained lobbying campaign by Aylmer of the more evangelical members of the privy council, the bishop of Lincoln was compelled to commission a survey of the state of the diocese's churches, paying special attention to church fabric. The main body of these accounts shows a picture of clear, if perhaps slow, conformism to the Elizabethan order for communion. From this body, 143 entries have survived without serious archival damage, 128 of which mention the altar.[32] Of these 128 parishes, only two mention an altar still standing at the time of the commission. The majority of parishes listed no date for altar destruction, but for those that did, more than half had complied within eighteen months of the injunctions. Reformation was not immediate. Its slow pace infuriated almost all evangelicals and most members of the episcopate. But in the scheme of the enormous change being undertaken, it was relatively quick and relatively effective.

Despite large-scale observance of the injunctions, the picture painted by the Lincoln survey – our best window into the change the entire country was facing – is uneven, chaotic, and messy. The parish of Belton, on the Isle of Axholme, reported it had yet to break or deface the altar stones, but hastened to add that it had defaced the mass book two years earlier and its altar cloths were "Rotten in pieces in the bottom of a chest."[33] Such unpaved and undefaced stones may well have been a sign of churchwardens hedging their bets against the possible reconstruction of the altars in a few years with yet another change of religion. In the fervent excitement of the 1569 Rebellion of the North, parishioners of both St Margaret's and St Giles in Durham took up altar stones hidden in the choir floor to resurrect into an altar.[34] But lack of destruction did not necessarily indicate religious resistance. The parishioners of Witham noted that they had pulled down the altar stones, and while two lay unbroken and undefaced, the third had been sold to John Harrington to use as a "fire back." This is less evidence of reverent sequestration by recusants than of sheer Tudor thrift.[35] Churchwardens often detailed the secular uses to which former altar stones were put: "Mr Sheffield haith made a sink of it in his kitchen"; "we have made stepping stones of [them] at our church yard stile"; "to keep Cattle from the Chapel wall"; "which altar stones lieth on broad bridge to bear up the bank."[36] A few accounts positively glow with evangelical fervour. The chapel of Kelbie in the parish of Haydon

Bridge reported its altar stones were "defaced and Laid in high ways and serveth as bridges for sheep and cattle to go on so that their now remaineth no trash nor trumpery of popish peltry in our said church of Kelbie."[37]

Removal of the altars, massive and visible furniture at the heart of sacramental architecture that they were, was the hallmark of physical compliance with the new order. That they fell more rapidly than other, less observable, tokens of traditional worship spoke both to their conspicuous presence and their symbolic value. By the end of Elizabeth's first decade on the throne, these altars, with all their symbolism, had largely disappeared. The reformed sacrament was now received on reformed furniture. Whatever the impetus behind such destruction, less than a decade after Elizabeth's injunctions had been issued, the material setting of the eucharist had been fundamentally changed.[38]

If the altars were largely dismantled by the mid-1560s, the pace of other destruction was uneven. Parishes often pulled down the altar and the rood loft at once, as in Steeple Aston, where the receipts for the two were side by side.[39] In some parishes, though, there was a significant gap between the destruction of the two. St Mary the Great in Cambridge saw its altar (just rebuilt after Edwardian iconoclasm) taken down in 1560, but its loft remained for almost four more years.[40] At Oxford's St Martin's, the altars were pulled down in 1559, but it took nearly fifteen more years before the rood loft was removed.[41] Again, the financial whiplash of the many phases of the English Reformation may well have caused wardens to pause, particularly in the early years of Elizabeth's reign. Shipdham, a small parish on the Norfolk coast about twenty miles west of Norwich, had dutifully followed the Edwardian prescriptions of 1547: the wardens had sold off its silver, taken down its icons, destroyed the images from the altar cloths, whited the church. Over the next few years, they must have destroyed its Catholic architecture; though the accounts from these years are missing, so too were the altars and the rood by the time of Mary's accession just six years later. Dutifully, again, they followed orders. The rood was rebuilt in 1555, the passion cloth of the altar repainted, the cross painted on the loft, and images of Mary and John and the All Hallows were outlined and painted in 1557. Two years after that, the altar was pulled down again. In 1561, the rood came back down.[42] It was an incredibly expensive business, with investments made and unmade every few years. Experience encouraged caution.

Figure 3.2 Royal Arms were frequently painted on the inside of parish churches by the mid-Elizabethan period. This depiction is from the parish of Ludlow, Norfolk, and was superimposed over an earlier painting of Christ's crucifixion. The caption translates to "I am not ashamed of the Gospel of Christ – long live Queen Elizabeth."

Despite this destruction, the Elizabethan church remained heavily decorated – this too an expensive business. At the holiday season, many parishes were strewn with holly and ivy. The floors were covered throughout the year in reeds, swept and renewed each spring. The walls were painted again, now with elaborate tables of the Ten Commandments and, by the mid-Elizabethan period, with pictures of the royal arms. In 1554, the churchwardens of Swaffham had paid 2s. 8d. to paint a crucifix on the centre of the rood loft. The rood screen was taken down, but the loft survived. In 1570, however, the wardens commissioned the Queen's Arms to be painted at the centre of the loft. In doing so, they tapped into the large number of artists who practised their crafts in the parish churches across the country; Bob Tittler's remarkable database of Early Modern British Painters shows well over seventeen hundred named painters working in the Elizabethan years alone.[43] Moreover, parishes were decorated with images of local laity, particularly in increasingly elaborate tombs and funerary monuments. Such memorials to the "better sort" of the parish multiplied in their complexity, sometimes riots of colour and symbolism as they celebrated the life of those who had died.[44] It was a very different aesthetic of ornamentation than that of its Catholic forebears, but the parish church remained a place of visual import.

When the ecclesiastical authorities heard accounts of the retention of Catholic church ornament, they brought their most powerful judicial mechanisms to bear. The Court of High Commission, that ecclesiastical corollary to Star Chamber, periodically heard cases involving the retention of vestments and Catholic ornament.[45] The matter took on increased urgency following the Northern Rebellion of 1569, where reappearance of altars and holy water stones particularly worried the authorities.[46] It must be noted, however, that these items had to be resurrected: they had been effectively removed from the parish in the previous decade. The altar stone in the parish of St Oswald's, Durham, had been "broken in three and underlaid with a piece of timber."[47] The parishioners of St Margaret's, Durham, "took a through stone out of th' pavement of the church floor."[48] The altar stone of Pittington was "upon the kirk floor," while the parishioners of Sedgefield "helpt to draw with ropes the said alter stone from Gibson garth into the church."[49] Even in those areas where loyalty to the old religion ran high, the first decade of following the Act of Uniformity had systematically dismantled Catholic architecture in the pre-Reformation spaces of worship themselves.

In its place, architecture deemed crucial for the spreading of the gospel was retained or rebuilt. Church pulpits were intimately tied with the privileging of the spoken word in the church, and as such they were an anchor in the parish-church fabric.[50] Some new pulpits had been constructed in Edward's time, and Elizabeth's 1559 injunctions mandated their presence within the church. Pulpits became increasingly technologically sophisticated, with sounding boards that allowed the congregation to hear the words of a sermon or a homily. They were also enormously expensive. Elaborate new Elizabethan pulpits were constructed in some parishes, as in St Matthew Friday Street, London; there, wardens paid £3 15s. for the joinery of the new pulpit, 8s. 3d. for "making the way to the pulpit," and a further 6s. to the smithy for decorative ironwork.[51] Parishes were also sites of the written word. As we will see shortly, by the mid-Elizabethan period they had evolved into small libraries, with Bibles, homilies, prayer books, song books, catechisms, Foxe's *Acts and Monuments*, and various reformed texts required by bishops, like Erasmus's *Paraphrases* or Musculus's *Commonplaces*.

For ease of reading, Bible stands were constructed, as in the parish of Tilney All Saints in 1563.[52]

Perhaps the most remarkable transformation in the nave of the parish church was the proliferation of parish pews across the country.[53] The rapid spread of fixed church seating, in pews or in boxes, has been attributed both to the new primacy of preaching and to the growing desire to order society.[54] While it is clear that there was medieval precedent in the construction of pews and the payment of parishioners for assigned seating, the erection of fixed seating became increasingly common over the course of the Elizabethan period.[55] Indeed, they were fixed in two ways: first, permanent seats, rather than temporary stools brought out for longer services or infirm parishioners; and second, allotted and assigned. Elizabethans did not just sit in any seat, they sat in a specific seat, often paid for like any other piece of property. There was a sense of ownership over these seats. This was compounded by the large costs of building these pews, especially for the more elaborate seating allocated to the wealthier members of the parish. In St Michael Cornhill, London, the 1569 construction of four new pews, including one for the alderman, cost over £6 10s. Expenses included green satin, red lace, copper nails, and a lock for the alderman's pew.[56] This was, of course, an extreme of luxury; far more common was the cost of 6s. 8d. for an elegant, but not luxurious, pew in St Michael's in Bedwardine.[57]

Pews had a much deeper social valence than merely providing a place for the parishioners to sit. The construction of pews was part and parcel of the growing definition of community within the parish church. They reflected the wider social order, with finely calibrated social gradations reified in the new fixed seating plans that placed the most prestigious seats closest to the pulpit.[58] This was part and parcel of a broader Elizabethan mania for ordering and ranking, one only encouraged by the growing power of the middling sort and their increasing identification with and affinity to local elites. Such a hierarchical order not only preserved ranking, it also helped to create a stricter definition of who belonged to the parish and who did not. Everyone had a place, and everyone's place was known. Those who sat in others' pews could be fined or, in extreme instances, brought to court; moreover, as the literature of the past forty years has amply demonstrated, personal disputes over pews often spilled over into questions of honour and insult, with many ending in defamation and litigation.[59] Crucially, in

Figure 3.3 The interior of Langley Chapel, built in 1601. Note the pews, in both bench and box form, which were arranged strictly according to rank. Pews allowed the congregation to focus on the sermons – and the wardens to notice anyone missing services.

those cases where the initial recourse was to the courts rather than to parochial argument, litigants tended to focus on a sense of defining the proper boundaries of the community. In many cases, neither custom not past payment for pews was enough to secure the rights to seating in perpetuity. Instead, one maintained the right to seating through use. For instance, in one case heard before the Northern Court of High Commission in 1596, the defendants argued that that the plaintiff, Robert Kaye, had ceded his right to a pew after he had moved away from the parish. Upon his return, he attempted to claim his customary seating, only for the defendants to refuse to yield the pew on the basis that, in leaving the parish land, he had abrogated his rights in the community.[60] Pews were not simply about ordering, but also tools of inclusion and exclusion.

Importantly, this new rigidity of spatial seating occurred simultaneously with an increased ecclesiastical interest in monitoring church attendance and restricting sacramental participation to the population of the parish. As we saw in chapter 1, the issue of *belonging* to a parish was politically charged in new and important ways. The ecclesiastical authorities, determined to measure conformity, mandated attendance at a specific place: one's own parish church. What pews did was to narrow the space still further: not just to a parish, but to a seat within that parish. The drive to fix people so precisely was not exactly a religious one. The vestry of St Michael Cornhill, anxious to preserve the privileges of those who had paid pew rents, charged a fine of 2d. for those sitting in seats not their own. But the results of this fixedness did aid an enforcement of Protestant conformity. In order for the vestry to levy any fines for breaking seating rules, their churchwardens had to have a precise awareness of their parochial roster.[61] Again, everyone's place was known, precisely. As a result, assessing conformity to attendance was rendered far more visible and its policing far easier. In the chaos of flexible, mixed seating – or, even more, in parishes without seating – rigorous accounting of those absent from church would have been difficult. In a parish like St Michael's in Bedwardine, however, which by 1595 had assigned seating for almost every parishioner, recognizing the absent must have been relatively easy.[62] If everyone's place was known, everyone's behaviour could be monitored and reported.

Pew construction was thus a distinctly Elizabethan movement, combining the push toward a Protestant, preaching-based religious service with the drive for greater social ordering and discipline. These impetuses were grounded, at least in part, in fear of chaos. For those authorities worried about conformity, pews created a legible public. For reformers who worried about the spiritual health of a nation splintered by thirty-odd years of oscillating liturgy and doctrine, pews focused the congregations of England on a steady diet of homily and sermon. For those concerned about increasing internal migration and the socio-economic strains of a growing wealth gap, pews allowed a site for articulating a clearer social hierarchy. Here, then, we again see the interplay of the social and the religious helping to facilitate the easy surveillance of conformity. While pewing the parish tended to spring from local initiative, it played into the needs and desires of the central state church.

The major architectural shifts of the Elizabethan church, then, were not blind destruction, but rather violent reconstruction. In the place of Catholic interiors rose the mandated Protestant architecture of pulpits and communion tables, and new pews.[63] The articulation of a Protestant aesthetic was deliberate, reflecting the priorities and theologies of the

Elizabethan church. The importance of the new aesthetic is reflected in the growing emphasis of the visitation articles not on the destruction of Catholic material, but rather on the construction of reformed fabric. Starting in the 1570s, visitations began to shift their focus toward the provision of reformed church goods. The fourth inquiry in the articles from the 1571 London visitation articles asked after the presence of a detailed list of items, including books, the communion table, communion plate, a poor box, and a table of the Ten Commandments; it was not until question thirty-three that any inquiry was made about the presence of Catholic adornment.[64] By 1580, many visitations entirely omitted questions about Catholic icons or images, instead simply inquiring after the presence and maintenance of the reformed fabric.[65] While fears of extra-parochial recusancy intensified, concerns about the presence of pre-Reformation ornament within the church walls faded away. In its place, the ecclesiastical authorities focused on the material life of the reformed aesthetic.

In doing so, they found that while major architectural changes, like the destruction of the altars, had been relatively easy, auditing the more movable goods of the church proved an altogether thornier issue. In clothes, books, and plate, authorities faced not simply ideological opposition but the practical difficulties of both providing and maintaining materials that were altogether more frangible than pews or tables. Ceremonial clothes appear frequently in inventories and, when lacking, in visitation presentments. Some vestments were retained from those purchased in previous religious orders, albeit transformed from their old purpose into a new. Vestments were defaced and turned to reformed purposes: albs into surplices or rochets, altar cloths into communion cloths, copes into pulpit covers.[66] These conversions may have been a way of preserving beloved liturgical garments in the new world of the Elizabethan church, but if so, parishioners would have had to see them used for radically different – and ideologically charged – purposes. A memory, perhaps, but not a continuity of devotion.

Rather than recycling, many churches decided to purchase new vestments, to start from scratch. Despite the expensive bulk purchase of church linen in Mary's reign, the wardens of St Michael's in Bedwardine authorized the 1566 acquisition of two new surplices at a cost of 34s.[67] The provision for church linens could be extensive. In 1584, the wardens of Pittington had "iii linen table clothes and one buckram table clothe … two surplices, one new and one olde."[68] This pales, however, in comparison with St Peters, Hertfordshire, whose Elizabethan inventory listed: "ii clothes of crimson and green velvet pained … both lined with blue buckram, one hearse clothe of white and crimson satin … one hearse cloth of crimson and black velvet embroidered and lined with blue buckram; one back part of an offray of a vestment of gold and silk embroidered, one old clothe for the pulpit of blue velvet fringed and lined; two cushions of crimson velvet, three linen table clothes, [and] one communion table cloth of linen.[69] As colourful as such description might be, it is not a matter of mere antiquarian interest. Purely on a practical level, provision and maintenance of such expensive furnishings place significant financial strain on the parishes. As the chapter will later discuss, such costs forced churchwardens to engage in complicated economic strategies that bound the parishes churches even more closely to their communities.

Moreover, such materials were fundamentally devotional in nature. Though sumptuous, they reflected the status quo of the reformed Elizabethan church; nowhere on this list is mentioned any item that would have been prohibited by injunction. There are no images, nor are there any albs or other specifically Catholic vestment. Instead, we see the complicated interplay between high ceremony and reformed doctrine that underpinned public prayer in the Elizabethan church. Such grand vestments would have infuriated the evangelical wing of the church. However, the wide latitude in devotional practice granted by Elizabethan injunction allowed for a certain flexibility in terms of local usage. As long as services were being conducted according to the Book of Common Prayer and the church was purged of explicitly Catholic ornament, churchwardens were free to purchase and to keep the church goods of their liking. In a parish with a strong godly influence, this may have resulted in fine, but plain, linens. In more traditional parishes, more ornate items could be used. In either case, it was conformity to the basic practices and prescriptions of the injunctions that was important to church authorities, leaving individual parishes a great degree of control in the design and outlay on linen, vestments, and the like. As with methods of electing churchwardens, flexibility was permitted within clear bounds. Diversity of experience was a feature, not a bug.

Books were another expensive item that parishes had to provide. The Elizabethan church required the purchase and maintenance of an extensive array of texts, all of which underscored the essential doctrines of the church. The Injunctions of 1559 required all parishes to purchase a large Bible within three months following the first visitation of the parishes. Moreover, within a year, parishes were to provide Erasmus's *Paraphrases*.[70] The latter text was particularly associated with the more radical tendencies of the Edwardian Reformation, and the inclusion in the parish church with the accompanying note that the text should be "set up in some convenient place within the said Church … whereas their Parishioners may most commodiously resort to the same, and read the same, out of the time of common service" was particularly galling to traditionalists.[71] By 1563, with the passage of the Act of Uniformity through parliament, the Book of Homilies and Book of Common Prayer were added to the list of required texts.[72] In both the purchase and the placement of such texts, the church's injunctions made a fundamental statement about the centrality of reformed doctrine and learning in the worship of the parish church.

While having profound ideological consequences, these new requirements also had serious practical repercussions, requiring another round of extensive financial outlay. In the parish of St Martin's, Leicester, for example, the first five years after the injunctions saw the purchase of two books of prayers, a book of homilies, two psalm books, a table of commandments and calendar, and a chain and staples to hold the English Bible.[73] The receipts for these books totalled £1 2s., or roughly a month's salary for a best-paid craftsman.[74] The most expensive required book was the Bible, with large volumes often costing a full pound or more on their own.[75] In enforcing textual conformity, the church yet again encountered the ramifications of thirty years of religious changes. Books mandated in 1547 had been forbidden in 1555, only to be required again in 1559. When the Royal Visitation of 1559 surveyed the parishes of Yorkshire, most of the parishes deemed textually deficient reported that their Edwardian copies of the *Paraphrases* or communion books had been burnt by Marian officials.[76] One Norfolk parish had spent nearly £2 in 1554–55 on two mass books, an antiphon, a little gradual, and a great gradual. Less than three years later, they had to destroy them all and buy a new round of texts.[77] Churchwardens had seen Reformations come and go before, and they were wary of investing too much capital into the purchase of reformed texts until they could be sure that the Elizabethan injunctions would stick.

Figure 3.4 The frontispiece of the 1569 Bishop's Bible, depicting the crown and the church as a unified force. The image at the bottom shows diligent parishioners assembled to hear the Word.

In response to this vacillation, early Elizabethan churchwardens employed strategies for conserving costs related to books. Despite their eager embrace of Marian material culture, the wardens of Shipdham in Norfolk seem to have preserved their Edwardian Prayer Book, unearthing it early in 1559 and spending a mere shilling for its repair.[78] Others purchased new but inexpensive texts in the early years. The parish of Ludlow in Shropshire was quick to purchase the required Bible, with an account entry from May of 1559 listing an expense of 12s. 5d. "for a Bible, and the carriage of the same from London."[79] Though this satisfied the requirements of the injunctions, it seems to have been a relatively cheap, and possibly flimsy, copy of the text. A decade later, in 1569, the wardens paid a full pound "for the exchange of a new Bible."[80] In Prescot, Lancashire, wardens paid only 3d. for a copy of the communion book in 1559; in 1568, they spent 5s. 4d., nearly twenty times as much, on a finer copy.[81] The parish of St Edmund, Salisbury, spent a seemingly large sum of £1 3s. 4d. on a Bible in 1560, only to buy a "great Bible" for £2 1s. 6d. in 1570.[82] Indeed, the wardens of St Edmund found canny ways of avoiding extensive book-related expenses early in Elizabeth's reign. In 1560, they recorded a payment of 18d. for a "loan of a book named the paraphrases," thereby both fulfilling the injunctions and forestalling financial risk.[83]

In each of these parishes, it is important to note that the letter of the law was being followed. Indeed, for most of these parishes, there seems to be little ill intent behind the purchase of inexpensive books. The rapidity with which the parishes purchased their first copies of the texts indicates a relatively strong conformity to the injunctions. Nevertheless, it took a full decade for these parishes to feel secure enough in the settlement to make extensive financial outlay for its key texts. It was not until the early 1570s that many parishes across the country seemed to have enough confidence in the stability of the new rule to invest heavily in the purchase of fine presentation copies of reformed books. By the 1590s, while a few parishes were still under-provisioned, the primary presentations for book defaults most often lay in the poor quality, not the absence, of the Bible. The parish of Old Byland, two miles east of the ruins of Rievaulx Abbey, was noted in 1590 as having a torn Bible and psalter, while five years later Gate Helmsley, close to York, was presented for an insufficient Bible that was soon replaced.[84]

Where books were missing, they tended to be supplementary rather than central texts. Books such as Andreas Musculus's *Commonplaces* or Jewel's *Apology*, though not required in every parish across Elizabethan England, were often locally encouraged or even mandated by diocesan officials.[85] In the 1593 visitation of the rural deanery of Norfolk, for instance, a number of parishes that had sufficient bibles and psalters were missing either the *Commonplaces* or the *Apology*.[86] However, the requirements for these texts were rather more fuzzy than strict; at least three parishes were able or ordered to substitute the missing *Apology* with Thomas Bilson's more recent defence of the Elizabethan church, the *Perpetual Government of Christ's Church*.[87] Moreover, the focus on these supplementary books by both visitors and wardens suggests they were generally assured that the key central texts – the Bible, the Book of Common Prayer, and the Homilies – were provisioned. On the whole, though with some exceptions in a tiny minority of locations, the English parishes at the turn of the century were sufficiently, if not extravagantly, supplied with the central confessional texts.

Perhaps the most expensive conveyable requirement was the provision of church plate. It was also one of the first casualties of each successful wave of English Reformations. Monastic plate was seized by Henry during the Dissolution, but parish plate was by and large left intact. Edward's destruction of the mass led to the large-scale parochial liquidation of chalices, candlesticks, communion plate, and other items of parochial silver. Mary's reign again saw a policy shift, with a special emphasis on the restoration of chalices for the proper furnishing of the mass. With the Elizabethan church, the parishes of England faced yet another change: chalices, many just purchased and extraordinarily costly, were to be eliminated and replaced with elegant but less-ornate communion cups. Compliance was hugely burdensome, and the whiplash of selling and buying plate strained even the most eager parishes. Full conformity was slow in coming. Some parishes purchased communion cups immediately, but, as with Bibles, bought more elaborate and expensive cups a decade or so later. These secondary purchases were extraordinary expenses for parishes. The parish of North Elmham spent almost 40s. on a cup in 1567, about half of all expenses for the year.[88] The 1571 purchase of the new cup in the parish of St Michael in Bedwardine, Worcester, accounted for nearly 70 per cent of that year's total receipts, while a cup purchased in 1570 in Prescot, Lancashire, cost more than the renovation of the roof.[89] By the mid-1570s, while a few parishes were cited for missing covers, almost all had been satisfactorily provisioned with the communion cups needed for the new ceremonies. It was a statement of growing confidence in the church, with wardens again willing, and able, to invest significant funds into church plate.

The transformation of the parish church into something approaching the ideal set out by the Elizabethan injunctions was, as we have seen, neither uncomplicated nor inexpensive. Its pace was often cautious and occasionally subverted. Perfect national conformity was never achieved: there was always a parish with a torn book, a missing communion cover, a moth-eaten vestment. However, by the early 1570s, most parishes had been brought in line with at least the essential requirements of the Queen's Injunctions. Nevertheless, they continued to be monitored, reported, and repaired throughout Elizabeth's reign. In other words, in terms of material culture, the Elizabethan Reformation was not an event, nor was it even an evolution toward a fixed and finite goal that, once achieved, was completed. Instead, it was a perpetual, infinite condition: not acquiring, but sustaining.

It was also a massive undertaking that relied on the participation and acquiescence of localities across the country, each of which had its own traditions, values, and liturgical affinities. While the injunctions may have taken a decade to percolate through the parishes of England, the result was the transformation of the public religious sphere by around 1570 – contested, sometimes resented, occasionally resisted, but transformed. Private spaces – households, private chapels, even consciences – may have remained complicated, but the public parish churches by and large conformed. Here, then, *communities*, if not individuals, were transformed. And this change was expensive, calling upon the contributions, willing or not, from nearly the entire population. The people of England had to fund their own Reformation.

The dramatic transformation of the parish church, with its attendant attractions of contested iconoclasm, material opulence, and doctrinal controversy, has attracted the bulk of the historical scrutiny into churchwardens' accounts. And yet, peering deeper into the accounts of the parishes, we find most records accounting for the kinds of expenses described in those 1566 records of Tilney All Saints: nails, mortar, paving stones and rushes, and the unceasing payments for the upkeep of the bells. Maintenance was mundane, endless, and absolutely fundamental to the functioning of the Elizabethan church. Bell ropes, baldrics, paving stones, and roof leads may have been unglamorous, but they were the essence of the Reformation.

With few exceptions, the transformation of parish architecture into a model of Protestant aesthetic was completed by around 1570, about a decade after Elizabeth's accession. Nevertheless, the expenditure on church fabric continued to dominate the accounts of most parishes for the rest of her reign. Indeed, while the more ideologically charged changes of the first decade preoccupy much of the literature, the more routine expenses of maintaining the church placed a far greater strain on parochial budgets. Two particular items seem to have caused particular problems: the bells and the roof. The lists of receipts were constant, petty, and exhausting to read (and one suspects to keep). They were also vital.

Bells pealed throughout Elizabethan England.[90] They kept the time, they called people to services, and they were deployed for special moments of celebration. When enemies were captured or defeated, as with the Babington Plot in 1586, the Spanish Armada in 1588, and a victory in Ireland in 1601, bells rang out. They could mark the arrival or the passing by of notable people, like bishops, monarchs, or local nobles.[91] The most regular celebration marked by the bells was Elizabeth's coronation day, November 17, with notations regularly made of payment, bread, and ale given to bellringers upon the day.[92] Payments toward the upkeep and repair of the bells run throughout all parochial records. This is perhaps predictable; proper use of the bells entailed extensive and violent collisions. Bell ropes, clappers, and baldrics (the strap connecting clapper to bell) had to be purchased regularly. The Tewkesbury accounts for 1580–83 are illustrative, with payments made for bell pegs (4d.), for baldrics (5s. 2d.), for mending the bell wheel (2s. 6d.), for mending and replacement of the clappers (15s. 3d.), for rehanging the bells (7s. 2d.), for bell grease (2s.), and for bell buckles (6d.).[93]

Keeping the parish roof free from leaks was another expensive business. Above and beyond great capital projects of rebuilding the entire roof, yearly repairs had to be made to prevent serious damage. Few years went by in any parish without some payment for tiles, lead, solder, or payments to the "plumber" for his work on the church or other parish buildings. The roof of St Michael in Bedwardine was retiled in 1559, 1566, 1571, 1580, 1584, 1590, 1594, and 1598.[94] In the parish of Prescot, Lancashire, wardens recorded payments for roof repair or roofing supplies for all but six years of Elizabeth's reign.[95] Maintaining the roof required constant vigilance on the part of the wardens.

Such attentiveness necessitated the sustained employment of local craftspeople to provide materials and workmanship for the churches. As such, the parish church remained a serious economic force in the local community, providing extensive employment and engaging the skills of a sizable portion of the community. The extraordinarily detailed accounts of St Martin's, Leicester, underscore the breadth of a church's economic reach within the parish. In the first five years of the Elizabethan records alone, at least sixty-five named individuals received income from the wardens for either goods or services.[96] Payments ranged from just 2d. (to John Busthe for paper) to 40s. (to Robert Butler "for laying in ye beam").[97] In the small rural parish of North Elmham in Norfolk, at least thirty-two different people were employed by the church, for everything from writing the account to cleaning the steeple stairs to keeping poor children to providing communion wine.[98] Some payments were one-off expenses for extraordinary renovations, but many more indicated the regular employment of a host of craftsmen and labourers for the maintenance of the church. The expense of constant renovations made the parish church an economic engine in Elizabethan England, employing everyone from the most skilled guild members to those poor of the parish given a small stipend for washing of linen or sweeping of the nave. Thus, maintaining the church required not only the efforts of the wardens, but also the sustained employment and labour of the parish.

Maintenance was a clear concern for contemporary authorities. Ecclesiastical visitations inquired about the state of the church almost without fail. The Metropolitical Visitation of 1563, one of the first large disciplinary surveys of the Elizabethan church, demanded to know "whether your Churches be well adorned and conveniently kept without waste, destruction, or abuse of any thing … whether your Churchyards be well fenced and cleanly kept, [and] whether your chancels and parsonages be well and sufficiently repaired."[99] This language echoes throughout decades of Elizabethan visitations, metropolitan, diocesan, and archidiaconal alike. Some thirty-five years later, the articles of the Bishop of London's visitation inquired "Whether is your Church or Chapel, and the Chancel well and sufficiently repaired and kept without abuse of any thing."[100] In some cases, the language of the 1563 metropolitan visitation is copied almost exactly, as in the rather strict articles of Archbishop Grindal's 1576 visitation, to which is added the incisive coda, "And if any part thereof be in decay, through whose default it is so."[101]

What this leaves us with, then, is a robust and regular survey of church maintenance. An analysis of visitation records in the Province of York, for instance, shows remarkably few people presented to the ecclesiastical courts for allowing the church to become dilapidated. Though the area of the North Riding was notorious for its slow adoption of Protestant reforms and for its lingering Catholicism, it seems as if the church fabric was relatively well maintained. Of the 2,632 laypeople from these deaneries presented to the ecclesiastical courts in 1590, 1595, and 1600, only 118 – fewer than 5 per cent – were presented for neglect of church maintenance.[102] It is impossible to calculate with complete accuracy what proportion of total parishes these neglected parishes comprise, as the visitation books vary in their comprehensiveness and often include chapels-of-ease as separate entries. However, a rough calculation places the percentage of parishes in this region with any sort of presentment for decay or missing ornament at as little as 12 and no more than 18 per cent in the last decades of Elizabeth's reign.[103] In an area derided as poor, sparsely populated, and deeply resentful of religious change, this is a surprisingly low presentment rate. To put it another way, over 80 and close to 90 per cent of parishes and chapels in the late-Elizabethan North Riding were declared by their churchwardens to be in good working order.

This was not a case of parishes engaging in a mass silence of pious perjury. If wardens had a consistent policy of avoiding the interference of church authorities into the material lives of their church, we would expect the only dilapidations presented to be those so obviously egregious as to demand declaration. In some cases, such decay is apparent: the 1590 returns present the churchwardens because "the steeple of Bagbie Chapel is in decay," while the tithe farmer of Brafferton was, in 1600, presented for not repairing the "great decay" of the chancel and tithe barn. However, most of the presentments are for issues far less serious: the Oswaldkirk churchwardens were reported for having a churchyard "not well fenced," the Warthill churchwardens for having a torn communion book, while Thomas Barton, a layman of Riccall, was presented particularly for not fencing "his part of the church yard." Some presentments were even cautious, or politic, such as the churchwardens of Over Silton, who declared that "it is thought by some that they should … repair the houses and chancel."[104] Rather than wholesale decay, these presentments depict a vast majority of parishes engaged with a constant, unglamorous battle against the ravages of time and nature.

In addition to showing a startling lack of presentments for dilapidations, these records show a vigorous bureaucratic institution keen on accountability. Records indicate that clergy and laymen alike were required to provide proof that they had corrected the offenses recorded in their presentments. The churchwardens of Bilsdale, Yorkshire, for example, were ordered to repair their decayed chapel by the feast of St Martins, "or else show cause why they defer the repair of it."[105] The case was dismissed when a certificate showing completion was sent to the court. Such certifications litter the Act Books, depicting a rigorous system of accountability. In general, by the later sixteenth century, there were few major repairs to be made, and most of them were made quickly. The Elizabethan church may not have been as lavishly outfitted as it was in the seventeenth century, but it had been preserved.

This preservation was deeply enmeshed in the language and rhetoric of religious reformation. Church authorities recognized, and indeed emphasized, the strong links between the prosaic and the devotional. When the 1571 Canons outlined the requirements for repairing the church fabric, they emphasized that the duties of the laity in maintaining the parish church had specific and concrete liturgical impact. Thus, as we have seen, the roof was to be repaired so that bad weather would not interrupt "the holy ministry and worshipping of God"; the Bible, Book of Common Prayer, and 1570 Homily against Disobedience were to "be whole and clean … lest it breed irksomeness or contempt amongst the people"; the walls were painted with verses from Scripture "that by the reading and warning thereof, the people may be moved to godliness."[106] In this iteration, the practical, everyday duties of the churchwarden were explicitly linked to divine purpose, and ordinary action was filled with devotional intent.

In a sense, this connection can be said to represent continuities with pre-Reformation lay devotion. The historiography of the past half-century has amply demonstrated the ways in which practical action by the pre-Reformation laity had serious religious intent.[107] The maintenance of the church flock to fund altar lights, for instance, has been described as an act of communal lay piety.[108] What the 1571 statutes did was to make explicit a direct link between action and intent in the *reformed* Church – to make plain the devotional consequences of everyday action. As in the pre-Reformation era, churchwardens' actions represented not only practical deeds but also ideological objectives; that is to say, routine activity was prescribed with specific theological or doctrinal purpose. What differed was that this activity was centred on the role of the warden and that it expressed the clearly *reformed* priorities of the church's institutional framework. Neither this Reformation nor this rhetoric was universally accepted, of course, and it would be ludicrous to argue that every warden paying for church repairs did so in order to improve gospel preaching. And yet there was the potential, and certainly the intention, of a bleed between action and doctrine, between window sealant and godliness.

Paying for the Church

Maintaining the parish church to the specifications and standards required was manifestly an expensive business. From the regular receipts for bell ropes and washing to occasional large capital outlays to the singular costs of transforming the church to its new Protestant aesthetic, costs quickly added up. The majority of these expenditures were nothing new: roofs had always needed tiling, windows had always needed repair, linens had always needed washing. Certainly, the enhanced efficiency and regularity of visitations had extended a deepened oversight of such repair, but the demand for funds to finance church fabric was a constant in the parish. The Reformation had, however, eliminated many of the traditional avenues for parochial fundraising. Doctrinally, gifts to the church could no longer be counted as good works, removing the redemptive potential of donations. Parish gilds, which had often adopted the maintenance of church fabric as their special charge, had been largely eradicated in the late 1540s.[109] The Marian reforms had, as much as possible, allayed the costs of re-Catholicizing the parishes by forcing a compulsory return of goods confiscated during the earlier Edwardian iconoclastic wave, and some of the pre-Reformation parochial organizations were revived, but the expenses were still staggering.[110] With the accession of Elizabethan and the reinvigoration of Protestant doctrine, however, the salvational possibilities of good works were firmly rejected. As such, wardens had to turn to other means to fulfill their obligations.

In the face of these rising costs, many parishes turned toward the regularization of finances through the imposition of a church rate. Such local taxation is often placed historiographically in direct opposition with the more "popular" methods of raising funds, such as church ales or similar celebrations.[111] In contrast, rates are seen as either part of the bureaucratization of the church or as evidence of growing puritanical influences.[112] In this description, the imposition of rates marks the Elizabethan church as fundamentally different from its communal, pre-Reformation incarnation. Qualifications to this argument, however, must be made. Popular celebrations of saints' days were indeed banned across most of England in the 1540s, but ales as church fundraisers were not generally forbidden by church authorities until much later in the century. Especially in the first twenty years following the settlement, ales continued to provide important funds for the parish. The town of Mere in Wiltshire raised £17 3s. 1½ d. from ales in 1559–60, while South Tawton, Devon, raised £40 8s. 8d. in 1564.[113] In Stanford-in-the-Vale, Berkshire, the May ales actually increased in profitability over the course of the 1570s; the net profit from ales averaged 318d. from 1570–74 and 587d. from 1575–59, in almost every year, representing the single largest source of income for the parish.[114]

While some parishes continued to rely on church ales to raise funds for their parishes, in areas with a strong godly population, many began to shy away from ales and revels in the 1570s.[115] The rhetoric surrounding the prohibition of ales was distinctly sabbatarian. William Keble, preaching to the JPs in Dorset in 1571, reminded his audience of the pleas of a minister "who understanding what great disorders there were commonly at these Church Ales upon the Sabbath day, required his flock … that they should not assemble the people together, to offend God by their ungodly behaviours, but rather give themselves upon the Sabbath day to serve God, according to their duties.[116] And yet, the larger push toward prohibiting church ales did not begin until the 1590s. Where visitation articles of the 1570s and 1580s discussed ales and alehouses, their proscriptions generally referred only to the service of alcohol during the time of divine service.[117] The prohibition of church ales was thus piecemeal, reflecting the religious tenor and proclivities of localities rather than a systematic dismantling of the pre-Reformation fundraising system. Insofar as a chronology can be traced, it again reflects a growing generational shift in the mid-Elizabethan period, with the religious tenor of the 1560s markedly different from that of the 1590s.

Church rates were undeniably of a different character than church ales. Leaving aside questions of jollity and joy, they represented a compulsory, rather than a voluntary, form of fundraising. This seems much in line with Elizabethan measures that enforced a mandatory church attendance and required triennial partaking of the sacrament. Indeed, the most regular levy in most parishes was not one based on population or landholding, but a collection from parishioners at Easter communion. In the parish of St Botolph, London, parishioners received a communion token in return for a payment of 2d., which raised £14 13s. for the parish.[118] Other parishes continued a reformed version of the holy loaf, raising money for communion through explicit donations for supplies around Easter; in Mere, Wiltshire, some version of this was collected throughout the entire Elizabethan period, though its name changed from "holy loaf" to "communion bread" by 1591.[119] Most parish accounts do not offer such a clear-cut method of collection, but the relative constancy of collection amounts from year to year suggest a formal or informal understanding of the amounts due each Easter.[120] The importance of this regular levy to their accounts must have given wardens further impetus to encourage participation in communion amongst their fellow parishioners.

On top of regular yearly offerings, special circumstances occasionally required additional sums to be gathered. Unsurprisingly, these circumstances often had to do with the repair of church fabric, as such capital projects were usually costly and many times unanticipated. In such cases, levies were to be agreed upon by the parishioners; wardens themselves had no legal basis to impose a levy without the consent of the vestry at the least.[121] Only after the assessment was agreed upon could those refusing to contribute be brought to court or presented to church authorities for lack of payment. In the 1595 visitation of the North Riding of Yorkshire, for example, some twenty-eight people were reported for nonpayment of church dues.[122] However, the levying of the rate itself relied upon the voluntary participation of a large portion of the parish.

In cases where disputes arose, churchwardens were keen to stress the participatory nature of the process. In the case of Orston in Nottingham, for example, serious repairs needed for decayed walls and windows galvanized "the parishioners of the said parish church … or the most part of them, [to] divers times assemble themselves and meet together, and [to] procure at sundry times very skillful workers and others of very good credit and skill to view and survey the said parts.'[123] In turn, the parishioners held a series of open meetings, at which point it was agreed by them – or, again, the "most part of them" – to levy a fine of fourpence for every house and for every "oxgang." This is a far more energetic and open process than we might expect: the meetings were open to all the inhabitants, and it seems as if those assembled voted on the measure. Importantly, the case refers to the "inhabitants" or the "parishioners" rather than "principal" or "substantial" inhabitants – indicating a relatively broad participatory experience.

Similar language can be found in the case of Jeffrey v. Kenshley and Foster, the precedent of which was cited in Edward Coke's *Reports* and became part of common law. When William Jeffrey, a local gentleman, challenged the right of the wardens to assess his lands in the parish of Hailsham, Sussex, the wardens protested that the rate had been agreed to by a general meeting of the parishioners. They provided evidence "that notice of such meeting was given in the said church, and also proclaimed in the market," and that the decision had been made collectively. The court found for the wardens, arguing that though Jeffrey had his home in another parish, he farmed his land in Hailsham directly and thus could have attended the meeting had he so wished.[124] Again, precedent here was grounded upon eligibility to participate in the process of assessment. Payment was compulsory, but agreement was collective. Jeffrey could have participated in the decision, so he must participate in the contribution.

A vein of communal activity runs throughout the churchwardens' accounts. Payments for food and drink for the wardens and sidemen was common, both at the visitations but also at meetings. And while little merriment might be anticipated in the minute accounting of the churchwardens' quarterly reports, the parishioners of St Michael in Bedwardine seem to have celebrated with a tab at the local alehouse open to all, as they did again to celebrate Easter and even occasionally after the distribution of poor relief.[125] Here, accounting was a communal activity. The line between the compulsory and the coerced is, in such cases, nuanced and blurred. Though accounting and collections may have been mandated, they were not necessarily resented. Indeed, many may have felt a sense of duty fulfilled upon the payment of their levies, especially when they resulted in a major improvement to the church fabric.

In addition to rates and ales, the reselling of the church fabric proved a lucrative fundraising device for the Elizabethan parish. This practice had certainly existed in the later Middle Ages, but its use had accelerated during the early Reformation with the vast array of riches culled from iconoclastic orders.[126] The years following the Queen's Injunctions proved no different. The massive changes described earlier in the chapter meant a chance for the parish to recoup some of its earlier devotional expenses. Elizabethan churchwardens' accounts are filled with receipts for the reselling of Catholic instruments of worship. The base of the rood loft of St Mary the Great, Cambridge, fetched 4s. in 1561.[127] In 1562, St Michael Cornhill, London, sold off its church plate and vestments for well over £5.[128] The parish of Ashwell, Hertfordshire, in 1563, recorded the purchase of 5s. 6d. of "old latten and brass."[129] In 1564, the churchwardens of Northill in Lincoln had a mass sale of church goods: that year alone, they recorded receipts for the rood loft, "two latten candlesticks," the pyx, two cruets, and a cross.[130] The churchwardens of Kilmington, Devon, seem to have exercised some circumspection in their accounts; in 1566, Sir William Abbot paid nearly £2 for objects simply listed as "certain stuff."[131]

It might be tempting to see a delay in the selling of church ornament as a sign of disapproval or disagreement with the reformed changes to church fabric. Ethan Shagan's thoughtful parsing of the sale of church ornament in the early Reformation must give us pause, however, when ascribing ideological motivations to iconoclastic actions; the factors motivating wardens to transform church interiors varied not only parish to parish, but also person to person.[132] Again, the evidence of the accounts requires a rather more nuanced depiction than that of eager iconoclast versus reluctant conformist. Take, for example, the parish of St Edmund in Salisbury. The wardens' payments for 1560 included 4s. for a communion book, 6d. for a Book of Homilies, and 3d. to John Atkins "for carrying off the latin books to our lady church."[133]

In the following two years, wardens also paid for the removal of the rood loft, another copy of the Book of Homilies, and "making glass windows."[134] This is, seemingly, a picture of perfect compliance with the Queen's Injunctions and the new, reformed church fabric. And yet, reading further into the accounts, it was not until 1568 that the more significant part of Catholic ornament was relinquished. The receipts for that year record the sale of candlesticks, a crucifix, a pyx, various Catholic vestments, a bowl for the holy water, a set of ewers, and the banners of St Eustace and St Nicholas.[135] The retention of such prohibited goods may well have been ideologically determined, evidence of a parish reluctant to leave its Catholic past behind. However, the early adoption of Protestant ornament, as well as numerous records of interaction with the episcopal and archidiaconal visitations, challenges the clarity of such a conclusion.

A similar case can be found in the parish of St Mary the Great in Cambridge, a church at the heart of one of the most evangelical towns in the country. As noted above, St Mary had destroyed its rood loft by 1561, while the altar had been replaced by a communion table as early as 1559, a remarkably rapid transition to reformed church architecture. Similarly, the 1559–60 accounts record the purchase of communion books, psalters, a Book of Homilies, Erasmus's *Paraphrases*, and a large, embossed Bible.[136] And yet, here too, extensive Catholic ornament was retained well into the 1560s. It was not until 1567–68 that most of these goods were sold: the receipts for this year include the sale of various vestments and plate, as well as "the holy water stop of pewter or lay metal with the Sprinkle," "all the Books at that time being which were in number 13 Small & great," "the crosse of Copper with Images of mary & John, a pax and a bell," "the chrismatory of pewter," and "the Image of our lady which was taken of the blue velvet alter clothe bi the commandment of the archdeacon."[137] Further goods, including the last remnants of the rood loft and vestments, were sold in 1569.[138] Even in a parish so eager to transform itself into a model of reformed aesthetic, Catholic church ornaments were held in the common stock for over a decade after the initial iconoclasm and rebuilding.

If it was not clearly ideological resistance, then why the delay? The sheer expense of such ornament offers another possible impetus for retaining the goods. The receipts from the sale of St Edmund's ornament totalled just over 42s., more than was raised in an entire year's worth of pew rents.[139] St Mary the Great received nearly £6 for its Catholic goods, more than half of the annual parish dues.[140] If the Elizabethan settlement had faded as quickly as that of Edward or Mary, the cost to recoup these items would have been extensive. Moreover, in both St Edmund and St Mary, timing of the sales coincided with the commencement of major capital projects, which called for extensive financial commitment. The year 1568 saw St Edmund begin a fundraising campaign to purchase a new organ, while St Mary the Great bought a new silver communion cup.[141] While it seems that the interiors of St Edmund and St Mary the Great were quite quickly brought in line with reformed policy, lay officials preserved their most substantial resources until such a time as the churches required their assets to be liquefied. Similar patterns can be found in parishes across the country, as in Swaffham in Norfolk, which in 1568 sold a pair of chalices to the Norwich goldsmiths for over £3 14s. and bought a new communion cup for £6 11s. The parishioners of Shipdham were even more efficient, making a new communion cup out of the melted remains of "the old chalice."[142] Again, as with the purchase of books, a new sense of confidence in the longevity of the Elizabethan church was emerging.

The selling of church goods, however, was not limited to the iconoclastic decade following the issuance of the Queen's Injunctions – nor were all the items ideologically charged. The church routinely sold old or disused supplies to local craftsmen or households, participating in a kind of recycled material economy. These items tended to be little more than scraps, well-used articles that could be flogged for a few pennies to add to the accounts. Entirely typical was the sale of "one crooked piece of timber" to Rhys Sawyer from the Oswestry parish church.[143] These small sums added up and helped to supplement church income. But even more than this, they encouraged a vibrant, interdependent economic relationship between parish and parishioner. People lived alongside the residue of their parish churches: old doors and bits of gate, frayed ropes and loose stones, roofing lead and discarded linens. There is no sense here that these ex-parochial items were considered holy or devotional. But the constant sale and repurposing of this miscellanea meant that parishes lived their everyday lives in a patchwork of repurposed church material.

This material could include goods that had clear devotional intent in the reformed church. Parishes were intimately involved in the second-hand religious literary economy, which burgeoned in the late sixteenth century as access to vernacular devotional texts increased.[144] The sums raised by these sales were not inconsiderable. The "old Bible" sold by the churchwardens of Tewkesbury in 1576 raised 10s., equivalent to the sum raised by rent of a "shop in the churchhouse."[145] When the wardens of St Michael's, Bath, purchased a "new bible" in 1572 for 20s., they sold off their old Bible to help balance the books; similarly, when the wardens of the Church of St Peter in St Albans, Hertfordshire, purchased a new Bible and psalter in 1586, they sold two old copies of the Bible for 8s.[146] In the parish of St Michael's in Bedwardine, the wardens sold off both their old communion book and old Bible to a Fulk Broughton, a local carpenter; this sale helped to fund the purchase of a "new Large Communion book" and "a new fair English Bible of the last Translation authorized in the church."[147] While copies of the Bible were easily purchasable in the market towns of late-Elizabethan England, the second-hand sales from the parish churches allowed cheap and easy access to finely crafted religious texts.

The parish church was thus intimately engaged in a second-hand material economy within their local communities. The level of detail recorded in these account books is stunning. In part, it points toward the careful parsimony of parochial officials, who knew any deficits could be raised from their own pockets. More importantly, though, it again suggests the constant intercourse between the parish as an economic community and the church as a physical institution. The extensive requirements for building materials and supplies not only benefited those from whom goods and services were purchased, but also helped to stimulate the local supply of easily accessible, inexpensive goods. In some cases, this may have had a more clearly devotional function; the purchase of old Bibles, for example, can be seen as part and parcel of the domestication of a reformed piety. However, more commonly, the items purchased by parishioners would have been purely pedestrian. Buying an old rope from the churchwardens to use in agricultural labour or to bind goods for market was not, strictly speaking, a devotional act. Nevertheless, in their participation in this second-hand economy, parishioners were providing a crucial source of funding for the church, which in turn used these funds to sustain a space for the reformed liturgy. The lack of ideological impetus behind the purchase of spare lead or scrap wood made it no less essential to church maintenance – or to the provision of Protestant rites and services. Thus, again, prosaic actions had profound consequences for sustaining the Elizabethan church.

Churchwardens found creative ways of establishing a more constant income. Chief amongst these measures was involvement with local agriculture. In some cases, churchwardens rented out parcels of land to local tenants. The small parish of Shipdham in Norfolk was, by the late 1560s, receiving almost all its income from the rental of land to over forty of its parishioners. These men and women may have been making a purely practical decision to augment their incomes, but in doing so, they were sustaining their church year in and year out.[148] Other parishes received their income by collectively owning and farming land or livestock to fund church needs. The parish of Stanford-in-the-Vale, located in the fecund and rolling landscape of northeastern Berkshire, managed both fields and flocks. In 1583, for example, the wardens listed income from barley, pulse, hay, and grass, as well as from the church sheep.[149] Interestingly, the system seems little different than that of pre-Reformation times, with profits from the sheep dedicated to the maintenance of the font. Indeed, the "font stock" seems to have been administered not by the wardens but by the "fontwives," a group of local women who managed both the animals and their proceeds. The system, with its medieval devotional trappings, was in operation through the end of Elizabeth's reign; the accounts list a sum of 8s. and 4d. raised by the wives in 1602.[150]

Similar communal responsibility for parochial agriculture can be found scattered throughout Elizabethan wardens' accounts. The parish of Pittington in Durham relied on communal maintenance of a church flock. In 1584, the vestry agreed that every man paying at least four pounds in rent for his landholdings "shall graze winter and summer one sheep, for the behalf of this church."[151] A generation later, the practice was still in effect; in 1603, the church flock included at least twenty-three sheep, which yielded over 30s. in wool and meat at the local market.[152] In Ashwell in Hertfordshire, the income in the 1580s was due almost entirely to the sale of grain and wood. While occasional payments were made to agricultural labourers, the accounts indicate some level of communality in the raising of these funds. The 1583 accounts, for example, note the agreements of local householders in the tilling of the church lands.[153] It must be remembered, of course, that the wardens were themselves drawn from local landowners and householders. Communality, then, was at the centre of parish finance, if only because the responsibility to hold office – and thus, at some point, to administer the church funds – rotated throughout the community. Again, a great number of parishioners may have been excluded from both the responsibility and the attendant prestige of contributing to persistent agricultural support. Nevertheless, in a parish like Pittington, the breadth of interest was far wider than the vestry. In the same year that the administration of the church stock was set down, the accounts record forty-eight husbandmen and yeomen in the parish; at the same time, the parish flock contained about twenty-five animals. If the parish cleaved to its own agreement, then, more than half of the propertied households would have been responsible for the raising and protection of one of the parish flock.[154]

Agricultural fundraising was all but impossible in market towns and cities. Here, the rental of church property, rather than communal farming, contributed most extensively to parochial income. Properties bequeathed specifically to the parish in the pre-Reformation era continued, for the most part, in the possession of the church.[155] To supplement this income, Elizabethan urban churchwardens frequently leveraged their surpluses toward the purchase of additional property. The expansion of population in urban areas made such properties valuable investments, resistant to the rapid inflation of the late-Elizabethan period.[156]

The accounts of the small parish of St Michael's in Bedwardine, as a small urban parish sited by the Cathedral of Worcester, provide a useful example of such arrangements. The parish owned two swaths of property, gifted to the church before the Reformation. One was a house in the city of Worcester, while the other was a parcel of land in the nearby town of Clifton. The latter property was particularly important to the parish's finances, regularly representing up to three-quarters of its income in the early years of Elizabeth's reign.[157] Maintaining this property was a priority for wardens, who periodically visited Clifton to inspect their land.[158] Not only did the Clifton land provide an annual rent, it also provided periodic large sums on the transfer of the lease to a new copyholder. In 1581, for example, a new lease was issued to a Thomas Salway for £25 13s. 4d., or more than seven times the total parish expenses of the following year.[159] Thus, property investment allowed not only for an annual income, but also for periodic windfalls that could be reinvested. The investment strategy chosen by the churchwardens of St Michael's was to expand their real-estate portfolio and extend their participation in the urban economy. The Salway lease more than paid for the complete rebuilding of the other pre-Reformation property, which pulled in over 26s. per year. These rents, combined with small legacies, allowed the 1599 purchase of a property in nearby Frog Lane; though this new tenement briefly landed the accounts in debt, it yielded a return of over 10 per cent per annum, a healthy return on investment. Thus, by 1601, the churchwardens received rental income of almost £4½ a year, or roughly 60 per cent more than they had been receiving in 1580.

It was a clear, sophisticated, long-term plan for financing, one that both leveraged the financial knowledge of the wardens and required a faith in the durable stability of the parish. Just half a century before, the chantries had been shuttered and their real-estate assets seized. Perhaps to our eyes, it seems obvious that the parishes would not be dissolved nor their assets seized. But from an Elizabethan perspective, having survived the dissolution of the monasteries and the chantries, the destruction of the gilds and confraternities, the removal of relics and the halting of pilgrimage, it must have seemed in the early years that nothing was off the table. To invest again in such assets reflected confidence, conviction, and security in the church and in their future.

The surplus was also used as a source of informal banking for parishioners. Wardens periodically lent sums to parishioners, with other parishioners serving as sureties for the amounts due. In 1560, the accounts of St Michael's list twenty-six debts remaining to the church, as well as the list of the guarantors.[160] In the 1590s, the wardens of North Elmham leant John Pierce a full twenty shillings, a notable sum, and received back seven shillings from John Handford in payment for a loan.[161] As was common in early modern England, many parishioners appeared both as debtors and as sureties, a result of the complicated system of personal debt and credit that supported so much of household finance at the time. As Craig Muldrew has so convincingly shown, however, such interpersonal debt relied on a careful construction of a concept of credit.[162] That is to say, personal trustworthiness and probity was a defining factor in the ability to access sources of credit. Such relationships must have been complicated by the participation of churchwardens, who simultaneously served as parish bankers and as ecclesiastically sanctioned monitors of moral and religious probity. Parishioners who disrupted sermons, who drank at alehouses on Sundays, who refused the communion, who absented themselves from services would be hard pressed to go, cap in hand, to ask for a loan from the wardens. Even more crucially, the practice of lending money embedded the institutional church even further in parishioners' lives. They counted on the church not just to survive, but to thrive. Parishioners were invested, quite literally, in the economic and institutional stability of their churches.

Urban churchwardens, then, were deeply involved in the kinds of economic investments, contracts, and opportunities available in the evolving early modern economy.[163] The complex contracts and arrangements that underlay multi-tiered tenancy agreements and frequent moneylending operations necessitated financial savvy and extensive planning. Service as a churchwarden required not only a willingness to participate in church affairs and to represent the parish in both secular and ecclesiastical courts, but also business acumen and facility with the increasingly complex world of the Elizabethan economy.

Yet again, we see the parish intimately involved in the practical affairs of its local community. As landlord and moneylender, just as employer and seller of goods, the parish church was woven closely into the web of the local economy and household finance. Moreover, the layering of disciplinary and financial responsibilities invested wardens with even greater political power within their parishes. As we have seen, wardens were increasingly called upon to enforce the tenets of the Elizabethan Reformation, as well as the general moral probity of their fellow parishioners. At the same time, they were intimately involved with the economies of those same parishioners. The role of the parish and its officials as a financial institution, one that provided a crucial source of liquid specie and ready funding, only tightened the relationship between notions of good credit and religious conformity in the Elizabethan parish.

The pews, another engine of conformity, created another key source of revenue seating within the parish church. Each parish was different in the relationship to the pews. Some sold seats; others rented them annually. But by the late-Elizabethan period, substantial income from the pews was common in parishes across the country. This type of income had manifest benefits. Unlike donations or legacies, it was regular income. But unlike a church rate, pew rents were not abstract.

One paid a rent for a particular seat, a kind of real estate of the nave. Collection was easy, and the connection between fees and benefit obvious. The clear pride that people felt in their pews – manifested in those elaborate decorations and the bitter disputes over church seating that made their way to the courts – only reinforced their utility as a fundraising device. Less obviously, though, pew rents were attractive to wardens because they could form one of the more flexible streams of income for the parish, with the rents able to be adjusted swiftly as need required. In contrast to long-standing tenancy agreements and contracts, or the similarly stable receipts from agricultural income, pew rents could be quickly increased in times of budgetary necessity.

The parish of Tewksbury, Gloucestershire, illustrates such flexibility nicely. Seat rents were, from the beginning of Elizabeth's reign, a steady source of income for the parish. In 1565, the rents raised just under 20s. for the church, with an average payment of 21.6p. per household. This income remained relatively even through the end of the sixteenth century; in the accounts of 1590–92, the average rent was 21d. per household, a statistically unimportant difference. The mid-1590s, however, saw an enormous capital outlay by the wardens. The roof of the church had to be replaced in 1595, and six years later the heavily decayed walls and windows of the church were repaired. In the midst of all this construction, the wardens decided to build a steeple on top of the church tower. The sums paid out in these years were remarkable. The outlay in 1590, a normal year of expenditure, was just under £8. In comparison, the roof cost over £43, the walls and windows £85, and the new steeple, £54. Little wonder, then, that the wardens' account of 1603 began by noting "in stock as in their hands remaining nothing because the church was to them indebted."[164] Despite gifts, levies, and a notable fundraising effort of producing "3 several stage plays within the abbey on the 3 first days of Whitson week," the churchwardens were desperately in want of additional money. In their need, the Tewkesbury wardens turned to pew rents. In 1602, the rent from the seats brought in almost 38s. in income. In contrast to the roughly 21d. per pew charged in both 1565 and 1590, the average pew-rent revenue generated per household in 1602 was more than 41d. In other words, though the rates had remained relatively steady throughout the Elizabethan period, the extraordinary capital expenditures of the late 1590s had resulted in pew rents nearly doubling in less than a decade. Above and beyond the social structuring and appeal of hierarchy that pews may have offered the churchwardens of Elizabethan Tewkesbury, their rents offered a temporary solution to their problems; though the 38s. would have put little dent into their overall debt, it prevented a further slide into arrears. The system of pew rents would have proved especially appealing in an age of increased parochial responsibilities and official oversight. The hierarchical system of rents, then, was encouraged not only by social, cultural, and religious factors, but also by the constant financial demands of the institutional church.

Finally, a note should be made about the continued importance of gifts in the financing of the Elizabethan church. To be sure, these bequests and legacies were nothing like those of the pre-Reformation church. The redemptive possibilities of good works were, of course, excluded in the reformed church, and the destruction of both the doctrine of purgatory and the Catholic veneration of the saints sincerely undermined avenues of fundraising.[165] Nevertheless, periodic gifts and bequests to the church can be found periodically throughout the Elizabethan accounts. In some cases, these were simple gifts of money, like the 10s. left by Thomas Coleman to the parish of Shillington in 1588.[166] In other cases, the legacy was far more substantial; St Michael's added to their property portfolio in 1594, when a Dr Hare left the legacy of his townhouse, which provided 14s. a year in rent.[167] Such legacies to the parish were not uncommon, and they helped to rebuild church endowments dented by the material expenditures of the mid-century.

In times of crisis, gifts – as distinct from assessments – could be solicited from the localities. In the midst of the extensive capital projects in Tewksbury, for example, the wardens raised over £6 10s. from an in-kind fund drive of parishioners and beyond.[168] Moreover, parishes levied not only cash but also gifts of labour from their parishioners. When the parish of Helmsley in North Yorkshire needed its steeple replaced in 1569, the parishioners provided the necessary labour: "They have helpen with their wains and draughts to carry timber stone and lime to and for the reparation of the said church like as other parishioners did and have done."[169] In such gifts, we can see a kind of continuity with late-medieval practices. If the shepherding of the pre-Reformation parish flock was an expression of piety and devotion to the church, we can read similar motivations into the voluntary, communal labour gifted to repair the steeple some seventy years later.

The largest growth in gift funds came to help the poor. In Elizabethan England, provision for the poor increasingly came under the purview of the parish and placed a significant strain on the wardens' accounts. The increase in bequests to help the parish church aid the poor has been much studied in the historiography and needs only a brief explication here.[170] In summary, Elizabethan parishioners gave extensively to charities involving poor relief. Despite complicated rhetoric involving worthiness and merit, bequests made to aid the poor increased markedly over the course of the sixteenth century. W.K. Jordan's landmark, though highly contested, survey of over thirty-five thousand Tudor bequests indicate this shift clearly: in 1480 to 1540, only 13 per cent of charitable donations were made specifically to aid the poor, while Elizabethan England saw 39 per cent of such donations given to poor relief.[171] These were not merely gifts to the poor; they were also gifts to the parish. As the parish was increasingly responsible for the sustenance and maintenance of the poorest parishioners, charitable bequests helped ease the new pressures placed on parochial finances.

As multiple historians have shown, gifts to the poor were part of a public transcript of reputation, piety, and patronage.[172] Nowhere is this clearer than in bequests made to the poor for attending funerals. Repeatedly, pious Elizabethans donated money to be distributed at their funerals, exchanging, in a sense, attendance for relief. The 1602 will of Robert Cudnor, a former churchwarden in the parish of St Christopher le Stocks, London, is exemplary.[173] An explicitly evangelical document, the will includes detailed and unambiguous funerary directions. Cudnor asks to be buried in St Christopher near the grave of his daughter, insisting "that there shall not be any black or mournings given or made at the time of my funeral at the charge of my Executors."[174] Instead, the sum that would be spent on funerary gifts was to be "given and distributed to and amongst Three hundred poor people that shall be at my burial, fifty shillings in single Two pences." Moreover, Cudnor left a legacy of 2s. 6d. for four poor men to carry his coffin and £3 to the children of Christ's Hospital, a sum which was contingent upon their attendance at the funeral: "so that some certain number of them do accompany my body to Church at my burial Three pounds, and not otherwise."[175] Though later in the will Cudnor left a tenement worth 40s. a year to the churchwardens, in order to provide perpetual poor relief for the parish, the focus on the public performance of grief and patronage by the objects of his charity is notable.[176] While the extensive detail of the bequest is remarkable, its sentiments were not: poor relief was often sited at funeral sermons, underscoring the close relationship between patronage, social hierarchy, and religious observance.[177] Gifts made to the church to support the poor were part and parcel of a larger program of crafting and maintaining personal reputation and piety. As such, the church finances were yet again intimately involved with the construction of social identities.

ഗ

As a whole, the evidence from Elizabethan churchwardens' accounts and visitations indicates a reasonably robust and responsive program of church repair. Certainly, the evidence reveals a more concentrated attention paid to church fabric than the literature generally suggests. Why then, contrary to our historiographical understanding, did the late sixteenth century see so much expense and effort expended on regular church maintenance? Four main strands are suggestive.

First, the institutional and bureaucratic systems of the Elizabethan church were indeed powerful weapons of authority. As explored in chapter 1, development and scope of the visitation system created a relatively effective tool of church discipline. By the late sixteenth century, these visitations had become far more regular and organized, with elaborate systems of certification and reinvestigation. By including pointed and precise questions about the state of church fabric, bishops and archdeacons were able to keep a relatively strong control on local programs of church repair. This did, of course, vary, dependent on larger concerns of church authorities or even on the simple efficacy of particular ecclesiastical authorities, but the system remained generally efficient.

Second, the church exercised enormous economic power, both on a grand scale of rents and tithes and on a piecemeal, local scale. Other than manor houses, churches were probably the largest single purchaser of goods. In the tiny fenland parish of North Elmham, a single year's records reflect sums paid for day labour, for payments to local craftspeople, for purchases of bread, sod, rushes, glass, solder, and nails.[178] It was in the economic self-interest of many for the church to be well maintained, both figuratively and literally. This is obvious for those whose livelihoods depended on the parish: the clerks, for instance, had a deep and vested interest in its welfare. But reading through the churchwardens' accounts, it becomes clear that the economic entanglements were far deeper. From the women who washed the linen and swept the aisles, to the pest catcher who sniped pigeons or hedgehogs, to the skilled crafts of the glazier and the plumber and the campanist, to the day labourer who hauled rubble for a few pennies and some bread and ale – the economic pull of the parish church was profound. And the parish was not just an employer, but also a customer, constantly purchasing goods; a retailer, recycling church material; and a landlord, renting fields or houses to its parishioners. It collected taxes and distributed poor relief. It held church ales and accounting banquets, sponsored apprenticeships and fundraised for international disasters. In sum, the church was embedded in the parochial economy. And this meant that everyday economic relationships, seemingly secular, became part and parcel of the Elizabethan settlement.

Third, less direct but perhaps no less powerful, were the interests of the "chief inhabitants," who most often served as churchwardens and were thus directly responsible for the upkeep of the church. Even when not churchwardens themselves, these men saw the church as a site for social legitimization. Pew repair and improvement is a common theme in these records, and such projects were usually underwritten by the lessee-occupant of particular seats; the village oligarchy could be deeply invested, both financially and socially, in the maintenance of the church. The church emphasized the twining, interconnected rhetoric of social responsibility, communal respectability, and godliness in its homily on "Repairing and Keeping Clean and Comely Adorning of Churches," one of those included in the 1571 *Second Book of Homilies*. As in the other officially promulgated homilies, it was to be read once a year to the parishioners assembled for Sunday service. Throughout the text, the homily equated upkeep of the church with "common honesty," deserving of "good report," and godliness, with the repair of the church linked to the respectability and reputation of the parishioners: "if ye have any common honesty … keep your Churches in good repair, whereby ye shall not only please God, and deserve his manifold blessings, but also deserve the good report of all godly people."[179] The village elite were thus encouraged to think of the church as an extension of their social well-being, and could thus be co-opted into wholeheartedly supporting maintenance of the church. In the hierarchical world of

Elizabethan England, such support mattered. But such buy-in was not limited to the better sort: the church was an expression of the community, and those who paid its penny rates could feel as entitled to its spiritual and communal benefits as those sitting in the box pews.[180] The Elizabethan church could be the site of harsh social hierarchy and moral condemnation. It could leverage social anxieties and obligations and notions of credit to enforce conformity. But it could also serve as a spiritual equalizer. Rich men may have sat in a finer seat, but all heard the same sermon. Rich men may have their memorials in the church, but all (or almost all) could haul stone to rebuild the steeple or graze a sheep to fund the font or buy an old bell rope to subsidize the parish. It all mattered.

Finally, we must allow that the church remained the centre of ritual and religious life in the parish, the locus of those fundamental events – births, marriages, deaths – that shape the rhythm of life. There was a general acknowledgment that this use required a certain financial responsibility for parishioners. The communal obligation for the parish was in part based on a sense of reciprocity and ownership. Those who worshipped in the church, who were married there and were buried there, who sought salvation within its walls, had a duty to preserve its fabric. To put it another way, there was a common understanding that church fees were legitimized through use. This rhetoric is nicely underscored in a case heard in the York ecclesiastical courts in 1570. Those attending chapels-of-ease in the large, mountainous parishes of the North Riding often protested rates and assessments raised to support the mother church of the parish. As one parishioner described his chapel, they had "all the right [*sic*] of a parish to the same belonging, as the burying of the dead, Baptizing of children, solemnizations of marriages, and ministration of divine service and all other sacraments and sacramentals in the same."[181] Thus, he argued, levies could reasonably be raised for support of the chapel, but *not* of the parish church, which provided none of the spiritual or ritual comfort of his own place of worship. A place where he did not worship nor experience life's rites had no claim on his money. His donations, instead, were meant to support the services that he attended, that shaped his life – services that were, of course, now communal rituals and rites based on a distinctly reformed doctrine. The levies of the church were not merely an expression of a collective obligation, but of an obligation to a Protestant Church.

Understanding parish finance, then, at once presents a picture of both continuity and of change. Churches were maintained, at least in part, because they remained important in the lives of everyday English men and women. The continued emphasis on participation involved parishioners still further, giving even the issues of repair and administration a social valence, a sense of belonging, and even a communal piety. That piety, however, was the expression of a reformed sensibility. The Elizabethan parish church had a different vernacular architecture, one that conformed to the priorities of Protestant doctrine. And the entire system of accounting and maintenance, of fundraising and repair, was monitored by the authority of the state Church.

Here, then, we see the fundamental interplay between the state and the parish in Elizabethan England. The central authority issued requirements and policed compliance, but the operations of parish finance were dominated by the decisions and needs of the individual parishes. Wardens employed methods of fundraising most appropriate to the economic, social, and doctrinal constraints and proclivities of their parishes. Decisions were made both pragmatically and ideologically, with the understanding that every penny spent on church fabric had to be raised from its parishioners. If provision of Protestant ornament and maintenance of the fabric was compulsory and universal, the strategies employed were collective and local.

The economy and the social structure of the community were deeply enmeshed in the operations of the parish church, and the wider parish was intimately involved in sustaining the church. They were wardens and congregants, assessors and ratepayers, craftsmen and labourers, tenants and volunteers alike. They gathered to make assessments, they attended church ales, they paid their dues at Easter, they rented pews, and in their last wishes, they gave gifts to their parish. We cannot know what was in the hearts and minds of these parishioners as they rebuilt their churches. Some must have been moved by piety, others by obligation, still others by fear of compulsion. Nevertheless, in their support, in their decisions and their strategies and their methods of collection, they not only maintained the parochial fabric of Elizabethan England, they built, together, a new church in England.

4

Taxing the Parish

Change came to the parish of Rowley in the third decade of Elizabeth's reign. A rural parish just northwest of Hull, Rowley had survived through the turbulence of the mid-Tudor years in relative peace. Their rector, Henry Browne, was presented to his living in the winter of 1540. There, he ministered to the congregation of St Peter's, a small, solid church that looks out over the low hills of the East Riding, for two generations. He arrived "young and lusty," and there he stayed, a steady presence through the many religious changes of Henry, Edward, Mary, and Elizabeth, until he "waxed old," dying in the summer of 1583.[1] Another death came three years later, and with it another change. From time out of mind, the lords of the local manor had been the Ellerker family.[2] They had a long record of service to the Tudor crown, which elevated them in turn. They fought (and died) at Flodden and in France, raised loyal troops in the Northern Rebellion, were elected members of parliament and mayors of northern cities, and were appointed as sheriffs and commissioners and justices of the peace. Edward Ellerker had been lord of the manor since he inherited at the age of nine, following the death of his father against the French in the last years of Henry's rule. In December of 1586, he too died, buried alongside his ancestors in the corner of the church known to this day as the Ellerker chapel.[3]

Both Browne and Ellerker had shaped life in Rowley for forty years or more. Now they were both gone. In their place came two very different men, much younger men, each determined to set his stamp on the parish. The new minister could hardly have been more different than the late Reverend Browne. James Gayton had graduated with a BA from Cambridge in 1570, quickly followed by an MA in 1573.[4] He was almost certainly the same James Gayton who made a name for himself a few years later in Bury St Edmunds, where as a hired preacher he embarked on a campaign of godly reform that so antagonized a faction of the town that they began sending children to his sermons to spy and make note of anything that smacked of illicit radicalism.[5] He left that parish precipitously in 1582. A year later, he was in the pulpit of Rowley, in a parish seemingly a world away in character and temperament from the heady zeal of the East Anglian avant-garde. But there was familiarity here, too. He owed his post to the presentment of Dame Winifred Hastings, aunt of Henry Hastings, the notoriously puritan Earl of Huntingdon.[6] There was safety in Rowley: a stable living, a pulpit of his own, protection provided by the president of the Council of the North himself. There Gayton not only preached but also served as a living model of godly learning for the county more broadly; in 1590, the sullen vicar of Brantingham, just down the lane, refused to come to be taught by him, as the authorities requested.[7]

Ralph Ellerker, on the other hand, represented a fundamental continuity with the past. He was in his mid-twenties when he inherited his father's estates – old enough to run them, but young enough to rely on his father's old retainers. He would rule as his father and grandfather had done before him, if slightly less prominently.[8] He surrounded himself with men who knew the rhythms of the land very well, who occupied the "lands thereto belonging first for sir Raphe Ellerker knight, who dyed about xxxij yere ago and after for Mr Edward Ellerker his son for diverse years together and since that time … for Mr Raphe Ellerker."[9] This is not to say that Ralph was not a man of his own time. He followed tradition, but he was also keen on improvement. Almost immediately after his father's death, he enclosed a piece of land of four or five acres on the edge of his estate, "so barren a hill that they bare no corn of many years," and started to farm it.[10] This was sharp thinking in line with the leading landowners of the day, who saw the immense possibility in turning waste to profit in a time of skyrocketing grain prices and plummeting labour costs. Ralph Ellerker was young, and he was traditional, but he was not a fool.

A conflict between Gayton and Ellerker is not, perhaps, surprising. Gayton was an interloper from another world; Ellerker was the scion of centuries of service and lordship. Gayton was a radical, a southerner, clearly proud of his education, eager to reform, and quick to admonish. At least one of his parishioners, Henry Browne (himself the nephew

Figure 4.1 Sir Ralph Ellerker, whose legal dispute with godly James Gayton reveals the fine-boned tensions involved with tithing practice. The painting is the surviving Victorian copy of the original.

of the late minister), was forbidden the communion "because the parson denied to minister the same unto him."[11] Ellerker was by all indications a religious conservative, though a conformist.[12] Both were young, ambitious men eager to put their mark on the world. Gayton had left Cambridge in his mid-twenties, ready to take on the sinners and the slack in Bury; Ellerker brought that same energy to his estate, which he began to rework toward efficiency and profit immediately upon inheriting. They were confident, determined, and fundamentally incompatible.

When the fight came, it came over tithes. It was not an issue of nonpayment: Ellerker's estate, Risby Hall, paid £3 a year as its portion of the rectory's overall takings. But he paid in cash, and Gayton wanted to be paid in kind: a portion of the grain, the animals, and, most importantly, the wool that Risby Hall raised each year. So, in 1590, James Gayton took Ralph Ellerker to court.[13] The case dragged on for months, with interrogatories from each side and ten separate witness statements. The witnesses to a man supported Ellerker's defence. Most were either his tenants or his servants, but as with most Elizabethan court cases, they also represented experience and long memory. George Pettus and Robert Freeman were in their sixties, and both John Sutton and Christopher Sutton (their relationship unclear) were seventy-six, "born and brough up within half a mile or thereabouts of the [said] manor of Risbie and hath dwelt there ever since."[14] The rector didn't stand a chance. While no sentence was recorded, the matter was soon moot. James Gayton quit the parish shortly thereafter, leaving the ministry to Henry Picard, formerly his curate, himself both a Cambridge graduate and a Yorkshireman.[15]

Tithe disputes, as anodyne as they might seem, provide a key to unlocking the full effects of the late Reformation. There, amidst the endless listing of prices for peas or turkeys or fleeces, lies a complicated and charged political, social, and economic landscape. Tithes preoccupied reformers, who worried they were insufficient to support an educated ministry. They also dominated the business of the church courts. The number of such cases skyrocketed over the course of the Elizabethan period, making up as much as a third of the total caseload in the period.[16] Spiritually significant, the tithe was nevertheless grounded in the more practical and pragmatic aspects of parish life: maintenance, sustenance, and the vagaries of pre-industrial economics. They provided the clerical income necessary to inculcate any type of reformed doctrine, but they were also subject to the socio-economic pressures felt across sixteenth-century England. In Elizabethan England, these pressures were compounded by the continued reliance on pre-Reformation parameters and structures in a rapidly changing world. This intersection of continuity and change produced a system that was simultaneously fundamental to the operation of the church and rife with conflict.

Despite this, tithes have played relatively lightly across the historiography. Few texts on Reformation history writ large mention them in anything more than passing.[17] They have been parsed more carefully by scholars of the institutional church, particularly the ecclesiastical courts, and in some excellent studies on clerical provision.[18] Perhaps the deepest footprint in the debate comes from Christopher Hill, who placed tithes and the lack of tithe reform at the heart of his *Economic Problems of the English Church*. For him, as for Elizabethan evangelicals writing four hundred years earlier, the system of English finance was corrupt and fundamentally damaging to the ministry.[19] Hill was no doubt correct, as were the evangelicals, that the ministry was insufficiently funded. That this problem was not new is perhaps not the point: the Reformation church was requiring more from its ministry than ever before, including new educational profiles and new skills in preaching, while also permitting the clergy to marry for the first time. An ecclesiastical income had to stretch further than ever before, enough to support a family and recompense for what could be an expensive education. Old problems intensified with the new realities of reformed ministry.[20]

And yet, analyzing tithes as provision alone leaves us curiously blinkered. To start with, tithes were only part of clerical income. There were, of course, glebe lands, which were owned by the benefice and farmed directly to provide money to the incumbent.[21] Ministers could also pick up piecework within their parishes, particularly for teaching or for scribal work. A few raised money through writing tracts or delivering visiting sermons in a preaching circuit. And some had other outside income, including inheritance and investment.[22] Tithes formed a crucial aspect of their funding, but they were by no means the sole source of remuneration. Looking at tithes merely from the angle of clerical provision is to ignore the complicated realities of clerical finance. Moreover, tithes very often did not involve the clergy directly at all. As we will see, a large portion – even a majority – of tithe disputes occurred between the laity, not between the laity and the clergy. While the income was certainly tied to the state of the church, very often the political, social, and economic stakes at play were primarily a lay concern.

What this chapter does, then, is to recentre our discussion of tithes and integrate it into the larger picture of parochial finance and the microeconomics of parish relations. We have seen the ways in which the practical financial realities of the church – the need to repair roofs and windows, say – had profound effects on everything from social ordering to religious ceremonies, and vice versa. The same approach is needed here. Focusing on two of the most important and contested of economic components of church finance in the Elizabethan parish – the payment of tithes and the impropriation system that allowed laity to purchase and control ecclesiastical taxation – will allow a holistic integration of tithes into broader discussion of custom, memory, inflation, devotion, and provision. The entangled relationships among parishioners, clergy, lay impropriators, and ecclesiastical expectations had a profound effect on the late-Reformation world. From a microscopic perspective, this often manifested in conflict. But more broadly, just as with church repairs and pew rents, it created strong economic bonds that tied Elizabethans ever further to the institutional Church and the reformed parish.

Tithes in the Pre-Elizabethan Church

The most entrenched difficulties of tithing in Elizabethan England were the legacies of choices made decades earlier. The process of tithing and the proliferation of local custom evolved over the course of centuries. Revised, as we shall see, by Henry and Edward, statutory law regarding tithes barely changed over the second half of the sixteenth century. Tithe law went entirely untouched in the early Elizabethan religious legislation and for a decade thereafter, and later attempts at change were inextricably linked to programs of godly reform that rendered them dead in the water on practical, political, and ideological grounds. Insofar as tithe legislation ever passed through an Elizabethan parliament, it was merely in the recapitulation of earlier statutory law in specific private bills.[23] In the rapid and dynamic world of Elizabethan England, tithes were explicitly, deliberately medieval. This choice, which prioritized stability and profit over forward-looking flexibility, had enormous, unforeseen consequences.

The basic mechanics of tithes, if tedious, were not particularly complicated. Tithes were categorized twice, determining both the source and the recipient of the income.[24] First, tithes were classified as one of three kinds: predial, personal, and mixed tithes. Predial tithes comprised a tenth of the yield from crop-based agriculture and timber or "that which doeth arise and grow by reason and virtue of the grounds."[25] Personal tithes were due on any income made through manufacture or trade, "that which doeth arise and come by means of lawful and honest commodity obtained and procured by Art, science, & the manual occupation of some person."[26] Mixed tithes were to be paid on the yield of agricultural products that had been developed by man, including animal husbandry and its products.[27] Thus, for example, corn and hay were assessed as predial tithes, income from crafts as personal, and wool and milk as mixed tithes. Tithes were further divided into two classes, great (magnae) and small or lesser (parvae). Great tithes comprised corn, hay, and timber, while lesser tithes were composed of all other predial, personal, and mixed tithes. Even clerical titles were defined in part by what income streams they received: the rector of the church received the great tithes, while the vicar received the small tithes.[28]

One can imagine an idealized parish in which this system worked perfectly and rationally. Rural and crop-based, the majority of its economy would be based on grain agriculture, with supplemental agrarian income garnered from milk and cheese, and smaller portions from a few skilled craftspeople and tradesmen. The grain, as a predial and great tithe, would be due to the rector, while a tenth of the dairy products and of the income of the craftspeople would be due to the vicar. The reality, however, was far messier and murkier, complicated by hundreds of exceptions, variations, and local customs, as well as the influences of the sixteenth century's changing economy and rapidly shifting demographics. The situation was further complicated in urban spaces, where oversight of personal income routinely proved difficult. In these areas, tithes were often commuted in favour of raised rates, paid annually or at certain festivals, or by an early form of property tax.[29]

The pre-Reformation church, then, had an already-complicated relationship with the tithe system. In part, this was due to the vagaries of custom and local agricultural patterns; coastal towns relying heavily on fisheries had quite a different tithe yield than great grain-growing parishes of the flatlands or the sheep-filled hills in the Peak district. The rectory of Ottham in Kent, for instance, saw more than seven times the amount of corn tithes than wool tithes.[30] In the enormously wealthy rectory of Manchester, wool and calves made up well over half of the total tithed goods.[31] Tithes reflected such localized diversity. At the dawn of the Reformation, tithing of fish in Scarborough was broken

Figure 4.2 Parishioners' agricultural life was wound tightly together, from funds raised through communal sheep-rearing to provision of timber for parish repairs to tithes paid to the rector and vicar. This woodcut, taken from Spenser's *The Shepherd's Calendar*, shows a hive of agricultural activity.

down by species; some parishes were tithed for lead and tin, with others exempted; pea tithes exceeded wheat tithes in Ely; and eggs were tithed in Holme-next-the-Sea in Norfolk but not in Harlow, Essex.[32]

More structurally important, however, was the impact of religious houses on the economics of the pre-Dissolution church. To begin, monastic estates were themselves generally not tithable. While the Fourth Lateran Council had exempted only certain orders, grants from the king and parliament had generally elided this distinction, with the majority of monastic land excused from tithe payments.[33] Parishes with land owned by religious houses, therefore, would see significantly smaller rates of tithe payments than those without such exempted land. Even more importantly, late-medieval England saw a growing incidence of parishes appropriated to religious houses. When a parish was appropriated to a religious house, the institution itself became the rector of the parish, and thus was entitled to its tithe profits. A rector was, to put it simply, the administrator of the parish, coordinating both its spiritual and practical management. Religious houses held rectories not as individuals but as corporations, collectively serving as rectors for their parish. While responsible for the provision of sacramental and pastoral services, rectors were not responsible for performing the ceremonies themselves. Instead, they appointed ministers as the local vicars or curates, who received a small stipend (and often the small tithes) for their services. In exchange for this provision, the rector received the great tithes of the parish.[34] Rectors were thus often disconnected from the day-to-day life of the parish, managing and administrating from a distance.[35]

Pre-Reformation corporate rectors were not solely religious houses: church officials, cathedral chapters, the universities, and local clerics also served this role. Monastic houses, however, were notable for the volume and concentration of parochial power that they wielded. Though lay gifts of appropriations were officially forbidden by the Statute of Mortmain in 1279, this law was routinely circumvented by licences granted from the crown throughout the fourteenth and fifteenth centuries.[36] Religious houses controlled a significant portion of the tithes raised in the pre-Reformation parish; by the late sixteenth century, roughly 37 per cent of parishes were held by religious houses.[37] This number is made more remarkable by its comparison to the total number of late-medieval parochial benefices, which shrunk in the face of the Black Death's demographic devastation and longer-term changes in agricultural practices and mobility patterns: while the number of parochial benefices dropped by 7 per cent in the period from 1291 to 1535, the number of appropriations skyrocketed by over 60 per cent.[38] Such a concentration of economic power was even more pronounced in the most heavily-monastic counties, such as Yorkshire, where religious houses held nearly two-thirds of all parishes.[39] Religious houses thus occupied a special and privileged place in the pre-Reformation ecclesiastical economic landscape. They were exempt from paying tithes in any parish where they might hold land, while also receiving tithed income from those parishes that they claimed by appropriations. Added to the inconsistencies of local custom, these exemptions and appropriations helped create a medieval English tithing system that was byzantine in its particulars.

Such convolution and opacity were only compounded by the legacy of monastic privileges and land ownership. From the beginning of the Dissolution, Reformation statutory law fused the medieval tithe rights of religious houses to the rest of ex-monastic property. The rights to appropriated parishes – that is, the rights to collect tithes as the rector of a parish – could be bought and sold like any other piece of the ex-religious estate. Parishes with these lay rectors became known as *impropriate* parishes, with the lay rectors known as the *impropriators*. Moreover, tithe exemptions granted to monastic property were granted to this land in perpetuity, regardless of current owner. As the Act for the Dissolution of Monasteries and Abbeys put it, "every of them, according to their estates and titles, [are] discharged and acquitted of payment of tithes, as freely, and in as large and ample manner as the said … ecclesiastical governors and governesses … enjoyed the same."[40] Thus the crown was exempt from paying tithes on confiscated land, as were future purchasers or grantees of this land; indeed, the value of ex-religious estates was augmented by these statutes, making grants of monastic estates that much more attractive.[41]

While reform presented an opportunity to modernize and centralize economic provision for the ministry, it was a road not taken. Instead, statutory law of tithes under both the Henrician and Edwardian parliaments privileged continuity over change, property owners' profits over clerical enrichment. It was a fundamentally ironic position: tithe statutes recalled the past at every turn, but it was a past that the very same legislative body had fundamentally transformed. The customs and laws of medieval tithing were fossilized at nearly the exact moment that the institutions that governed so many of them were dissolved. This essential disconnect between pre-Dissolution structure and post-Dissolution reality created a situation in which the influence of laymen was ever more deeply embedded in the economics of the English church. Now, instead of a country full of monastic rectors, there was a country full of lay impropriators, collecting the tithes from local parishes and paying stipends to vicars or curates.

It was an irony only compounded in the Edwardian statutes, the last significant tithe reforms in the sixteenth century. Edward's parliaments began where Henry's left off, again exempting ex-religious land from the payment of tithes.[42] However, Edwardian statute also recognized the shortcomings in the Henrician law, which had largely focused on monastic tithe rights and ignored larger tithe questions. There had been little acknowledgment to this point that the entire tithe system might have been called into question by such massive institutional and doctrinal change. The 1549 Act for the Payment of Tithes addressed this lapse. It did so by again privileging continuity and looking to the past. Tradition took precedent. Parochial tithes were to be paid according to custom, defined "as hath been of right yielded and paid within forty years next before the making of this act."[43] Tithes in Edwardian England, then, were to be paid as they were in 1509 – a Reformed church grounded firmly in pre-Reformation custom. In an age of innovation and iconoclasm, the appeal to a vanished past is all the more striking.

For all the entrenchment, however, the Edwardian statute did reflect the agricultural changes percolating through the English countryside. The sixteenth century saw the beginnings of what has commonly become known as the agricultural revolution, with its concomitant diversification of crops, increase of yield, and fundamental restructuring of land rights with the growth of enclosure.[44] To strand tithes on an antique agricultural island would be to undermine any benefits the church could reap from these innovations. As such, Edwardian statute allowed barren ground, once improved, a seven-year exemption from increased tithe payments, after which time crops raised on this land were to be fully tithable.[45] While some scholars, most notably Christopher Hill, have criticized this statute as deleterious to the economics of the church, this assessment is short-sighted.[46] To begin, tithe exemptions for newly cultivated land were not unfamiliar. In the pre-Dissolution church, monasteries routinely increased their income by cultivating new land, or *novalia*. This was a way of augmenting their non-tithable estate in the face of parliamentary strictures following the Statute of Mortmain, which had been meant to limit the land that could be donated to the church and thus out of the reach of secular taxation.[47] This was of continual benefit to religious houses, not a one-off windfall; as part of the monastic estate, profits from this land would avoid tithing in perpetuity. The Edwardian statute, on the other hand, limited the exemption to just seven years, long enough to serve as an inducement but short enough to guarantee profits would return to the parish. Indeed, just as modern-day tax abatements promote residential and commercial redevelopment in economically depressed cities, Edwardian tithe exemptions for reclaimed land could actually be seen as an ambitious program to increase clerical revenues in the long run. By creating an abatement on wasteland, the Edwardian statute encouraged cultivation and, within a decade, increased the amount of tithable land.

Nevertheless, the heart of these early tithe laws lay in the past, not in the future. In putting such a keen emphasis on precedent in a time of such rapid change, they allowed for a continuation of customs that amplified crown estates and political goodwill while forestalling widespread resistance amongst those who had purchased ex-monastic property. As we will see in the following section, there was significant political resistance to stripping monastic estates of their tithable land, and such a position certainly made sense for the economic interests of the crown. But the Edwardian statutes were also put into place to address larger concerns over landlords and taxation that motivated both the commonwealth debate and much of the popular protest in the late 1540s. Locking tithes into ancient custom was in part a way to satisfy anxieties about the "pitiful complaint & righteous cause of the poor oppressed" and the prices "so high … as they were never wont to be in times past."[48] Appeals to the past were comforting to both the landed interest and reformers alike. This nostalgic policy, though, would have significant effects for years to come. With Elizabethan statute not changing Edward's compromises, the customs and traditions of the early sixteenth century were calcified into the law.

There was one significant innovation in the 1549 statutes: the enforcement and prosecution of tithe rights in the ecclesiastical courts. Tithe cases brought in instances of nonpayment were, according to An Act for the Payment of Tithes, to be prosecuted in ecclesiastical rather than common-law courts. Moreover, the Act allowed for plaintiffs bringing cases in ecclesiastical courts to receive what were essentially damages of two to three times the value of the unpaid tithes, further encouraging litigants to use the ecclesiastical justice system.[49] Some cases continued to be presented in courts of equity, most especially Chancery and Star Chamber, but these represented a minority of Elizabethan cases, largely limited to suits involving wealthy participants, extensive tracts of land, or, on less frequent occasions, particularly contentious cases. By 1550, the overwhelming majority of tithe cases were prosecuted in the ecclesiastical courts.[50]

Cases adjudicated in such courts were largely brought by the plaintiffs themselves rather than by ecclesiastical officers. The Act had forbidden the use of personal or corporal oaths in tithe cases, which had the perhaps unintended result of forcing these cases to be heard as instance suits rather than ex-officio prosecutions; that is to say, rather than being brought as correction cases by ecclesiastical officers, which would have required the use of the forbidden corporal oath, tithe cases were brought by the plaintiff, as in civil courts.[51] Thus, the Act not only compelled tithe cases to be brought before ecclesiastical courts, but it also obliged rectors, lay tithe farmers, and impropriators to bring these suits themselves. In practice, this brought a tidal wave of new litigation and new litigants in front of ecclesiastical magistrates. In some areas, the number of tithe suits doubled and even tripled in the twenty years following the legislation.[52]

This surge continued well into the late sixteenth century, only increasing in the years following Elizabeth's accession. Such dramatic a rise was clearly not due to new legislation, of which there was none. If the law of the land remained the same, then, why was there such a surge in tithe litigation in the Elizabethan church?

Tithe Resistance and Litigation

It is tempting to link the explosion of tithe litigation to disapproval of the church or its clerics: tithe resistance as a form of popular protest. This was certainly true on the Continent, where clashes over tithes broke out into violence and rebellion. Objections to tithe payments in early 1520s Germany stirred the beginnings of the uprising that became the German Peasants' Revolt of 1525. Abolition of the small tithe was a key demand of the Twelve Articles of the Upper Swabian Peasants, and tithe refusal spread rapidly in the rebelling regions.[53] Throughout the mid-sixteenth century, the French countryside was gripped by regular tithe strikes, quite possibly inspired by the German revolt.[54] In 1573, collective and violent tithe resistance was found in regions as distinct as Croatia and Sweden.[55] In each case, a confluence of economic and religious tensions produced mass violent opposition to the tithe.

There is little evidence, however, of sustained mass political or religious resistance to tithes in England after the split from Rome. Wycliffite lines of attack that tithes were a relic of Mosaic laws and that "in the new law neither Christ nor any of his apostles took tithes of the people nor commanded the people to pay tithes neither to priests nor to deacons" faded when the clergy being supported were themselves preaching reformed doctrine.[56] In a national framework, tithes were never at the centre of large-scale rebellion at any point in Tudor England. There were, to be sure, references to tithes in both the 1536 Pilgrimage of Grace and Kett's Rebellion of 1549, but in both instances tithe protests were overshadowed by larger economic concerns. The religious conservatives of the Pilgrimage of Grace placed far more emphasis on opposition to enclosure, to royal taxation, and to the raising of entry fines – an inheritance or sales tax paid upon first tenancy of land – than on tithe rates.[57] Attacks on tithe barns seem to have been reactions to particularly harsh or lacklustre landlords, especially, in these days before full dissolution, those owned by monastic appropriators.[58] Thirteen years later, Kett's evangelical rebels asked for tithe reform rather than abolition. Acknowledging the sometimes-contentious effect of tithe collection on parish relations, the manifesto included an item requesting "that no proprietary parson or vicar, in consideration of avoiding trouble and suit between them and their poor parishioners, which they daily do proceed and attempt, shall from henceforth take for the full contentation of all the tenths which now they do receive but viii d. of the noble" – in other words, a tenth of the existing tithe.[59] This demand, shoehorned between an item calling for the end of copyhold renting and another for fencing of rabbit warrens, was far from the focus of the rebellion. More pressing were the calls that "no lord of no manor shall common upon the Comons" and that rents and prices should be fixed as they were fifty years earlier. Meanwhile, complaints about the ministry focused largely on their capabilities and provision of duties rather than their tithe collections.[60] The actions of the rebels mimicked their demands. Where rioters destroyed property, they targeted enclosed land rather than tithe barns.[61]

Thus, while both rebellions made significant religious and economic demands, abolition of tithes was not among them: where any call for tithe reform was present, it was eclipsed by other more pressing and more radical calls for change. This stands in marked contrast to explicit tithe rebellion on the Continent. Instead, English tithe resistance, where it occurred, was largely individual. And while such resistance may well have had doctrinal undertones, these were almost never explicit. Court cases trying to recoup tithes almost always consisted of issues of legality or tenancy, quantity or quality, not the legitimacy of the tithe itself. The case of James Lockey, vicar of Little Ouseburn, is archetypical: Lockey sued Reginald Batey for payment of tithes on firewood. While Batey acknowledged that the tithes were unpaid on this firewood, he argued that he had "refused to pay the same because he believeth that by Law it is not due unto [Lockey]."[62] The reason he gave for refusal, however, had nothing to do with religious reform and everything to do with traditions of payment, from which this particular firewood had long been exempted.

Similar rhetoric flows throughout tens of thousands of pages of depositions. A few examples will suffice. We see it in the defence of Ralph Ellerker against James Gayton's claims that his tithes should be paid in kind not cash: not for a second does Ellerker claim that he does not owe a tithe or that he dislikes Gayton's preaching (although he almost certainly did), but merely that, according to precedent, he did not owe Gayton a cash crop as claimed in the lawsuit. And he was not alone. In 1572, Edward Richardson testified that "he believeth that he is discharged by the statute of this Realm from paying any tithe at all because the said wood was xxx years growth" and thus exempt.[63] Francis Atlay defended himself by arguing that tithe money "for the tithe hay of which two closes … hath not been paid at any time during the years aforesaid."[64] As R.B. Outhwaite puts it, withholding of tithes "did not represent hostility to the church; it betokened the reluctance of people to give away part of their hard-won surpluses and to pay what were in effect taxes."[65] It is unsurprising to hear this rhetoric made by the defence – only the most principled self-saboteur would plead opposition to the church in front of the ecclesiastical courts. But crucially, such accusations are absent from nearly all plaintiffs' libels as well.[66] If there were widespread evasion due to religious nonconformity, it would have been a potent weapon for the plaintiff's case. (Just imagine this in front of the church courts: "He owes me tithes but refuses to pay because he thinks the reformed service to be the work of the devil.") Its absence in plaintiffs' allegations seems to indicate the generally non-ideological nature of tithe disputes in the Elizabethan period.

If the rise in tithe litigation was not a result of mass anticlericalism or religious protest, we must consider more secular causes: the changing economic and demographic realities in late-sixteenth-century England. The Elizabethan period, especially in its later years, was notorious for rapid population expansion, wage stagnation, inflation, and an increasingly centralized and connected economy.[67] With real agricultural incomes decreasing in the mid-sixteenth century, landlords attempted to maintain their holding's value by increasing rents and employing some forms of enclosure.[68] Smaller farmers found themselves increasingly pinched, with rising rents to answer for in an age of increased inflation. Tithes, as "the heaviest direct tax on farming," could not have escaped the influence of this strain.[69] In the most acute times of anxiety, local organized resistance emerged. The loudest and most violent of these – and thus the most legible in the historical record – were grain riots, common in times of bad harvest and dearth.[70] One might expect tithes, as a regressive agricultural tax, to be a focus of outrage in the rhetoric of rioting. Remarkably, however, tithe collectors and tithe barns do not seem to have been a common target of subsistence rioters in the Elizabethan period. Antipathy was instead directed at grain profiteers, who stockpiled grain and artificially inflated prices in times of starvation.[71] Tithes remained far less targeted by popular protest.

Why, then, did tithes largely escape blame in times of dearth? To begin, those who would have felt famine the sharpest might have avoided tithe payment altogether. Since the passage of the Edwardian statutes, "common day-labourers" were exempt from tithe payment, alleviating the payment burden on one of the most vulnerable sections of society.[72] Wage stagnation and rising grain prices had left labourers, especially by the end of the sixteenth century, dealing with increasingly narrow margins of subsistence. With as much as 90 per cent of a labourer's wages spent on food costs, even in times of plenty, the rapid inflation of grain prices in times of dearth left them starving.[73] With privation comes resistance, and it is no surprise that many of the grain riots in the later sixteenth century were composed of the labouring poor, who targeted grain profiteers as those whose actions had a direct impact on their desperate situation.[74] Tithe exemptions for labourers, then, may well have forestalled extensive local organized opposition to payment, violent or otherwise.

Nor does litigation seem to be a reaction to quieter protest against tithes. At first glance, it would be tempting to see the rise in tithe prosecutions to be a response to large-scale refusal to pay during times of dearth, a shadowed footprint of political action. Nonpayment here would be a tool to negotiate power and authority, a kind of moral economy of tithe payment that underpaid the tenth (or outright rejected payment) in times of need.[75] If this were the case, we would expect to see two things. First, tithe litigation would follow the patterns of dearth, with more prosecutions sought in times of economic crisis. This certainly occurred in criminal prosecutions, which tended to spike in times of dearth, as people broke the law to sustain their families' needs.[76] To give one small example, prosecutions of theft in late-Elizabethan Essex more than doubled in times of dearth.[77] Second, cases would target those who felt dearth most acutely, particularly the smaller farmers who led so much of the more vocal and violent grain protests.

A closer look at the contours of prosecution, though, reveals a far more complicated picture. The 1590s – a decade with a notoriously volatile economic landscape – serve as an especially useful sample of the effects of economic crisis on tithe prosecution. The period opened with two poor summers, resulting in grain prices surging to 41 per cent above average in 1591. Prices normalized the following year, with relative prosperity from 1592 to 1594. The year 1595, however, saw the first of four consecutive disastrous harvests. These were years of great poverty, and at their peak in 1597, grain prices had spiked to almost 130 per cent above average.[78] Coming on the heels of three decades of rapid demographic expansion – the population had grown by nearly a quarter between 1560 and 1590 – the pressures were too much for the economy to bear.[79] This was hardship of the most acute and basic kind: people quite literally could not afford to eat, and regional mortality in the northeast as much as quadrupled.[80] By 1599, however, harvests improved, prices dropped, and the crisis eased. The acuity with which we can trace times of dearth and times of plenty in this decade makes comparative study particularly valuable.

A rough analysis of the tithe cases prosecuted in the York courts during the 1590s shows little reliable correlation between years of dearth and numbers of prosecutions.[81] No clear pattern can be found here. Healthy harvests produced as many, if not slightly more, prosecutions as years with poor harvests; 1593, for instance, saw more tithe cases brought than in the rough years of 1594–96. Nor is there a clear model of prosecutorial reaction lagging a year or so behind dearth. If that were the case, we would see the 1597 spike in prosecutions drag on for another year or two before harvests eased, but they dropped almost immediately. Tithe litigation, then, did not clearly follow patterns of dearth.

Nor, indeed, did the cases target those who felt dearth most acutely, the kind of men who led the grain riots in the south, who might be tempted to take part in a silent protest of withholding. Impoverished husbandmen were not the main objects of complaint, and hidden crops were not the main accusation. While on a theoretical level all produce was to be tithed, the structural realities of enforcement would have

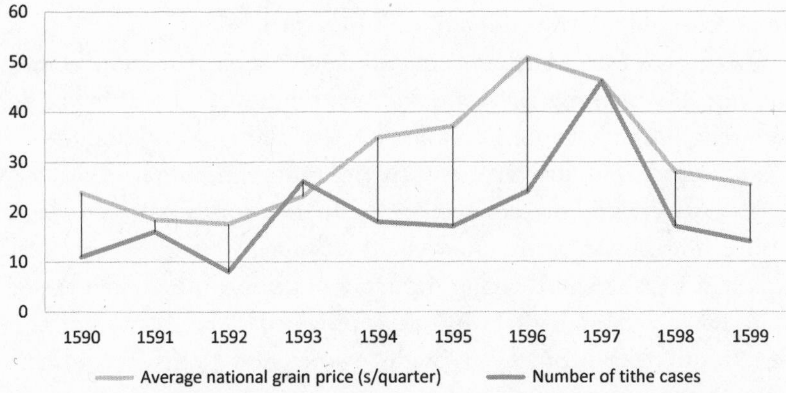

Figure 4.3 Tithe prices and prosecutions in the ecclesiastical courts of York, 1590s. Grain prices taken from W.G. Hoskins, "Harvest Fluctuations and English Economic History, 1480–1619," *Agricultural History Review* 12, no. 1 (1964): 46.

discouraged extensive prosecution of minor claims. As the statute-law restrictions ensured that almost all cases would be brought as instance suits, or privately instigated disputes between the parties, the plaintiff was forced to bear the costs of prosecution until a verdict was rendered. In cases involving long-standing conflict, large quantities of tithable goods, or issues of ownership, such prosecution made financial sense. In cases of a few eggs or a small plot of land, the cost of a suit would have exceeded even the triple damages that the courts might award.

Where such minor prosecutions did exist, they were often symptoms of deeper conflict. In Elizabethan England, litigation could be wielded to prosecute grudges and feuds as much as contractual failures. Though far from the clerical ideal espoused by sermon writers and conduct books, clerics were routinely drawn into such clashes. In such instances, payment and prosecution of tithes became tactics of dispute. The case of Edmund Marsh, vicar of Sherburn in Elmet, is a particularly vivid example of such dispute. Marsh sued his parishioner, Thomas Taylor, in the summer of 1590, for tithes due on a few bushels of apples and other incidental produce. Taylor rebutted these charges, declaring that he had paid his apple tithe and that the suit was simply retribution for another dispute. Marsh, Taylor stated, "when he had slandered this Respondents wife & her mother and fallen out with them he in malice took forth a Citation against this respondent to answer him for tithes & served the same upon him."[82] In return, both Taylor's wife and mother-in-law took Marsh to court for slander and defamation, at least one case of which was successful.[83] Here, the tithe had nothing to do with religious or economic conflict, but was simply a tool brandished in an interpersonal struggle between vicar and parishioner.

Not all clerics were so out of charity with their congregations. Indeed, lack of prosecution of the poor could also have had an ethical basis. Tithes in Elizabethan England did retain at least some of their sacred character, including charity: while tithes provided for ministers, ministers were to use their incomes to provide for the poor.[84] Visitation articles, Convocation decrees, and injunctions all required clerical charity and care for the poor.[85] The connection between tithes and charity even extended to impropriate tithes, which in turn were meant to support the minister. In the 1601 Poor Relief Act, poor rates were required to be paid by "every inhabitant, parson, vicar and other, and of every occupier of lands, houses, tithes impropriate or propriations of tithes." Remarkably, the poor rate was the only local levy for which impropriated lands were liable; they were exempt from all local obligations other than their duty to the poor. In addition to routine hospitality, some ministers provided extraordinary charity to their parishioners, especially in times of dearth. Noted evangelical Richard Greenham not only sold his own corn to the poor for 40 per cent of market price, he also convinced local farmers "to hire a common granary, and therein to lay up corn for the poor … every man according to his ability."[86] Few ministers exercised such extraordinary charity: in addition to potential personal foibles of greed or indifference to parishioners, ministers had a responsibility to provide for their own families and households. Nevertheless, relentless prosecution of one's struggling parishioners hardly fit the spiritual ideal of clerical charity, and ministers may well have overlooked occasional withholding in times of need.

Ministers might have had a pastoral reason for not prosecuting their poor parishioners, but interestingly, the same patterns extended to the laity collecting tithes on ex-monastic land. Though these lay impropriators were keen to protect their interests when dearth sent grain prices skyrocketing, they also rarely prosecuted tithe cases against the most vulnerable. Instead, they too focused on substantial farmers and estates. Lay impropriators had to contend with the same practical, if not perhaps the same moral, restrictions as clerical tithe collectors.[87]

Lawsuits were costly and time-consuming. Even more importantly, lay impropriators generally collected only the great tithes, especially grain tithes – those which saw the greatest price spikes during the years of dearth – and were largely unconcerned with the kind of subsistence agriculture that composed much of the economy of makeshifts and yielded much of the small tithes. It was the vicar, or his tithe farmer, who had to contend with the collection of a rope of onions here, a bushel of apples there, and a tenth of the gallons milked from cows kept on common land. Ministers were more than twice as likely to be plaintiffs in suits involving apples or milk than hay or wheat.[88] Lay impropriators, very often substantial landholders themselves, tended to bring suit against other wealthy estates, who may have also been profiting from rising grain prices.

Looking carefully through the libels and depositions, then, it becomes clear that the target for tithe prosecutions in times of dearth were usually aimed not at embattled smallholders, but rather at large-scale, relatively wealthy landowners. These were men like Ralph Ellerker, with his wheat and rye and barley and wool and livestock. William Carrington, taken to court for grain tithes in 1597, came from an old Cheshire family and had inherited the manor of Spaunton from his father-in-law.[89] In 1594, the rector of Brandesburton brought suit against John Wensley, part of the family that had held the manor since at least the time of Edward IV.[90] The Walter Strickland brought to court by the tithe farmers of Appleby-le-Street was almost certainly the son of the famous, godly MP whose seat at Hildenley Hall was in the next parish.[91] By no means, however, were all those prosecuted such nationally important figures, and some plaintiffs chased after more modest prey. The tithe farmers of Silkstone in the West Riding, for instance, took Percival Thornton to court for nonpayment of tithes in 1596. His responses to their accusations paint a picture of a comfortable, but by no means wealthy, yeoman farmer of Yorkshire. He harvested seven wains of hay, and with his wife and family raised forty sheep, some milk cows, and a handful of pigs, geese, and hens. In a good year, his profits from these goods alone ran around £8 to £9.[92] Such a sum made Thornton eligible for jury service and the franchise, and it indicated an estate worth somewhere in the range of £50 to £60.[93] It did not compare, though, to local gentry like Ellerker, whose estate within the bounds of Rowley alone was worth at least eight times more.[94]

Despite this disparity, the cases of Percival Thornton and Ralph Ellerker had identical motivations for prosecution: cash payments for tithes. This was a compounded problem of the backward-looking nature of tithes in Reformation England. Not only did statute law lock tithe collection into the institutional structure of the late-medieval church, it also locked payment schemes (whether in case or in kind) into an eighty-year-old pricing model. This was patently ridiculous. The economy of the 1590s looked far different from that of 1509. In the early years of the sixteenth century, grain was plentiful and harvests were good. Cash, not crop, was prized.[95] Over the course of the next decades, deals were made between rectors and their parishes to collect cash payments in lieu of crops. This was particularly true for the great predial tithes of grain and cereal from larger estates. Rectors liked the system, as it obviated the need for complicated accounting of sheaves and stocks and wains (and the need to act as a grain merchant), and they may have accepted a slight discount to ensure a steady stream of income, a win for all.

A good bargain for a rector in 1509 was a disaster for the rectors of 1590. They were locked into ninety-year-old deals that no longer met the economic reality. Grain was worth more than five times as much in the last decade of the sixteenth century than in the first. During the dearth of the mid-1590s, the prices were even higher, almost ten times as much as they were at the beginning of the century.[96] Edward's compromise, meant to appease both potential land purchaser and landless peasant alike, had disastrous consequences for those who inherited these earlier bargains. James Gayton brought suit against Ralph Ellerker because Ellerker's estate paid him only £3 in cash each year, less than half as much as he could have brought in had the payment been made in kind.[97] Nor was Gayton alone. Cash payments, long a matter of contention in a century of quickening inflation, became a flashpoint during times of crisis.[98] The case of Edward Whitacre, rector of the Thornhill parish, is particularly acute. In a case brought before the court in December of 1597, Whitacre sued Edward Copley for refusing to pay in-kind on his fields. Copley admitted that his harvest of wheat, rye, and oats had yielded £126 3s. 4d. on the market over the past two seasons but claimed tithes of "the same are not due unto [Whitacre] but xx*s*. in money yearly."[99] This was a breathtaking discrepancy. If strictly tithed, the harvest should have generated over £12 for the rector;

instead, Copley offered forty shillings, or two pounds – less than a sixth of the worth of an in-kind tithe. Such disputes were repeated, albeit generally with less dramatic particulars, in cases throughout the height of the harvest crisis.[100] These tithe suits were not a matter of refusal to pay, but about attempts to negotiate the complicated legacies of statute laws' reliance on customary payment. The mid-century conciliations, in the long run, promoted conflict rather than peace.

Tithe litigation, then, was not aimed at those seeking to escape famine by eating their tithes, but at those attempting to leverage outdated economic relationships to profiteer from harvest crises and inflationary prices. Indeed, the vulnerable party in these suits was often the plaintiff himself. The value of ministers' livings, especially those of the vicars, was often far from generous: enough to keep a minister comfortable, but certainly not enough to afford extravagant surpluses or indifferent attention to income. Clerical probate records show the rural clergy to have an average estate of around £50 by the mid-Elizabethan period, placing them among the more substantial farmers in the local area; a survey of Oxfordshire households in the same years show only 46 of 248 (18.5 per cent) inventories valued at more than £50.[101] There were, however, a significant minority of much poorer clergy: a survey of Cornish ministers in 1586 valued a little over 10 per cent of livings at under £30, while a similar survey in Berkshire put the number at over 20 per cent.[102]

In many cases, then, tithe suits were brought to *prevent*, not enforce, exploitation of the vulnerable. James Gayton's prosecution of Ralph Ellerker was in no way an economic contest amongst equals. Better educated Gayton may have been, and well connected to the great political patrons of the north he certainly was, but he had no landed estate, no loyal tenants. His previous position as a visiting lecturer in Bury was prestigious, but it was paid on sufferance from voluntary contributions collected from the townspeople and local godly gentry.[103] Gayton's angry insistence that a £3 tithe was insufficient income from the parish's largest landowner was no doubt correct.[104] Some of the rising tide of litigation was indeed a response to a growing economic stratification, especially in times of heightened grain prices. However, this stratification often left the clergy, not just the laity, desperate to protect their economic security. The clergy, far more literate and well versed in bureaucracy than the average tenant farmer, was perhaps better able than most of their parishioners to resist landholders' efforts to improve their profit margins. Here, tithe litigation was, if not a weapon of the weak, a weapon of the weaker.

There is no real evidence of mass tithe resistance as a form of popular protest. There was little organized violence directed at tithe collections or collectors, certainly not on the scale seen on the Continent. Tithes exacerbated, but did not provoke, the great religious rebellions of the mid-century. Nor did tithe disputes map cleanly onto short-term economic crises, as criminal prosecutions so often did. While concerns over cash payments were indeed rising over the last quarter of the century, they tended to be reactions to two larger structural problems: growing inflation and the earlier political compromises. At least in court, rectors and impropriators were largely battling the wealthy, not the poor, in these lean years.

Economics, however, cannot entirely explain the rise of tithe litigation in the period. As we have seen, years of plenty produced as much if not more litigation than years of scarcity. While general concerns about economic stratification were present throughout Elizabeth's reign, acute apprehensions began accelerating only in the last two decades of the sixteenth century. Incidence of tithe litigation, on the other hand, increased steadily throughout the second half of the sixteenth century. Why this disparity? Here too, earlier compromises yielded unexpected results. The Edwardian offer of trebled damages upon successful prosecution of a tithe case was a clear inducement to bring suit, particularly against wealthier landlords, since the value recouped might be as much as an annual income of an estate.[105] Litigation surged. Tithe cases were by no means alone in this; Elizabethans were entering the ecclesiastical courts at an unprecedented pace across the board.[106] But tithe suits were also rising relative to total rates, and only defamation saw anything like such a spike in prosecutions. In 1561, thirteen tithe causes were entered in the consistory court in York; in 1601, the number had risen to 133.[107] In an increasingly litigious culture, at a time of economic strain, the lure of trebled damages saw tithe cases – especially of more sizable estates – enter the courts more frequently than ever before.

The appeal of prosecution was only enhanced by the Edwardian statute's insistence on the primacy of precedent.[108] This may well, as some have suggested, have led new tithe owners keen on establishing their rights to the land to bring suit in the courts.[109] Practices left unchallenged could become new custom, which, while technically illicit, could nonetheless become ingrained. Establishing custom was an inherently charged process; as Andy Wood puts it, "the process by which customs were laid down was always political."[110] What made tithe practices particularly difficult, and particularly fraught, was the statutory reliance on a past long vanished. Custom here *was* the law. To have that custom formalized and acknowledged in the church court was a quick way to prove precedent and assert power over the process. A final court sentence was not necessarily the goal. Litigation was often a springboard for less-formal arbitration, and suits were frequently abandoned before the final sentence in favour of an agreement that might be more equitable and would certainly be far cheaper than a full judicial decision.[111] This was as true for tithes as it was for secular lawsuits over debt.[112] Merely to bring a lawsuit, then, was a step in a political game. It might end in treble damages. But it might also force and formalize a change in practice that could be as beneficial – perhaps even more so – than any judicial sentence. The courts became a forum not simply to adjudicate the dispute of the moment, but also to set the practice for the future: a future grounded deeply in the past.

Remembering the Pre-Dissolution Tithe

Nowhere is this paradox clearer than in the fundamental problem of former monastic estates. The great swathes of land once owned by the monasteries continued to be exempt from tithe payments even once they were sold or leased by the crown to the laity. This was as true in 1599 as it had been in 1499. The difference, of course, was that the world of 1499 no longer existed. To some extent, the past was always lost. New tenants farmed the fields as old families died or moved away; estates were bought and sold; lands were enclosed. But the dissolution of the monasteries had wreaked an epistemic change. What had been destroyed was a *way of life*, not just a landlord. The institutional memory of these religious houses was also dissolved. It was not, however, destroyed, but rather disintegrated into the wider world. And this memory, the memory of the pre-Reformation, was consciously and constantly resurrected in Elizabethan tithe disputes.

Reformation required conscious forgetting. Here, as Andy Wood describes, the ruptures of religious change create "an assault upon local memory" and a "sense amongst the people of late Tudor and Stuart England that they were separated from their pre-Reformation ancestors by a yawning chasm, a breakage within the remembrance cultural that hitherto had bound their communities together."[113] This is a moving invocation and effectively describes the wrenching disconnect and enforced silence that the Reformation could and did impose upon communities. So too does Judith Pollman's work on the necessary acts of oblivion that followed religious change, which are needed to give a way to move forward following such massive disruption. Such acts, she writes, "say that past events are *not* acknowledged as a legitimate reason for action of the present; they are *of the past*."[114]

And yet, from a resolutely practical standpoint, total discontinuity was impossible. This was particularly true in tithe litigation. Tithe suits required memory. Both the statutory construction of tithe legislation and the larger English legal reliance on custom and precedent meant that memories of the past were a constant presence in Elizabethan courtrooms. Contrary to Pollman's picture, the past was constantly, perhaps even uniquely, a legitimate reason for action in the present. In fact, both past and future were predicated upon it. Historians have carefully described how important memory and custom were to traditional rights of grazing and gleaning.[115] What is less realized, though, is just how true this was of pre-Reformation religious systems, structures, and institutions. Here too, memory and custom reigned – not secret, illicit memories, hidden away from grasping religious authorities looking to ferret out any hints of the old world, but live, vivid, and authoritative recollections. And these memories were not merely discussed, but actually sought after, not by recusants or rebels but by the heart of conformist, statist religion and its institutions: church courts, episcopal visitations, and courts of equity.

Most tithe cases included testimony that drew on collective knowledge of precedent. But in cases where the land in question had been held by religious houses in the years before the Reformation, tithe cases required a wholescale resurrection of the past: a past that was not just gone, but that had been actively dissolved. Earlier compromises had enormous consequences. Huge measures of land, as much as a third of all estates in places like Yorkshire, continued to be exempt from tithe payments, even once sold or leased by the crown to the laity. But the institutions that had guaranteed those exemptions were gone. The suddenness of the change was rehearsed in court testimony, like that which recalled "that the said monastery divers years immediately before the suppression thereof, and also even at the day of the suppression … had occupied the said arable demesne lands in their own hands, and … occupied and tilled [it] … also before the suppression of the same by the space of a hundredth [or] CCCCC years."[116]

By the Elizabethan period, the estates once held by religious houses had often changed hands several times, subdivided and amalgamated as the century progressed. In practice, this led to intense contention over which parcels of property could legitimately withhold the tithe. In case after case, defendants in tithe suits argued that their land was exempt from tithe payment because it had formerly belonged to a religious house. The claims of Gregory Waterhouse in 1588 are entirely typical: "that the said prior and Convent of Lewes at the time of the dissolution of the said monastery and their tenants by privilege were freed and discharged of and from the payment of any tithes … whereof he the said Gregory by the Laws and statutes of this Realm is also by reason of the said privilege freed and discharged from payment of tithes."[117] Some fifty years after the last monastic houses ceased to manage their land, the echoes of their influence continued to reverberate in courts across the country. Without the institutional continuity of the religious houses, however, these echoes led to contention. Whether fearful of allowing a customary exemption to gel or simply desperate to eke all value from their livings, tithe owners filled the courts with suits against owners of former monastic estates.

The reliance on memory and local custom took on shadings of urgency with the passage of time. Those who could testify first hand as to the arrangement of finances in religious houses were, simply put, dying. It is nearly impossible to calculate accurately the population of the religious orders in the pre-Reformation period. The numbers of ex-religious receiving a governmental pension is useful but not complete; many opted to become secular clerics, receiving benefices or cures, while the more well-heeled could be absorbed back into their families without state support. At least two thousand former religious went unpensioned after the Dissolution, and historians have estimated that between a quarter and a third received no state support.[118] Nevertheless, the relative decline of ex-religious receiving a government pension gives a rough sense of the pace of loss. In Yorkshire, the population of the religious eligible for pensions at the time of the Dissolution was at least 840.[119] By 1556, the number receiving pensions had dropped to 724; by 1564, to 190; by 1582, 49. By the end of Elizabeth's reign, only a single eligible pensioner still lived.[120] Though the figures themselves cannot be complete, the pace of decline is obvious and provides a useful measure for the presence of the ex-religious in Elizabethan life. The early reign would have seen them as an aging but relatively common portion of the population, with roughly a quarter still alive; by 1580 they would have been exceptional.

With settlement on tithe disputes resting on the details of payment from the pre-Dissolution years, first-hand knowledge of monastic finance was a particularly useful form of testimony. The ex-religious are found throughout the cause papers and depositions of the early Elizabethan period, testifying to pre-Reformation patterns of tithe payments and arrangements. Their testimony was clearly valuable: the level of detail to which they could attest was remarkable. Of particular import were former monastic office-holders who had specialized knowledge of monastic finance or landholdings. Robert Hall testified in 1561 that as "the officer and Receiver of saint Leonard's vij years together before the Dissolution," he "never paid to the said bowser of sanit mary abbey or any other officer there the sum … articulate."[121] An elderly Robert Scolay testified in 1574 "that for the space of xxty years or thereaboutes next and immediately before the dissolution of the monastery of Munckbretton this examinate dwelt and continued in the monastery of munck Bretton and was sexton of the said monastery during the same time by reason whereof he saith he very well knew all the desmesnes of the monastery of munckbretton aforesaid."[122] Witnesses were keen to stress their former authority, as in a rare case featuring testimony from a former nun. The witness, Joan Cockell, pointed out "that she being an officer in the said monastery or nunnery by and during all the time aforesaid must needs have known if any tithes had bene paid at all of any commodities whatsoever coming chancing growing or renewing of in or upon any the grounds aforesaid or at the least have heard tell thereof which she never did."[123] In a system based on custom manifested as common knowledge, such testimony provided powerful credit to a litigant. In the courtrooms of Elizabethan England, monks and nuns had institutional authority again, albeit of a very different kind.

These ex-religious provided a bridge to pre-Reformation life that spanned the ruptures of the Dissolution. Testimony like that of Elizabeth Burnett – who declared she knew that no tithe should be due on land once belonging to Moxby Priory, Yorkshire, because "that she her self did yearly for the most part in hay time help to straw and cock the hay growing in the said grounds and see the same led away the tenth part with the nine parts" – brought back to life a vanished past.[124] But such evidence was rapidly disappearing. By the mid-1580s, such testimony had all but vanished from the records. The past was handed now into the memories of the layman. New testimony emerged. The 1583 deposition of John Gawtree based his knowledge of the Priory of Kirkham's tithing lands on what "he hath heard Richarde Aslabie then tenant of the said close at the time of the Dissolution say."[125] In 1592, Thomas Wright recalled a childhood memory, wherein "he hath known and seen the prior … sell some of the corn grown in same grounds before the dissolution" of the Priory of Healaugh Park.[126] John Staines testified in 1602 that the land in question had never belonged to the Priory of Gisbrough because "Rowland Staynes [his] father was farmer of some part of the said grounds" and had paid his tithes elsewhere.[127]

Memory here functioned not as a memoir or a memorial, but a practice, something that had to be constantly maintained and negotiated. Tithe cases were still litigated in the courts long after the last monk, or even lay servant employed on the monastic estate, had died. But in the sea change of the 1580s, custom was becoming no longer first-hand testimony of a world that was gone. It was a second-hand resurrection. Memory remained, but it was the memory of a memory. Even in a system so thoroughly and deliberately grounded in the past, the future had come.

Laicization of the Tithe

By the final decades of the Elizabethan period, the laity dominated tithe litigation. Witness lists were increasingly dominated by testimony from the laity. Sporadically, ministers served as witnesses to tithe cases, but such statements were relatively rare; in the ecclesiastical courts of York, for example, less than 9 per cent of surviving Elizabethan cause papers list a cleric as any sort as a witness.[128] Coupled with the slow, steady erasure of ex-religious testimony from the records, the body of evidence rested firmly on the shoulders of the laity. Perhaps more importantly, the clergy more rarely served as plaintiffs in these suits. In many cases, the suits were brought by the lay impropriators who had purchased the right to tithes once collected by monastic rectors. In other cases, tithe suits were prosecuted by the collectors employed by clerics to deal with the difficult work of managing, gathering, and selling the tithe products. Though ministers owned the tithe, they often outsourced its collection. For a cut of the profits, tithe farmers would deal with all complications, including the messy business of conflict and litigation. Tithe farmers could also be employed by lay impropriators, who similarly contracted out their gathering. At times, this resulted in cases of a layman (the tithe farmer) prosecuting another layman (the parishioner) on behalf of a third laymen (the impropriator) – all over the clerical tenth. Laity dominated the prosecution of tithe cases, in some places making up nearly two-thirds of such litigation.[129] In this, as in so many other areas of the Elizabethan church, a strong lay influence on procedure and institution flourished.[130]

Despite the laicization of a good portion of the tithe business, it would be a mistake to characterize the tithes as secular. As discussed earlier, there is little evidence of significant avoidance of tithe on doctrinal, rather than practical, lines. The surge in tithe dispute had far less to do with religious protest and far more to do with institutional and economic concerns. And yet, this did not render tithes a secular concern. Those involved may have been laity: lay rectors, lay farmers, lay defendants. But there was an understanding that the purpose of tithing was, in the end, to support the ministry. And it is clear that tithe payment provoked expectations of clerical provision. The parishes of Elizabethan England felt that they should get what they paid for: a clergy member who discharged his obligations.

This was a complaint heard amongst the godly. Their primary grievance against tithes was, of course, their insufficiency to provide a proper preaching ministry. As one of the bills written during the final presbyterian push of the 1586 parliament plainly argued, "it is not to be looked for that all Churches should be furnished with learned ministers except a sufficient and competent living be provided for [their] maintenance."[131] Historians have focused on this argument, and excellent, careful studies have been produced to prove the puritans right or wrong.[132] Less well noticed, though, was a godly lay complaint: that parishioners were being cheated by paying tithes to bad ministers. One of the petitions drummed up in preparation for this contentious parliament argued that livings were sufficient, but the ministry was not. "We allow so much and receive so little," the godly Cornishmen complained. For these protestors, it was not that the livings were inadequate but that tithes had to be paid whatever the quality of the clergy. Parishioners still had to pay negligent ministers: "the poor labourer must pay the tithe of his hands, the servant of his wages, the wife of her eggs, or else no sacrament can be had at their hands."[133] In their eyes, good wages should result in good ministry.

If the expectations of the godly were unusually high, the *idea* of an expectation itself was not unusual. Take the case of the churchwardens of St Martin's in Beverley, for instance. By 1592, they had reached the end of their tolerance for the vicar of the parish, Thomas Utie.[134] Utie had refused his ceremonial duties: "to bury their dead, & Christen their Children, & to marry such persons as were to be married." The core rites of the church, those that marked the life cycle and built a community, were disregarded by Utie. Most egregiously, he had left a young child unburied, forcing the child's father "to make sure to Mr Mayor of Beverly to get some minister to bury it." Furious, the churchwardens sued their vicar in the Consistory Court of York for neglect of duty and benefice. Utie's refusal to perform services had absolutely nothing to do with doctrine, however, and everything to do with structure (and a fair share of greed). The case was an administrative labyrinth, complicated by the tangled repercussions of the Reformation. Utie was technically vicar of St Mary's, which in the fourteenth century had been annexed to the altar of St Martin's, which in turn was attached to the collegiate church of St John's.[135] St Martin's had served as a de facto parish church in the late-medieval era but had been torn down in the years following the Reformation, leaving St Mary's the recipient of the dues and duties of the former St Martin's. Thus, to be precise, the churchwardens wished Utie to bury not the parishioners of St Mary's, but those of the former St Martin's – in the grounds of the still-standing St John's. It was this sort of snarled chain of service and command that was the practical parochial legacy of the English Reformation. Utie claimed that he had no responsibility to provide services in the parish. He was happy to do so at St Mary's, but St Martin's was not his responsibility.

In the churchwardens' eyes, however, the matter was clear: Utie received the tithes, and thus he ought to perform the duties. Just as parishioners had a duty to pay for fabric repairs to the place where they worshipped, the receipt of tithes created another kind of obligation, that of the cleric to his congregation. As one witness put it: "that he the said Thomas Utie being vicar of St Mary's … should say divine service, minister the sacraments, bury the dead, christen the children & discharge all other ecclesiastical rites to & for thinhabitantes & parishioners of St Martin aforesaid … And this examinate for his part … hath in that Consideration yearly paid unto the said Mr Utie or some of his servants or deputies the tithes of his kyne [cow], hens, & garths within the same parish of St. Martin & he hath seen diverse other his neighbours of the same parish pay for the like tithes to the said Mr Uties use for the Considerations aforesaid."[136]

The parishioners paid their vicar with their tithes, and they expected services and ceremonies in return. Tithes may have been paid to "servants or deputies" – or farmers or impropriators – but they were meant to maintain the church both clerically and ceremonially. If Utie would receive the stipend, he had to perform his duty. Technicalities about administration paled next to this clear moral imperative. This was one of those rare tithe suits brought all the way to sentence: the churchwardens won.

Thus, the payment of tithes generated lay expectations of clerical service. They created a contractual relationship between minister and parishioner, with the latter expecting the services of the former. This was perfectly normal in early modern contract theory (indeed, in any contract theory). But what made tithes different, of course, was that the services being demanded were far from secular. Instead, they were religious rites that were imbued with a distinctly reformed doctrine. The eucharist that the churchwardens of Beverley explicitly demanded, as we will see in the next chapter, rejected the real presence of Christ *and* reinforced the message of the queen as a divinely inspired monarch. These sermons, sacraments, and ceremonies were not only rituals of community or even of personal salvation, but were also methods of inculcating reformed theology and belief in their parishioners. The payment of tithes and the expectations generated by such payments bound parishioners ever closer with both the institution and the doctrines of a Protestant church in England.

Impropriations: An Overview

The encroachment of the laity into the ownership of tithes – the impropriations – created perhaps the most contentious aspect of Elizabethan ecclesiastical finance. Here, too, the problems and debates of the Elizabethan church were rooted in the decisions of the early Reformation. With the monastic manorial land sales of the Dissolution came the selling and reselling of those rectorial tithes that had once been appropriated to the monasteries. The scale of this enterprise was enormous: on the eve of the Dissolution, around 3,300 of roughly 9,000 parishes were appropriated to monasteries; by the end of the Elizabethan era, the number of impropriated benefices had reached nearly 3,850.[137] Thus, a large portion of tithes paid by English parishioners were diverted not to the ministry, or even to the lessees of the clerical property, but directly to members of the laity.

Such a practice has been condemned both in contemporary literature and in current historiography. Impropriations were censured both by centrist and evangelical figures in the Elizabethan church. As with tithe practice more generally, impropriations were especially singled out by Victorians engaged in debates over tithe reform.[138] More recent criticism has largely followed Christopher Hill, who placed impropriations at the heart of the *Economic Problems of the Church*.[139] Hill argued that impropriated tithes siphoned crucial resources away from the ministry and fundamentally weakened the English church, describing a church rapidly degenerating in its fabric and foundation as a result of impropriatory greed. Such an argument must be taken seriously. The ownership of such a vast amount of church property by the laity *did* have a profound impact on both the economic and social dimensions of the Elizabethan church. But things were far more complicated, and far more nuanced, than the gloomy picture of rapacious laity suggests. In fact, it is apparent that impropriators on the whole did tend to their parishes. And while the critics were no doubt correct that ministerial livings would have prospered without impropriated tithes, there was an unexpected consequence to their continuance. Impropriation tied lay interest to the fate of the church far more closely than ever before.

Impropriations became a key line in evangelical critiques of the Elizabethan church. These attacks sprung in large part from practical theological concerns: if funds were leeched away from spiritual livings to fill the coffers of the laity, they argued, these benefices could not attract the quality of minister needed to enact a true Reformation. Nearly every major evangelical minister gave a sermon or wrote a tract denouncing impropriations. Edward Dering, in a sermon preached before the queen in 1569, decried impropriations as "abominations" that had "defiled" benefices.[140] Dudley Fenner warned that, if these "sacrileges of Abbeys" were not reformed, those who "stand with this provision, shall be guilty of the blood of all them that perish through the default of teaching."[141] John Field's *Admonition to the Parliament* demanded that impropriations be removed to reform the church's "deformities."[142] Anthony Gilby called impropriations "wicked," "evil," and "Popish."[143] Arthur Dent painted them as the creations of the "filthy villains" of religious houses who had "devoured all the fat morsels every where" by getting "the church-livings into their hands: they first made impropriations."[144] In a 1589 sermon that may have forced him to move across the country to Bristol due to its vehemence, Norwich's William Burton exclaimed "now many congregations will hardly maintain one good preacher of the gospel. And no marvel, for then there were too many foolish bees that brought al their honey into the popes hive, and now we have too many drones that suck all the honey out of the churches hive: nay now we have too many horseleeches, which always cry give, give."[145]

A rhetorical success, impropriation reform remained a legislative failure. As early as 1563, speeches in parliament denounced the ill-effects of impropriated livings. The Speaker of the House himself, Thomas Williams, decried abuses of impropriations, arguing that "The universities are decayed, and great market towns and others without either school or preacher," while "the poor vicar hath but only £20, and the rest, being no small sum, is impropriate."[146] A parliamentary campaign against impropriations continued in some earnest for the first half of Elizabeth's reign. At least three separate bills attempting to reform the impropriation system were drafted in this period: a "Bill for Reformation of the abuse that cometh by impropriations" in 1563; an "Article for an Act in Parliament, touching Impropriations" in 1572; and "Articles for an Act of Parliament touching impropriations" in 1576.[147] As with most legislation bent on reforming the church in an evangelical or presbyterian manner, none of these bills were passed into law.[148]

Impropriation reforms were also bundled in omnibus evangelical bills. The notoriously presbyterian "Bill and Book" legislation brought by Anthony Cope in 1586, for example, suggested an end to lay control of tithing as part and parcel of the complete dismantling of "the Queens supreme authority & government ecclesiastical."[149] Opposition speeches in parliament focused closely on the implications of impropriation reform, especially as couched in such radical legislation. The three speakers marshalled by the crown to contest Cope's bill were a testament to the overwhelming hostility to impropriation reform: Christopher Hatton, Lord Chancellor, queen's favourite, and a religious conservative, whose speech was effectively ghost-written by the arch-orthodox Richard Bancroft; Anthony Mildmay, Chancellor of the Exchequer and noted evangelical; and Thomas Egerton, Solicitor General and frequent prosecutor of recusants.[150] A short analysis of the rhetoric used in these speeches demonstrates the main impediments to any sort of impropriation reform: a potent entropic combination of economic interests, state power, and religious factionalism.

The overwhelming and obvious obstacle to impropriation reform was the sheer volume of economic interests opposed to any alteration of the status quo. Impropriated tithes, like all monastic property, had been sold and resold in the years since the Dissolution, long since becoming a cornerstone of family estates and economics.[151] Furthermore, thousands of people who did not own the tithes were heavily invested in their right to tithes; the prevalence of tithe farmers and rectorial lessees extended the economic influence of these impropriated benefices. Impropriations and their leases were part of a system too entrenched and entangled in the English economy for reform to be considered seriously.

Indeed, the last large-scale economic transformation of the country – the dissolution of the monasteries – had succeeded politically in large part due to the very same propertied interests challenged by reform. Not even Mary, who was less than overly politic in matters of religion, had seriously ventured to annex former monastic property.[152] As Hatton argued in his speech, those who sought to increase clerical salaries by revoking impropriated tithes undermined the estates of many in the political class: "for the enriching of them selves, they labor … to impoverish us."[153] The connection of economic interest and opposition to reform was not unique to Hatton. Some dozen years earlier, when trying to explain lack of progress in increasing clerical salaries, John

Whitgift had written, "That this was a certain and sure principle, that the temporality would not lose one jot of their commodity in any respect, to better the livings of the church."[154]

Both lay and ecclesiastical investment in impropriations was so significant as to render any scheme of elimination untenable. In addition to extensive holdings by the crown and by members of gentry, rectorial tithes were held in great number by the episcopate itself; the province of York, for instance, collected over a quarter of its income from rectories at the beginning of Elizabeth's reign.[155] Such a proportion had only increased following the laws of 1 Eliz., c. 19, which had allowed the crown to exchange its own rectorial holdings for any episcopal estates held by a unoccupied see.[156] John Bridges, dean of Salisbury and stalwart defender of Elizabethan orthodoxy, answered the presbyterian call for an end of impropriations, arguing that the end of impropriations would threaten the economic security of both church and secular society: "Whereby not only Bishoprics, Colleges, Cathedral churches, and Hospitals, but all the estates, even the highest and all in civil policy (under pretense of reforming the church and dividing the church livings) might be called in the compass of this new division … therefore the devise of this division may not be attempted, without the incurring greater inconvenience than our brethren would shun."[157] To supplement the income of the parochial ministry, many of the most powerful lay and clerical officials would suffer deep financial injury.

The economic arguments against impropriations reform did not, however, rest entirely on personal interest. Opponents argued that larger issues were at stake, including a burgeoning sense of property rights and the larger security of the state. When Hatton told parliament that impropriation reform "toucheth our inheritances," he was pointing not simply to individual economies but to the larger tenets of property law.[158] Proposals to seize tithable income were, at their heart, a radical restructuring of property. Such restructuring, some argued, was entirely illegitimate. As Bridges wrote of these proposals, "which to be done without the owners good wills, that peradventure also bought it with their money, or by exchange with the Prince for other lands, by what title should we term this restoring?"[159]

All three parliamentary speakers pointed also to the crippling effect that such reforms would have on the crown. Egerton noted that the proposal meant "The Queens revenues … shall be decayed and taken from hir."[160] Hatton argued that "her majesties strength standeth very much upon her revenues … Now what a loss … if as hath been said, all her impropriations should be taken from her."[161] The stakes for undermining the state were enormous and pressing, especially from an international standpoint: fears of Catholic plots were rising across the country; Mary, Queen of Scots, had been executed not a month earlier; and the worry over the threat posed by the Spanish was quickly building. Undermining the crown at such a crucial juncture was self-destructive. After all, as Mildmay plainly put it, "we live here under a Christian Princess."[162] Impropriation reform, he argued, would cause an erosion of state economic power that could ultimately backfire; those who disliked the rule of Elizabeth certainly would like the rule of a Catholic monarch far less. This may have been baldly cynical xenophobic rhetoric, but in the context of a sharpening international political crisis, it remained compelling logic.

The final nail in the coffin of impropriation reform was its fundamental association with radical religion. An awareness of the weaknesses of the Elizabethan church was widespread – after all, even such defenders as Whitgift himself had bemoaned the deleterious effects of impropriated tithes – but, as anti-reformists argued, reclamation of impropriations was merely part of a larger project of radical reform. Presbyterians of the 1570s had been explicit about just such a connection. Field's *Admonition* sought the elimination of impropriations in order to free parishes to choose their own minister: "Your wisdoms have to remove Advowsons, Patronages, Impropriations, and Bishops authority … and to bring in that old and true election, which was accustomed to bee made by the congregation."[163] This connection tainted all proposals for impropriation reform, at least in the eyes of episcopal defenders. Whitgift was deeply suspicious of calls for tithe reform, which he thought cloaked the truly destructive intent of its presbyterian backers. Though he felt that impropriated tithes encouraged some abuses, he thought the status quo a necessary evil: "And therefore his judgment was, to keep that they had; for better they should not be; they might be worse; and that he thought by many was intended."[164] As time went on, he became even more explicit in his condemnation of these proposals. As he put it, "he feared, lest under the pretense of reforming the one, the dissolution and utter undoing of all the other would be sought for. Which, he added, would be the ruin of the church at last, the fall of religion, and the decay of learning."[165] It is tempting to think of this as merely a rhetorical device to protect vested economic interests, but the actions of the religious radicals themselves confirmed Whitgift's suspicions. By centring impropriation reform in virulently anti-episcopal legislation like the Bill and Book, they ensured that even potentially sympathetic evangelicals like Mildmay would reject any overhaul of the system.

Complaints against impropriations were not new; they echoed complaints against monastic appropriations made decades before dissolution.[166] And yet, as the debate around Cope's bill makes clear, the stakes of this debate were higher and more sharply defined in the Elizabethan church than in pre-Reformation years. Both supporters and opponents of impropriation reform argued that they were trying to preserve and protect the Protestant church in England. For the reformers, impropriations stood in the way of a learned and pure church, impoverishing the ministry and undermining the development of a godlier England. Anti-reformers, while often conceding the faults of the Elizabethan ministry, argued that impropriations were part of the larger hierarchy of social and religious order; attempts at further reform, they argued, were part and parcel of a dangerous radicalism that threatened the security of the church and of England itself. Here again, then, the Elizabethan attempts to enforce continuities with the early Reformation came into conflict with attempts to finish a "half-started" Reformation.

With the legislation going nowhere, impropriations remained a way of life in the Elizabethan parish. On the whole, the basic economic complaints of the evangelicals were warranted. To be certain, from the time of the Dissolution vicarages had been generally worth less than rectories, with the stripping of the great tithes having a significant financial impact. Jeremy Collier's summary of the Henrician valuation of church property, the 1534 *Valor Ecclesiasticus*, gives a useful overview of the situation at the end of the period of monastic appropriations.[167] Of the 8,803 parishes, around two-thirds were rectories and a third vicarages. Vicarages made up a disproportionate percentage of the poorest parishes, with around 42 per cent valued at under £10. More moderate parishes – those worth between £10 and £20 – were represented almost exactly proportionally. The wealthiest parishes, however, were almost exclusively rectories: rectories composed 76 per cent of parishes worth between £30 and £40, and 80 per cent of those worth over £40.[168] It is difficult to make iron-clad conclusions based on these figures; as historians have noted, the *Valor* does not take into account clerical tithe leases (resulting in diminished returns) or pluralities.[169] Nor do these valuations account for ways in which pre-Reformation clerical income could be supplemented, such as fees for sacramental services.[170] Nevertheless, it is clear that impropriated benefices were, on the whole, less valuable livings for their clerical incumbents.

Tracing the values of benefices into the Elizabethan period is difficult and inexact. Though reports were commissioned on the wealth of high ecclesiastical officials, no survey equivalent to the *Valor* was made during Elizabeth's reign.[171] Indeed, the *Valor* remained the basis for many valuations well after changes in agricultural practice, ecclesiastical structure, and inflation rendered its sums useless. For example, a valuation of the Diocese of Norwich commissioned in the 1580s is, upon closer inspection, identical to the valuations made a half-century earlier.[172] Though it is tempting to use larger surveys, like those conducted by godly ministers in 1586, these present their own problems.[173] Leaving aside the political biases of the authors, who were apt to judge their fellow ministers harshly, there seemed to be a general state of ignorance, or at least confusion, about the worth of benefices; as the Berkshire ministers wrote, "The value of each of the benefices before named from the beginning may be other wise, for in this behalf we have nothing but by conjecture."[174] Nevertheless, some general observations can be sketched. The economic disparity of rectories and vicarages generally continued into the Elizabethan period and may indeed have grown slightly; while the value of the livings, on the whole, matched or exceeded the rapid inflation of the sixteenth century, vicarages' worth generally grew at a slower rate on average than did those of rectories.[175] Importantly, though, the poorer benefices of the Elizabethan church were also those that had been poorer in the pre-Reformation years. The Elizabethan church did not so much see an expansion of clerical poverty as an entrenchment of earlier economic realities.[176]

The image of a rapacious laity happy to gut their impropriated benefices of desperately needed funds ran throughout evangelical literature. This trope has been picked up by modern historians, especially those who relied most heavily on printed and pamphlet literature. This is, of course, most true in the case of Christopher Hill, whose magisterial work on ecclesiastical finance features relatively little in the way of actual archival economic evaluation. Despite this, the power of Hill's analysis has successfully dominated the literature of the past fifty years. However, in order to truly understand the relationship between rector and church, we must turn away from the pamphlets and toward the lived reality of the Elizabethan parish.

The most visible sign of rectorial influence on the parish lay in the upkeep of the chancel, the area of the church once considered most holy, and thus funded by the great tithes of the church. With the advent of the reformed services and a new focus on a communion table in the nave of the church, the relative spiritual and ceremonial significance of the chancel had declined. Nevertheless, like so much of Elizabethan ecclesiastical property law, the pre-Reformation traditions stood, and the liability for chancel upkeep remained the responsibility of the rector.[177] If in reality lay impropriators were roundly neglecting their ecclesiastical responsibilities, one would expect chancels to be largely dilapidated, especially in areas such as Yorkshire, where impropriated benefices were plentiful.

At first glance, this is indeed the situation. Every visitation includes entries that bespeak wholesale neglect of church fabric by the rectors. The churchwardens of Kirkby Moorside in Yorkshire complained in 1575 that "the chancel is in great ruin and decay (and hath bene so these vij years) both in the walls, glass windows and leads thereof; and it hath bene often complained upon and no redress had."[178] The same visitation found the parish church of Adwicke-by-the-Street with "their chancel and high choir … in ruin and decay (the Queen's Majesty being patronne) so that divine service cannot be said in it, nor the Communion there ministered for danger of falling down upon their heads."[179] Sparham had a chancel so decayed in 1578 that "rain come in."[180] The chancel of Thirling in Norfolk was described as being "in very great decay of the Roof and glazing and also the seats therein are decayed, so that it lieth like a dovehouse."[181] It is clear that some churches suffered greatly from the negligence of their rectors. Compelled to come to church, parishioners would have to sit in churches without windows, with crumbling walls, subject to the whims of wind and rain and even the occasional bird.

And yet, to a remarkable degree, lay impropriators provided for the material needs of their parishes. Taking a more comprehensive view, the picture is far less extreme than anecdotal evidence implies. Of the 506 parishes and chapelries reporting in Archbishop Grindal's

1575 visitation of the province of York, only 14.8 per cent presented their chancels in any sort of decay.[182] Similar figures can be gleaned from the 1587 visitation of the archdeaconry of Nottingham (14.6 per cent), the 1594 episcopal visitation of Somerset (9.5 per cent), and the 1597 visitation of the diocese of Norwich (12.1 per cent).[183] The relative rate of chancel dilapidation remained strikingly stable in the last thirty years of Elizabeth's reign. In the archdeaconry of Cleveland, a reasonable sample of Yorkshire parishes, the rate of presentment remained relatively steady throughout the Elizabethan period: fifteen presentments were made in 1578; thirteen in 1590; nine in 1595; and twelve in 1600.[184] Larger surveys of Yorkshire, although spottier in their archival survival, point to a similar steadiness. J.R. Purvis's analysis of Yorkshire visitations shows a dilapidation rate of 15.6 per cent in 1586 and 14.3 per cent in 1594.[185] Perfection, these parish churches were not. Somewhere between 10 and 15 per cent of them seem to have been in some way damaged. But even so, these figures suggest a situation far from the disastrous picture painted by Elizabethan controversialists. It is easier to see when the numbers are reversed: 85 to 90 per cent of chancels were in good repair.

Indeed, even these relatively low rates of deterioration can be qualified. Visitations reported various levels of decay, from the ruinous examples given earlier to far more mundane presentments for minor dilapidations. These less serious dilapidations are often presented generically: "in some decay" or "a little decayed." In other entries, though, the disrepair is more specific. Presentments were made because the chancel was "in some little decay in the tiles" or "not decently whited"; in other cases it was the pavement that was "to be amended."[186] Of particular trouble were the windows, constantly broken by the wind or by storms; dozens of chancels were presented for "want of glazing" or windows "slightly in decay."[187] While it would be unwise to read too closely into the descriptions of chancel dilapidations given in visitations – most of which simply record the chancel as "decayed" – it is possible to get a rough sense of the relative severity of their disrepair. While many presentments are generic, the direst are often qualified as being in "great decay" or as "ruinous." As a whole, cases of severe neglect are quite rare. Of those Cleveland chancels reported in 1575 as dilapidated, for example, only five are listed in great decay: a mere 3.8 per cent of all parishes.[188] In the archdeaconry of Norwich in 1597, only thirteen parishes were presented for ruinous chancels, or 4.9 per cent of all parishes.[189] Only a small minority of impropriators neglected their duties.

The kind of grasping greed bemoaned by godly ministers and contemporary historians alike was certainly present in the Elizabethan impropriator. Nevertheless, rectors seem to have been relatively responsive to church maintenance. While some chancels were left in neglect over the course of a long period, most were fixed by the time of the next visitation. The deanery of Sparham in Norfolk illustrates this case nicely. In the episcopal visitation of 1593, five parishes were reported for chancel dilapidations. Of these, three were minor: Foulsham was "not sufficiently repaired," Sparham's chancel windows "want some glasinge," and Little Witchingham was simply listed as having decayed windows. Two, though, were in far worse repair, with Wood Norton described as "very ruinous" and Thurning as in "very great decay."[190] Four years later, in the next episcopal visitation, only one of the presentments was repeated. Thurning was reported, ironically enough, for the mess created by construction: "The Chancel is very undecent within both for want of whiting and also filthy with dirt & stones ever since it was mended."[191] The cold, whipping winds of north Norfolk worked their worst on the deanery of Sparham, and in the 1603 archidiaconal visitation, four of the six chancels presented for decay were repeat offenders, having been reported for disrepair at some point over the previous decade. On the surface, it looks like neglect; upon closer inspection, it was more probably the grinding reality of maintaining public buildings. Of these four, only one, the parish church of Brandiston, seems to have been suffering from dilapidations that had remained stubbornly unrepaired. The others were presented not for failing to mend an old problem but instead for new damages. The parish of Haveringland, for instance, had the earlier presentment dismissed by the courts upon proof of window repair; six years later, the windows had broken once again.[192] It was a constant struggle.

Indeed, evidence of active repair was often noted by the church courts. The churchwardens of Halifax presented that "the church and chancel are something in decay, but are begun to be furnished."[193] In Farnham, Cheshire, the visitation's scribe commented that "the chancel is somewhat decayed but preparation is made for repair of it."[194] The report made by the parishioners of Little Bytham indicated that "by order taken with the parishioners and with Mr Wymberley my l. Bishop of Lincoln his farmer of the parsonage a speedy repair will be had, the same being already in hand."[195] Though the chancel in Hillfarrance needed its tiles to be repaired, the visitation book recorded that the fault "through the late tempestuous weather wants covering, but they say it shall be repaired forthwith."[196] Impropriators, or their agents, were often active in parochial restorations.

Such repair could be quite expensive. As the rector of Great Ryburgh, Norfolk, testified, "I have also glazed at mine own proper cost & charge all the windows in the Chancel. Which are in number v & those very large & great, which did cost me with the scripture written within the said Chancels walls more than xx *li*."[197] Leonard Pilkington, parson of Middleton-in-Teesdale, Durham, petitioned the crown for building supplies to supplement his own expenses laid out to repair the "chancel off that kirk, which cost me at the point of 40 *l* at one time."[198] Indeed, in cases where chancels were deeply decayed, the cost of reconstruction could outstrip the profits yielded by the benefice. Natural disasters or the neglect of previous rectors could lead to costs totalling several years' income. Even the regular upkeep of a chancel reduced the net profit of an impropriated rectory. A rare account of annual chancel repairs illustrates standard costs for upkeep: "paid for two hundred of tyle or slate," 3s 4d; "for 16th sacks of Lyme," 6s 8d; "to the Taylor for viijth days work Laying the tyle," 7s; "paid to one that served the tailor for viij days," 3s 6d. With additional minor repairs made for the windows, the pavement, and other areas of the chancel, the bill submitted for compensation was almost 53s.[199] Such upkeep could easily consume a substantial portion of the income.

None of this is to say that chancel disrepair was not a real problem for the Elizabethan church. As noted above, chancels could be decayed to the point of danger for the congregation; even in places with far less damage, a deteriorated chancel was hardly a symbol of the kind of devotion hoped for by English reformers. And there were indeed cases of serious neglect, such as in the coastal parish of Owthorne in the East Riding, which was presented in 1567 for decay; 1591 for decay; 1596 "utter ruin and decay, like to fall and endanger the body of the church"; and 1600, again for decay.[200] However potent the anecdotes, it was not the reality.[201] As we have seen, rectors tended to care for their parishes. If the value of impropriate rectories were merely in their rents – if this were merely a matter of gross self-interest – we might expect a far higher degree of dilapidation than the records actually reflect. That the rate of dilapidation was so low, especially in the face of the real expense that repairs required, indicates that greed was held in check either by internal or external compulsion.

Internally, rectors could be motivated by their own religious impulses. The personal confessional proclivities of patrons could strongly influence their choices of ministers.[202] Impropriated benefices, with their concomitant control of clerical purse strings, were particularly attractive. In some cases, rectorial tithes were sought precisely to advance the impropriators' personal religious interests. The notably evangelical Henry Hastings, fifth earl of Huntingdon, took a twenty-one-year lease of Whitby's rectory for precisely such a purpose: the lease was made "to the intent that a godly learned and sufficient preacher may continue to be there resident during the time and term aforesaid."[203] Though ideologically opposed to impropriated benefices, many godly patrons saw no need to cut off their noses to spite their faces; they too would take impropriated rectories, if only to prevent them falling into the hands of less assiduous patrons.

Externally, the expansion of the visitation system, with its increased regularity, organization, and diligence, resulted in lay impropriators being held in greater accountability by the state church. Failure to repair the chancel would bring one into the orbit of the ecclesiastical courts, with all their attendant costs, inconvenience, and power of moral discipline. If the property rights to a rectory were transferred by sale or by death, the new rector could sue for the costs of any dilapidations, as well as for the court fees engendered by the suit.[204] Moreover, even if one did not own a rectory oneself, good stewardship of the parish might have economic ramifications. The rights to continue to lease or farm a rectory, for example, could be influenced by evidence of having taken good care of the church fabric during a past lease. The lessees of the parsonage of Astonfield, Staffordshire, for example, requested a renewal of their lease based partly upon the "great sums of money lately expended by them in repair of the chancel."[205] Upkeep of a chancel and relative care for a parish's incumbent could help to ensure the continuance of profitable leases, and the economic and institutional consequences for dilapidations tempered the wisdom of squeezing all possible profit from a rectory.

In terms of the continuing stability of the church, the involvement of lay rectors mattered. It is true that the reformed ministry suffered from the short-term effects of having potential clerical income diverted to the laity; while godly complaints of clerical poverty were perhaps overstated, the extra income would certainly have made ministry a more remunerative profession and might have encouraged better-educated clergy to join poorer or more rural parishes (what reception they would have found is left to speculation). However, what undermined clerical capital may in fact have bolstered the security of the church more generally. Monied interests were making a serious investment in the Elizabethan church, both literally and, to an increasing extent, figuratively. Gentry, nobility, merchants, guildsmen, ambitious yeoman farmers, land speculators, and all others involved in the leasing and farming of church property had new obligations to church property. Such involvement has long been recognized by cultural historians, who point to monuments and church iconography as evidence of the construction of a godly lay identity flourishing by the later Elizabethan period.[206] Impropriations, too, were a mechanism that could tie the "better sort" to the church. Just as the sale of monastic property had put a serious dent in the Marian efforts to resurrect Catholic infrastructure, the continuance of impropriation rights under Elizabeth helped to cement a relationship between economic and religious interests. There was a vested financial interest in maintaining reformed English confessional stability.

Impropriations may have stood in the way of a fully reformed church. The diversion of income from the preaching ministry remained the core complaint of the evangelical pamphleteers throughout the Elizabethan period. And yet, the system of impropriated tithes tied together the fortunes of the church and the landed laity. That such economic interest may have fortified support for the church is recognized.[207] But the extent to which the practical responsibilities of these lay rectors were taken seriously has been vastly undervalued.[208] Some certainly did exploit the system of impropriations for their economic gain and did so at the expense of the parish. The great majority, however, remained largely diligent in their maintenance of church fabric. Fighting a constant battle against the depredations of nature and the decay of ancient buildings, these lay rectors provided for the physical needs of their churches to a remarkable level. Thus, the continuities of rectorial tithing preserved by the Elizabethan church and state allowed for an ever-deeper weaving of the English church and the wealthier segments of the laity, both on a macroeconomic and a minutely practical scale.

Conclusion

At its core, the Elizabethan church was in relatively good repair. The destruction and iconoclasm of the mid-sixteenth century – a pattern certainly present in the early years following the settlement – gave way to a program of repair that was at once unglamorous and fundamental to the health of the church. In the space opened up by the Reformation's rents in the social and physical fabric of the parish, new bonds between church, state, and society were knit. For, if the Reformation was destructive, it left in its wake huge opportunities for development, expansion, and a *new* kind of creation.

Despite the gloomy reports of the tract writers and the equally gloomy perspective of much modern historiography, the economic realities of the Elizabethan church were far from a disaster. To be sure, there were real problems: an underfunded ministry, a lack of clerical control of ecclesiastical income, and in some places serious material dilapidations. On the whole, though, the church coped rather well. If underfunded, the ministry was nevertheless of a far higher standard than in pre-Reformation years; if the clergy lacked control of finances, the vast majority of lay impropriators fulfilled the basic duties they were assigned; if dilapidations occurred, they were for the most part fixed quickly and effectively through the combined effort of rector and parish. There was much to be admonished and much to be disparaged, but these problems were both acknowledged and managed. That the church failed to live up to the expectations of its puritan critics is far from a surprise, and modern historians must ask themselves to what standard they are holding the Elizabethan parish. If the parish was far from ideal, it was also far from broken.[209]

Indeed, it was contention, not consensus, that drove much of the Elizabethan continuity in ecclesiastical economic policy. Impropriations, for example, were widely contested both in print and in parliament. Paradoxically, however, it was often this very debate that led to the cementing of the status quo. Desperate to avoid instability that could threaten both the crown and the church, ecclesiastical officials and the queen herself routinely rejected calls for economic reform. Whether these efforts might have been more successful if not tied to more radical rhetoric is questionable; a host of other interests, including the economic interests of many members of parliament, were closely aligned with a continuation of these compromises. Nevertheless, the connection between reform and radicalism left such proposals dead in the water. The rising debate made constancy a more appealing option, not a less appealing one.

This continuity brought its own problems. Many of the struggles the Elizabethan church faced were a long-standing legacy of the early Reformation. Compromises made in the first tumultuous decades of religious change fundamentally shaped the parameters of the late sixteenth century. This was true practically as much as spiritually. The political and economic decision to transfer tithe rights from religious houses to the impropriators reworked structures of power, placing much of the responsibility for the church's economic security on the laity. And while the reliance on custom and the continuation of pre-Reformation tithe exemptions may have promoted stability in the short term, it set the stage for extensive legal wrangling. This was particularly true as the old economic models of the early sixteenth century gave way to the new economic realities of the late-Elizabethan period. New strains were placed on the laity by rapid inflation, a demographic explosion, and a sharpening economy. The growing social stratification, fuelled at least in part by the seismic shifts in the property market caused by the reallocation of ex-religious land, could engender significant conflict. We have seen the effect of economic pressure on the rise of tithe litigation in the Elizabethan parish, but this was a single symptom of a much larger problem. But these elites could not simply leave the parishes behind. Whether compelled by the church courts, by their ideological beliefs, or by their sense of social status and obligation, they invested in the parishes.

The economic life of the Elizabethan parish demonstrates the increasingly important role played by the laity in the English church. Large swathes of ecclesiastical property were maintained, administrated, and supported by the laity. Both conflict and community tied the laity closer to the inner workings of the church: from the consistory court to the accounting ale, rectors and parishioners alike had an expanded accountability and responsibility for its conservation. In turn, this gave the laity a greater stake and agency in the church. This was a process of laicization and not secularization. The context and the expectations for lay participation in the church were essentially religious: those gathering to collect the church rate were engaging in a new iteration of late-medieval communal piety; tithe payments, whether made to layman or vicar, still financed the ministry and the upkeep of the chancel. Participation may have been compulsory, but in its practice the laity were drawn closer to the church than ever before.

5

Receiving in the Parish

In 1601, Christopher Sutton, the young vicar of Caston in Norfolk, published a book of meditations on the sacrament of the Lord's Supper for his patrons' eldest daughter, Elizabeth Southwell.[1] After several meditations focusing on the spiritual and soteriological virtues of the rite of communion, he wrote, "The fourth effect is to stir up in us the love of God, and our neighbour. Of God, who first loved us, of our neighbour, for his sake that said, He that loveth God, should love his neighbour also."[2] This was a thoroughly Elizabethan sentiment, and Sutton was a thoroughly Elizabethan clergyman. Born just a few years after the Act of Uniformity had passed, he was raised in a conformist mode. His studies in Oxford were deeply coloured by Richard Hooker, to the point that one Victorian described Sutton as Hooker's "younger brother in divine things."[3] What Sutton was describing here – the eucharist as at once an individual connection to God and a collective expression of divine love – was the culmination of forty years of struggle, change, and the long, hard process of stabilization.

By 1601, communion had become perhaps the ultimate action and symbol of conformity to the new state church – but also a symbol of social conformity. The Elizabethan years saw the construction of a rite that twined together godliness, obedience, and community. At its heart, the Elizabethan sacrament was fundamentally an expression of parochial collectivism. Compelled by a state that saw its reception as a tangible sign of orthodoxy and loyalty and by a church that saw its reception as spiritually essential, the Lord's Supper became part of the rhythm of parochial life, a rite that expressed a community of belonging. By the time that Sutton wrote his *Godly Meditations*, the eucharist had become a hallmark of a new, Protestant order in the English parish.[4]

Traditionally, the place of sacraments as a whole within the Elizabethan church has been undervalued, with the rise of ritual conformity placed firmly in the lap of the Laudians of the 1620s and 1630s. Conrad Russell's assertion that "the stress on the sacraments instead of preaching" was the province of a "lonely and often submerged group, not of the mainstream Protestantism of Elizabethan England" is emblematic.[5] More recently, scholars have argued for a broader acceptance of the ceremony in late-Tudor England.[6] Though the historiographies of the English and Continental Reformations remain largely divided, a similar effort to understand the cultural and popular religious effects of the sacrament has developed in the latter as in the former. John Bossy's seminal work on the service of mass as a communal experience in the late-medieval church inspired a host of examinations of popular sacramental practice in the Catholic Church.[7] More recently, historians have turned to a focus on the cultural developments of Protestant ceremony.[8] Though divergent in their conclusions, these texts have sought to undermine the idea of Protestant sacramentology as hollow or secondary to processes of Reformation. These interventions are crucial and persuasive, but in making them, scholars tend to focus on expansive, asynchronous approaches to the sacrament. We come away with the impression of a vital parochial engagement with the eucharist, but we have much less sense as to the development of conformity in the English church, or indeed why it might change over time. Moreover, these newer accounts avoid significant discussions of state intervention or coercion in discussions of the sacrament, painting this enormously charged ceremony as remarkably unpoliticized.

We need, instead, a new way of thinking about this vital ceremony, because it is within a study of the sacrament that we can best understand the full dynamics of the Elizabethan Reformation, where we can truly understand how and why England became a Protestant nation. Here, all the themes of this book are drawn together: the unintended consequences of early compromises; the unexpected continuities with the past; the laicization of church practice; the tensions and connections between local and centre; and, above all, the robust communalism of Elizabethan church life. It is a story of how conformity was built, how it was weaponized, and how it was enforced.

Conformity was born out of the twin desires for stability and salvation: a single standard for religious practice in the moment of the massive upheavals of the Reformation and the ultimate fate of English souls after death. Not everyone involved in the debates over the eucharist cared about each equally, of course. Arch-instrumentalists were particularly concerned with outward signs of loyalty (or at least submission) to the state. Ardent reformers sought to perfect a rite that brought the people closer to God; many, perhaps most, doubted that real conformity was ever close to having been achieved. Elizabethan critics were constantly issuing grave calls about the "backwardness" of religion and disobedience amongst the populace. Historians, reading these sources, meet claims of compliance with a skeptical eye. And yet, record after record, archive after archive, discloses an overwhelming conformity to the Elizabethan sacrament by the last years of the sixteenth century. Churchwardens' accounts, visitations, surveys, token books, Easter lists, censuses: each reveals extensive participation in this central rite of the English church. It was by no means perfect conformity. A segment of the population, whether for reasons of ideology, ability, or temperament, did not accept the sacrament. But that segment was a vanishingly small minority of the population. Their resistance, defiance, or even absence for reasons of practicality rather than principle, is important. It should, and has, been studied and discussed. But it was not the experience of the Elizabethan parish writ large. By 1600, the communal norm was conformity – conformity with the reformed eucharist that so encapsulated the Elizabethan church.

This chapter approaches the question of the eucharist from two different, equally important, angles. The first half explores the pace and shape of sacramental conformity within the Elizabethan church. It examines the blend of the political, the doctrinal, and the social that gave conformity its weight and its meaning, and it traces that conformity over time, finding patterns of behaviour that suggest a fundamental hinge of change in the mid-Elizabethan period. The next section looks to the lived experience of the sacrament in the Elizabethan parish. If the first half of the chapter seeks to establish the fact of conformity, the next asks why exactly the people conformed. Only by placing sacramental reception in the context of financial credit, political allegiance, personal salvation, ideas of neighbourliness, and the construction of community, charity, and reputation can we begin to understand why this change occurred. The pressures placed on the values of neighbourliness and community from *within* the church created a symbiotic relationship between religious and social orthodoxy. When Christopher Sutton wrote of the value of the sacrament in awakening love of one's neighbour, he was pointing to the basic bonds of collective life in the Elizabethan parish. Taking of the sacrament became a sign of being a good Christian *and* a good neighbour – and above all, perhaps, a good English subject.

Prayer-Book Eucharist

The mass was the living, beating heart of late-medieval Catholicism. Nearly everything – the holidays, the music, the gilds, the chantries, the devotionals, the rituals of birth, marriage, and death – radiated out from the divine miracle of transubstantiation, where, for just a moment, the body and blood of Christ lived once again on earth. It inspired the great music of the day, as well as much of the great art, metalwork, and even woodcarving. Corpus Christi celebrations had bloomed since the early fourteenth century, with elaborate masses, cycles of mystery plays, and the procession of the consecrated host through the streets and squares of parishes across the country.

In the years immediately following the split from Rome, the mass was much debated and little changed. Henry VIII was devoted to the mass and resisted any and all attempts at substantial alterations.[9] When Edward came to the throne in 1547, reformers saw a new opportunity to transform the liturgy. England had by this point become a refuge for some of the leading Protestant thinkers on the Continent. Thomas Cranmer personally invited men like Peter Martyr Vermigli and Martin Bucer, asking them to come be "a labourer with us in the harvest of the Lord."[10] Once they arrived, he promptly put them in positions of major institutional power: Peter Martyr took up the Regius Professorship at Oxford, Bucer the same at Cambridge.[11] Cranmer's evangelical, Continental approach was soon turned toward constructing a new service, one in the vernacular that would transform the entire liturgy of the church. The first Edwardian Book of Common Prayer that emerged was a stake to the heart of the traditional mass. The two versions that followed – the more radical Edwardian version in 1552 and the Elizabethan in 1559 – differed in many respects, but they each rejected the pre-Reformation mass in favour of a new eucharistic service. Each edition of the Prayer Book – the Edwardian editions of

1549 and 1552, and the Elizabethan edition of 1559 – reimagined a new, Protestant eucharistic theology and rite. Just what *kind* of Protestant sacrament the English church would embrace changed dramatically from edition to edition, as the politics and participants themselves changed, debated, and rose again. The "chief reason" why the Prayer Book reforms had taken so long, an exhausted Peter Martyr wrote to Heinrich Bullinger in the early Oxford summer of 1552, "was that the subject of the Sacraments stood in the way … A work of so great labour it is to bring back into the church pure truth." But what remained clear, to Peter Martyr as much as to modern historians, was that an essential line had been crossed: "As far as regards transubstantiation, or the real presence … concerning these things there seems to be now no controversy as it regards those who profess the Gospel."[12] While the details of the rite were hotly contested, no one doubted that the rite had fundamentally broken from the past and had been deeply influenced by Continental reform.

The changes were apparent from the very beginning. The eucharistic formula of the 1549 Book of Common Prayer was both radical and conservative, the kind of compromise that satisfied exactly no one. (As Bucer put it in a letter to Cranmer, "both the Divine Scriptures and daily experience teach us, that Satan omits no opportunities of involving in bitter contentions."[13]) Serious breaks were made with the Catholic mass, including the use of the vernacular, communion in both kinds, and absence of elevation of the sacraments. And yet, the overall structure of the mass was retained and the question of the real presence neatly circumvented. Liturgically broad, the formula had the minister utter upon reception, "The body of our Lorde Jesus Christ which was given for thee, preserve thy body and soul unto everlasting life … The blood of our Lord Jesus Christ which was shed for thee, preserve thy body and soul unto everlasting life."[14] The vagueness as to whether the wafer and wine were themselves the body and blood of Christ – that is, whether they had been transubstantiated – was left to the work of an article: "the body" not "this body." Attempting to appeal to Protestants while not antagonizing Catholics, the Book and its formulae were roundly rejected by both.[15]

The most tangible sign of the ensuing fury came in the Prayer Book Rebellion that summer, where the West Country rebels insisted (amongst many other demands) that the mass stay in Latin, that the sacrament be at the high altar for due worship, that communion be of one kind, and that the "Sacrament of the altar but at Easter [be] delivered to the lay people," following the common medieval pattern of sacramental reception but once a year for most of the laity[16] These were demands that the eucharist remain a mystery, a miracle, far away from the earthly and the mundane. It was an imagining of the sacrament as too holy, too otherworldly, for regular lay exposure or consumption. The rebels did not want the new service that was "but like a Christmas game," but the older rhythms of Latin and procession, at once more familiar and more extra-ordinary. Their efforts failed completely.

It was the last gasp of a shuttering world. Three years later, in 1552, a new Book of Common Prayer was issued, and in it even the nods toward Catholic tradition were gone. Here, the Prayer Book was explicitly reformed, maintaining that the eucharist was simply a moment of remembrance, godly but not miraculous. The formulas for reception of both bread and wine insisted upon the symbolic rather than the real, without the subtle slippage of an article. The memorialist, demystified nature of the reformed eucharist was underscored even more heavily in the hasty addition of the "Black Rubric," the result of a clash between Thomas Cranmer and John Knox over the suitability of kneeling during the sacrament. Though it defended traditional kneeling, in line with Cranmer's wishes, the rubric took pains to decry any reminiscences of the medieval mass. Kneeling was "not meant thereby, that any adoration is done, or ought to be done, either unto the Sacramental bread or wine … or unto any real and essential presence there being, of Christ's natural flesh and blood … [which] remain still in their very natural substances, and therefore may not be adored."[17] To underscore the very earthly nature of this memorial communion, it mandated that the bread was to be a loaf, not a wafer, with the excess of eucharistic supplies given to the curate to supplement his dinner table. A mystery, it was not.

The Elizabethan Prayer Book of 1559 embraced the disconnect between the two Edwardian Prayer Books – and the host of political and theological rifts it encompassed – by creating a pastiche of the two ceremonies. Its formula for communion combined the sacrificial language of the 1549 ceremony with the memorialist language of the reformed 1552 text. The effect was jarring. The doctrinal implications of the ceremony changed suddenly, mid-ceremony, leaping from the rich ambiguity of the former to the clear denial of the real presence in the latter: "The body of our Lorde Jesus Christ, which was given for thee, preserve thy body and soul into everlasting life: and take and eat this in remembrance that Christ died for thee, and feed on him in thy heart by faith, with thanks giving."[18] This was a classic early Elizabethan construction: a compromise, to be sure, but a clearly Protestant one. It was not a radical formulation, but it was a brave one. Unlike the first Edwardian ceremony, the liturgical language made little effort to truly appease Catholic communicants. Its explicit denial of the real presence was untenable in Catholic eyes, satisfying neither the theological experts in Convocation nor, one can imagine, those who shared the perspective of the rebels of the West with their adoration of a miraculous host. What it *did* do, though, was bridge a gap between more conservative Protestant doctrine and the more radical reformers, while also appealing to a Calvinist sacramentalism, thus creating a coalition of Protestants willing to content themselves with the new ceremony.[19]

The appeal of the sacrament to as wide a spectrum of Protestant understanding as possible was important not just on a political level, but also as a symbol of a comity and commonality. Communion as a rite of community was central to the Elizabethan liturgy. This idea was not new; as John Bossy argues, the mass had long been both a religious and a social institution, and public eucharistic services were outlined in the earlier Edwardian Prayer Books. Indeed, the Elizabethan Prayer Book expressed a kind of essentialist social continuity with earlier eucharistic ceremonies.[20] The sacrament was to be given only when a large section of the parish was gathered together, with no service held "except there be a good number to communicate with ye priest."[21] The eucharist was not to be taken as an emblem of individual piety, particularly not one reserved for a priestly class, but rather as part of a group of both laity and clergy expressing a shared commitment to the spiritual and social goals of the Lord's Supper.

As with the earlier reformed service, community was centred throughout the liturgy, with the language of parochial peace and common good running throughout the text. Those partaking in the sacrament were exhorted that "if ye shall perceive your offences to be such, as be not only against God, but also against your neighbours: then ye shall reconcile your selves unto them, ready to make restitution and satisfaction … for other wise the receiving of the Holy Communion doeth nothing else but increase your damnation."[22] Communion without community was not merely useless, but doom. Those who had reconciled properly, in a kind of social repentance, were to take the sacrament "before this congregation here gathered together in his holy name." Those who refused to reconcile, or who refused to communicate, "stand[ing] by as gazers and lookers at them that do communicate, and bee no partakers of the same," were accused of a great unkindness to God Himself.[23]

Rhetoric of the sacrament as a communal undertaking was reinforced by the practical prescriptions for the Order of Communion. First, financial provision for communion supplies was to be provided by the curate and churchwardens, with funds collected from the entire parish.[24] This marked a significant change from the 1549 Prayer Book, in which provision of the bread and wine was to be made by clergy alone, circumventing the involvement of the laity entirely. A change first seen in the reformed 1552 text, this shift of sacramental responsibility to the laity writ large – the churchwardens to assist in gathering and provision, the congregation to fund it – reflected the communal and memorial focus of this new Order of Communion.[25] No longer was this the preserve of a separate, clerical sphere, but instead shared with the laity.

Indeed, the compromises of the 1559 Prayer Book, particularly as they extended to eucharistic practice, were a far more radical act than the traditional historiographical language of tepid *via media* might suggest. At its core, the doctrine of the service, particularly the second half of the eucharistic formula, was consistent with Calvinist – rather than more conservative Protestant – thought. The language of feeding by faith echoes directly Calvin's own formulation, which contains thanks for "this worthy memorial of our redemption wherein thou haste nourished and fed our souls with the body and blood of thy dear son."[26] Even the exhortation to community recalls Calvin's description of the Lord's Supper as a great unifier: "since He has only one body of which he makes us all to be partakers, we must necessarily, by this participation, all become one body."[27] Community here was not simply an expression of collective bodies but of collective souls, a spiritual unity that imitated Christ even as it memorialized Him.

The Elizabethan Prayer Book was shot through with these congruences with Calvin. Ceremonially, though perhaps more conservative than some evangelicals would have liked, it fell in line with the letter, if not the full spirit, of reform. Though the Genevan consistory would insist upon direct participation of the laity in the administration of the sacrament, Calvin's *Institutes of Christian Religion* formally categorized most details of reception – the type of bread, the method of distribution, the office of the dispenser – as *adiaphora*.[28] Some of the godly wing of reformers may have preferred the communion service to use coarse brown bread, received standing. But in fact, the Elizabethan formula was roughly consistent with the *Consensus Tigurinus*, which Calvin and Bullinger had written a decade earlier as the general reformed position on sacramental doctrine. The Elizabethan eucharist was a demonstrably reformed sacrament. Indeed, as John Jewel reassured Peter Martyr during the complicated process of legislating the Prayer Book, "all our articles of religion and doctrine … have not departed in the slightest degree from the confession of Zurich."[29]

No English Catholic had any doubt about this. The insistence upon a vernacular liturgy with communion in both kinds, surrounded by a sermon and delivered with an explicitly memorialist formula, was anathema to their eyes. The vituperative reaction of the still-Catholic Convocation of 1559 to the Elizabethan Prayer Book's Order for communion made it quite clear that anything but the traditional service was unacceptable. They insisted on a service that stressed the doctrine of transubstantiation and an understanding of the host as a "propitiatory sacrifice for the living and the dead."[30] This was an identical position that the Catholic clergy had taken on the second Edwardian Prayer Book; nothing would conciliate except a return to the full traditional Mass.[31] The Elizabethan service was insupportable.

A vocal minority of reformers, both English and Continental, agreed with this assessment. Here, though, the objections were reversed. The ceremony, they claimed, was not nearly pure enough. The use of vestments, the kneeling, and other reminders of an English Catholic past were an abomination to the godliest amongst them, several of whom were already considering refusing ecclesiastical office if forced to wear the "rags of Rome." And yet, the Protestant cause had not been sufficiently established to allow such infighting. Even Continental divines recommended participation in the rite, which they viewed as polluted but not untenable. As Peter Martyr wrote to Thomas Sampson, "I think however that if peace could obtain between the churches of Saxony and our own with respect to doctrine, this sort of garments would never cause a separation; for though we should by no means approve of them, we would bear with them, congratulating ourselves upon having got rid of them."[32] The Elizabethan church, with its general doctrinal harmony with the *Consensus Tigurinus* and its attempts to unite the Protestant cause in the face of ex-Marian opposition, was just the kind of church with which most Continental reformers could ally, if lament.

What this meant, at its core, was that the sacrament was ideologically charged and deeply political. Its reception was not a hollow chamber that could be filled with any doctrinal intent: it was an explicit affirmation of reformed doctrine, not simply an empty gesture of institutional conformity. It was also not optional. Perhaps most importantly, the 1559 Prayer Book mandated compulsory thrice-yearly participation in the Lord's Supper. Annual reception, taught in the late-medieval church, prized by the protestors in the West, and characterized by Calvin as an "invention of the devil" that encouraged complacency, was rejected.[33] Though Calvin would have, no doubt, resisted the requirement of triannual reception as similarly prone to leading toward a rote apathy, this new requirement was a shock to the traditional ritual calendar. The mandating of a public, memorialist, communal ceremony as a more regular feature of the liturgy marked the Elizabethan eucharist as a fundamental break from the kind of conservative Protestantism found in the 1549 Prayer Book. In Elizabethan England, parishioners would be exposed, regularly and routinely, to this clearly Protestant rite. Here, the Elizabethan Prayer Book was once again following in the footsteps of the second, more radical, Edwardian Book. But this time, the Prayer Book's prescriptions were given teeth. Edward's precipitous death had left little time for legislating the sacrament. The 1563 Act of Uniformity, however, codified and legislated mandatory, triannual reception. The sacrament would become not just a memorial of Christ's sacrifice, but a symbol of fidelity to both the queen and her new church – the Lord's Supper as loyalty test. Reception of the eucharist, mandated by Prayer Book and parliamentary statute alike, became a public performance of conformity to the expressly reformed, memorialist ritual *and* to the state that required it. Taking the Lord's Supper in the Elizabethan church was an explicitly political act.

By the mid-1560s, the matter had been settled, at least as far as the Supreme Governor of the church was concerned. And it would stay that way for the next forty years of her reign, throughout which Elizabeth rejected any attempt to reform this liturgy. Those who challenged any aspect of the Prayer Book communion service drew the fire of the crown and of a significant proportion of the episcopacy. Reformers and nonconformists were shouted down, castigated, fined, deprived of their living, even imprisoned. Attempts to legislate changes to the eucharistic rite were met with utter intransigence, including the queen's veto and members of parliament thrown into the Tower.[34] Following John Whitgift's accession as Archbishop of Canterbury in 1583, the clergy was subjected to greater discipline for any variation of the ceremony, and visitations became ever more interested in clergy who sought to alter the service. Such resistance to change was, of course, part of a larger Elizabethan policy that emphasized stability over purity. As she told parliament in no uncertain terms in 1586, following the introduction of the radical plan to transform church governance known as Cope's Book and Bill, "Her Majesty thinkest that though it were granted that some things were amiss in the church … [yet] to make every day new laws … were a means to breed great lightness in her subjects to nourish an unstaid humour in them of seeking still for exchanges."[35]

The official policy of stability reigned, and it became increasingly focused, increasingly predicated, upon conformity with the sacrament. The godly never stopped "seeking still for exchanges." Catholic recusants continued to refuse to take Calvin's Supper. But all this resistance merely encouraged Elizabeth and her increasingly conformist bishops to entrench her commitment to the Prayer Book eucharist. Indeed, it increasingly signalled not merely one's personal faith, but instead loyalty to the crown and fidelity to the church. Orthopraxy became orthodoxy. And the ritual life of the Elizabethan parish fundamentally changed.

Communion in Practice

An Englishman walking into his parish church to take communion on a Whitsunday morning in 1580 would have known exactly what to expect. The rhythms and rites of the church no longer held novelty – they had fallen into a pattern set for nearly two decades, practised over and over, year after year. There may have been changes, here and there. An earnest young curate might have added an extra communion service each month for the particularly pious. A preacher might have recently passed through, invited by parson or patron or even the churchwardens. New pews might have risen up over previously vacant space; the Bible might have been newly purchased or the floors newly washed. But our parishioner could come to the church with expectations, an understanding of the familiar ceremony of which he was about to partake.

Let us imagine our parishioner, perhaps an Englishman born in the tumultuous mid-century years of the Edwardian reforms, walking into his parish church to take communion on that Whitsunday morning. The service would have been instantly familiar to him. Indeed, if he were a young man, he had been preparing for it all his life. Only those who came to the sacrament with at least a basic knowledge of church doctrine could be admitted to receive. The standards for this understanding were simple and commonly known (they were included from the very first Elizabethan visitation): none was to receive "before they can perfectly [say] the Lords prayer, the articles of the faithe, and the x commandments in English."[36] If he had been paying even the slightest attention in his youth, he would be able to perform these with ease. Ministers were enjoined to repeat them to their congregation on a regular basis, and this oration was to be supplemented by parental instruction and the recitation of catechisms. Catechisms were increasingly popular in Elizabethan England, read aloud to the illiterate and read devotedly by those who could.[37] And they were tied intimately to the practice of sacramental reception. One 1580 catechism made this point immediately, with a startingly on-the-nose title: *A breefe catechisme so necessarie and easie to be learned even of the symple sort, that whosoever can not or wyll not attayne to the same, is not to be counted a good Christian much lesse to be admitted to the Supper of the Lorde*. In such texts parishioners learned the rudiments of common Christian principles: the commandments, Christ's sacrifice, the mercy of God. But they also learned a distilled reformed doctrine, which taught that "we are saved by Jesus Christ only, & not by our own works" and "there are two Sacraments, Baptism and the Supper of the Lord."[38] Communion here was an affirmation of faith and fidelity, a touchstone in the uncertainty of life: "In the Supper of the Lorde, I am by the spirit of God assured, that as the bread broken, and the wine poured out be delivered unto me, even so was the body of Christ broken, and his blood shed, as a full recompence to God for my sins."[39]

Preparations for the sacrament, though, did not stop there. Anyone who wanted to receive would first have to clear his or her conscience. This process began in oneself. The method was interior and private, and its records are few and undeniably elite. The most common descriptions come not from spiritual diaries (though some survive) but from printed explorations and exhortations of sacramental preparation. Christopher Sutton enjoined his readers "to become surveyors of our selves, and call a little consistory in our own souls."[40] Those who "presume rashly, negligently, and unadvisedly to receive the holy Sacrament without due examination of themselves," wrote an anonymous pamphleteer in 1580, "eat and drink, not the body of Christ … but their own damnation."[41] This message was not just read, but preached and taught. It is in the records of the surviving sermons that we can best hear the ideal as it might have been preached to our English parishioner – deliberately distributed, intentionally didactic on a broad scale. In 1580, energetic, determined Bishop Cooper of Lincoln wrote a homily that was to be read throughout his entire diocese (or at least those without a licensed preacher) before each communion service. The parishioners assembled were warned "that we ought to be very careful, so to prepare our selves, that we may be worthy guests for that blessed table … we must look unfeignedly into our selves."[42] Bartemius Andrews, preacher at Yarmouth, taught the inhabitants of the city that they could only come to the sacrament with repentance, which could be found only "if I examine and prove my heart, and am truly grieved for my sins, confessing them before God, and forsaking them."[43] Hundreds of miles away in Giggleswick, Yorkshire, the parishioners of Christopher Shute were taught that to receive the grace of God in the sacrament, "first I must consider the grievousness of my sins … secondly, I must try and examine my self whether I have a true faith in the promises of Christ."[44] This was the message heard and repeated throughout the parishes of England, from at least the mid-Elizabethan period on: the sacrament was to follow on the heels of soul-searching.[45]

Notions of self-examination preoccupied the devout.[46] Those obsessed with cataloguing their sins found preparations for the sacrament a particularly acute moment of awareness of their own depravity. Samuel Ward was a bright and sharp, if distractible, graduate student when he began a diary of spiritual self-reflection (and flagellation) in the heady atmosphere of 1590s Cambridge.[47] In June of 1595, he wrote one of his longer entries, castigating himself for "my negligence in preparing myself for the receiving of the Sacrament … [I] Think if thou cannot receive Christ by faith, in the Sacrament … that commeth of my negligence in preparation by prayer."[48] The idea of preparation before the sacrament was not, of course, particularly unique to the Elizabethan church; it recalled, though it fundamentally reshaped, the late-medieval notion of confession and penance before reception.[49] If it was not new, though, it was essential. It changed the sacrament from empty show to true transformation. Some were cynical as to whether this serious preparation ever moved to the wider population. Arthur Dent's sour assessment of the ignorance of English parishioners – "they have a deep insight into earthly things, and doe wholly delight to talk of them … but come once to talk with them of Gods matters … you shall find them the veriest dullards & dunces in the world" – saw Elizabethan capacity for reflection in the most pessimistic terms.[50]

Self-examination, however, was not the end of our parishioner's preparation for receiving the sacrament. From the individual and private, he next had to turn to the communal and public. Clearing one's conscience involved not only reconciliation with God but with one's neighbours. Reception of the sacrament required peaceful relationships within the community, and all were to reconcile disagreements before coming to the table. No less an authority than the actual order of communion service in the Prayer Book required it: "The same order shall the Curate use, with those between whom he perceiveth malice and hatred to reign, not suffering them to be partakers of the lords table, until he know them to be reconciled."[51] By the 1560s, this prescription had made its way into visitation articles, where churchwardens were examined as to "whether any of your ministers doth or hath admitted any notorious sinner or malicious person out of Charitie, without just penance done and reconciliation had, to receive the holy Communion."[52] Communion was clearly, deliberately communal. It was an expression of the grace of God, to be sure, but it was also an instrument of parochial peace. Lawsuits, feuds, quarrels, rivalries, squabbles, vendettas, grudges, factions – these were the bugbears of that quintessential early modern value, neighbourliness. To our Elizabethan parishioner, neighbourliness was not *next* to godliness; it was a form of godliness itself.

By Whitsunday 1580, our parishioner would walk into a church that was materially and liturgically different than anything his father or grandfather would have experienced. As we saw in chapter 3, the interior of the church had been fundamentally transformed by 1580. Gone were the altars at the east end of the church. In their place sat stout, handsome wooden tables. He sat in his fixed pew, a seat that belonged to him and his family, for which he paid an annual rent.[53] Surrounding him was his parish community in its fullest extent: nearly every man, woman, and child who could physically attend. There would be gaps, of course. Unchurched women – those who had given birth but not yet received a requisite postpartum blessing or purification – would be absent, as would some of the very aged or infirm. In the middle of the annual agricultural employment season, it is unlikely that there would be a host of new faces or the absence of familiar ones, recently arrived or departed for work in neighbourhood parishes, but others might have been drawn away on business. There could be one or two absent for other, more disreputable, reasons. The "notorious drunkards" of the parish might be absent, or a youth who played at games rather than attending. And, of course, there might be a principled recusant family, who stayed away from the reformed service whenever possible. But all of these were exceptions, not the rule. The rest of the parish would have been there: yeoman farmers, employers of the agricultural labourers; smaller tenant farmers and their families; the craftspeople who lived near the centre of the village; wives and widows and servants; the very poor, who relied on the charity of their neighbours; maybe even a local gentleman and his large household.

The communion table stood in the centre of the church, or perhaps in the chancel, dressed in a long, white cloth of linen. The minister stood at the north end of the table – very deliberately not facing east, as he would have done at an altar – dressed in his full gown and surplice.[54] The congregation knelt as the minister began to pray, working his way through the ten commandments and leading the people as they begged for mercy for their transgressions, together in one voice. He would read the collect for the day and then, in a piece of stunning statecraft, would read a special collect for the queen. The words were a potent blend of monarchism, piety, and power. The minister would pray that Elizabeth ("knowing whose minister she is") would seek to glorify God. In return, her subjects "duly considering whose authority she hath may faithfully serve, honour, and humbly obey her in thee, and for thee, according to thy blessed word and ordinance."[55] The message was entirely clear: God had laws, and so did the queen. Serving one was serving the other.

Further prayers followed, along with the creed, and then a sermon. If the minister was no preacher, then a homily would be read – at least once a year again stressing duties of obedience to the queen. Next was an exhortation for help of the poor, at which point the churchwardens would gather a collection for the poor man's box, walking the aisles or passing the plate. Ministers who were concerned that those assembled would choose not to communicate at this particular service were enjoined to read another long sermon on the manifold benefits of the sacrament. Those who would "stand by as gazers and lookers on them that doe communicate, and bee not partakers of the same" were called despisers and mockers of Christ's Testament.[56] Those who did choose to communicate were warned that they must have a clear conscience, being both in charity with God and with their neighbour.

Finally, the moment of communion was ready. Those who would receive knelt, humbly and penitently, and shared in a collective recitation of their sins and unworthiness. This was not the specific, sacramental confession of the pre-Reformation church. It was, instead, an expression of communal sin and repentance. Devoid of the personal, it stressed the universal depravity of the congregation. Indeed, even the very form of the confession was shared: one man (sometimes the minister; sometimes a layman) would recite the confession "in the name of all those that are minded to receive."[57] Personal confessions were to have been made in the heart before the table was approached; in the mutual address, the congregation together heard aloud the comprehensive nature of sin and pleas of mercy. The minister could not absolve. But he could pray to God, asking for mercy to "pardon and deliver you from all your sins."[58] The minister would receive the communion first, delivered to himself in two kinds, and then give it to any other clergy in attendance. Communicants would come forward, kneeling, receiving the bread and then the wine, there in the body of the church. Together, all would say the Lord's Prayer. And then they would depart, with the blessing of God ringing in their ears.

This was the Elizabethan sacramental rite. It was deeply and deliberately communal and collective. It rang through with exhortations to live fully with the community: to serve as subjects, to help the poor, to join in common confession. The liturgy explicitly spoke of mutuality and of neighbourly peace and reconciliation, "for otherwise the receiving of the holy Communion doeth nothing else but increase your damnation."[59] The space for the individual was internal and private. The service required corporate participation, and explicitly rested upon

Figure 5.1 Communion lay at the heart of the Elizabethan ritual calendar. Plain yet elegant and expensive communion cups, like this one from the 1580s, were a major purchase for any parish.

lay activity. This extended far beyond reception in two kinds. The prayers were responsive, a true litany. The churchwardens had an explicit role to play, and they served as representatives of the parish in their performance of duty. A lay congregant might read the confession aloud to all. It was, in short, an encapsulation of so many of the aspects of the Elizabethan church we have read about throughout this book – and not just an exemplar, but itself a catalyst. It was a uniform service that inculcated the essential values of the late Tudor church: obedience, coherence, unity, fidelity.

This was, in any case, what the Elizabethan policy of unchanging conformity intended. There were, as we shall see in the next section, struggles against it, by the laity and clergy alike. But the standards were clear, the ceremonies described, and the aesthetics prescribed. A decade into Elizabeth's reign, those who deviated did so knowingly and deliberately. Accidental nonconformity had been squashed. To conform, or not to conform, was now a political act. To be sure, there were those who simple *could* not obey: the infirm, for instance, were noted but rarely punished for missing a communion service, and children were not considered ready to receive. But, for the rest, accepting (or rejecting) the sacrament was both a spiritually and politically charged act.

Accepting the Sacrament

For some, acceptance of the reformed eucharist was made eagerly. They rejoiced in a sacrament of two kinds and a vernacular ceremony. Henry Smith, a godly cleric known as the "Silver-Tongued Minister" and both promoted and protected by Burghley, equated it to the holiness of the Bible: 'The Word and the Sacraments are the two breasts wherewith our mother doth nurse us," he wrote. To him and his ilk, the Lord's Supper was not tolerated but embraced, almost rapturously. Smith, though taking pains to condemn transubstantiation over and over again, wrote of the sacrament as a way to come close to God: "when the faithful receive the Bread and Wine, one like the Son of God seemeth to come unto them, which fills them with peace and joy, and grace, that they marvel what it was which they received."[60] Smith, and the godly like him, did not merely accept, they embraced.

For others, of course, acceptance was at best begrudging and at worst a product of a serious program of institutional and social coercion. Reluctant to publicly break with orthodoxy, as the Prayer Book rebels from the West Country had done decades earlier, they found small ways to subvert the process. Some staged elaborate fictions of dissent with their neighbours to avoid eligibility for the sacrament. Others pleaded illness or absence to avoid reception. Still others took the sacrament but did so reluctantly, their discomfort and even disgust as opaque to us as it may have been to their neighbours. (We too cannot make windows into men's souls.)

In some cases, though, the repulsion was obvious. Katherine Lacy was well known to the parishioners of St Hilda's in Sherborn for her hatred of "the Religion that is now set furth by public authority" and her love of the saints and the old ceremonies "or such like superstitious things," as testimony against her read.[61] But even she gathered with her parish to receive the sacrament at Easter in 1569. Even she conformed to this public rite. In the end, though, it was quite literally too much to swallow. After the minister gave her the bread and moved a dozen people down the line, "the said Mrs Lacye, who had received … [took] further of her mouth the said bread … and did convey the same behind her." Caught, Katherine pleaded that she meant "no evil" and "no harm," but was put under the churchwardens' watch.[62] Her mother even came to the minister to beg him to forgive Katherine, "who although she had done foolishly, yet she would be ready to amend the same."[63] The regret was too little and too late. Such public rejection was an "evil example unto all the parishioners" and "a great dishonour to the same Sacrament, being so abused and so lightly Regarded."[64] Katherine was prosecuted that fall, the sentence lost to us.

What is interesting here is not that a woman in deep Yorkshire on the eve of the Northern Rebellion tried to avoid taking a Calvinist sacrament. That is, of course, entirely unsurprising. But what the case of Katherine Lacy reveals is that even the most reluctant recusant, a woman who publicly proclaimed her affinity for traditional religion and her animosity toward the new church, might feel compelled to attend the public communion service. Even if she could not, in the end, bring herself to ingest a sacrament she hated, she had made the attempt. She was unlucky enough to be caught by the minister, but who knows how many others followed in her quiet footsteps, not just present but participating, only to expel the sacrament surreptitiously.

However, reception of the sacrament – or lack thereof – was not always imbued with ideological intent. Some who wanted to accept the Lord's Supper would have been unable to do so, pulled away by illness or poverty. The very aged and infirm were often given tacit licence to miss the public ceremony, while unchurched women were forbidden from attending. And though the reformed sacrament was intended as an expression of deliberate egalitarianism, levelling the difference not just between the laity and the clergy but also among those across all stations of life, some survived too close to the margins for full conformity. Many of the young, the indigent, and the jobless moved locales in a seemingly ceaseless peripatetic cycle, migrating in hope of better employment or family support; that they might miss a triannual communion is easy to imagine. And some that did receive the Lord's Supper may have done it not with conviction or repulsion but almost by rote, accepting it as merely part of one's life.

For each example we find in the archives, a counter-example will appear. There is rich fodder for an historian wanting to prove nearly any argument about Elizabethan opinions on the sacrament. Ritual acceptance was rarely catalogued in any great depth. Narrative accounts tend to depict nonconformity, as in prosecutions of people like Katherine Lacy, or pious fervour, as in the diary of Samuel Ward. (Routine, as Eamon Duffy so beautifully puts it, "leaves few records, even though most of what is fundamental to ordinary existence is a matter of routine – undocumented, invisible and as a consequence, far too easily discounted by the historian seeking to touch the texture of the life of the past."[65]) But where we may not have description, we do have data. Churchwardens' accounts, visitations, privy council reports, and censuses all allow us to answer fundamental questions about the acceptance of the Lord's Supper: were the orders of the Prayer Book accepted into parish communities? And if so, how fast, and to what extent? Only after we have some concrete answers to these questions can we turn to attempting to unpack the patterns of acceptance they reveal; only then can we really ask *why* they unfolded as they did.

At first, such questions themselves seem to be almost impossible to solve. Though by the end of Elizabeth's reign some churchwardens kept careful track of the number of communicants in their parishes and their patterns of reception, such records are largely absent for all but a very few urban parishes. And even in places where we know such records were kept, like St Mary the Great in Cambridge, they have vanished from the historical record, tantalizing in their loss. Nevertheless, it is possible to approximate, in some cases quite finely, the spread of basic conformity with the new communion order. Churchwardens' accounts, visitation books, and episcopal surveys present evidence of the incorporation and enforcement of the Prayer Book's sacrament. This dual perspective – acceptance and scrutiny – is vital, allowing the question of conformity to be evaluated from both a positive and negative view, creating a more holistic picture of change. That is to say, only by considering both active participation with conformity *and* prosecution of nonconformity can we begin to glimpse a real picture of the patterns of acceptance of the Elizabethan Lord's Supper.

The prescriptions of the Prayer Book were an ideal, and the Elizabethan church was neither uncontested nor bureaucratized enough for rapid, full-hearted adoption of the new liturgical order. Compliance tested not only the adaptability of an individual's religious practice, but also parochial systems of ordering and governance. And as we shall see, tracing patterns of eucharistic practice through the surviving records reveals a wide variety and pace of experience and observance across English parishes. In some, the new ceremony was adopted quickly and wholeheartedly; in others, conformity slowly emerges from reluctance or even sheer chaos. It was a wholescale change of calendar, rite, ritual, liturgy, donation, outlay, provision, and of an understanding of the clergy, of the divine, and of the fundamental relationship between the soul and Christ's sacrifice. Even when welcomed, it took time – and it was not always, or perhaps even often, welcomed. And yet, from this disarray, patterns begin to emerge. Looking at the transformation of the physical architecture of the church, at shifts in overall rates of reception, and of changes in the liturgical calendar, a new picture develops. By the latter half of Elizabeth's reign, the new order had become rooted in the English parish, fundamentally changing the experience of the sacrament in England. By the end of her reign, there was vast and overwhelming compliance with this new reformed sacrament.

Taking Communion: Reception Patterns

Tracking changes in behaviour is a far more slippery and elusive enterprise than tracing changes in the physical fabric. It is clear that, by the mid-1560s, the overwhelming majority of parishes in Elizabethan England had removed their altars and replaced them with communion tables. The extent to which this furniture was used, and in what way, is less certain. First-hand diaries of religious behaviour by those other than the spiritual elite are vanishingly rare, and even when they exist, they offer only one small window into liturgical practice and understanding – a window that tends to favour the pious, the devoted, or the rebel. Instead, it is to institutional documents that we must turn to sketch the outlines of sacramental reception in Elizabethan England across a broader swath of society.

Churchwardens again ride to the historian's rescue. Here, amidst payments for roofing tiles and linen and laundry and Bibles, some of their accounts regularly record payments for sacramental bread and wine. These payments allow the tracing of eucharistic practice, at least along the roughest lines. In some accounts, wardens recorded each individual purchase of communion supplies across a fiscal year, leaving a footprint of their liturgical calendars and sacramental observance. Though other accounts merely listed annual totals for "bread and wine," these too are revelatory: by comparing holistic expenses on communion supplies over time, we gain a general sense of their growth and large-scale patterns of reception.

An examination of receipts for bread and wine offers a window into sacramental conformity. It is an imperfect view. Most churchwardens' account books have been destroyed or damaged over the centuries. There are geographic gaps, with few accounts that span the whole period surviving for the far north of England; while extant visitation records and depositions indicate that accounts were faithfully kept, they have been lost to time. Many of the surviving Elizabethan account books contain large gaps or record summary total parochial receipts only, particularly in the early years. And even detailed churchwardens' accounts that reveal vibrant and active engagement with the sacrament may not include payments for communion supplies, which could be purchased by the curate rather than directly by the wardens.[66] Discovering the holistic growth of sacramental supply is, however, still possible. Over two dozen Elizabethan accounts include a detailed, regular record of the purchase of communion supplies over the decades following the implementation of the Prayer Book – and they reveal a startlingly similar picture. While the small surviving sample means the evidence can never be definitive, it is compelling and it is constant. In parish after parish, from small villages in Norfolk to teeming neighbourhoods in London to urban parishes of Midland towns to the remote moorlands of Devon, the general pace of change follows the same patterns.

Each of these parishes saw a soaring growth in receipts for communion supplies in the first two decades of Elizabeth's reign. The numbers are staggering. Over and over again, the amount spent on providing the eucharist skyrocketed between 1560 and 1580. The churchwardens of Yeovil paid 11s for communion wine in 1568; twenty years later, they paid Augustin Exall, vintner, 38s 10d for the same.[67] In the remote Dartmoor parish of Ashburton, communion receipts grew by nearly threefold between 1560 and 1580; nearly identical relative growth can be found in the account books of busy St Michael's in Bedwardine in Worcester.[68] The coastal parish of Snettisham, Norfolk, paid 3s. 9d. for bread and wine in 1561; twenty years later the receipts recorded 15s. 7d., a fourfold increase.[69] St Peter-le-Bailey in Oxford spent 3s. on wine in 1563–64 and 15s. 7d. ob in 1586–87.[70] St Mary the Great in Cambridge spent 10s. 6d. in supplies in 1564, a number that more than doubled less than two decades later.[71] Kilmington, near Axminster, saw its expenses more than triple in this period. The wealthy market town of Swaffham nearly quadrupled its communion payments between 1561 and 1582, from just over 9s. to 32s. 6d.[72] Receipts from Chudleigh, Devon, in the mid-1560s averaged 4s 3d; two decades later, the average expenditure was north of 22s.[73] The wardens of Tintinhull in Somerset saw their expenditure grow from 3s. 1d. in 1568 to over 7s. in 1585.[74] The tiny fenland parish of Tilney All Saints laid out nearly four times as much for their Lord's Supper in 1585 as they had just fifteen years earlier.[75] Something had changed by the 1580s. Across England, parishes had vastly increased the amount spent to provision the sacrament.

After this point, however, the expenses largely plateaued. St Mary the Great, Cambridge, spent just 26 per cent more in 1600 than they had twenty years earlier.[76] The churchwardens of St Peter-le-Bailey, Oxford, had seen communion expenditure grow more than fivefold in the first two decades following Elizabeth's accession; between 1586 and 1601, however, the number grew just over 20 per cent.[77] Between 1560 and 1583, the wine receipts of St Nicholas Warwick grew from 8s. 10d. ob to 21s. 7d.; by 1602 the total wine expenditure had risen by less than a shilling more.[78] In London, St Stephen Walbrook's churchwardens averaged just over 6s in communion expenses for the first five years of Elizabeth's reign. By the early 1580s, that number had nearly doubled to an average of 11s. 6d. In contrast, the last three years of Elizabeth's reign showed an average expenditure of 15s. 5d., an increase of only about a third.[79] In short, the breakneck climb of communion expenditure had slowed considerably by the final two decades of Elizabeth's reign.

In parish after parish, the pattern remains the same: dizzying growth from 1560 to 1580, followed by a steady levelling off of expenses. It is tempting to explain away this progression as merely a consequence of population increases or inflation. Comparative socio-economic data, though, undermines this explanation. To be sure, it was a period of marked demographic expansion, but the best estimates show the population rising by about six hundred thousand people in the first twenty years, or roughly 16 per cent. This, along with difficult harvests, also caused inflation, but here again the figures are between 9 and 15 per cent, far from the spiralling cost of providing supplies. Moreover, none of this explains the flattening from 1580 onward, when the population continued to expand and prices continued to rise, but the meteoric growth in communion expenses markedly slowed.[80] Neither demographics nor inflation is sufficient to explain this pattern. It was practice, not secular factors, that accounted for the rise in communion expenses.

The Elizabethan requirement of communal, regular reception of the sacrament took root in the parishes in the first two decades after the Act of Uniformity was passed. It was in this period when the real change happened, when the reformed sacrament was woven into the rhythms and traditions of the parish. The process was, as with all things, uneven and unpredictable. In some towns, the transformation was nearly immediate. The Dartmoor parish of Ashburton doubled its expenses in just a decade, while Chudleigh did so in just five years.[81] In others, like the parish of Winterslow, the process was more gradual, only reaching significant change by the middle of the 1580s.[82] Nor were the patterns of growth particularly predictable. That St Mary the Great in Cambridge, the market church of the university town most responsible for the development of the evangelical agenda across the sixteenth century, would quickly and heavily embrace a reformed sacrament is entirely unsurprising. That a tiny parish near the Vale of the White Horse or on the edge of Dartmoor would do so presses us to reconsider our assumptions about conformity to the new eucharistic practice.[83] In each of these cases, though, it is clear that, by the middle of Elizabeth's reign, acceptance of the Lord's Supper had undergone a sea-change. A new liturgical norm was born.

The bulk of these supplies were purchased for Easter or, more carefully put, for the Easter season. Paschal communion remained at the heart of the sacramental calendar, as it had been for generations before, mirroring the pre-Reformation practice of pious annual reception. This was a continuity, of course, not just with the late-medieval church but with the Last Supper. The godly were keen to stress this connection to the early church. As Henry Smith wrote, "he hath given us another Lame to eat … that is himself, upon whom all do feed … when they devised mischief against him, & sought all means to destroy him, then he consulted how to save them, and instituted this night this blessed Sacrament."[84] It was a rare liturgical overlap between traditionalists and the godly, each finding value in the paschal sacrament. Moreover, in the requirement for triennial communion, the church mandated that at least one of these had to be during the Easter season.[85] And so, up and down the country, Easter remained the cornerstone of the eucharistic experience.

The account books reflect this emphasis on Easter. The Elizabethan parish accounts that detail their communion receipts (rather than simply noting a lump sum for the year) invariably recorded their largest eucharistic expenses during the Easter season.[86] In some, there were multiple communions held in the weeks leading up to Easter Sunday and even the weeks after. The parish of St Peter Cheesehill in Winchester held at least six communion services between 20 and 28 March in 1596.[87] Wootton St Lawrence had services on Palm Sunday, Shrove Tuesday, "Easter Even," and Easter day itself.[88] And the numbers here could dwarf communion expenses for the rest of the year. In North Elmham, Norfolk, for example, the 1566–67 receipts record the purchase of a pint of wine each for Michaelmas, Christmas, and Whitsunday, with "one bottle of malmsey and iij quarts of Redd wine against ester."[89] Even discounting the bottle of malmsey, the churchwardens ordered twice as much wine for Easter as they did for the rest of the year's communions combined. Few records contain such detailed descriptions of type and volume of communion wine, but other accounts do list the receipts for individual purchases. In the late 1580s, Tintinhull in Somerset spent 42d. on the Easter season and just 18d. for the rest of the year, while the churchwardens at St Nicholas Warwick spent at least twice the amount on Easter wine as they did the rest of the year.[90]

Indeed, the pre-eminence of the Easter communion has led historians to argue that, as Arnold Hunt puts it, "there certainly seems to have been little popular demand for communion services outside of Easter."[91] J.P. Boulton's influential analysis of two poor and crowded London parishes shows all but Easter communion as scantily attended, leading Diarmaid MacCulloch to describe "a silent consensus in modifying official liturgical practice" in resorting to only a paschal communion.[92] There is some truth to this. Easter communion not only dominated account books but also marked a baseline of conformity with the Elizabethan church.

And yet, a close look at churchwardens' accounts reveals a more nuanced picture of reception. While it is clear that Easter dominated Elizabethan sacramental practice, many parishes quickly moved beyond the minimum triennial communion to a far more frequent sacramental experience. The parish accounts of Swaffham in Norfolk show as many as nine different receipts for communion wine by 1561.[93] Urban parishes picked up on this trend with similar speed: the vestry of St Michael, Cornhill, decreed that the parish would offer monthly communions as early as 1563, while the 1567 accounts of St Mary the Great, Cambridge, recorded no fewer than twelve separate receipts for communion bread.[94] Nor was this pattern limited to teeming city parishes or rich, godly market towns. Many smaller rural parishes were also offered more frequent communions. The 1564 accounts of Shipdham, that small coastal village in Norfolk, depict the sacrament adapted for the festive calendar: wine for Christmas, Candlemas, Lent, mid-Lent, Good Friday, Easter, Whitsuntide, Corpus Christi, St James's Day, St Bartholomew's Day, St Matthew's Day, St Faith's Day, All Hallows.[95] It was a festal list remade for the reformed sacrament, with at least thirteen communion services in just a year. In the tiny Worcestershire parish of South Littleton, just beyond the Cotswolds and about a half-mile from the River Avon, the church of St Michael's held communion eight times in 1568 and at least seven times in 1569. In Tintinhull, the wardens recorded at least seven services by the mid-1580s.[96] The churchwardens of Mere in Wiltshire recorded fifteen different communion services in 1578 alone.[97] This went far beyond the requirements of the Act of Uniformity and speaks to a larger sacramental piety.

Thus, while Easter communion remained the cornerstone of the eucharistic experience, and Easter remained the most expansive and expensive communion service in almost all parishes, the idea of paschal monopoly of the sacrament found in the literature is only one narrative of Elizabethan practice. This too was changing over time. In many parishes, the end of the sixteenth century saw Easter as the pre-eminent but not exclusive sacramental experience. And in rare cases, Easter communion seems to have been dwarfed by a more balanced liturgical calendar. The early accounts of Northill in Bedfordshire, for example, at first glance seem to fall in line with the picture of annual communion familiar in the historiography. To be sure, there were an unusually large number of services for the time – as many as eight by the mid-1560s – but Easter dominated the calendar. Michaelmas wine cost the wardens only 3d., while the "Hallow tyde" communion receipt was for 5d. Easter, on the other hand, totalled 3s 4d – more than half of all receipts for the year for one Sunday alone. This pattern held through the early years of the 1570s, as the parishioners of Northill adjusted to the new liturgical order. By the 1580s, however, things had again changed. Now Northill held ten or more communions every year, giving broad access to the sacrament. And Easter, while still the heart of the calendar, no longer dominated it. By the 1580s, Easter receipts were making up just a third of the total communion expenses; by 1600, it was less than a quarter. More frequent reception of the Lord's Supper was becoming the norm in Northill.[98] Not only were multiple communions provided, but they also seem to have been attended.

The motivation for such frequent communion services differed among parishes. Rationalized, monthly services allowed pious individuals to regularly experience the reformed sacrament and make their communion with God – to gain that peace and joy and grace that Henry Smith so craved. But more frequent communions also allowed for the creation of a newly invigorated festal calendar. Perhaps unsurprisingly, parishes held communion services to celebrate civic events. Most notable amongst these were communions tied to Elizabeth's Coronation Day. In addition to the ringing of the bells, which was common throughout the country, parishes like Yatton in Somerset or Mere in Wiltshire marked the day with the Lord's Supper.[99] One can imagine the Prayer Book invocations of Elizabeth's divine favour and role in the preservation of the church resounding particularly clearly on 17 November. More commonly, additional services allowed communities to highlight moments in the liturgical calendar. Common dates for non-paschal services included Candlemas, Whitsunday, Michaelmas, All Hallows, and Christmas.[100] These were highly traditional dates, invested with meaning both religious and secular, marking the passing of the year or the stages of the harvest. And tradition could wend its way even further into this reformed rite. In one of the most startling surviving entries in an account book, the churchwardens of Wooton St Lawrence, near Basingstoke, noted in 1600 that they held a communion service "after the king ale," a raucous parish festival, usually held in the long summer light of Whitsuntide, more familiar in the late-medieval parish.[101] Side by side lived the meat and drink of merry England and the bread and wine of Calvin's Supper.

It at first seems a curious paradox that such a reformed sacrament might be used to such traditional ends, gathering the community in celebration of ancient harvest rhythms or even a day most associated with the purification of the Virgin. And yet, this was the Elizabethan Reformation in a nutshell. The sacramental *via media* was not a true compromise. Communion was mandated by the state and closely observed by its bureaucracy – the *via sola* again. The service placed the queen as both governor of the church and as guided directly by God in her spiritual authority. The liturgy was unequivocally and unapologetically Protestant; if it was not as reformed as some puritans would have hoped, if it still contained kneeling and if the minister still wore a surplice, its doctrine was deeply inflected with Calvinist teaching. But the past was neither broken nor forgotten. It was instead a *repurposing* of tradition for explicitly reformed ends, a transformation of familiar form with new weight and intent. It was a form of evangelism that emphasized conversion and transformation rather than repudiation. By allowing each parish to create its own sacramental customs, as long as the minimum obligation was meant, the Elizabethan settlement created space for parishes to adapt the liturgical calendar and – within very clear boundaries – to shape the sacrament to their needs.

Overall Rates of Participation

It is clear that by the mid-Elizabethan years, the sacrament had become rooted in the Elizabethan parish. But while the increase in communion expenses (and in some cases the number of services themselves) is clear, we still lack a sense of proportion. Were these increased expenses the result of full participation with the sacrament, or were they simply the cost of a small portion of the congregation fully receiving? Was this relative growth, or was it truly an expression of general acceptance? One could certainly imagine a scenario in which a parish that recorded a tripling of their eucharistic budget actually only saw regular sacramental participation grow from 10 to 30 per cent of the adult congregation – an impressive growth, to be sure, but nowhere near the kind of eucharistic observance that the Act of Uniformity required. While churchwardens' accounts can suggest that sacramental practice was changing, we must look to other sources to reveal a true picture of Elizabethan conformity.

In a very few cases, parochial figures are available through the study of token books, records kept by the churchwardens of the exact numbers of communicants at each ceremony. Though various parish accounts make mention of such books, almost none survive in the archives. Their very existence points to the gravity with which some parishes took the question of attendance; the parish of St Mary's in Cambridge, for instance, paid half a shilling a year to someone like "mr norkotts boy for writing the Communicants," a process that evidently required an annual door-to-door survey of households in anticipation of Easter.[102] Jeremy Boulton's analysis of a rare surviving book, that of the poor urban parish of St Botolph's, Aldgate, reveals that such attention could yield an astonishing degree of compliance: despite the grossly overcrowded and transient nature of St Botolph's, the annual communion rate was roughly 94 per cent of eligible adults.[103] It is startling, if specific, evidence of real conformity.

While such books have rarely survived, broader data can be gathered from episcopal visitations. The Elizabethan church was deeply invested in surveying and monitoring full participation in the Lord's Supper. In the first decade, visitation articles focused on whether the communion was properly provisioned and held: whether "the holy Sacraments be … ministered reverently," whether "you have in your parish churches all things necessary and requisite for Common prayer and administration of the Sacraments," "whether your Alters be taken down," "whether they do use to minister the Communion in wafer bread," and "whether the communion table be decently covered." Faults in lay reception too largely lay with the minister, and the articles inquired whether any unrepentant sinners had been permitted to receive. Suspicion of the laity largely focused on private masses or searching out illicit services and far less on reception in the parish.[104] By the late 1560s, this had changed. Now visitation articles explicitly asked whether parishioners were communicating "thrice every year at the least."[105] By the 1570s, the formula most often replicated was whether any in the parish had not received "thrice at the least this year, and namely at Easter last, or there about for once, and what their names are."[106] This question was asked by and large in the same form until the end of Elizabeth's reign.[107] For nearly thirty-five years, visitations from archdeacons, bishops, and archbishops alike regularly gathered the names of those who did not receive, a kind of rogue's gallery of nonconformity.

The data gleaned from these visitation reports indicates levels of conformity in line with Boulton's study of Southwark. Bishop Redman's visitation of Norwich in 1597, for instance, produced similarly startlingly low numbers of non-communication. In the entire city, only twenty-seven people were presented for not attending communion; of these, three presented certificates testifying to the contrary and had their charges dismissed.[108] With a conservative estimate of seven thousand potential communicants in Norwich, the visitation saw the presentment of only 0.4 per cent of the eligible population.[109] Certainly some non-communicants would have slipped through the disciplinary cracks, but on the whole the level of scrutiny was noteworthy. Four men from the parish of St Clement, for example, were presented for not having received communion "thrice this last year."[110] Assuming these men represented an anomaly in their parish, it seems as if St Clement, at least, was meeting the triennial standards of the Elizabethan Prayer Book. More broadly, even imagining that the numbers presented were off by a power of ten (a very conservative estimate), this would indicate a communication rate in late-Elizabethan Norwich of some 96 per cent, not far from Boulton's assessment of London's congested St Boltoph's.

If this was the standard for a notoriously godly city – albeit a dense and crowded one – we might expect to see far greater rates of non-communication in rural parishes, especially those known for recusant nonconformity with the Elizabethan Prayer Book. However, even here presentations for non-communication were remarkably low by the later years of Elizabeth's reign. The 1594 visitation of the diocese of Somerset returned just 176 names for not receiving communion, out of 304 parishes.[111] In the 1590 visitation of the deanery of Doncaster, only twenty people (from a total of seventy-five parishes) were presented for not attending Holy Communion, while the 1593 visitation of the archdeaconry of Sudbury in Suffolk presented just thirty-five for the same offence.[112] Larger surveys confirm this. An analysis of the 1590, 1595, and 1600 episcopal visitations of the Archdeaconry of Cleveland in the North Riding of Yorkshire reveals no more than ninety people explicitly presented for non-communication in any given year. If one includes those presented for recusancy, the number presented increases but never rises over four hundred in any visitation.[113] (This is no doubt not the full picture of communicant numbers, but as we have seen in chapter 1, visitations were a relatively robust system of surveillance; moreover, the statistics fall roughly in line with more comprehensive surveys of the church, as we shall see.) These visitations by no means revealed complete conformity. Recusancy and separatism were real, and the underground networks of each were robust.[114] Many resisted taking the communion, some for deeply principled reasons. Their experiences matter, both in painting a full picture of Elizabethan religion and in trying to understand the near-panicked response of the Elizabethan state. What these visitations do uncover, though, is the creation of a new sacramental norm by the end of the sixteenth century: by 1600, resistance to the reformed sacrament was fervent but vanishingly small.

The scrutiny of sacramental nonconformity did not end with routine visitations, which were inefficient for the needs of central state authorities. The purpose of visitations was, at its heart, to correct misbehaviour; their emphasis was on confession and penitence, albeit in a strictly reformed mode, and their goal was to eliminate error. The central state, particularly as manifested through the Privy Council, was less interested in repentance and more interested in surveillance. There was a desperate desire amongst these councillors to *know*: to know whether their rules were being followed, to know areas and patterns of resistance; to know just what threats the stability of the realm might face. In terms of monitoring religious obedience, here too the focus landed squarely on communion. Conformity to the sacrament, that public and communal loyalty test, became a stand-in for a broader obedience to the state.

The sacrament was often used as a test of the willingness of potential recusants, particularly those in positions in power, to conform to the state. Men suspected of "papistry" or of abstaining from church would be asked to take the sacrament as proof of their convictions. The ecclesiastical commissioners of Chester allowed suspected recusant Cuthbert Clifton to go free in 1570, providing that "before or on thisside [of] the feast of the blessed Trinity next ensuing" he would "in his parish church … in the face of the congregation Receive the holy and blessed communion and thereof make true certificate to the said commissioners."[115] Such certificates were common in the ecclesiastical courts, but by the 1580s they were also coming in to the Privy Council.[116] Henry Edyall, being questioned in late September about his involvement in the Babington plot, claimed that "touching his behaviour towards the state, and namely in matters of religion," he was not a Papist. As proof, he noted that had received communion for twenty years "openly" in his parish church, "and so is ready to do again … if it be tomorrow, for testification of his assent and good liking [of] the religion now professed."[117] Within a fortnight, he had been freed.[118] In each of these cases, communion served as a public proclamation of both individual conscience and of loyalty to the state.

The public reception of communion was also used as a means of testing radical Protestant nonconformists. In 1573, the ex-cleric and recent publisher of Thomas Cartwright's notoriously Presbyterian tracts, John Stroud, was hauled before the High Commission. "Are thou contented to receive the communion in open churches according to the order that is prescribed in the book of common prayer?" he was asked. When Stroud affirmed that he had, Commissioner Goodman then demanded, "Name one church where thou hast received the communion." "You seek my undoing," Stroud replied. (The desolation rings across centuries.) Stroud then admitted that he avoided the sacrament for conscience's sake, as "there can no fruit be taken" from an unfit ministry; he was let go upon promising that he would "receive the Sacrament of the L. Supper according to the order prescribed."[119] Francis Marbury, erstwhile radical and now conformable minister in Lincoln, sought Lord Burghley's help in lifting an old inhibition on preaching, arguing that "to the uttermost extent of my private vocation I have long and still do exactly communicate in prayer, sacraments, and … rites."[120] The inhibition seems to have been lifted soon thereafter, and Marbury spent the next two decades preaching and building his not inconsiderable reputation.[121]

Sacramental reception, then, was not merely a matter of personal spiritual probity or even communal consonance. It was also a tool of state. And it began to be used not just in individual cases, but as a blanket, anticipatory tool. To take but one example, in 1586, a minister was appointed to the Court of Marches with explicit orders to offer the sacrament to all of its officers: "It is her Majesties pleasure and express commandment … that they shall not from henceforth after one term ended permit or suffer any person or persons whatsoever to have or occupy any place or office in the said courts … that shall either refuse to take the oath for her majesties supremacy or to come to Church and communicate."[122] Here, the sacrament was an oath in practice, an overt conformity to the state church no less powerful than a public statement of the Oath of Supremacy. Moreover, to ensure that the communion requirement was taken seriously, the minister was to hold a public communion every court term with all court officers present, "that it may appear … if any there be that will refuse it."[123] This was not the Lord's Supper as a sacred commemoration of divine sacrifice; this was not eucharist as an individual's pious communion with Christ. This was sacramental conformity at the tip of the sword, orthopraxy as a brand of political loyalty.[124]

The Privy Council took this logic one step further. Rather than simply targeting individuals and testing their loyalty with communion, they began to actively seek out large-scale reports of those who failed to communicate: not post-facto examinations but active surveillance. The motivation was political and ideological, to be sure, but it was also a practical way of enriching the crown. In 1577, amidst a push to refocus the queen's attention from godly prophesyings to the Catholic threat, John Aylmer wrote to Francis Walsingham with a new plan.[125] Aylmer, then Bishop of London and clear contender for the next Archbishop of Canterbury, thought that anti-Catholic measures had been too gentle. (In a breathtakingly obtuse line, he even complained that imprisonment in fact aided the recusants "by sparing of their housekeeping greatly to enrich them."[126]) The best way to punish them would be heavy fines, but here he was hamstrung by the law that already imposed a twelvepence fee for missing church: "for if we should directly punish them for not coming to the Church, they have to allege that the penalty being already set down by statute … is not by us to be altered, nor aggravated."[127]

Instead, Aylmer advanced a new plan. Rather than simply punishing non-attendance, the Privy Council should impose huge new fines "for contemptuous refusing of receiving the Communion according to our order & Commandments."[128] Aylmer's plan of targeting those who refused the sacrament with a separate fine from those who refused to attend church never came to full fruition.[129] But it did intrigue the Privy Council, which proceeded a few months later with a national survey that required bishops to certify the names of all those in their diocese who did not attend regular services and "also the value of their lands and goods."[130] Returns were ordered to be sent just one week after the receipt of the letter. Partly as a result, the numbers and names reported to the council were limited both in scope and in detail. They focused on the most prominent recusants in the county, particularly the gentry and richer yeomanry. In all, roughly fifteen hundred names were reported from most dioceses, the universities, and the Inns of Court.[131] It was, as everyone understood, a limited list. The commissioners completing the survey from the Bishop of Rochester's visitation listed only seven recusants, each worth over one hundred pounds, concluding "And this is as much as, for the shortness of time, we can testify."[132]

While this limited scope renders these surveys useless as statistical metrics for understanding conformity with communion, the exercise as a whole nevertheless reveals an enormous amount about sacramental conformity in the mid-Elizabethan period. First, such information was *available* to the bishops on startlingly short notice. The first reports started trickling in by October 20, just five days after the certificate had been issued; by the end of the month, most dioceses had reported to the council.[133] This efficiency was in large part due to the pre-existing mechanisms of surveillance available to the bishops, particularly the visitations. In some cases, the evidence from the bishops came from their own interactions with noted recusants, like Thomas Cooper in Lincoln who presented recusants whom he himself had met.[134] More commonly, though, it was explicitly drawn from the visitations, underscoring just how robust and vital this edifice of surveillance had become.

Second, the demographics of those listed is more nuanced than might at first be expected. To be sure, wealthy landowners are the primary targets of most lists. And yet many people of significantly more modest means were also included in the reports. Returns from the city of York included potters, butchers, tilers, saddlers, and carpenters.[135] These were, of course, perfectly respectable and often profitable professions, but they were a far cry from the countess of Cumberland or the daughter of the earl of Shrewsbury, both listed at the beginning of the same certificate.[136] In some cases, those reported were quite marginal economically, like the late Nicholas Cassinger in Southwark, "a poor husbandman, and his wife now married to one of like poverty," John Cooke, alias Puddinge, of Gloucester, "worth nothing," or Agnes Wigan of St Dennis, York, a widow valued at "nil."[137] Many of those listed were women, and married women at that, suggesting that the old scheme of conformist heads of household cloaking recusant dependents was coming under greater scrutiny. In short, while the list skewed heavily toward those who could potentially pay extensive fines, Elizabethans from across the social scale were in the sights of both their bishops and even of the Privy Council. This was a granular level of surveillance.

Finally, by the 1570s, absence from communion itself was sufficient to be accused of recusancy. While the directive from the Privy Council asked merely for certificates of those who did not attend church, sacramental participation preoccupied the bishops. Those who sent back detailed reports and not simply lists of names and incomes frequently included patterns of reception. A few examples are indicative of the whole: John Strangemen and his wife, the widow of the John Felton executed for hammering a copy of *Regnans in Excelsis* onto the Bishop of London's palace, were noted not only as absent from services but that "neither have the said John and his wife received the Communion since they were married."[138] In Berkshire, Francis Morris of Coxwell was listed as one who "doth neither Come to the church to hear divine service, nor receiveth the Communion."[139] Lincoln's Inn reported that they had "sequestered from our fellowship" those "for suspicion had of their religion, for not Receiving the Communion."[140]

Moreover, a few of those reported to the Privy Council were acknowledged to attend services but not receive the sacrament. Mr Burdett of Sunning "Commeth now and then to the church, but receiveth not the Communion."[141] In Essex, William Worthington of East Hordon was someone "who sometimes cometh to church, but never doth communicate,"[142] while Nicholas Saundar of Evesham was listed as a person who was occasionally absent but also did not take the sacrament.[143] The list of recusants in Oxfordshire was divided between those who avoided all services and "those that have not bin known to receive the Communion this year and more; but come sometime to the church."[144] The returns of Hadleigh in Suffolk included "Two poor weavers, viz Thomas Stansby and William Hach, which do come to the church, butt refuse to communicate. They are in prison in Newgate for that matter."[145] In such cases, mere attendance at services was considered insufficient proof of conformity. As Bishop Scambler put it in his letter to the Privy Council, "if you had charged me … to certify you of those that refuse to receive the communion" rather than merely those who did not attend, "you should have had a larger certificate of persons dangerous in mine opinion."[146]

This was an extraordinary conclusion by the bishops. As we shall see in the next section, there was no statutory law at this point that compelled attendance at communion – it was an *ecclesiastical* offence, not a secular one. And while the head of the secular state and the head of the ecclesiastical state were indeed united in the person of the queen, there were clear lines of demarcation between the two, particularly to royal eyes.[147] In turning over the names of those who had followed secular law, the bishops were working far beyond the remit of the Privy Council's order. In doing so they were deeply attuned to the idea that communion was the purest test of true conformity.

More data on recusants was collected over the following decades. New legislation cracked down on recusancy – specifically and particularly on Catholic recusancy – and mandated significant fines for not attending church services. Names of recusants and fines levied from their estates were collected by the Exchequer, first scattered amongst the generalized accounts of the Pipe Rolls and then specifically in separate Recusancy Rolls. The numbers here run in a similar vein to the 1577 reports; the most comprehensive figures, from 1592–93, name around 3,600 recusants across the country.[148] This stands in comparison to a population of roughly 2.3 million potential communicants.[149] Though comprehensive in geography, and collected with a keen monetary motivation, these rolls still have modified value for a true understanding of sacramental conformity. Officially, recusants were merely those who had not attended regular services, and the rolls record little in the way of detailed offences. The targets were generally either wealthy or significantly contumacious, and often both, an unrepresentative sample.

The national picture thus seems tantalizingly out of reach. And this would be true, if not for Archbishop John Whitgift. Whitgift was a man who prized information and control above all else. Though initially one of the bright young godly things of Cambridge, he had marked himself out as an establishment man by opposing the radicalism of Thomas Cartwright.[150] His subsequent ascent to power was swift, and at each step of the way, he made new rules and orders, which he expected to be obeyed. When named vice-chancellor of Cambridge, he instituted new statutes that concentrated power in the hands of his office.[151] Appointed as a member of the High Commission for Ecclesiastical Causes, he became one of the few commissioners who consistently investigated and ruled on cases.[152] As Archbishop of Canterbury, he extended orders for obedience to the state further than they had ever reached. He had Star Chamber issue a decree for new "rules and ordinances" of the printing trade, which gave him the right to control all printing presses and censor any text they printed.[153] And perhaps most famously, in 1583 he issued to the godly clergy the three articles of prayer-book conformity, which caused petitions, protests, and mass resignations.[154]

All of which is to say, obedience was Whitgift's raison d'être, and cataloguing this obedience became his obsession. In his eyes, the easiest way to create conformity was to control behaviour. As he put it in his very first sermon at St Paul's as archbishop, "Many now a days do profess and protest obedience in word, and in a generality … but they will not do that which they command. These men give *reverentiam subjectionis*, but not *obedientiam actionis*, as one saith. They say, and do not."[155] Visible actions were measurable and reportable in ways that thoughts and words were not. For Whitgift, information was control, a way to breed compliance. It made problems assessable; what could be counted could be disciplined and regulated. His register is full of requests for reports, accounts, and certificates, haranguing his bishops and archdeacons for what he saw as undue lethargy: "you may not fail hereof, nor deal otherwise in your certificate then you will be able to stand to and justify," he wrote to the elderly bishop of Gloucester, "And notwithstanding you have peradventure made some such certificate heretofore unto me … but you must again certify … and in that due order and form."[156] Deeply involved in the Privy Council, the High Commission, and the Star Chamber, Whitgift sat at the nexus of information, power, and government.

Whitgift's fondness for public demonstrations of compliance and conformity made Elizabethan communion his perfect vehicle. Early in his tenure as archbishop, he planned to make provision of quarterly communion mandatory for all preachers, in large part to catch out godly radicals and separatists who might have attempted to avoid interaction with the Book of Common Prayer by becoming roving preachers.[157] Whitgift also hoped to root out Catholic recusancy through public ceremonies.[158] The desire for information, for conformity, and for public acts of obedience culminated in one of the greatest pieces of surveillance in early modern England. Known to history as the Ecclesiastical Census of 1603, it compelled every bishop to require every archdeacon to seek from every minister the answer to seven questions posed by Whitgift. It was, strictly speaking, not an Elizabethan measure; indeed, it was very likely commissioned just after her death, in the summer of 1603, as a way to provide the new king with vital information about the state of his church and to counter puritan messages about its dire straits.[159] What the census gives us, though, is the clearest, most far-reaching picture of the level of sacramental reception at the end of Elizabeth's reign, a picture of how far the country had changed since Elizabeth ascended to the throne.

The ecclesiastical census was the extensive capacity of the episcopal surveillance state on full display, and it set the Lord's Supper as the hallmark of religious orthodoxy. Its latter questions asked about clergy, patrons, and benefices, but the first three questions explicitly focused on sacramental conformity, inquiring as to:

1 The certain number of those that do receive the communion in every several parish.
2 The certain number of every man recusant inhabiting in every several parish … without specifying their particular names; and likewise the certain number of every woman recusant, distinct from the man, in manner as afore.
3 The like inquiry to be observed also, as well what the certain number is of every man as afore, who doth not receive the communion, as also the certain number of every woman … who doth not receive the communion, without specifying their names.[160]

Notably, Whitgift asked for a list of non-communicants *over and above* a list of mere recusants: this was a net that would catch men like William Worthington or Thomas Stansby, who came to church but who refused to communicate. It placed the sacrament, not just the service, at the heart of conformity. Its scope was unprecedented. This was the first time that a national, comprehensive listing of communicants had been sought. An earlier survey of the population, also through the bishops, merely asked for returns of the number of households. Here, the population's sacramental conformity was being listed.[161] Unlike visitations, exchequer rolls, even the 1577 returns, this was not meant to target specific individuals: it truly was a national census, meant to allow the state to know its population more intimately.

This census thus gives perhaps the best glimpse at the breadth of sacramental reception by the end of the Elizabethan era. To be sure, this data should be qualified – no historian should be so credulous as to take it at face value. Some diocesan reports omitted ecclesiastical peculiars from their surveys, counting only those parishes under their direct control; some returns were presented as general summaries rather than as detailed local records; some saw suspicious rounding of parochial population calculations to the nearest ten or twenty, suggesting estimation rather than exactitude.[162] Not all non-communicants may have been reported correctly, whether through ineptitude or intrigue.[163] Moreover, the census returns were collected in the middle of a particularly deadly outbreak of plague, one that caused Thomas Dekker to lament: "a stiff and freezing horror sucks up the rivers of my blood: my hair stands an end with the panting of my brains: mine eye balls are ready to start out, being beaten with the billows of my teares: out of my weeping pen does the ink mournfully and more bitterly than gall drop on the palefac'd paper, even when I do but think how the bowels of my sick Country have bene torn" – not an ideal time for a head count.[164] Nevertheless, this census has been widely used by historical demographers and other social historians as the best measure of the population at the turn of the seventeenth century. Breathtaking in its scope and its ambition, it remains the best hope for understanding the holistic picture of England's population – or of its religious temperature – at this time.

What the 1603 census reveals is a staggeringly conformist country. Among the overall number of adults living in England, only a tiny handful of the population were listed as recusants. In total, the census reported slightly over 2.25 million communicants in England. The total number of recusants listed was 8,500.[165] The number is shockingly low, just .4 per cent of the total eligible population. To put it another way, the census records that more than 99.6 per cent of potential communicants were conforming. Even if we were to imagine these reports were undercounted by a factor of twenty – that there were twenty times more recusants in actuality than were listed in the reports – that would still put the overall conformity rate at around 93 per cent of adults.

The most detailed surviving returns from the census paint a similar picture of overall conformity to the sacramental order. In the charmingly named Turners Puddle, Dorset, there were two non-communicants to fifty-four communicants.[166] Down the coast, Lyme Regis saw sixteen men not receive, in comparison to the estimated 1,100 adults who did. The parish of Uffculme, Devon, reported "about the number of thirty" who did not receive in the previous year – and around eight hundred who had.[167] The entire city of Norwich listed just ten non-communicants, other than those "as are already in the Gaole."[168] Five days' ride away, Babworth, Nottinghamshire, noted only two non-communicants "above 16 years old" out of a total of fifty-nine adults.[169] The market town of Stroud in Gloucestershire recorded one man and two women as non-communicants – and nine hundred others who did receive the sacrament.[170] Goudhurst, just outside Tunbridge Wells, had just one out of nine hundred of its adults refuse the Lord's Supper.[171] These specific examples are reflected in larger returns. More substantially, the entire diocese of Durham reported only 119 non-communicants, and 526 recusants, out of a total adult population of nearly sixty-nine thousand, a conformity rate of over 99 per cent in a deeply conservative area.[172] In the diocese of Gloucester, there were nearly fifty-nine thousand communicants to seventy-one recusants and ninety-eight non-communicants – 2 per cent reported for not conforming.[173] Again, even if these reports undervalued recusancy at a rate of twentyfold, the conformity rate would be 96 per cent. From tiny rural parishes in Devon and Nottinghamshire to bustling cities in Dorset and Norfolk, report after report indicates an overwhelming conformity with the sacrament.

These are exhausting figures. The relentless recital of them runs together, numbing their impact. (Spare a thought for the men who originally compiled these lists, without calculator or spreadsheet to hand.) The overall impression, though, should not be lost. In these highly detailed surveys, almost every single parish and every single diocese saw close to full reception of the Lord's Supper by the early seventeenth century, with only an atypical handful refusing to conform.

There were, to be sure, notable pockets of nonconformity. Warblington in Hampshire, once the home of Margaret Pole and later the noted Catholic George Cotton, reported twenty-four recusants and six non-communicants to 150 communicants – a conformity rate of just 84 per cent.[174] The parish of Boarhunt, in the same county, also had a manor owned by a recusant family, this time the Henslowes. Ralph Henslowe had been a client to the notoriously Catholic earl of Southampton, and all the women in his family had been reported as recusants in the 1577 survey.[175] Unsurprisingly, perhaps, the 1603 census returns reported nearly a third of adults in his parish as either recusants or non-communicants.[176] But such parishes were an anomaly in Hampshire. The entire diocese of Winchester, to which most Hampshire parishes belonged, reported an overall conformity rate of about 99 per cent, in line with the other dioceses of the province of Canterbury.[177] The picture that emerges is of a conformist nation with hyper-localized concentrations of serious recusancy. More broadly, receiving the Lord's Supper had become the liturgical and parochial norm.

The sheer conformity of it all feels difficult to swallow, and the sensible and wary historian falls back on the caveats enumerated above: uneven recording, underground resistance, plague, politics – a survey not to be trusted unquestioningly. However, it is important to remember that the 1603 census did not materialize from thin air. It was the product of a well-oiled machine of surveillance that regularly and routinely reported recusancy and non-conformity. The apparatus of the state church had become accustomed to scrutinizing its population. The bishops had also been well-prepared for requests of information from their archbishop, who had spent nearly two decades demanding certifications of data. Moreover, the numbers in the 1603 census did not come from a hurried scramble to report, as had the 1577 numbers. Whitgift had given the bishops plenty of notice that such a survey was coming. In the previous three years, he had repeatedly asked for general lists of recusants to be sent to his office – albeit in a far less comprehensive fashion than the census – and had hinted at this new, massive survey in the six months leading up to its order.[178] This census as a process, even as a format, was in no way an anomaly.

Moreover, even the most skeptical should note the similarity of these national numbers with the parochial and diocesan data discussed earlier in the section. From the crowded warrens of Southwark to the wide moors of the North Riding to the godly streets of Norwich to the rolling hills of the West Country, record after record seems to indicate rates of sacramental conformity far greater than we might originally imagine. Pulling these numbers together, it is a reasonable, perhaps even conservative, claim that, by the final decade of Elizabeth's reign, at least 90 per cent of English adults received the sacrament at least once a year. Indeed, the numbers may have been far higher, upwards of 97 or 98 per cent of the adult population. This is the context of the rising communion expenses in the parishes of England. The Elizabethan church was far from uniform. There were local traditions, parochial quirks, individual disputes, personal consciences. But by the end of the sixteenth century, it was, fundamentally, conformist.

We are, perhaps, overused to the exception: to the radical separatist, to the pious recusant, to the morally suspect, who ended up hauled before the ecclesiastical courts. These were the men and women who wrote, or who at the very least were written about. They have the most exciting stories, and they leave the clearest trace on the historical record. The dutiful man who comes to his parish church and receives the sacrament as he ought to have done, every year from his youth to his old age, who farms diligently and conforms generally, avoiding lawsuits and summonses as best he can, raising his family against the rising tide of economic stratification and dimming prospects, of skyrocketing prices and falling incomes – he touches the records lightly and our imaginations little. But he is still worth counting and still worth remembering. His conformity was still a political act, if an act of obedience rather than rebellion, which changed the world in which he lived.

Refusing the Sacrament

If the sacrament was so widely enforced and widely accepted, the question remains, why did some people refuse the sacrament, and what effect did that refusal have on the creation of a liturgical identity within the church? This focus should not suggest that refusal of the sacrament was somehow more important than its reception; they are, in many ways, two sides of the same coin. But as with most aspects of Elizabethan religion, it was the misdemeanour, not the observance, that left the deepest mark on the records. By examining just why people *refused* the communion, we can gain a better understanding of the place of the sacrament within the Elizabethan parish.

Not all absence from the communion had any real ideological intention. At its most basic level, many people who did not come to communion did so because they could not. As we saw in chapter 1, churches often served large geographical areas, making the trek to services miles rather than minutes. Simply getting to church could be a struggle: as one Westmorland man described: "the ways [to the church] were dangerous and troublesome in winter time by reason of great inundations and waters and winter weather."[179] Those living on more distant farms would have often encountered difficulty in travelling to church at such times, forestalling their ability to take the sacrament as required. The focus on the sacrament at Christmas and

Easter, neither of which time of the year can be particularly noted for good English weather, must have caused additional disruptions to eucharistic conformity.

Those at the margins of society – the ill, the aged, the poor – were often also presented for missing communion. In some cases, this was simply a description, such as the entry for Jane Mitchell, "a poor woman, presented to be excommunicated and not to have received the Communion at Easter last."[180] More commonly, however, churchwardens seem to have been making a special pleading for such non-communicants. The 1595 presentations for the parish of Wheldrake in the North Riding presented three people for not communicating, but noted that "Brayes wyfe, is a Recusant, [but] thither two had Mr Palmer sayeth, are very miserable poor persons and have communicated since at their parish church."[181] Here, the distinction between those who refused to communicate on ideological grounds and those who had failed to communicate due to life circumstance was made perfectly clear. Such consideration can also be found in those ecclesiastical courts responsible for sentencing non-communicants. When the widow of Thomas Cooper was presented in 1597 for not attending church or taking communion for an entire year, for example, the archdeacon's court summarily dismissed the charges, due to her ill health.[182] Similarly, the charges against John Atkinson of Yarm in Cleveland were dropped after he produced a note from his churchwardens confirming that he "did not communicate at Easter last being sick."[183] Longer-term illness was also recognized, as in the case of Elizabeth Cordingley, "a woman distracted [who] received not the Communion since she fell distracted."[184] Conformity may have been crucial, but both lay and ecclesiastical officials recognized the difference between defiance and deficiency. Ecclesiastical discipline was harsh, but it did not lack discretion.

Others who did not receive were morally, if not materially, marginal. John Barner and his wife were accused of both avoiding communion and keeping their alehouse open on the Sabbath.[185] Other non-communicants were noted for their sexual immorality. The churchwardens of Reedham presented John Goldworth for not receiving Easter communion and for having "a childe in base about Whitsuntide last by one Alice Blasie."[186] Such records abound in the visitation returns, and these joint presentations served to magnify the delinquency of the offender on both counts. That those who defied moral orthodoxies might have also ignored liturgical strictures seems relatively straightforward, but such avoidance might well have been grounded in fear (speculative or realistic) that they would not have been permitted to receive the communion; ministers could and did withhold the sacrament on a temporary basis as a punitive matter for similar offences.

Other kinds of social disorders could lead parishioners to exclude themselves from communion, most notably the transgression of personal quarrels. The communion was a symbol of a unified body of believers, and as such was prohibited to those out of charity with their neighbours.[187] Such prohibition was taken seriously, and unreconciled neighbours often chose to abstain from receiving the eucharist.[188] Thomas Ryedall of Bolton in Yorkshire, for instance, "being out of charity did not receive the [communion] last Easter."[189] These scruples exerted a powerful influence over the early modern parishioner and were generally recognized as a valid reason for refusing to take the sacrament. The Lord's Supper served as a rite not only of communion with God, but also of communion with one's fellow parishioners. Refraining from communion in the Elizabethan period, then, was a visible and outward sign that one had strayed from the normative conception of good order.[190]

At times, such abstention reflected neither unorthodoxy nor disorder, but rather a profound respect for the sacrament. Many tried to mend their quarrels before the Easter communion, in order to avoid being seen as contumacious and rebellious. The rector of Tatham, Lancashire, used the coming Easter communion to reconcile two warring parties who then "openly professed in Assembly that … they were in charity & sufficient Motives (on both sides) for me … to admit them to the Communion."[191] Such attempts at reconciliation were common, with the paschal sacrament in particular serving as a means to leverage a resolution – or at least a ceasefire – regarding parochial relations.[192] Those who refused to do so were banned from communion. Though accepted by church courts as an ideologically sound reason for refusal, pleading contention nevertheless marked a parishioner as lacking "neighbourliness," that warp of the early modern English social fabric.[193] Thus, ties began to form linking social, moral, and liturgical probity, intertwining the idea of a communion-taker as part of the ordered community, and, conversely, of a communion-avoider as antagonistic.

In the minds of authorities, abstention could mask a still-deeper separation from the community. Because the excuse of contention was legitimate, it served as a perfect cover for Catholics wishing to avoid the penalties of recusancy. Many Catholics who attended church drew the line at taking communion; in Alexandra Walsham's words, they "felt that mere churchgoing might be stomached, but not Calvin's Supper."[194] Indeed, like the bishops in the 1570s survey, their contemporaries saw refusal of the sacrament as a hallmark of recusancy; as William Burton preached ironically, "should [I] refuse to administer the Lords supper, because some Church papist in my parish will never receive the communion."[195] With the increase in fears over closet Catholicism growing in the Elizabethan period, refusal of the sacrament was increasingly seen as an indication of unorthodox political, as well as social or religious, character. Abstaining from the eucharist, even when claiming lack of charity, brought one under greater scrutiny. Church courts questioned closely those who tendered the excuse of contention, and testimony revealed a common understanding of the ties between recusancy and abstention. Richard Easte of Suncombe, Oxfordshire, protested to the archdeacon's court in 1584 "that he did not communicate this last Easter because his conscience was troubled bye the evil speech of Katherine Ginacre, but doth not refuse the Lords table upon any scruple in religion or otherwise."[196] The very defensiveness of such testimony points to the increasing stakes of refusal to conform.

Many outside official channels soon became suspicious of those who self-excluded under the excuse of being out of charity with neighbours. A generation after Elizabeth's reign, John Earle would write that a church papist's "main policy is to shift off the Communion, for which he is never unfurnish't of a quarrel, and will be sure to be out of Charity at Easter; and indeed lies not, for he ha's a quarrel to the Sacrament."[197] The roots of such rhetoric lie in the Elizabethan period, where a similar connotation began to reinforce the rite of communion as a hallmark of true Protestant belief. Indeed, Alexandra Walsham and Arnold Hunt have argued persuasively that communion became a key part of godly identity by the late sixteenth century, embraced by centrists and evangelicals alike as part of a Protestant identity.[198]

Such argument, however, needs to be developed within the context of social dynamics within a parish. Communion became not only part of a godly identity, but part of a communal identity, a collection of everyone in the parish except those out of charity, disordered, or unorthodox. Refusal of the sacrament on ideological grounds placed one in the company not only of the immoral or marginal, but perhaps more importantly also in the company of those who could not get along with their neighbours. If abstention was a sign of uncharitable behaviour, then taking the sacrament was a sign of being a good neighbour, in charity with the wider community; as recusants refused to communicate, they could be associated with *lack* of neighbourliness. Early modern Englishmen and women may have been perfectly able to differentiate between those refraining for ideological reasons and those who were fundamentally contentious; a good Catholic could still be a good neighbour. And yet, the enforcement of compulsory communion and the growing association of abstention with contention increasingly marked recusants as being different than their neighbours, of being an "other." In the decades following the Elizabethan settlement, a new association of community and Protestantism was forged. If exclusion from the sacrament marked one as being out of charity with one's neighbours, then the persistent self-exclusion of recusants could only drive a further wedge between Catholics and their local communities. In a sense, then, annual communion served to isolate recusants in all but a few parishes and to cast them as unneighbourly, contentious, and disordered.[199]

Through illness, contention, scruples, or even simple neglect, early modern English parishioners might abstain from their communion service. In doing so, they set themselves apart, not just politically but also socially and spiritually. Indeed, in the early modern mind, these latter two ideas were fundamentally intertwined in the communion. As Bishop Cooper of Lincoln preached of the sacrament in 1580, "we teach that it is a link of unity among our selves, and a spiritual engrossing of us, into the mystical body of Christ."[200] The Lord's Supper served as the temporal and spiritual expression of community. Those who chose not to receive the eucharist at least annually were subject to both social and judicial scrutiny, vulnerable to presentation by churchwardens or to being cast as immoral or marginal: abstention, however scrupled, became suspect.

Suspension and Exclusion

Exclusion from the sacrament was not always voluntary, and those who hoped to receive could find themselves nevertheless turned away from the communion table. The Book of Common Prayer clearly instructed its ministers to refuse communion to unworthy parishioners: "If any … be an open and notorious evil liver, so that the congregation by him is offended, or have done any wrong to his neighbours by word or by deed, the curate having knowledge thereof, shall call him, and advertise him, in any wise not to presume to the Lord's table."[201] These prohibitions were soon extended to include those who were ignorant of basic Church doctrine, most usually displayed by the recitation of the Ten Commandments, the Lord's Prayer, and other articles of faith.[202] Succinctly described by Christopher Haigh in his brilliant article on exclusion from communion as "sin, malice and ignorance," these three offences could lead to an informal exclusion (or sanction) or, eventually, to a more formal excommunication.[203] Though, thanks to excellent historical work over the past two decades, we have a good sense of the parameters of those crimes that rendered the Elizabethan parishioner unfit for reception, looking closely at these offences underlines the importance of community at every stage of the suspension process.

A whole host of immoral behaviours could lead to suspension from the sacrament. The 1598 visitation articles from Lincoln, for example, asks the churchwardens to report those who took communion while considered an "open and notorious blasphemer, fornicator, adulterer, drunkard, or evil liver, by whom the congregation is offended."[204] That lay immorality was punished in the church is no great surprise; the church courts had reigned over the judgment of such crimes for centuries, doling out corporal punishment, pecuniary charges, or public penance as they saw fit.[205] But crucially, the Elizabethan church emphasized the involvement of the community even at this stage of the suspension process. The Prayer Book, and the visitation articles that drew from it, relied on a communal sense of decency to differentiate between those worthy to receive the sacrament and those who should be excluded: the minister was to forbid those "by whom the *congregation* is offended."[206] Exclusion from communion was built on a rhetoric of communal displeasure and disapproval, a powerful symbol of isolation from a collective morality.

Nowhere is this isolation clearer than in cases of malice. If some self-excluded over neighbourly contention, not all felt such scruples so deeply, attempting to communicate despite their disorder. The church empowered ministers to turn away such delinquent communicants on the basis of their lack of charity with their neighbours, "that the congregation may thereby be satisfied."[207] This informal suspension often involved the common fame of the parish. In 1579, Elinor Awd of Elwick, Durham, was repulsed from the sacrament because "she is not in love and charity with hir neighbour, Isabell Wardon, the wife of William Wardon; neither would she forgive nor ask forgiveness of the said Isabell when the curate and churchwardens of the same parish did exhort."[208] The collective activity described in such an account is conspicuous. Not only was the sacrament used to try to leverage peace in the community, but such appeals also came from a combination of clergy and laity. In Elinor's case, both the curate and the churchwardens intervened in the dispute. The individual dispute was given public scrutiny, and the failure to reconcile to communal norms was met with rejection from the communion table.

This is not to say, of course, that these norms were in any way politically neutral. From an elite, national perspective, allowing parochial churchwardens to intervene in questions of the sacrament seems a wildly egalitarian notion. From a local perspective, however, this system placed extraordinary power in the hands of a small portion of the community. Historians of the past forty years have carefully parsed the politics of authority in early modern parishes.[209] Sacramental exclusion, however, needs to be understood as part of this process: a potent weapon in the contestation over power. It tied together the potential for serious spiritual ramifications (separation from Christ), political ramifications (state attention), and even, as we will see in a moment, social ramifications. Wielded by a subset of the parish population, set within the context of a state church increasingly consumed with punishing lay nonconformity, the ability to exclude congregants from the Lord's Supper had enormous political capacity. Communion was not, however, a unidirectional tool of subordination. It could be used to enforce customary norms of support and obligation. Richard Purdy of Mettingham, Suffolk, was presented to the Archdeacon's Court for not taking communion during the Easter service of 1596. The witness testifying on his behalf said this was not for lack of trying, swearing "that he saw the said Purdie offer himself to the minister to receive the communion, but the minister would not admit him for that he said that Purdie was hard to the poor."[210] The minister would not give the Lord's Supper to a man who would let his neighbours starve. Purdy was literally out of charity – he did not extend the support for the poor that was expected of all good neighbours.[211] Exclusion thus became a subtle, supple instrument for both reinforcing and negotiating systems of power within the parish.

The third reason for exclusion, ignorance, at first seems little to do with the communal ideals expressed above, and far more to do with what Haigh called a desire "to prevent profanation of the sacrament."[212] And yet, this too was communal. Education in the basic Christian tenets was seen as a collective, not an individual, responsibility. As Paul Griffiths has suggested, the young were seen as particularly amenable to moral and social formation through education, and catechism was meant not only to increase religious knowledge, but to help raise "dutiful and obedient children" and "faithful and diligent subjects."[213] Knowledge of the church's basic tenets and doctrines was considered an essential component of adult life in early modern English society. Parents, masters, and ministers were supposed to instruct their charges through regular catechizing. The influential evangelicals of Dedham, Essex, had hopes that such education would remain a collective endeavour, with "every governor of household … to resort to their minister to the church at times conveniently appointed for the same, to assist the minister in the godly examination and due preparing of them and theirs to the Communion."[214] This plan was, of course, a godly ideal, but education was a preliminary criterion for participating in the communal eucharist.

Visitations required those who took communion to be able to prove their familiarity with the basic tenets of the church. Levels of understanding were compelled by age, generally with all those over fourteen required to say the catechism and those above twenty to add the Ten Commandments, the Articles of the Faith, and the Lord's Prayer (in English).[215] A presentment from 1579 Durham was entirely typical: in Brancepeth, William Brasse was "repulsed from the Communion because he could not say the 10 commandments," a sentence which was lifted upon proof of recitation.[216] In the same parish, Thomas Cheswicke, "lacking the catechism did thrust in amongst others and received, being commanded to the contrary."[217] Even in areas of the country like Durham, where reformist tendencies were limited, a basic level of religious understanding was required to partake in the sacrament.

Here too, then, we see the beginnings of the creation of a Protestant identity among the parish. While reciting the Ten Commandments or the Lord's Prayer might have been a simple display of Christian knowledge, catechisms were endowed with clear ideological perspectives. The instruction necessary for communion was not simply a Christian education, but a basic *Protestant* education. If communion was, as we have seen, an expression of communal cohesion and of being accepted as a member of a functioning community, the ties of religion and neighbourhood were bound ever more closely: to be considered a fully-fledged adult and a functioning member of the community, one had to be capable of expressing the most basic principles of Protestant doctrine. Recitation was, of course, not the same as belief, but communion provided another opportunity to inculcate the fundamental tenets of the reformed Church. With the passing of generations whose membership in the adult community was marked by their reception into the parish church – a reception that required evidence of reformed doctrine – the sacrament served as a powerful link between reformed learning and communal identity.

The power of the minister to judge who was fit to take the sacrament led some of the clergy to overexercise their privileges of exclusion. Some demanded far higher standards of godliness than required by any Prayer Book, injunction, or article of canon law. The radical members of the Dedham cohort began to make spiritual and moral interrogations of their congregations in the days leading up to the communion service, examining their parishioners' state of grace and extracting their promises of upright behaviour.[218] These evangelicals no doubt saw their actions as permitted by the requirement for education. However, any system that smacked of "closed communion" was deeply troubling to church authorities. They had much sympathy with Calvin's position that perfect faith and charity were impossible bars to sacramental reception; as he put it in his *Catechism*, "this supper had been a thing ordained in vain, if none were meet to come to it, unless he were thoroughly perfect."[219] Moreover, such restrictions may have purified the body of receivers, but it also stripped the communal sanctions from the sacrament and thus threatened both liturgical orthodoxy and the power of the eucharist to act as an indication of basic conformity. In almost all cases, such ministers were brought before the church courts and forced to distribute communion to their broader congregation.[220] Other clerics abused the power of exclusion to settle personal conflicts or pursue vendettas. As Christopher Haigh has noted, contemporary moralists feared that exclusion might be seen as a personal affront, as in the 1582 case of David

Dee, who rejected parishioners for "private occasions of offence between Mr. Dee and the parties, though they have willingly offered reconciliation."[221] Personal parish conflicts between ministers and parishioners could turn into punishments of exclusion, supported by accusations of contumacy or disorder but motivated by personal animus.

To counter the power of the ministry over the sacrament, the church authorities empowered the community to have a part in the sentence of exclusion. To begin with, suspensions were to be made only if there was a common fame or rumour of misbehaviour.[222] Even when the reputation of a parishioner was uniformly negative, a minister could still be enjoined to discuss the matter with his congregations. For example, the 1577 injunctions of the Bishop of Lincoln – certainly no evangelical – cautioned that exclusion should only occur after consultation with some of the leading men of the parish: "to the end the same may be quietly done, and without offence, no parson, vicar or Curate shall proceed thereto, before he hath opened the whole cause to the churchwardens, and some other of the best staid of his parishioners, who he shall think meet to call thereto, if there shall by them any stay be made, or any controversy rife, that the matter be certified, either to the reverend father or to some officer of his that order may be taken therein."[223] Thus the church used the community to provide oversight to ministerial justice, amending sentences that were considered harsh or unjust. When a minister could not prove the common fame or consent of the community, the church courts could overturn his exclusion or even punish him.[224] The community itself could apply pressure to overly strict clergy, with churchwardens using the visitations to protest tyrannical power. If the community could mitigate overly harsh sentences, they could also protest ministers who were too lenient. Ministers who allowed the unworthy to communicate were, in essence, declaring them to be fit members of the parish. In some cases, complaints against these ministers seem like the work of a few godly churchwardens disgusted by the laxity of a local curate. The Bishop's Visitation of Norfolk turned up several ministers who distributed the sacrament to the ignorant, such as John Gibson, curate of Terrington St John, who "receiveth to the Communion those which have not bene confirmed."[225] These presentments allowed the leading congregants some agency in the regulation not only of the probity of the parishioners but also of the behaviour of the clergy.

Such communal involvement underscores the primary consequence of exclusion: shame. To be excluded from communion was to be found unworthy, both by the minister and by a section of the larger community. The rules and laws of exclusion meant that being refused the sacrament was not only a sign of "sin, malice or ignorance," but also a sign that the community considered such an assessment to be true. It was, in a sense, an officially sanctioned defamation. When Richard Crowley pronounced his sentence of exclusion upon the Soden brothers of Oxfordshire, they railed at him, "ye go about to shame us before the whole people."[226] The Soden brothers recognized that being barred from communion would humiliate them, not just internally or as a matter of conscience, but "before the whole people." Puritan minister John Dod later vividly described such degradation: "the shame of departing from the table without the sacrament: all the congregation looking on them, and the minister passing by them."[227] Public humiliation was fundamental to exclusion.

In early modern society, shame entailed far more than simple emotional humiliation. As has been discussed in great detail by a number of social historians, the systems of credit and reputation were the underpinnings of a society.[228] Damage to an individual's reputation had a profound practical impact on the lives of early modern Englishmen and women. As Dan Beaver has elegantly summarized, "A reputation consisted of a variety of elements, combined to produce a stock of honour or credibility, and the possession of honor influenced the response to requests for economic aid or aspirations to political leadership."[229] Without honour, without a good reputation, one could suffer financial hardship, removing one from the "economy of obligation."[230] Loss of reputation could also lead to a more general alienation from the community; in a society where community was ever-shifting and defined in large part by exclusion, a bad reputation could result in social isolation.[231] The consequences were immediate, damaging, and often indelible. Margaret Cotton's angry outburst to the Cambridge Commissary Court – that those who take away their neighbour's good name "is a robber" – is a testament to the stakes at hand.[232] Thus exclusion, a sanction marking one as separate from the community and intimating a questionable reputation, could be an enormously powerful punishment in the English parish during this period.

Excommunication

The most serious form of exclusion was excommunication. More than a temporary suspension, it was a permanent and mandated isolation from church and from community. Serious crimes warranted automatic excommunication, including drawing blood in the churchyard or clandestine marriage.[233] Those standing excommunicate could be arrested by the civil authorities and thrown into prison, although this was subject to the judgment of the bishop or the ecclesiastical court and was only occasionally enforced.[234] Moreover, excommunicates were technically banned from attending church services and from the society of their neighbours. It was, in essence, the ultimate sanction of the church.

The sentence was most commonly used in the Elizabethan period to censure those who ignored the commands of the church; offenders presented to the ecclesiastical courts, even for such insignificant offences as unpaid church taxes or fees, had to attend upon pain of excommunication.[235] Though the church authorities claimed that they were punishing the sin of contumacy, some contemporaries derided such routine excommunication as diluting its efficacy and undermining its severity. As Francis Bacon wrote in 1604, "Excommunication is the greatest judgment upon the earth … and therefore for this to be used unreverently, and to be made an ordinary process to lackey up and down for Fees, how can it be without derogation to Gods honour, and making the power of the keys contemptible?"[236] This led to the traditional historiographical position that excommunication was a penalty easily given and lightly ignored.

However, more recent research has emphasized the efficacy of such sentences. As we saw in the first chapter, Martin Ingram's exhaustive study of church courts has shown that most of those presented to ecclesiastical commissions did in fact answer their summons, thus voiding or avoiding the sentence of excommunication. The Archdeaconry of Chichester, for example, showed an appearance rate of 83 per cent in 1594. Nor was this an anomaly: similar rates of attendance were noted in the Diocese of Ely and, to a slightly lesser extent, the Archdeaconry of Leicester.[237] Such rates are even more remarkable when considering that many of those called before the ecclesiastical courts were vulnerable or marginal members of parochial society or stood as openly recalcitrant in the face of conformist efforts. If even the disordered or unorthodox were largely responsive when faced with excommunication, such a sentence must have been even more efficacious for those who strived toward moral or religious order.

To put things in perspective, take the 1575 metropolitan visitation of York, which examined all parishes within the province. In this survey, 1,212 people were presented for offences; using a conservative estimate of 150,000 communicants in the province, those presented represent only 0.8 per cent of the population. In response to the visitation, all but 383 visited the archbishop's court or presented an acceptable excuse in writing. In fact, if one ignores the troublesome archdeaconry of Pickering, the response rate upon pain of excommunication was 89.6 per cent.[238] In all, only 0.025 per cent of the 1572 communicating population of Yorkshire was left standing excommunicate after the metropolitan visitation. As large and troublesome as contemporary writers may have painted the problem, the real number of those who stood excommunicate in Elizabethan England was relatively slight.

Nevertheless, excommunication loomed large in contemporary minds. The primary punitive consequence of excommunication was spiritual: those forbidden from taking the eucharist suffered a disharmony with God. As such, it remained, in both the public imagination and the preacher's invocation, a central part of a parishioner's relationship with God. To receive the eucharist was to receive Christ, whether literally or metaphorically, and to be without such communion, such assurance, was to risk damnation. For the devout, the type of person represented in Christopher Suttons's 1601 dialogue as "the spiritual man," open and free communion was fundamental to faith: "unless I should often communicate without doubt I should be worse and worse, and happily at this hour I should burn in hell fire."[239] We must not underestimate the real fear that such a ban could engender. Susan Bate, an excommunicate who had borne a bastard child, pled to the justices at Ely for her reconciliation with the church: "[she] by the space of 2 years last past hath been and yet is debarred of her access to the church to hear gods divine service and to receive his holy sacrament, to her great grief and terror."[240] The genuine panic radiates through the centuries. For some Elizabethans, removal of the sacrament had real and genuine spiritual consequences.

The punitive force of exclusion from communion, however, was perhaps even more clearly pronounced in the earthly sphere. For those whose professions depended on a certain ecclesiastical support, excommunication could present a threat to their livings: schoolmasters, ecclesiastical lawyers, clerks, sextons, even the linen washers, bell ringers, and nave sweepers of the parish. The clergy themselves could also be threatened by the sanction of excommunication: those not fit to receive communion were not considered worthy to grant it. Norwich's Archdeaconry Visitation of 1597 noted that Mr Knighte, the minster of Worlingham, Suffolk, stood "excommunicate by law for striking and drawing blood in the churchyard of Wyrlingham on Easter Eave anno dni. 1594." Horrified to find that the rector nevertheless "ever sense read service, preached and ministered the sacraments," the Archdeacon's court immediately withdrew him from the parish.[241] Excommunication also had its effects higher up the chain of ecclesiastical command. When archdeacon John Pilkington was punished in 1586 for avoiding a synod, an official came to visit his church to prohibit him from holding the visitation itself, "for that he then stood excommunicate and was an excommunicated person."[242]

Most parishioners, of course, did not receive their living directly from church authorities. Nevertheless, the punishment of excommunication had immediate, palpable, and deleterious social consequences for lay parishioners, far greater than simple exclusion. People standing excommunicate were supposed to be avoided by their neighbours, an officially-mandated communal shunning. It was, in a sense, an incarnation of the metaphor of Holy Communion: those who did not participate in the union with God were to be forbidden union with their neighbours. Articles of Visitation in the late sixteenth and early seventeenth century were preoccupied with the degree of intimacy between excommunicates and their communities. By the 1590s, ecclesiastical courts had begun to require churchwardens to report anyone who consorted with excommunicated parishioners.[243] Excommunication was contagious: those who associated with known excommunicates might not only face possible presentment, but on rare occasions suspension or even their own excommunication.[244] Excommunicates were, in effect, to be socially quarantined, cut off from the networks of neighbourliness, kinship, and community upon which they relied.

Other bonds of social network were similarly threatened by the sentence of excommunication. Being admitted as a godparent was contingent upon receiving the eucharist, and by the late sixteenth century, archdeacons' visitations routinely inquired after the spiritual rightness of those standing as godparents.[245] This seems a perfectly reasonable position for the church to take; after all, if a godparent were ignorant of the basic tenets of the doctrine or out of harmony with the church, it stands to reason that he or she could not provide necessary and proper spiritual guidance. However, like so many of the strictures on the excommunicate, this was a position of sound ecclesiastical sense that resulted in profound social consequences. Godparentage was a crucial tool in the construction of social networks. Those who chose family and friends as godparents could strengthen and formalize pre-existing ties of obligation and kinship, while those who sought godparents of a higher social rank could create links of patronage. Such benefits were reciprocal: the godparents, in addition to any mutual benefits of intensified bonds, also gained social prestige in their role as benefactor and spiritual guide.[246] Moreover, the Elizabethan period saw a surge in bequests to godchildren, indicating economic and as well as emotional bonds forged through godparentage.[247] Excommunicates were thus further isolated from the normal practices of social bonding.

Nor were excommunicates permitted to participate in formal legal procedure: they could not bring lawsuits, give testimony in a case, and were even barred from serving as executors of wills.[248] Such restrictions were not limited to ecclesiastical courts; excommunicates lost the right to sue in civil courts as well. In 1596, for instance, defendants appearing before the Court of Chancery were able to avoid answering the plaintiff's bill of complaint until the plaintiff proved to the court that his excommunication had been absolved.[249] These restrictions left excommunicates deeply vulnerable. If cheated or slandered, they could not bring the case to court; in an increasingly litigious society, this penalty must have been particularly appreciated.[250] Nor could they control the bequests of a spouse or sibling, instead yielding such power to others. Excommunicates were thus denied the basic protections of the common civil law, just as they were isolated from the broader help of their neighbours. Indeed, even in death, they were to be separated from their communities. The diocese of London banned excommunicates from being "buried in christian burial, not having before his death sought to be absolved, and testified the same to some honest and discreet man, who shall upon his oath signfy to the Bishop of the Diocese."[251] This sentence may have been an ideal rather than a lived reality (records here are few), but it was one that excluded the excommunicate in perpetuity.

Excommunicates heartily protested such ostracism. In some cases, this simply meant coming to church despite the prohibition of attendance. Churchwardens' presentments are full of accounts of parishioners refusing to be banished from services. The parish of North Elmham in Norfolk had a rash of stubborn churchgoers, with six such people presented to the archdeacon's court in a single visitation.[252] The churchwardens of Great Ellingham presented John More as one who "hath stood excommunicated this xij months & yet cometh to church to hear service, although Mr. Holden [the vicar] hath forborne to read service."[253] These parishioners silently asserted their right to take communion, despite their sentence, merely by their presence. Others were far less quiet in their protest. Thomas Abbott, hauled before the Oxfordshire Archdeacon's Court in 1584, confessed "that he disturbed the minister in the time of divine service because there was an excommunication denounced against his wife." Charged with "brawling in the church," he was sentenced to a heavy schedule of public penance.[254] Perhaps even more contentious was Jane Hayward of New Buckenham, Norwich. When she appeared at services, the churchwardens attempted to escort her from the service. However, "she refused to the great disturbance of their minister in his ministration [*sic*] of service, & further used many Railing & opprobrious speeches, calling him black sooty-mouthed knave."[255] Excommunication was clearly a punishment worth protesting.

Such a zealous defence often baffles historians, especially in light of a historiography that tends to emphasize the general lack of interest in the sacraments. For Christopher Haigh, the motivation for such actions was primarily religious; he argues that exclusion "deprived some Christians of a communal custom or a seal of the covenant or a means of grace."[256] John Spurr is more openly puzzled by this paradox; as he writes, "Strangely, in view of the general lack of enthusiasm for the sacrament, there was often as swift and adverse reaction from parishioners when a minister attempted to limit admission to the Lord's Supper. It was as if the sacrament was seen as a service which should be available to all in the community if they wanted it."[257] Both of these theories have a good deal of truth to them: parishioners seemed genuinely concerned about their spiritual welfare, and some of the strongest displays of affinity to the sacrament appear when admission to communion was limited. However, neither truly appreciates the social context of excommunication.

Excommunicates faced the litany of social barriers described above: the normal bonds of neighbourliness and obligation were forbidden to them, they were not allowed to participate in litigation or to sign wills, and they were not admitted as godparents. Their reputation was diminished, their credit tarnished, a situation compounded by rules that made their sentences deliberately and clearly public. By the late sixteenth century, ministers were required to announce the names of excommunicates at services and sermons at least every six months, and sometimes more often than that.[258] Joseph Haworth, curate of Batley in the West Riding, was presented to the church courts for not promptly reading such an excommunication. It was not, he protested, that he did not wish to read it, but that it had been "delivered and tendered at an inconvenient time even when he was in his surcloth ready to begin the morning prayer" and unable to properly peruse the document. He hastened to add that "upon the Sunday following" he denounced his parishioner "when a great number of people were present."[259] It was just such a denunciation – a public, routine disgrace, explicitly marking the excommunicate as a social pariah – that goaded Thomas Abbott into disturbing the divine service in 1584 Oxfordshire to defend his wife's good name.

Such disgrace could be rapidly and easily curtailed. While the effects on a person's reputation might echo for years, the immediate injunctions were removed immediately upon confession of a crime and performance (or payment) of penance.[260] As we saw in chapter 1, penance itself could be public, humiliating, and profoundly shaped by the power of the state church. As the Bishop of Lichfield put it, the excommunicate was to give "christian public satisfaction."[261] But it was also a mechanism by which people could quickly return to the fold. The ease with which this penalty could be rescinded might seem to undermine the seriousness of the sanction. However, a closer reading shows precisely the opposite: part of the power of excommunication lay in its ease of cessation. Unlike corporal punishment or the payment of a fine, the sanction was reversible. It was a punishment that continued only so long as the offender stubbornly continued to offend. Those who stayed excommunicate and were announced as such during services were repeatedly and publicly declared not only to be outcasts but also to be people unwilling and uninterested in readmission to the community. To remain an excommunicate was, in essence, to scorn your neighbours. This placed added pressure on the sensitive excommunicates to redeem themselves as quickly as possible in the eyes of the church and the community, to rejoin their neighbours, to regain their reputations. Redemption was possible as soon as misbehaviour was corrected. Excommunication was thus the perfect mode of social control – not only isolating those who strayed outside the bounds of acceptable behaviour, but also making readmission to full function in society contingent upon reformation. Moreover, the cycle of excommunication and redemption perpetuated the legitimacy of early modern social codes: to rejoin the community, one had to reaffirm the validity of its moral structure and its authority of judgment. It served as a tool of both coercive rehabilitation and of restorative justice.

Some have argued that such a tool would have limited effect on those who did not already have some care for the sacrament – a punishment, essentially, that preached to the converted.[262] There were certainly those who seemed to care little about such a sanction. Some approached their excommunication with a light heart; Henry Daynes, as the churchwardens reported, "maketh a jest of it saying he shall save a hundredth mile going in the year, because the church is a mile from his house."[263] And yet, the sentence seems generally effective. It was avoided, it was protested, and it drove people to court to have the censure lifted.[264]

Such a tool had an effect on rich and poor alike. Excommunication provided an obvious threat to the better sort, who stood to lose their social position in any hint of scandal. However, such a sanction could also have a devastating impact on the poor of the parish, who were those most frequently presented for offences.[265] Poor relief was, of course, distributed in the parish church, often by the same churchwardens who were so deeply involved in the visitation process. It was subjective, not automatic, charity. By the late-Elizabethan period, poor relief was becoming increasingly contingent upon judgment of worth by the overseers of the poor, a worth defined not only on circumstance, but also on moral character and piety.[266] Even the moment of charity had been tied to eucharistic conformity, with some parishes beginning to distribute relief at the very services where excommunicates' names would be read.[267] Poor people who refused the sacrament made themselves intensely vulnerable. This was as true for those who needed occasional help as those who required weekly support. Those in exceptional circumstances could turn to local authorities to petition for extraordinary relief. Magistrates judged such petitions in large part upon the proof of a claimant's good reputation, as attested to by fellow members of his or her community. In 1600, for example, forty-seven people, including the vicar, testified that Thomas Fawtless, a poor blacksmith, "is and hath ben in all his actions of good Decent and honest usage Demeanour and behaviour."[268] It is hard to imagine the vicar and the reputable parish going to bat for a poor man whose name was routinely read for standing outside the communion. With a sentence of excommunication, those already on the brink of poverty could be thrust into a world of financial desperation. Excommunicate John Sutton wrote that a local magistrate "doth utterly refuse to absolve your said Orator … to the utter impoverishing of your said Orator."[269] Standing excommunicate, then, rendered a poor person intensely vulnerable at a time of increasing economic privation.

If excommunication had an impact on all levels of society, such influence was distinctly *local*. The Church mandated that congregants should communicate only within their own parish church, and asked the churchwardens to report congregants who did not "resort unto their own parish church" and ministers who allowed strangers to receive the sacrament.[270] Even orthodox communicants who attended more convenient services outside their own parish boundaries could find themselves reported to the church courts. John More of Gorleston, Suffolk, when presented by churchwardens for irregular attendance, protested "that he is Corpulent and fat and dwelleth nearer Yarmouth than Gorleston church, and by reason thereof he repaireth to Yarmouth church, he and his wife, and there gave and do most commonly hear divine prayers read." Unmoved, the court ordered him to attend services, nearby or no, in his own parish.[271] The community was thus defined precisely by the boundaries of the parish.[272] The reasons for such restrictions were clear. Without boundaries, the state Church could not regulate orthodoxy of attendance, ceremony, or doctrine. Though religious instruction of the laity was certainly a priority, especially for those ministers who wished for a stronger preaching ministry, the biggest fears of the central Church lay in the dissenting minorities, both traditionalist and radical. The argument of Francis Kenton of Thetford illustrates the danger clearly: "he refuseth to receive the communion at ye Ministers hands … [and says that] if two ministers be in the town & the one a preacher & theother non he willbe at his choice to which he will go." When asked why he would not receive in his own church, he answered that he had judged his minister to be a "profane man."[273] This sort of personal agency was not welcome in a church that saw such decisions as steps toward nonconformity and even separatism.

Authorities were aware that those who moved outside the boundaries of their parish could easily disassociate themselves from the sanction of excommunication. It was a real fear, almost impossible to know, whether migrants had faced suspension from their previous congregation. Martin Ingram argues that the anonymity of migration allowed excommunicates to slip "back into normal life without securing a formal absolution."[274] Officials did the best they could to publicize the names of excommunicates, though one suspects it was an uphill battle. Nevertheless, they tried. The litany of excommunicate persons, read by the minister before the congregation, spread the news throughout the area, a rumour that could pass from parish to parish. Visitation articles, too, pushed ministers to ensure, however they could, that new members of their congregations had been absolved. The bishop of London asked his ministers to gather "testimony from the minister of the place where [new congregants] dwell, what they be, that it may appear that they be not persons excommunicate or otherwise infamous."[275] What is fascinating here is not just the expectation of surveillance, but also the idea that those sentenced to an excommunication would not live happily outside the church, but instead seek to rejoin the congregation in the sacrament. The fear was not of those avoiding communion but those trying to avoid the shame and punishment that excommunication could bring. The expectation is that the sacrament would be sought.

There would always, of course, be those who did not care about their exclusion from the sacrament, be it excommunication or more informal suspension. Some lived in the slippery margins of society, evading official condemnation or the deepest pressures of communal expectation. Others proudly flouted authority, on ideological or personal grounds. And yet, annual participation in the ritual of the Lord's Supper in

Elizabethan England remained not only the norm, but a hallmark of belonging: belonging to God, belonging to one's community. It was a contested community, shot through with sharp politics and changing circumstances. But it was also a community of neighbours, of their mutualities and obligations, of their shared, communal, public sacrament. The bonds between social conformity, political conformity, and spiritual conformity were knit tight by the sacrament. And England would never be quite the same.

Conclusion

When our parishioner walked into his parish church on a midsummer morning in 1580, he was entering a world unlike any England had ever known. Gone was the mass of the late-medieval years, the miracle witnessed more than partaken of, the old Latin rite and the great stone altars at which it was sung. In its place was an English ceremony, not just vernacular, but proudly patriotic, celebrating the power of the divine and of the crown. Gone was the separation, figurative and literal, between the ministry and the laity. The rood was dismantled, the altar stones broken, and in their place sat a sturdy table on full display in the nave, where all who were permitted received both bread and wine. Gone was the chaos and uncertainty of the mid-Tudor years; the rapid changes of that era's liturgical practices replaced by Elizabethan consistency, year after year of the same cadence, the same words, the same litany. And gone were the vestiges of any distance between church and state, supplanted by the heavy guiding hand of obedience and surveillance. This the world of the late-Elizabethan church, and the sacrament that the parishioner received represented a changed England.

From its beginnings in the 1559 Prayer Book, the Elizabethan sacrament was personal, but it was by no means individual. Instead, it was deliberately, even coercively, communal. It represented communion with Christ, the relationship between the human and the divine. It represented communion with the country, a uniform service praising the queen heard throughout the land, a reflection of the special bond between God and England. And it represented communion with the parish, a collective experience of the full and bounded community. The memorial meal was eaten with one's neighbours, a society of believers on earth. This conception of the sacrament as public and communal was underscored by a state church determined to enforce a uniformity of practice across the spectacular diversity of local parishes. In the face of challenges from both Catholic recusants and Protestant separatists, and driven by a fear of fragmentation, the Elizabethan church increasingly sought to regulate conformity to the sacrament in terms of collective and shared reception.

This regulation was, on the whole, successful. Parochial and diocesan records demonstrate the incorporation of the new reformed sacrament within the two decades following the Elizabethan revision of the Prayer Book. Some of the attendant changes were rapid; renovation of church interiors, for example, was largely completed within five years and almost entirely adapted by 1570. Others were slower; communion expenses indicate the expansion of eucharistic participation could well take twenty years to come to fruition. By midway through Elizabeth's reign, however, reception of this reformed rite was the new norm. Piety and obedience were deeply linked to sacramental participation, and the Lord's Supper became a hallmark of religious orthodoxy and acceptance, however coerced, of the new ecclesiastical order. Receiving – or not receiving – was an explicitly political act. To receive, however reluctantly, was to legitimize the state church and its power to shape liturgy. To abstain, however benignly, marked one as an aberration. Every parishioner became a political actor.

At the same time, communion served as a site for reconciliation and communal harmony within the social ties of the parish community. Communicants took admonitions to resolve parish conflict before reception seriously. The accessible but consistent standards for reception – charity with your neighbours, a basic understanding of church tenets, overall moral probity – placed added pressure on the parishioner to communicate. Not communicating – or, even worse, being refused communion – was a sign of separation from the moral and social order of the parish. Exclusion was humiliating, and it carried with it real and serious consequences for participation in early modern society. Excommunication was particularly damaging, carrying with it deep legal and economic vulnerabilities. Participation in the Lord's Supper, then, also became a hallmark of social orthodoxy, and a tool of micropolitical subordination and negotiation.

Communion was, in the Elizabethan church, the ultimate expression of community – and a community redrawn along specific ideological lines. While the communion order of the Elizabethan Prayer Book had allowed some conceptual flexibility, it was latitude within a larger Protestant debate. Similarly, this new sense of parochial community, and the concomitant participation in the Lord's Supper, was grounded within a fundamentally Protestant identity. Conforming to the Elizabethan church meant accepting this new sacrament; accepting the sacrament meant participating in the reformed ritual; and denying the sacrament meant a separation from society. Thus the ties between religious and social orthodoxy in Elizabethan England were drawn ever closer, and the Elizabethan parish wove a new, reformed communal fabric, supper by supper, and with it, made a new church.

Conclusion

We end where we began, in Wiltshire.

Between 1559 and 1561, the parish of Mere stripped its altars. It also took down the rood screen; whitewashed a picture of the Trinity; bought a Book of Common Prayer, a psalter, Erasmus's *Paraphrases*, and several pricksong books; and outfitted the minister with a new surplice. The churchwardens attended multiple visitations to prove their work, bringing prepared bills with them as evidence. It was not a clean destruction. Just a year earlier, the wardens' election had been postponed by the twin disruptions of the "occasion of the Alteration of some part of Religion and of the service and Ceremonies of the church" following the death of Queen Mary and the "occasion of some variance and Contention among certain of the parishioners." Exactly what that contention was – doctrinal, ideological, personal, secular, economic, political – was left unsaid. But then, when Elizabeth came to the throne, new wardens were elected, "according to the Ancient usage of the parish," and the accounts returned to normal order.[1]

It is tempting to declare this the moment of the Reformation, done and completed. The material culture was converted; the protestant books purchased; the wardens functional; the parish presenting the results to the state visitation. It was nothing of the sort. The transformation of the parish took years, even decades, to put into place. Changes trickled in over time. The rood loft came down in 1563.[2] In 1569, they had to go to Salisbury to sort out difficulties with old chantry lands.[3] By 1570, they were formalizing the selling of church seats, located precisely and specifically within the body of the church: "sold one seat in the midst of the church unto John Forward, son of Roger Forward, which was Ralph Permans seat."[4] Payments for bread and wine began to be recorded; in 1575 alone, they held seven different communion services.[5] That same year the accounts record a decree that the wardens should build new pews "in a void place in the western part of the quire" but that that the "authority" to choose who would sit there would rest in "the whole parish at the church reckoning day."[6] The sounds of the church multiplied and grew. By the late 1570s, they had refurbished the troublesome old organs with new pipes and were ringing the bell for Queen Elizabeth's accession day.[7] Communion services had grown too: at least one Supper a month, with three more for Easter weekend.[8] In 1579, they exchanged their "Chalice" for a "new Cup."[9] The mid-1580s saw new rationalization of the churchwardens' roles in light of their increased duties.[10] The church ales that had sustained the parish until at least 1581 faded from the records for some time, but were revived in at least the 1590s, before fading again.[11] They were joined by other regular sources of income: the holy loaf, seat rentals, funerals, and legacies.[12] Poor relief increasingly crept into the records.[13] Throughout it all, wardens reported constantly to the visitors, making bills and presenting them to ecclesiastical authorities. And the tiny repairs, of seats and windows and ropes and cloths, continued inexhaustibly.

The accounts of 1599 showed a Mere transformed from four decades earlier: not just in the obvious aspects, like rood lofts or English Bibles, but in habits, expectations, authority, and power relationships.[14] Money flowed in through funds that fixed conformity in people's lives. Seat sales and rents composed the bulk of the income. As we have seen, such fixed seating engendered a sense of ownership within the church (this is my seat, which I have paid for) and a specific belonging within a community (this is what my seat indicates about my social status and family relationships). In doing so, it made the community and attendance legible, monitorable, and reportable. And the pride and belonging with which these parishioners clung to their spaces – going so far as to sue for their rights to sit in a particular place – created a stable listening audience for Protestant sermons or homilies on obedience to the queen. They raised money through regular rates, an expression of the independence and authority of the wardens, overseers, and auditors who issued annual local taxation and distributed for church and community needs. Small sums came from the leasing of property, twinning the parish to the local harvests. And income came from communion bread, no longer called the "holy loaf," supporting at least seven communions scattered throughout the year, plus the Easter season. Here, parishioners gathered openly, as a community, to take a Calvinist Lord's Supper together. This public reception marked them as good neighbours, obedient Englishmen, and unabashed Protestants.

The expenditures were similarly reconstructed.[15] To be sure, there were continuities: to the plumber and the clerk, for candles and clappers, for "an ell and a quarter of white cloth for Richard Kendall's childs shroud." But much had changed. There were the regular expenditures on communion bread and wine, from a small 12p. service to a 38s. "barrel of wine against Easter." The church ale had transformed into new communal celebrations, to "make the Lord of Gyllingham drink" and "for making of the ringers drink." The accounts noted an increasing connection to the broader world and an understanding that parishes should be explicitly involved in national charity: regular payments to the poor in the gaol at Salisbury and frequent payments for wounded and maimed solders, most injured in the quasi-religious wars in the Low Countries and Ireland – Protestantism and patriotism entwined again. The churchwardens seem to have avoided a visitation that year, after an expensive outing a few months earlier, with books sent from the dean of Salisbury and substantial funds laid out for a trip to the dean's ecclesiastical court.[16] But the sinews of power here were clear, with a heavy load of duties: to manage the funds, pay the vendors, employ the clerk, keep track of church seating, monitor their fellow parishioners, report to authorities, organize the communion supplies, carry out government orders, provide for the poor.

These were the agents of the English Reformation. Not to them, or even with them, but *through* them, the parish had been transformed – transformed under a state church that had given them generational consistency for the first time since the break from Rome, which demanded performative conformity and which crafted a compulsory community. The Protestant nation was made in tithe collections and pew disputes; in church ales and churchwardens' elections; in pest control and shilling loans and hopes of social advancement. It lies with the women who were paid tuppence a week to sweep the church clean; with the parishioners who purchased well-worn copies of parish Bibles for their own daily use; with the poor who knelt before their parish governors in the chancel to receive their relief; with the unmarried pregnant girls reading out their penance before the congregation;

with churchwardens marching door to door to collect funds for their church; with the craftsmen painstakingly repairing broken windows and leaking roofs. It lies with tithe collectors gathering eggs, bell ringers marking the accession of the queen, painters decorating the walls with royal arms, vintners making a fortune from communion in two kinds. It lies with everyday people negotiating new avenues, new powers, new authorities, and a new conception of just what it meant to be English. And together, they build a new experience of religion, of politics, of society. Together, they built the English church in the Elizabethan parish.

Notes

Introduction

1 TNA PROB 11/97/219; Crittall, ed., *History of the County of Wiltshire*, 239–50.
2 WSHC PR118/1660/14.
3 WSHC PR207/2944/44; LMA P69/BOT2/B/012.
4 WHSC PR118/1660/14, 3.
5 Ibid., 12.
6 Christopher Haigh, *English Reformations*; Diarmaid MacCulloch, *Later Reformation*; Peter Marshall, *Heretics and Believers*; Alec Ryrie, *The Age of Reformation.*
7 Haigh, *English Reformations*, chap. 10.
8 34 & 35 Hen. VIII c. 1 s. 9.
9 Haigh, *English Reformations*, 157–67.
10 An erudite discussion of the various influences of Swiss Reformers can be found in MacCulloch, *Thomas Cranmer: A Life*, chap. 14. MacCulloch argues that, though Cranmer was particularly influenced by Bullinger, there were nevertheless strong elements of Calvin and even Bucer in his conception of the sacraments.
11 Duffy, *Stripping of the Altars*, 448–77; Shagan, *Popular Politics*, Part 3.
12 MacCulloch, *Later Reformation*, 11–17.
13 The brief attempt to put Edward's cousin, the Protestant Lady Jane Grey, on the throne met with famous disaster; she has been known to generations of schoolchildren as the Nine Days' Queen.
14 Haigh, *English Reformations*, 203–34; MacCulloch, *Later Reformation*, 17–23.
15 Duffy, *Stripping of the Altars*, 524–55.

16 Eamon Duffy, for one, believes that the tactics of the Marian regime had been largely successful and were effectively turning the tide toward Catholicism; for Duffy, it was the twin deaths of Queen Mary and Cardinal Reginald Pole – who died on the same day – that undermined the Catholic restoration. (Duffy, *Fires of Faith*.)

17 Patrick Collinson's comprehensive *Elizabethan Puritan Movement* is illustrative in this regard, especially when placed in the context of Norman Jones's analysis of the co-operation between conservative and radical Protestants in the crafting of the Elizabethan settlement. (Jones, *Faith by Statute*.)

18 1 Eliz. I, c. 1.

19 1. Eliz. I. c. 2. A few fundamental changes to the 1552 edition were made; see chapter 3 for a closer analysis of the doctrinal basis of these changes.

20 *Articles* (1563).

21 MacCulloch, *Later Reformation*, 28.

22 D'Ewes, *The Journals of All the Parliaments*, 329. Cf. also MacCulloch, *Later Reformation*, chap. 4; Collinson, *Elizabethan Puritan Movement*, Part 5.

23 For a fuller account of the historiography, see below, note 33, and chapter 5 of this book.

24 Haigh, *English Reformations*, 251–3.

25 MacCulloch, *Later Reformation*, 121.

26 Haigh, *English Reformations*, 263.

27 Shagan, *The Rule of Moderation*, 113–15, 154–5.

28 Duffy, *Voices of Morebath*; Duffy, *Stripping of the Altars*; Hutton, *Rise and Fall*, chap. 1–2.

29 Hartley, *Proceedings in the Parliaments*, 1:240. Cf also Walsham, *Church Papists*, 11–12.

30 Elton, *Parliament of England*, 201–3.

31 Kaufman, "Process of Protest."

32 Archer, *Pursuit of Stability*; Black, *English Nationalism*; Brenner, *Merchants and Revolution*; Brooks, *Law, Politics, and Society*; Brooks, *Pettyfoggers*; Gowing, *Domestic Dangers*; Griffiths, *Lost Londons*; Hindle, *On the Parish*; Jewell, *Education in Early Modern England*; Kent, *English Village Constable*; Lockwood, *Conquest of Death*; Muldrew, *Economy of Obligation*; Stretton, *Women Waging Law*; Shepard, *Accounting for Oneself*; Shepard, *Meanings of Manhood*; Wall, "Greatest Disgrace"; Wrightson, *English Society*.

33 Cf. McGrath, *Papists and Puritans under Elizabeth I*; Bossy, *The English Catholic Community*; J.C.H. Aveling, *The Handle and the Axe*; Pritchard,

Catholic Loyalism; Dures, *English Catholicism*; Walsham, *Church Papists*; Wooding, *Rethinking*; Dillon, *Construction of Martyrdom*; McClain, *Lest We Be Damned*; Questier, *Catholicism and Community*; Shagan, ed. *Catholics and the "Protestant Nation"*; Tutino, *Law and Conscience*; Corthell, ed. *Catholic Culture.*

34 The most influential work on Elizabethan puritanism is undoubtedly Patrick Collinson's *The Elizabethan Puritan Movement.* Other works on this subject (and on the related, though certainly not coterminous, subject of more radical separatism) in Elizabethan England include: Pearson, *Thomas Cartwright*; Seaver, *Puritan Lectureships*; Lake, *Moderate Puritans*; Collinson, *Godly People*; Lake, *Anglicans and Puritans?*; Martin, *Religious Radicals in Tudor England*; Acheson, *Radical Puritans in England*; Marsh, *Family of Love in English Society*; Pearse, *Between Known Men*; Spufford, ed. *World of Rural Dissenters*; Lake and Questier, *Anti-Christ's Lewd Hat.*

35 Cf. especially Neale, *Elizabeth I and Her Parliaments. vols. 1 and 2*; Collinson, *Archbishop Grindal*; Hudson, *Cambridge Connection*; Jones, *Faith by Statute.*

36 Shagan's *Popular Politics*, referenced several times in this section, is a notable exception to this. Cultural history, especially the history of non-written sources, has been far more influential on Reformation historiography than on social history.

37 Marsh, *Popular Religion*; Jones, *English Reformation.*

38 Shagan, *Popular Politics*, 11.

39 Wood, *Riot, Rebellion, and Popular Politics*, 13.

40 Cf. Ethan Shagan, *Popular Politics*, and Kumin, *The Shaping of a Community.*

41 Cf. Zedeen, *Entstehung der Konfessionen*; Reinhard, "Reformation, Counter-Reformation, and the Early Modern State"; Schilling, "Confessional Europe"; and Boettecher, "Confessionalization," 1–10.

42 Cf. Marshall, "(Re)defining the English Reformation," 575–6, 583–6.

43 Shagan, *Popular Politics*, 25.

Chapter One

1 Wheater, *Parishes of Sherburn and Cawood*, 292.

2 BI Wis.1/Watson. The annual dates have been changed to reflect the current conventions; the language has also been silently modernized to allow ease of reading. These conventions will occur throughout the book.

3 Blair, *Church in Anglo-Saxon Society*, chaps. 7–8.

4 Margaret Clark, "Northern Light?" 56; Grierson, *The Companion Guide to Northumbria*, 257; Campbell, *The Landscape of Pastoral Care*, 237; Richardson, *Puritanism in North-West England*, 15.

5 There was a long-standing struggle to have St Nicholas recognized as a parish, which was not finalized by the end of our period. Beloe, *Our Borough: Our Churches*, 41–171, especially 155–61.

6 Walsham, *Reformation of the Landscape.*

7 The number of parishes in a deanery varied considerably. Victorian scholars saw the origins of the deanery in the Saxon church, and E.L. Cutts's *Dictionary of the Church of England* ascribes the etymology of *dean* to the Saxon tradition of dividing the secular jurisdiction of the *hundred* (on which rural deaneries were often mapped) into ten *tithings* (another, small secular jurisdiction). In any case, by the time of the Reformation, archdeaconries had replaced deaneries as the primary jurisdictional division. Cutts, *Dictionary*, 532–3.

8 While the new diocese of Oxford had a bishop in place for fewer than four years from 1558 to 1603, it did have long-standing church personnel, including archdeacons and deans of the cathedral, who managed in episcopal absence. Cf. Horn, *Fasti Ecclesiae Anglicanae*, 75–85.

9 TNA, SP 12/132, f. 61v.

10 DRO, Chanter/41, ff. 91–2.

11 Scargill-Bird, *Calendar of the Manuscripts*, 306; BL, Lansdowne Vol/11, f. 4r; TNA, SP 12/116, f. 45r-v and responses, e.g. SP 12/117, f. 25; BL, Lansdowne Vol/36, ff. 45r–49r.

12 Cf. chapter 5 of this book for more.

13 Owen, *Records of the Established Church*, 30–4.

14 Ingram, *Church Courts*, 44–5.

15 For medieval examples, cf. Cheney, *Episcopal Visitation*; Frere, *Visitation Articles and Injunctions.*

16 Take, for instance, the surviving episcopal records of the diocese of York in the Borthwick Institute, which begin in 1567–68. [BI, V.1567–8/CB.1-CB.2], or those of Norwich, which begin in 1555, but only become regular in the 1590s [NRO DN/VIS 1/1, NRO DN/VIS 2/1–DN/VIS 3/2].

17 SWHT, Somerset, D/D/ca/17, 22, 23, 24, 25, 27, 40, 41, 43, 68, 66, 82, 114, 120, 121, 122a, 133, 134.

18 Some records survive from earlier in the 1540s and 1550s as well. WSRO, Ep/I/18/9, 11, 13, 14, 16, 17–23, 25.

19 BI, V.1567–8, V.1571-2, V.1575, V.1578–9, V.1582, V.1586, V.1590–1, V.1594, V.1595–6, V.1600.

20 There is extensive evidence of visitations taking place before this date, but it is only from 1589 that the records survive in a near-unbroken streak. NRO ANW 1/9–ANW 1/16, covering 1589 to 1590, 1592 to 1593, 1596 to 1599, 1601, and 1603. Additional information is found in NRO ANW 1/21, which includes material from 1601 to 1612.

21 Cf. the volumes of the York and Norwich visitations mentioned above.

22 SWHT, Somerset, D/P/tin/4/1/1, ff. 185r–190v, quote f. 186v.

23 SWHT, Devon, 1048A/PW/38. Also cf. /46 and /53.

24 *Churchwardens' Accounts of Pittington*, 34–5. Prentice was the deputy of the Official of the Dean and Chapter, who oversaw the parish.

25 DUL, DDR/EV/VIS/2/1, ff. 8r–169v.

26 Kitto, ed. *St Martin in the Fields*, 452–3.

27 Usher, ed. *Presbyterian Movement*, 85, 88–9; Collinson, Craig, and Usher, eds., *Conferences and Combination Lectures*, 184.

28 Beatniffe, *A sermon preached at Torceter…*, A8v.

29 Ingram, *Church Courts*, 44–6; Owen, *Records of the Established Church*, 32–3; O'Day, *Routledge Companion*, 64–7.

30 Chaucer, "General Prologue," 659–60.

31 Shorrocks, ed., *Bishop Still's Visitation*, 4.

32 To give but one example, the eight parishioners presented from Felixkirk, Yorkshire, in 1600 were entered consecutively in the court books. BI V.1600/CB.1, f. 70r-v. Cf. also Marchant, *Church under the Law*, chap. 4, for a very detailed description of the process.

33 Cf. NRO DN/VIS 2/1 or BI V.1578–9/CB.1, e.g., for particularly nice examples of this structure.

34 BI V.1590–1, f. 186r.

35 Ingram, *Church Courts*, 45.

36 Strype, *Life and Acts of John Whitgift*, 447.

37 Price "The Abuses of Excommunication"; Hill, *Society and Puritanism*; Houlbrooke, *Church Courts and People.*

38 E.g. Stoughton, *An Abstract*, 251–8.

39 Usher, *Presbyterian Movement*, 88–9.

40 Ingram, *Church Courts*, 347–51.

41 Shorrocks, ed., *Bishop Still's Visitation*, 18.

42 Ibid., 19.

43 Ibid., 151.

44 Ibid., 355–8.

45 Herrup, *The Common Peace*, chaps. 3–6.

46 Churchwardens did volunteer some presentments between visitations, though this tended to be reserved for more acute cases. Whether wardens would have volunteered the same information that they presented at a visitation can be only a matter of speculation, as the system of visitations was robust and regular enough to render most other presentments unnecessary. Cf. Ingram, *Church Courts*, 44.

47 *Articles to be enquired in the visitation … anno 1559*, A2r.

48 *Injunctions exhibited by Iohn … Bishop of Norwich*, A2r-v.

49 The issue was present from the beginning of Elizabeth's reign, but first took concrete expression in the Convocation of 1563. Collinson, *Elizabethan Puritan Movement*, 60, 65–9.

50 *Articles to be enquired of in the visitation of … Matthew*, A2r-v.

51 *Articles to be enquired of within the dioces of Norwiche* (1567), A2r-v.

52 *Articles to be enquired of in the visitation of the dioces of London … 1571*, sig A2r.

53 Wrightson and Levine, *Poverty and Piety*; Underdown, *Revel, Riot, and Rebellion*; Ingram *Church Courts, Sex and Marriage in England*; Ingram, "Reformation of Manners."

54 Houlbrooke, *Church Courts and the People*, 75–8; Marchant, *Church under the Law*, chap. 6; Outhwaite, *The Rise and Fall*, chap. 7.

55 *Interrogatories for the doctrine and maners … in the churche*, sig A4r.

56 *Articles ecclesiasticall to be inquired of by the churchwardens and the swornemen within the dioces of Hereforde*, B2v.

57 *Injunctions given by … Edmonde … Anno do. 1571*, C1v.

58 *Injunctions given by … John … Bishop of Sarisburie* [*sic*], B3v.

59 *Articles to be enquired of, by the church Wardens … within the Archdeaconrie of Middlesex*, B2v.

60 *Articles to be enquired of by the churchwardens … within the deane of Shorham*, A4v.

61 This number includes those presented in the archdeaconry of Cleveland. Some 342 individuals were so presented for a primary offence, for crimes including fornication, adultery, sexual incontinence, and illegitimate children. [BI. V.1600/CB.1]

62 *Articles to be enquired in the visitacion in the first yere …* (1559); *Articles to*

be enquired ... of the ... Archebyshop of Canterbury (1563); *Injunctions with certaine articles* (1569).

63 *Articles to be inquired within the dioces of London* (1586).

64 *Articles to be enquired ... within the diocese of Lincoln* (1588).

65 *Articles ministred by ... Anthony ... Bishop of Chichester* (1600).

66 *Articles to be enquired of in the visitation of ... Matthew* (1563), A2r.

67 *Articles to be enquired of within the dioces of London* (1601), STC (2nd ed)/10254, sig A2r.

68 The London visitation of 1586 asks at least thirty questions of its ministry, as does the Hereford visitation of 1592, while the Winchester articles of 1570 contain twenty-nine. *Articles to be enquired of within the dioces of London* (1589); *Articles to be ministered by ... Robert ... Bishop of Winchester (1570).*

69 Similar articles appear in those visitations mentioned above.

70 Haigh, *English Reformations*, 243–4.

71 Ibid., 248. Cf. Foster, *The State of the Church*, 33–46.

72 Stevenson, *Calendar of State Papers, Foreign*, vol. 4, no. 323, 191.

73 Scargill-Bird, *Calendar of the Manuscripts*, no. 1024.

74 TNA, SP 15/11 f. 29r.

75 Haigh, *English Reformations*, 248–9.

76 Wenig, "The Reformation in the Diocese of Ely," 154.

77 Carlson, "Origins, Function, and Status of the Office of Churchwarden," 167–71.

78 NRO ANW/6/1, f. 21r.

79 See chapter 2 for a longer discussion of the office of the warden.

80 *A booke of certaine canons* (1571), C3r.

81 Cf. Haigh, *English Reformations*, chap. 8, and Carlson, "Origins and Function."

82 NRO ANW/6/1, f. 5r.

83 BI CP.G.2277; CP.G.2596.

84 Sheils, *Papers of the York Court*, passim. Cf. es BI HC.CP.1564/2 and HC.CP.1569/1.

85 NA SP 12/19 f. 74v; Houlbrooke, *Church Courts and the People*, 44–5.

86 Lockwood, *Conquest of Death*, chap. 5.

87 *Articles ministered in the visitation of ... John King*, B2r.

88 *Articles to be enquired of within the dioces of London* (1598), B3r.

89 NA SP 12/36 f. 86r.

90 Shorrocks, ed., *Bishop Still's Visitation,* 130.
91 Ibid., 16.
92 Gee and Hardy, *Documents*, 77, 416.
93 See Lake and Questier, "Introduction," *Conformity and Orthodoxy*, ix–xx.
94 1 Eliz., Ca 2, as quoted in Gee and Hardy, *Documents*, 463.
95 *Articles to be enquyred in the visitacyon* (1559), B1r.
96 *Articles to be enquired of in the visitation of … Matthew … Archebyshop of Canterbury*; Cf. also *Articles to be enquired of within the dioces of Norwiche* (1567), A4r.
97 *Articles to be enquired of in the visitation of the Dioces of London* (1571).
98 Collins, *The Canons of 1571*, 72.
99 Neale, *Elizabeth I and Her Parliaments.* Vol. 1, 386–9.
100 *Articles to be enquired of, within the prouince of canterburie* (1582), B4v–C1r.
101 *Articles to be inquired of in the ordinarie visitation* (1584), A2v.
102 *Articles to be enquired of … within the Diocesse of Lincoln* (1594), B2r.
103 *Articles to be answered of the sworne men in the Archdeacon of London* (1584).
104 DRO, Chanter/41, 565.
105 *Articles to be enquired of, within the diocese of Lincolne …* [1598] STC (2nd ed.)/10235, A4v.
106 Hindle, "Beating the Bounds," 227.
107 Wrightson, *English Society*, 40–4.
108 Slack, *Poverty and Policy*, chaps. 4–6.
109 Some of the most interesting discussions on this topic have been in Lake and Questier, *Conformity and Orthodoxy*, and Shagan, *Rule of Moderation.*
110 Rolle, *Here Begynneth a Lytell Boke*, A2r. This edition was printed in 1534, but dates to the fourteenth century. Rolle is an interesting figure, whose personal positions on penance were modified by his devotion to solitary life, but this is a reasonable popular understanding of the penitential system. Cf. Hughes, "Rolle, Richard."
111 An interesting ritual description can be found in Thomas, *Religion and the Decline of Magic*, 181–4. Here too, Thomas argues that penance was largely a public ritual. This portrayal has heavily influenced other historians' conceptions of popular penance – see, for instance, Bossy, "The Social History of Confession," 21–38. However, close examinations of both written and non-written sources point to a remarkable amount of privacy during the sacrament of confession. Nichols, "The Etiquette of Pre-Reformation Confession," 145–63.
112 Postles, "The Market Place as Space," 44–5.

113 Shagan, "Clement Armstrong," 64.
114 *Articles to be enquired of within the dioces of London* (1598), A3v.
115 Cf. Postles, "The Market Place," 44–8.
116 *Articles to be enquired of, within the diocese of Lincolne …* (1598).
117 Cf. Wrightson, "Mutualities and Obligations," especially 163–76; Shepard, "Manhood, Credit, and Patriarchy; Muldrew, *The Economy of Obligation*; Muldrew, "The Culture of Reconciliation"; Withington. "Citizens, Community, and Political Culture in Restoration England," 134–55.
118 CUL, GBR/0265/Comm.Ct. II.11, f. 27r–v.
119 Cf. Shuger, "The Reformation of Penance," 568–71.
120 BI Wis.1/Maycocke.
121 Ibid.

Chapter Two

1 Stowe, *A Survay of London*, 159.
2 Willis, *Church Music and Protestantism*, 94.
3 LMA P69/ALH6/B/011, f. 162v; also cf. ff. 80r–81v, 56r, and 69r.
4 Carlson, "Origins, Function, and Status." Craig's excellent "Co-operation and Initiatives" offers an anthropological take on the Elizabethan office; while sensitive and revelatory, it speaks much less to a sense of change over time or of fundamental shifts in the parochial landscape. More focus on change is in the final chapter of Kümin's *Shaping of a Community*, although its conclusions are not as detailed about the Elizabethan as the medieval office. Important studies of local office-holding have looked at the churchwarden in the context of other officials, though these have generally concentrated on the seventeenth century. Cf. French, *Middle Sort of People*; Wrightson and Levine, *Poverty and Piety*; Pitman, "Tradition and Exclusion."
5 Moorman, *Church Life in England*, 143.
6 Drew, *Early Parochial Organization*, 6.
7 Synod of Exeter (1287), c. 12, quoted in Wilkins, *Concilia*, 140.
8 Drew, *Early Parochial Organization*, 10–13.
9 French, *People of the Parish*, 69–72.
10 Carlson, "Origins, Function, and Status of Churchwardens," 169–70.
11 The best description of this can be found in Kümin, *Shaping of a Community*, chaps. 3–4.
12 It is unclear whether these were the earliest accounts or merely the earliest to survive.

13 SWHT Somerset, D/B/bw/1742.
14 Cox, *Churchwardens Accounts*, chap. 2; French, *People of the Parish*, Appendix.
15 Swayne, ed., *Churchwardens Accounts*, 13–16.
16 Amphlett, ed., *Churchwardens Accounts*, 92.
17 Overall, ed., *St Michael, Cornhill*, 206.
18 LMA P92/SAV/0001 ff. 7r, 9r.
19 French, *People of the Parish*, 76–9; CA P30/4/1 ff. 2–10.
20 Foster, ed., *Churchwardens' Accounts of St Mary the Great*, 95.
21 Bray, *Tudor Church Reform*, 137.
22 Ibid., 370–3.
23 Ibid., lxxiii–lxxvi.
24 Ibid., 349.
25 Ibid., 371–3, quote, 372–3.
26 Bray, *Anglican Canons*, 172–209.
27 *A booke of certaine canons* (1571), C1r–C2r.
28 Ibid.
29 Cf. Duffy, *Stripping of the Altars*; Duffy, *Voices of Morebath*; Marsh, *Popular Religion in Sixteenth Century England*; Haigh, *English Reformations.*
30 *A Booke of Certaine canons* (1571), C1r.
31 Ibid., C2r.
32 Ibid., C2v.
33 *Articles to be Enquired* (1563), A4v.
34 *A book of Certaine Canons* (1571), C2v. "Let" is used here in the sense of hinder or interrupt.
35 Ibid., C2v.
36 Ibid., C2r.
37 Ibid., C3r.
38 Ibid., C1v.
39 Inner Temple Library MS Collection, Unit 1, Petyt Col, Vol. 47 f. 50r. For more on Elizabeth's motivations in this regard, cf. Collins, ed. *The Canons of 1571*, 7–8.
40 Collins, *Canons of 1571*, 1–8.
41 Drew, *Early Parochial Organization*, xlv–l.
42 43 Eliz 1 c 2.
43 Drew, *Early Parochial Organization*, xi.
44 2 & 3 Philip & Mary, c. 8.
45 5 Elizabeth c. 13.
46 WSA PR350/3 3353/33, f. 44v.

47 LMA p69/STE2/B/008; WSA 1899/65; WSA 1271/18; SWHT Devon 4344A/add99/PW/1.
48 Day, ed., *Oswestry Parish Church*, passim, e.g., 4, 8, 9, etc.
49 Garry, ed., *Churchwardens Accounts*, 49.
50 WSA 1197/21, f. 30r.
51 SWHT, Devon, 2945A/add99/PW1, f. 21r; Brinkworth, ed., *South Newington Churchwardens Accounts*, passim.
52 SWA, 2944/44 f. 3r.
53 Alas, as was often the case in Tudor ecclesiastical courts, no sentence survives (and the matter was perhaps settled before one was given). BI, HC.CP.1594/4. For more on the High Commission, cf. Outhwaite, *Rise and Fall*, 13.
54 LMA P69/ALH6/B/011, ff. 162v, 158r.
55 Ibid., ff. 158v, 163r.
56 Carlson, "Origins, Functions, and Status," 189–91.
57 Foster, ed., *Churchwardens' Accounts of St Mary the Great*, 287.
58 Ibid., throughout, for instance at 168, 186, 211, 263, 267, 269, etc.
59 Andy Wood, *The Memory of the People*, chap. 2.
60 Foster, ed., *Churchwardens' Accounts St Mary*, 28.
61 Lambarde, *The Duties of Constables*, 46.
62 McRae, "Husbandry Manuals"; Oren-Magidor, *Infertility in Early Modern England*; Gallagher, *Learning*, chap. 2; Helen Hull, "Lowe and Lay Ministers of the Peace."
63 E.g., Exeter St Petrocks (SWHT Devon 2945A/add99/PW/3); North Elmham, Norfolk (Legge, ed., *Ancient Churchwardens' Accounts*).
64 *A booke of certaine canons* (1571), C1r.
65 Tate, *Parish Chest*, 85.
66 Ibid.
67 SWHT Devon, 3009A/add99/PW, f. 16.
68 Ibid., 256.
69 Ibid., ff. 16 and 29.
70 Ibid., ff. 15–38.
71 Freshfield, *Vestry Minute Book*, 14.
72 Webbs, *English Local Government*, 39.
73 Wrightson, *Earthly Necessities*, chap. 8.
74 John Walter, "A 'Rising of the People'?" 90–143.
75 LMA P69/CRI/B/012/MS04424, f. 115r.
76 Ibid., ff. 115r–116v.

77 Ibid., f. 116v.
78 Ibid., f. 117r.
79 Ibid.
80 *Injunctions Given by Edmonde … Archbishop of Yorke* (1571), B2v; *Articles Ecclesiasticall … within the Dioces of Hereforde* (1592), B1v.
81 Webb and Webb, *English Local Government*, 173.
82 Page, ed., *Victoria County History of the County of Durham*, vol. 2, 90–1.
83 Barmby, *Churchwardens' Accounts of Pittington*, 12–13.
84 Ibid., 13–18.
85 Webb and Webb, *English Local Government*, 190–1.
86 Farmiloe and Nixseaman, eds., *Elizabethan Churchwardens Accounts*, xi, 31, 44.
87 Wrightson, *Earthly Necessities*, 164.
88 CSP *Colonial*, vol. 2, 105–6; Clowes, *Royal Navy*, 16.
89 Ibid., 10–27.
90 Local analysis has shown adult men made up 23.9 per cent of the total burials in the early seventeenth century. Using a conservative metric of 20 per cent and a conservative population estimate of twelve thousand, this suggests that there were roughly twenty-four hundred adult men in Stepney parish in the last years of Elizabeth's reign – meaning the vestry represented 1.7 per cent of adult men. Hill and Frere, eds., *Memorials*, 28–9.
91 Hill, ed., *Memorials of Stepney Parish*, 19.
92 Ibid., 39–40.
93 Ibid., 28.
94 Ibid., 35.
95 Freshfield, ed., *Vestry Minute Book of St Bartholomew Exchange*, 33
96 Overall, ed., *St Michael, Cornhill*, 243.
97 Braddick, "State Formation and Social Change," 2–3.
98 *Articles to be enquired of within the dioces of London* (1598), B3r.

Chapter Three

1 Parkin, *An Essay Towards a Topographical History*, 79.
2 Gomme, *The History of Thomas Hickathrift*, i–xiii.
3 Stallard, ed., *The Transcript of the Churchwardens' Accounts*, 205.
4 Cf. *Stripping of the Altars*; Duffy, *Voices of Morebath*; Haigh, *Reformation and Resistance in Tudor Lancashire*; Scarisbrick, *The Reformation and the English People*; and, a notable example, Fincham and Tyacke, *Altars Restored*.
5 Aston, *Broken Idols*; Whiting, *Reformation*.

6 Stubbes, *A Motive of Good Workes*, 80–1.
7 Cf, e.g., Jordan, *Philanthropy in England*, 315.
8 BI V.1590, V.1595, V.1600.
9 BI V.1590/157r.
10 BI V.1600/225r and /239v. The visitation from 1600 presented nineteen parishes or chapels for dilapidations, out of an estimated number of roughly two hundred so visited.
11 Shorrocks, ed., *Bishop Still's Visitation*, 15–17.
12 Foster, *The State of the Church*, 219–36.
13 I am indebted to Bruce Gordon for emphasizing this point in conversation with me.
14 Cf. Drew, *Lambeth Churchwardens Accounts*, xxiii–xxv.
15 MacCulloch, "The Myth of the English Reformation," 12.
16 Eire, *War against the Idols*, 151–6.
17 Gee, ed., *Documents Illustrative of English Church History*, 428.
18 *Injunctions exhibited by John … the Bishop of Norwich* (1561), B2r–v.
19 *Articles to be enquired of in the visitation* (1563), A2v; *Iniunctions with certaine articles of the … Byshop of Norwich* (1569), A4r.
20 *Iniunctions geven by the Quenes Maiestie*, D3v.
21 Ibid.
22 *Articles to be Inquired of, in the Metropolitical Visitation* (1559).
23 *Iniunctions exhibited by Iohn … Bishop of Norwich*, B1r.
24 *Articles to be enquired of in the visitation of Matthew* (1563), A2r.
25 SWHT, Somerset, D/P/Yat/4/3/ff. 101–4.
26 SWHT, Devon, 4344A/add99/PW/1/f. 141r; *St Martin in the Fields: The Accounts of the Churchwardens*, 177; OHC, PAR 207/4/F1/1/f. 30r; Earwaker, ed., *St Mary-on-the-Hill*, 250; NRO PD 337/85, 125; WSHC, MSS 730/91/1/ff. 1559 (unfoliated); NRO PD 52/71, 170r; Holland, ed., *Cratfield*, 91; Overall, ed., *St Michael, Cornhill*, 149–50; Wright, ed., *Ludlow*, 94; North, ed., *S. Martin's, Leicester*, 86; LMA, P69/STE2/B/008/MS00593/002 f. 44r–v; Hanham, ed., *Churchwardens' Accounts of Ashburton*, 142–3; WHSC 2944/44/f. 9r; CA KP30/4/1 f. 121r; SWHT Devon 2915A/PW/1, ff. 105–6; Garry and Garry, eds., *St Mary's, Reading*, 37; Howse, ed., *Stanford-in-the-Vale Churchwardens' Accounts*, 47.
27 SWHT, Somerset, D/P/Yat/4/3, ff. 102–4.
28 Hutton, *Rise and Fall of Merry England*, 107.
29 Duffy, *Stripping of the Altars*, 570.
30 Hutton, *Rise and Fall of Merry England*, 108; Duffy, *Stripping of the Altars*, 570–1.

31 Duffy, *Stripping of the Altars*, 572; Henry Gee, *The Elizabethan Prayer-Book and Its Ornaments*, 147.

32 Peacock, ed., *English Church Furniture.* Several of these fifteen silent accounts suggest that the altar had indeed been removed – one, for example, mentions a communion table, and is also peppered with evangelical language and mentions table linen. (89). However, for precision's sake, this analysis looks only at accounts where the presence or removal of the altar is explicit.

33 Ibid., 46–7. The Isle of Axholme was so named as it was set on high ground, formerly surrounded by vast marshes.

34 DUL DDR/EJ/CCD/1/2, 168v–211r. *Depositions and other Ecclesiastical Proceedings from the Courts of Durham*, 167–75.

35 *English Church Furniture*, 166.

36 Ibid., 65, 93, 73, 48.

37 Ibid., 110.

38 Cf. Shagan, *Popular Politics*, chap. 5, for an analogue Edwardian iconoclasm. A very few altars were left undisturbed until later in the reign, especially in the border counties and in very rural parishes in the North. A note attached to the 1570 visitation of York noted that the parish of Masham, which lies between the great Yorkshire Dales and the North York Moors, lacked a communion table, while the nearby parish of Richmond used "an old chyste" instead of a formal communion table. (Purvis, *Tudor Parish Documents*, 63.)

39 WHSC PR278/730/97/1/1559 accounts.

40 Foster, ed., *Churchwardens' Accounts of S. Mary*, 146, 151.

41 OHC, PAR 207/4/F1/1, 80r, 43–5.

42 NRO, PD 337/85, 105–30.

43 Tittler, *Early Modern British Painters.*

44 Aston, *Broken Idols*, 980; Sherlock, *Monuments and Memory*, chap. 2.

45 For the High Commission, cf. Usher, *The Rise and Fall of the High Commission*; cases include BI HC.CP.1567/1; HC.CP.1570/4; HC.CP.ND/10.

46 Duffy, *Stripping of the Altars*, 583–6.

47 Nichols, ed., *Depositions and Other Ecclesiastical Proceedings*, 171.

48 Ibid., 173.

49 Ibid., 176 and 187.

50 Hunt, *The Art of Hearing*, chap. 1, esp. 21–5.

51 Cox, *Pulpits, Lecterns, and Organs*, 89.

52 Stallard, ed., *The Transcript of the Churchwardens' Account*, 194.

53 Whiting, *Reformation of the Parish Church*, chap. 12.

54 Flather, "The Politics of Place: A Study of Church Seating in Essex, c. 1580–1640"; Pittman, "The Social Structure and Parish Community"; Flather, *Gender and Space in Early Modern England*, chap. 5; Tittler, "Seats of Honour, Seats of Power," 218–23.

55 Flather, "Politics of Place," 10–13; Tittler, "Seats of Honour," 218–19.

56 Overall, ed., *St Michael, Cornhill*, 164.

57 Amphlett, ed. *Churchwardens' Accounts of St Michael's in Bedwardine*, xv.

58 Hindle, "Hierarchy and Community"; Marsh, "Common Prayer in England"; Estabrook, "Ritual, Space, and Authority"; Marsh, "Order and Place in England"; Flather, *Gender and Space*, chap. 5; Amussen, *Ordered Society*, chap. 5.

59 Ibid. Incidents of pew disputes are omnipresent in the archives. Some particularly vivid cases can be found in the following: TNA STAC5/08/5, STAC 5/L1/16, STAC5/L4/7; BI CP.G.108A, CP.G. 3064, CP.G. 3315, CP.H.778, HC.CP/1564/3, HC.CP1564/4, HC.CP.1573/1, HC.CP.1581/1, HC.CP.1597/2, and HC.CP.1597/11.

60 BI HC.CP.1597/2.

61 Overall, ed., *St Michael, Cornhill*, 230, 238.

62 Amphlett, ed., *Churchwardens' Accounts of St Michael's in Bedwardine*, xvi.

63 One such example can be seen in Overall, ed., *St Michael, Cornhill*, 246. Extensive discussion on this subject can be found in Collinson, *Birthpangs of Protestant England*. However, a historiography of iconoclasm in Elizabethan England is less examined, with notable exceptions including Aston, *Broken Idols*. Far more studied is the earlier Reformation iconoclasm, most notably in Duffy's *Stripping of the Altars* and Aston's *England's Iconoclasts* [Oxford: 1988], as well as discussions of destruction surrounding the Civil War (cf. John Walter, "Popular Iconoclasm"). This subject is treated more substantially in discussions of the continental Reformation. Some of the most important recent analyses of images and iconoclasm, from quite different methodological perspectives, can be found in Eire, *War against the Idols*; Wandel, *Voracious Idols and Violent Hands*; and Koerner, *The Reformation of the Image*. Bob Scribner's entire body of work is of course of significant impact, of which *Popular Culture and Popular Movements* and *For the Sake of Simple Folk* are exemplary.

64 *Articles to be enquired of in the visitation of the Dioces of London* (1577), A1v and B2r.

65 *Interrogatories to bee enquired of by the churchewardens … of Lincoln* (1580); *Articles to be enquired of … within the Archdeaconrie of Middlesex*; *Articles to be Answered of the Sworne Men in the Archdeacon of London … 1584*.

66 *English Church Finishings*, passim.

67 Amphlett, ed. *Churchwardens' Accounts of St Michael's in Bedwardine*, xix, 30.

68 Barmby, ed., *Churchwardens' Accounts of Pittington*, 12.

69 Palmer, ed., *Tudor Churchwardens Accounts*, 126.

70 *Injunctions geven by the Quenes Majestie* (1559), A3r.

71 Sheils, *The English Reformation*, 39; *Injunctions geven by the Quenes Majestie* (1559), A3r.

72 *Articles to be Enquired of in the Visitation* (1563), A2r–v.

73 North, ed., *The Accounts of the Churchwardens*, 91, 95–6, 103–4.

74 Woodward, *Men at Work*, 283, Appendix 2.6.

75 Amphlett, *Churchwardens' Accounts of St Michael's in Bedwardine*, 163; Wright, *Churchwardens' Accounts of the Town of Ludlow*, 135.

76 The parish of Watton, for example, noted that "the communion book and other books of service was burned in queen Mary's time." Similar notes can be found for the parishes of Bonyne, Lowdham, Estwaite, Stapleforth, Scarington, Edingley, Howton, Carlenton, Felkirk, and Hickton. In the entire province, nineteen parishes reported books destroyed or removed, while only four mentioned missing devotional texts that had not been destroyed. Kitching, *The Royal Visitation of 1559*, xxxv, 62–70.

77 NRO PD/337/85, 110–14.

78 Ibid., 125.

79 Wright, ed. *Churchwardens' Accounts of the Town of Ludlow*,104.

80 Ibid., 136.

81 Bailey, ed., *Churchwardens' Accounts of Prescot, Lancashire*, 45 and 65.

82 Swayne and Swayne, eds., *Churchwardens' Accounts of S Edmund & S Thomas*, 280 and 285.

83 Ibid., 105.

84 BI.V.1590/151V; BI.V.1595/93V.

85 Jewel's *Apology* was mandated nationally by Archbishop Bancroft in James's reign, but not earlier. The first extant visitation article requiring Musculus can be found in Richard Cox's diocese of Ely in 1571. *Iniunctions geuen by the reuerende father in God Richarde* (1571).

86 NRO DN/VIS 2/1.

87 Ibid., Brisley and Toftrees/3r and 4v; /Blofield/14v.

88 Legge, ed., *Ancient Churchwardens' Accounts in the Parish of North Elmham*, 82.

89 Amphlett, ed. *Churchwardens' Accounts of St Michael's in Bedwardine*, 69. The cup cost 42s. 2d., while total receipts for the year were £3 2s. 2d.;

Bailey, ed., *The Churchwardens' Accounts of Prescot, Lancashire*, 66–7. The cup and its retrieval cost £3 10s., while the shingling of the entire south side of the roof cost £3 3s. 4d.

90 Marsh, *Music and Society*, chap. 9.

91 Mears, "Public Worship," 11; Swayne and Swayne, eds., *Churchwardens' Accounts of S Edmund & S Thomas*, xxvii.

92 Swayne and Swayne, eds., *Churchwardens' Accounts of S Edmund and S Thomas*, passim, e.g. 297.

93 Litzenberger, ed., *Tewkesbury Churchwardens' Accounts*, 50–2.

94 Amphlett, ed., *Churchwardens' Accounts*, xii.

95 Bailey, ed., *The Churchwardens' Accounts of Prescot, Lancashire*, 48–144.

96 North, ed., *The Accounts of the Churchwardens of S Martin's*, 89–110. This number represents a minimum based on a conservative understanding of multiple spellings for similar names. It is possible that some of the more differentiated spellings may indeed have been receipts paid to two different individuals, driving the number still higher. The number also does not include payments to unnamed individuals or merchants.

97 Ibid., 90, 95.

98 NRO PD 209/154, 46r–48v.

99 *Articles to be Enquired of* (1563).

100 *Articles to be Enquired of within the dioces of London* (1598), A4v.

101 *Articles to be enquired of within the province of Canterburie* (1576), sig A2v.

102 It must be noted that the number of repairs may well have been underreported by the wardens. However, the systems of accountability and cross-checking employed by ecclesiastical officials would have helped to minimize concealment.

103 BI V.1590/CB.1; BI V.1595/CB.1; BI V.1600/CB.1.

104 BI V.1590/CB.1, f. 46v; V.1600/f. 84r; V.1600/CB.1, f. 225r; V.1590/CB.1, f.38r; V.1590/CB.1, 52v; V.1590/CB.1, 48v.

105 BI V.1590/CB.1/f. 157r.

106 Ibid., 66.

107 This is a main contention of the revisionists, especially Duffy in *Stripping of the Altars*, particularly 131–206.

108 Duffy, *The Voices of Morebath*, chap. 4.

109 Duffy, *Stripping of the Altars*, 144–7, 454–6; Palliser, *Reformation in York, 1534–1553*, 18–24.

110 Duffy, *Stripping of the Altars*, 547–50; Duffy, *Voices of Morebath*, 158–67.

111 Cf. esp. Underdown, *Revel, Riot, and Rebellion*, chap. 3.

112 Duffy, *Voices of Morebath*, 120.
113 Ware, *The Elizabethan Parish*, 72–3.
114 Howse, ed., *Stanford-in-the-Vale Churchwardens' Accounts*, 64–87. Ales were held every year but 1578, with net profits ranging from 160d. (1572) to 864d. (1579).
115 Underdown, *Revel, Riot, and Rebellion*, 48–50. Examples of ales held later in the period are included in Ware, *Elizabethan Parish*, 374–7.
116 Kethe, *Sermon made at Blanford Forum*, C3r–v.
117 *Articles to be Inquired of* (1573), A3v; *Articles to be Enquired of* (1577), B4r.
118 Boulton, "Limits of Formal Religion," 141.
119 WSHC, PR207 2944/44/1, 101.
120 The accounts for Stanford-in-the-Vale, Berkshire, for example, record payments of between 93d. and 104.5d. over the course of the 1570s. Thus, in the course of a decade, the contributions to Easter charity vary by less than a shilling, a remarkable rate of stability for anything but common understanding, informal rate, or silent assessment. (Howse, ed., *Stanford-in-the-Vale Churchwardens' Accounts*, 64–85.)
121 Palmer, ed., *Tudor Churchwardens' Accounts*, x.
122 BI V.1595/CB.1.
123 BI CP.G.2234A/4.
124 Coke, *Reports of Edward Coke*, 133–6.
125 Amphlett, ed., *Churchwardens' Accounts*, xxv.
126 Cf., e.g., Duffy, *Stripping of the Altars*, Part 2, especially 448–503; Shagan, *Popular Politics*, chap. 5.
127 Foster, ed., *Churchwardens' Accounts*, 149.
128 Overall, ed., *St Michael, Cornhill*, 154–5.
129 Palmer, ed., *Tudor Churchwardens' Accounts*, 3.
130 Farmiloe and Nixseaman, eds., *Elizabethan Churchwardens' Accounts*, 8.
131 Cornish, ed., *Kilmington Church Wardens' Accounts*, 25.
132 Shagan, *Popular Politics*, especially chaps. 5 and 7.
133 Straton, ed. *Churchwardens' Accounts*, 105.
134 Ibid., 106.
135 Ibid., 111.
136 Foster, ed., *Churchwardens' Accounts*, 146.
137 Ibid., 164.
138 Ibid., 169.
139 Though no pew rents were recorded in the receipts for 1567–68, which were arranged chaotically, the 1568–69 rents earned 33s. 8d. Swayne and Swayne, eds., *Churchwardens' Accounts of S Edmund & S Thomas*, 114.

140 In all, sales that year totalled £6 10s. 3d., while money collected in the Easter book totalled £10 11s. 9d. Foster, ed., *St Mary the Great*, 164–5.

141 Swayne and Swayne, eds., *Churchwardens' Accounts of S Edmund & S Thomas*; Foster, ed., *Churchwardens' Accounts of St Mary the Great*, 167.

142 NRO PD 52/71, 199r–200r; PD 337/87, 9–10.

143 Day, ed., *Oswestry Parish Church: The Churchwardens' Accounts for 1579–1613*, 41.

144 Watt, *Cheap Print and Popular Piety*, chaps. 2, 7, and 8.

145 Litzenberger, ed., *Tewkesbury Churchwardens' Accounts*, 36.

146 "Churchwardens Accounts of S Michael's Church, Bath," in *Somerset Archaeological Society's Proceedings* (1880), 129–30; *Tudor Churchwardens' Accounts*, 124, 129.

147 Amphlett, ed., *Churchwardens' Accounts of St Michael's in Bedwardine*, 121–2. Though his occupation is not listed at the time of the receipts, a "Fowlk Browghton" received 3s. for the building of pews in 1595–96 (129).

148 NRO PD 337/87, 19.

149 *Stanford-in-the-Vale Churchwardens' Accounts*, 96–7.

150 Ibid., 134.

151 *Churchwardens' Accounts of Pittington*, 15.

152 Ibid., 51.

153 *Tudor Churchwardens' Accounts*, 21.

154 *Churchwardens' Accounts of Pittington*, 13–15, 18.

155 For a description of tithe lands, please see chapter 5.

156 For a longer durée description of London rents and population densities, cf. Harding, "City, Capital, and Metropolis, 117–43.

157 Amphlett, ed., *Churchwardens' Accounts of St Michael's in Bedwardine*, xxxii. In 1562, for example, the rent and the sale of timber from Clifton yielded 53s. 4d., compared with only 14s. 1d. raised at Easter and 2s. raised in pew rents (47).

158 In 1566, for example, of the wardens laid out eight pence for wine "when we went to survey our church" land at Clifton.

159 Ibid., 89–91.

160 Ibid., 44.

161 NRO PD 209/154, 46r–49r.

162 Muldrew, "Interpreting the Market," 163–83; Muldrew, *Economy of Obligation*.

163 The best description of these changes can be found throughout Wrightson, *Earthy Necessities*, especially chaps. 6 to 8.

164 Litzenberger, ed., *Tewkesbury Churchwardens' Accounts*, 95.

165 Tittler, *The Reformation and the Towns*; Fleming, "Charity, Faith, and the Gentry of Kent"; Duffy, *Stripping of the Altars*, chaps. 4, 5, 10, and 15; Whiting, "For the Health of My Soul."

166 Farmiloe and Nixseaman, eds., *Elizabethan Churchwardens' Accounts*, 87.

167 Amphlett, ed., *Churchwardens' Accounts of St Michael's in Bedwardine*, xxxvi, 143.

168 Litzenberger, ed., *Tewkesbury Churchwardens' Accounts*, 93.

169 BI CP.G.828.

170 Slack, *Poverty and Policy*, 162–8; Hindle, *On the Parish?* 120–55; Ben-Amos, "'Good Works' and Social Ties."

171 W.K. Jordan, *Philanthropy in England*, 368. For a useful discussion of some of the methodological problems with Jordan's larger study, including his position on inflation, cf. McIntosh, *Poor Relief in England*, 23nn64–5.

172 McIntosh, *Poor Relief in England*, 23–5; Ben-Amos, *The Culture of Giving*, especially chap. 5.

173 Cudnor served as a churchwarden in 1589. *Accomptes of the churchwardens … of St Christofer's*, 16, 20–2.

174 TNA, PROB/11/101/f. 215v.

175 Ibid.

176 Ibid., /f.216r.

177 Cf., e.g., TNA PROB/11/69/f. 312v; PROB/11/60/f.117r; PROB/11/91/f.62v.

178 Legge, ed., *Churchwardens' Accounts in the Parish of North Elmham*, 80–1.

179 *The Second Tome of Homelyes* (1563), 84r–88v, quote 87r.

180 Cf. Christopher Marsh, "'Common Prayer' in England" and "Order and Place in England."

181 BI CP.G.1456/Kirke.

Chapter Four

1 BI CP.G.2595/Sutton; BI Inst. AB.3, f. 166v; "Browne, Henry (CCEd Person ID 115055)."

2 They had held the seat since the first years of the fifteenth century. Foster, ed., *The Visitation of Yorkshire*, 136–7.

3 The elder Sir Ralph Ellerker was kidnapped by the rebels during the Pilgrimage of Grace, perhaps with his own connivance, but he very soon continued his loyal service to the king, for which he was directly praised. BL, Cotton MSS Caligula B/II, f. 27; TNA, SP1/108, f. 221r; SP1/113, f. 69r–73r; SP 1/115, ff. 51r–54r; SP 1/217, ff.101v–102r; SP 15/8, f. 83r;

C142/213/122. Hall, *A History of South Cave*, 184–5; Hasler, ed., *The History of Parliament*, 85.

4 Venn and Venn, eds., *Alumni Cantabrigiensis*, 2:203.

5 Most of our knowledge of this comes from petitions by townspeople to have Gayton and his fellow minister, John Handson, reinstated. Cf. TNA, SP/12/155, f. 7, as well as a more lengthy discussion in Craig, *Reformation, Politics, and Polemics*, 89–91.

6 Indeed, Huntingdon was deeply involved in this presentment. He had written to his aunt in March of 1582/3, asking her to cede her presentation to Sir Henry Gate, himself a client of the earl's. It is unclear whether she tacitly acceded, but her name is certainly on the presentment in the archbishop's register. BI Inst. AB.3, f. 166v; Lowndes, ed., "The History of the Barrington Family," 10.

7 Marshall, *Face of Pastoral Ministry*, 14.

8 In 1598 he rode with four hundred men to protect the coast when rumours of a Scottish invasion came from local fishermen. Scargill-Bird, ed., *Calendar of the Salisbury Manuscripts*, 494. He was knighted by James at York upon the latter's progress to the capital in 1603. (Oliver, *History and Antiquities*, 508.)

9 BI CP.G.2595/Freeman. His math was wrong here – Sir Ralph Ellerker died in 1546, which was forty-five years before the deposition was taken.

10 BI CP.G.2595/C.Sutton.

11 For the full context of such a decree, please see the next chapter.

12 His family had been involved in putting down a number of Catholic uprisings against the Tudors, most recently in the northern uprising of 1569. There is no mention of him on the recusant rolls, nor had he marked himself as problematic by the time James knighted him. His wife was noted as a recusant in 1604, one of only two in the parish, but he was never noted as such. (Peacock, ed., *A List of the Roman Catholics*, 134.)

13 The full case can be found in BI CP.G.2595.

14 BI CP.G.2595/J. Sutton.

15 Venn and Venn, *Alumni Cantabrigiensis*, 3:358.

16 The Borthwick Institute's Cause Paper Database shows 3,022 total causes between 1560 and 1600, of which 1,045 were tithe cases.

17 Tithes are mentioned in small parts of the following (most substantial references only): Dickens, *English Reformation*, 70, 114, 190, 364, 429n23; Duffy, *Stripping of the Altars*, 356–7; Collinson, *The Religion of Protestants*, 173–4; Collinson, *The Elizabethan Puritan Movement*, 339–41, 450–1;

Haigh, *English Reformations*, 45–7; Shagan, *Popular Politics and the English Reformation*, 109, 122, 139; Marshall, *Heretics and Believers*, 44–6; Ryrie, *Being Protestant*, 453. They are omitted in Scarisbrick, *The Reformation and the English People*, and Walsham, *The Reformation of the Landscape*. None of this is a critique of these works, which by and large have different focuses than tithing practices, but the list demonstrates the light footprint tithes have left on the historical record.

18 Outhwaite, *The Rise and Fall*, chap. 3; Purvis, ed., *Select XVI Century Causes*; Ralph Houlbrooke, *Church Courts and People*; Sheils, "'The Right of the Church,'" 244–7; O'Day and Heal, eds., *Princes and Paupers*, particularly Cross, "The Incomes of Provincial Urban Clergy," and Zell, "Economic Problems of the Parochial Clergy"; Heal, "Economic Problems of the Clergy."

19 Hill, *Economic Problems of the English Church.*

20 O'Day and Heal, *Princes and Paupers*, 7.

21 D.M. Barratt, *Ecclesiastical Terriers*, introduction.

22 Zell, "Economic Problems," 37–9; Cross, "Incomes of Provincial Urban Clergy," 74–86.

23 So take, for instance, the 1576 record in Cromwell's journal of "a bill that privy tithes should be payd in Reading, according to the order payment of tythes in London sett forth 37 Henry 8." (Hartley, ed., *Proceedings in the Parliaments*, 1:483.)

24 This typography is of my own making and for clarity's sake. I borrow here from A.G. Little, who referred to the distinction between predial, mixed, and personal tithes as "of three kinds," and John Mirehouse, who referred to tithes "divided into two classes, great or small." Little, "Personal Tithes," 68; Mirehouse, *A Practical Treatise*, 2.

25 Clark, *Tithes and Oblations*, B3v.

26 Ibid.

27 Ibid.

28 Mirehouse, *A Practical Treatise*, 2; Toller, *A Treatise of the Law of Tithes*, 50–1.

29 Cf. Thomson, "Tithe Disputes in Later Medieval London"; Susan Brigden, "Tithe Controversy"; Ian Archer, "The Burden of Taxation."

30 *Valor Ecclesiasticus*, 1:60. Most entries in the *Valor* list tithes grouped together, not divided by type.

31 Turner, *Second Appendix*, xix.

32 Swanson, *Church and Society*, 210–15.

33 Clarke, *History of Tithes*, 99–100; Moorman, *Church Life in England*, 116.

34 Palmer, *Selling the Church*, 10–11.

35 The degree of disconnect between rector and parish, and especially between corporate rectors and parishes, was made even more pronounced by the regular leasing of tithe and other parish income. Leasing the parish allowed rectors to receive profit with a minimum of effort, and Palmer's convincing study has shown this becoming the dominant form of parochial land management in the years following the Black Death. By 1500, corporate rectors routinely made leases as long as twenty years, with leases of over thirty years not uncommon. While some of these lessees were clerics, a majority were laypeople who looked on tithe farming as a profitable investment. Cf. Palmer, *Selling the Church*, chap. 4, especially 88–92.

36 Thompson, *The English Clergy*, 111–12; Peter Heath, *English Parish Clergy*, 148–9.

37 Palmer, *Selling the Church*, 99.

38 Swanson, *Church and Society*, 44–5. The latter figure is of my own calculation, with Swanson noting that "between 1291 and 1535 the number of appropriated churches in England and Wales rose from under 2,000 to over 3,300" (44).

39 Thompson estimates that late-medieval Yorkshire had 622 parish churches, with at least 392, or 63 per cent, appropriated to monastic houses. *The English Clergy*, 115.

40 31 Henry VIII c. 13, s. 14 (1539).

41 For more on dissolution property, cf. Youings, *The Dissolution of the Monasteries*; Heal, *Reformation*, chap. 3.

42 2 & 3 Ed. VI, c. 13, s. 4. (1548).

43 2 & 3 Ed. VI, c. 13, s. 1. (1548).

44 Thirsk, *Rural Economy*; Outhwaite, "Progress and Backwardness"; Overton, *Agricultural Revolution*; Whittle, *Development of Agrarian Capitalism*; Wrightson, *Earthly Necessities.*

45 2 & 3 Ed. VI, c. 13, s. 5 (1548).

46 Hill, *Economic Problems*, 91.

47 Helmholz, *Oxford History of the Laws of England*, 450.

48 Becon, *New Pollecye* H1v and H3v–H3r. (NB: the original text incorrectly labels the latter quote as G3 rather than H3.) Outhwaite makes this larger point in *Rise and Fall*, 30–1.

49 Helmholz, *Roman Canon Law*, 91–4.
50 Outhwaite, *Rise and Fall*, 29–32; Jones, *Elizabethan Court of Chancery*, 395–9. This situation was in large part reversed in the seventeenth century, with the gradual encroachment of the civil courts of equity, but tithe cases remained the province of the ecclesiastical courts through the end of the sixteenth century. (Helmholz, *Roman Canon Law*, 89–104.)
51 Helmholz, *Oxford History*, 442.
52 Houlbrooke, *Church Courts and the People*, 273; Haigh, *Reformation and Resistance*, 59; Outhwaite, *Rise and Fall*, 26–7.
53 Buck, "Opposition to Tithes," 11–22; Blickle, *The Revolution of 1525*; Sea, "The Swabian League."
54 Ladurie, *The French Peasantry, 1540–1600*, 252–66; Burg, *A World History of Tax Rebellions*, 156–7; Heller, *Iron and Blood*, 57–9.
55 Kamen, *The Iron Century*, 333; Burg, *World History of Tax Rebellions*, 171–2.
56 *The Examination of Master William Thorpe*, E3r. For more, cf. Aston, *Lollards and Reformers*; van Engen, "Anticlericalism among the Lollards," 53–64.
57 Though taxes were protested, the focus was on first fruits and tenths (and the fifteenth and tenth, a smaller direct tax) rather than tithes. Elton, "Politics and the Pilgrimage of Grace"; Bush, *Pilgrimage of Grace*; Fletcher, *Tudor Rebellions*, 38.
58 Davies, "Popular Religion and the Pilgrimage of Grace," 81.
59 BL, Harley MS 304, f. 76v. A noble was the equivalent of eighty pence, and thus a request for eight pence of the noble was a request for only 10 per cent of the tithe.
60 Ibid., ff. 75v–77r, quote f. 75v.
61 Magagna, *Communities of Grain*, 114.
62 BI CP.G.2015/Batey [8 November 1581].
63 BI CP.G.1594/Richardson [2 May 1572].
64 BI CP.G.2104/Atlay [12 June 1583].
65 Outhwaite, *Rise and Fall of the Ecclesiastical Courts*, 32.
66 I have certainly never come across a case where the defendant is accused of rejecting the tithe system wholesale, though I would be delighted to find exceptions. At times, as is discussed later in the chapter, there are moments when failure of duty is given as an excuse for nonpayment, but this is vanishingly rare. This is a point that seems to be missing from the literature. Helmholz recognizes its absence from the defence, but not from the prosecution. Helmholz, *Roman Canon Law*, 103–4.
67 Wrigley and Schofield, *Population History of England*; Outhwaite, *Inflation*; Wrightson, *Earthy Necessities*, chaps. 5 to 7.

68 Hoyle, "Rural Economies under Stress," 444–7.

69 Kain and Prince, *The Tithe Surveys of England and Wales*, 6.

70 Some of the more notable examples include Wrightson and Walter, "Dearth and the Social Order"; Walter, "The Social Economy of Dearth"; Sharp, *In Contempt of All Authority*, esp. chaps. 1 and 6; Thompson, "Moral Economy of the English Crowd."

71 There are occasional references to tithe seizure, but these are generally cast as larger property or political disputes between gentlemen. For instance, in the lawless early years of Elizabethan Wigan, disputes between the bishop of Sodor and the mayor of Wigan erupted into violence (with the bishop's servant striking the mayor) followed by retaliation in the tithe fields, with local gentry stealing tithe corn. Similarly, in 1599, the new vicar seems to have taken up scythes against the fields of the Earl of Derby, with whom he was engaged with several legal proceedings. Wigan, however, is an anomaly amongst parishes, the majority of which left no record of similar violence on the records. Bridgeman, *The History of the Church*, 131–63.

72 2 & 3 Ed. VI, c. 13 (1548). This applied to personal tithes only, based on wages, not on any product that the labourer's family may have been able to raise. Moreover, there is no indication in this act that labourers would be exempt from other forms of collection, though some parishes may have decided to render them so.

73 Lawson, "Property Crime and Hard Times," 98.

74 Sharp, *In Contempt of All Authority*, 13–21.

75 Compare to the actions in Thompson, "Moral Economy of the English Crowd," 112–13.

76 Lawson, "Property Crime and Hard Times"; Sharpe, *Crime in Early Modern England.*

77 From 78.6 average p.a. from 1592–94 to 178.3 p.a. in 1595–97. Wrightson and Walter, "Dearth and the Social Order," 24.

78 Figures taken from Lawson, "Property Crime and Hard Times," 107–8. Hoskins saw prices peak in late 1596. Hoskins, "Harvest Fluctuations," 46.

79 Figures taken from Wrigley and Schofield, *Population History of England*, 208. They estimate the population to have grown from 2,984,576 in 1561 to 3,899,190 by 1591.

80 Slack, *Poverty and Policy*, 47.

81 These numbers are taken from a survey of the Borthwick Cause Papers Database, accessed March 2014. They count the number of separate cause papers first brought before the court between 1 May and 30 April of a given year; thus the 1590 figure represents all cause papers begun between

1 May 1590 and 30 April 1591. As some tithes were paid annually at Easter, this allows such tithes to be counted with the previous summer's crop; this seems the most accurate way to assess the effect of poor harvests on tithe prosecutions. In some cases, multiple sets of cause papers could be brought by the same plaintiff or against the same defendant; in order to give an overview, however, each cause paper is counted once. An exception to this is made for 1594, where the eleven separate cases are catalogued as part of one larger entry. Excluded are cases with general dates given (e.g., 1594 or 1560–1600), as their relationship to specific harvest years are impossible to ascertain. While these cases represent only a portion of those seen in front of the courts, they give a rough indication of the patterns of prosecution.

82 BI CP.G.2575/Taylor.

83 BI DC.CP/1590/11; BI DC.CP/1590/3.

84 43 & 44 Eliz., c. 2 (1601); Hill, *Economic Problems*, 134.

85 Heal, *Hospitality in Early Modern England*, 269–77.

86 Clarke, *A General Martyrologie*, quoted in Margaret Spufford, *Contrasting Communities*, 51–2. See also references in John Walter, "The Social Economy of Dearth," 110n98.

87 As Sheils mentions, the laity had fewer obligations toward charity and peace-keeping than clerical plaintiffs would have done. Sheils, "Tithe and the Courts at York," 238.

88 Figures taken from survey of Borthwick Cause Papers, 1560–1600, accessed March 2014, counting only those suits begun in this time frame with relatively certain dating (eliding those that were dated with estimations). Clerics were the plaintiffs in just over 16 per cent of wheat cases but nearly 38 per cent of cases in which apples were involved. This does not indicate the full extent of clerical involvement, as many of these cases may have involved tithe farmers directly employed by clerical rectors or vicars; however, ministers were far more likely to appear as plaintiffs themselves in these cases. BI CP G series and H series.

89 BI CP.G.3063; Weston, *History of the Ancient Parish Parish of Lastingham*, 31–2.

90 BI CP.G.2783; Hebditch, ed., *Yorkshire Deeds*, 41–2.

91 BI CP.G.2980; Waterson and Meadows, *Lost Houses*, 12.

92 BI CP.G.2864.

93 Shepard, *Accounting for Oneself*, 107–9. Shepard indicates income in this period ranged from around 10 to 25 per cent of total estate value.

94 BI CP.G.2595.

95 The most detailed figures on this can be found in Gregory Clark, "The Price History of English Agriculture," 42. For a more general survey, cf. Wrightson, *Earthly Necessities*, 53–5.

96 Bowden, "Statistical Appendix," 847–9.

97 BI CP.G.2595.

98 Helmholz, *Roman Canon Law*, 100–1; Hill, *Economic Problems*, 80–131; Outhwaite, *Rise and Fall*, 26–9; Sheils, "The Right of the Church," 244–7.

99 BI CP.G.2988/Copley. This profit is calculated from Copley's testimony of harvest yield and grain prices for wheat, oats, and rye over the course of two years.

100 Cf. for example: BI CP.G.2995, BI CP.G.3018, BI CP.G.3097, BI CP.G.3104, BI CP.G.3204, and BI CP.G.3205.

101 Cross, "Incomes of Provincial Urban Clergy," 76; Holderness, "The Clergy as Money-Lenders," 203.

102 Zell, "Economic Problems of the Parochial Clergy," 40.

103 Craig, *Reformation, Politics, and Polemics*, 90.

104 Indeed, Gayton brought another suit the following year; neither case record contains a final sentence, itself not unusual. BI CP.G.2654.

105 Outhwaite, *Rise and Fall of the English Ecclesiastical Courts*, chap. 3; Sheils, "Tithe and the Church Courts," 244–5; Helmholz, *Roman Canon Law in Reformation England*, 100–1.

106 Brooks, *Pettyfoggers*, chaps. 4 to 6.

107 Marchant, *Church under the law*, 62.

108 2 & 3 Edward VI c. 13 s. 1. (1548).

109 Outhwaite, *Rise and Fall*, 29; Marchant, *Church under the Law*, 63.

110 Wood, *Memory of the People*, 139.

111 Houlbrooke, *Church Courts and People*, 138–9.

112 Muldrew, "Culture of Reconciliation."

113 Wood, *Memory of the People*, 92.

114 Pollman, *Memory in Early Modern Europe*, 151.

115 Hoyle, ed., *Custom, Improvement, and the Landscape*; Wood, *Memory of the People*; Thompson, "Custom, Law, and Common Right."

116 DCL Raine MS 124, f. 27v.

117 BI CP.H.3921.

118 Hodgett, "The Unpensioned Ex-religious," 201.

119 Calculations taken from figures provided by Cross and Vickers, *Monks, Friars, and Nuns*, 4–13. The total number includes at least 610 monks and

canons and 230 nuns; the 200 friars mentioned are elided, as most friars were not eligible for pensions in 1539. Cf. 4–5.

120 Ibid., 13. The remaining pensioner was Isabel Coxson, who was nineteen at the time of Dissolution. Cross and Vickers note that she was still receiving the pension at the age of eighty-five and seems to be the last surviving professed member of a pre-Dissolution house in Yorkshire.

121 BI CP.G.806/Hall. Cf. CP.G.1075 for a continuation of the case.

122 BI CP.G.1775/Scolay.

123 BI CP.G.2216/Cockell. Cockell is quite possibly the former Joan Bentley. Three Joans seem to have belonged to the priory at the Dissolution, two of whom (Joan Ellarie and Joan Hunton) are described by Cockell herself in her testimony. Details about Bentley are missing from Cross and Vickers's detailed biographies of the former nuns of Moxby; while they mention Cockell several times (described as someone "who had lived in the nunnery for seven years" rather than as a nun), it should be noted that Joan Cockell is listed as a widow in the deposition's preamble.

124 BI CP.G.2216/Burnett.

125 BI CP.G.2116/Gawtree.

126 BI CP.G.2648/Wright.

127 BI CP.H.167B/Staynes.

128 The Cause Papers Database shows a total of 977 tithe causes dated at any point between 1560 and 1600, 83 of which included clerk testimony. In order to gain more accurate results, I have elided any case without a reasonable degree of date accuracy; for example, cases listed with dates from 1580 to 1620. With these elisions, one can make a very conservative accounting of 913 cases begun between 1560 and 1600, of which 81 – or 8.9 per cent – included clerk testimony. (Accessed March 2014.)

129 Outhwaite, *Rise and Fall*, 26–7.

130 The proportion of these lay impropriators changed markedly in different areas of the country, perhaps reflecting the legacy of medieval appropriations. Sheils, "Tithe and the Courts at York," 236–7.

131 *Seconde Parte of a Register*, 196.

132 Cf. O'Day and Heal, eds., *Princes and Paupers in the English Church, 1500–1800*, especially the chapters by Zell (19–43) and Cross (65–89).

133 *Seconde Parte of a Register*, 175.

134 The case is detailed in the depositions of BI CP.G.2667.

135 George Poulson, *Beverlac*, 724–5.

136 BI CP.G.2667/C.Jordan.

137 Swanson, *Church and Society*, 44; Hill, *Economic Problems*, 144–5.

138 Cf. Kain and Prince, *The Tithe Surveys of England and Wales.*
139 Hill, *Economic Problems*, chap. 6.
140 Dering, *A sermon preached*, E4r–v.
141 Fenner, *A briefe and plaine declaration*, 55.
142 Field, *An Admonition to the Parliament*, A4r.
143 Gilby, *A Pleasant Dialogue*, B4v, E1v.
144 Dent, *The Ruine of Rome*, O3v.
145 Burton. *A Sermon preached in the Cathedrall Church in Norwich*, C2v–C3r. This recalls Gilby's description of "you that be loiterers, to devour the church goods, the sweat of poor men's labors, and do allow proprietaries & improprietaries, drones to suck the Honey comb." Gilby, *A Pleasant dialogue*, D3v.
146 Neale, *Elizabeth I and Her Parliaments.* Vol. 1, 99. Cf. also Hill, *Economic Problems*, 139.
147 TNA SP/12/27, f. 226; TNA SP 12/88, f. 98, and TNA SP 12/107 f. 138.
148 See Introduction of this book for more details.
149 SP 12/199 f. 7v. D'Ewes's *Journal* described it as "a petition that it might be enacted that all laws now in force touching ecclesiastical government should be void. (D'Ewes, *Journal*, 410–12.)
150 A description of the legislation and its opposition can be found in Neale, *Elizabeth I and Her Parliaments.* Vol. 2, 148–65.
151 Youings, *The Dissolution of the Monasteries*, 130–1.
152 Neale, *Elizabeth I and Her Parliaments.* Vol. 1, 160.
153 SP 12/199/1, f. 3r.
154 Strype, *The Life and Acts of John Whitgift*, Vol. 1 [Oxford: 1822], 145. Cf. Hill, *Economic Problems*, 147–8.
155 Sheils, "Profit, Patronage, or Pastoral Care," 94. As Sheils points out, this put those bishops who disapproved of impropriations in a difficult position; they may have had ideological objections, but they were practically tied to the institution (97).
156 Hill, *Economic Problems*, 15; Sheils, "Profit, Patronage, or Pastoral Care," 93–4.
157 Bridges, *A defence of the gouernment established in the church of Englande for ecclesiasticall matters* [1587], STC (2nd ed.)/3734, 521–2.
158 SP 12/199/1, f.2v. Also quoted in Neale, *Elizabeth I and Her Parliaments.* Vol. 2, 160.
159 Bridges, 520. Hill notes that absolute property rights became an issue by the early seventeenth century, though these statements place their germination firmly in the Elizabethan period. (Hill, *Economic Problems*, 156.)

160 SP 12/199/2, f.7v.
161 SP 12/199/1, f.2v.
162 Neale, *Elizabeth I and Her Parliaments.* Vol. 2, 161.
163 Fields, *An Admonition to Parliament*, B3r.
164 Strype, *Whitgift*, 1:145.
165 Ibid.
166 Moorman, *Church Life in England in the Thirteenth Century*, 38–44; Palmer, *Selling the Church*, chap. 2.
167 Collier, *An Ecclesiastical History*, 362–3.
168 Some 1,895 of 4,543 parishes rated under £10. Comparatively, 58 per cent of total vicarages were valued at this very low level, while 48 per cent of rectories were so valued. Ibid., 362.
169 Hill, *Economic Problems*, 110.
170 Swanson, *Church and Society*, 215–16.
171 For an example of a summary valuation, see SP 12/96, f. 101.
172 NRO, DN/VAL 1/2. Compare with *Valor Ecclesiasticus*, 3:281–498.
173 These unofficial surveys, commissioned by evangelical ministers to support their claims for further reformation, attempted to account for the value of livings and quality of the clergy across England. They were, as noted, highly flawed, but they provide a provocative glimpse of the areas of church life most in contestation in the mid-Elizabethan period. For further information, cf. Collinson, *The Elizabethan Puritan Movement*, 280–3.
174 *Seconde Parte of a Register*, 144.
175 Zell, "Economic Problems of the Parochial Clergy," 38–40. It should be noted that Zell does use the 1586 survey for these numbers.
176 Ibid., 40.
177 John Addy, *The Archdeacon*, 22. Fascinatingly, a version of this liability stands today, enforced by the 1932 Chancel Repairs Act. In the past few decades, these provisions have been debated in the House of Commons and the British media, who delight in spotlighting cases such as the £230,000 repair of the Aston Cantlow parish church in Warwickshire. (Morris, "Church Bill" and 551 Parl. Deb. H.C. [5th Series] [2012–13] 130–1 WH.)
178 Sheils, ed., *Archbishop Grindal's Visitation*, 50.
179 Ibid., 33.
180 NRO ANW 6/1.
181 NRO DN/VIS 2/1, f. 8v.
182 Of 506 chapels, seventy-five presented for decay: thirty-five in the archdeaconry of Yorkshire, fifteen in Cleveland, twenty-two in the East

Riding, and three in the peculiars. Sheils, ed., *Archbishop Grindal's Visitation*, iv–vii.

183 Figures taken from Blagg, ed., *A Miscellany of Nottinghamshire Records*, 10–42; Shorrocks, ed., *Bishop Still's Visitation, 1594*, 9–15; Williams, ed., *Bishop Redman's Visitation*, 8–10. Eight hundred and six parishes made presentments, with 181 additional silently marked *omnia bene*; 119 parishes were presented for chapel default.

184 BI V.1578–9/CB.1; BI V.1590–1/CB.1; BI V.1595–6/CB.1; BI V.1600/CP.1.

185 Purvis, *The Condition of Yorkshire Church Fabrics, 1300–1800*, St Anthony's Hall Publications, No. 14 [York: 1958], 16. I have not cited Purvis's 1590 records, as the exclusion of figures from five of the deaneries skews the relative data.

186 *State of the Church in the Reigns of Elizabeth and James*, 224; Williams, ed., *Bishop Redman's Visitation*, 37; NRO ANW 3/2.

187 NRO DN/VIS 2/1, f. 7v.

188 Sheils, *Archbishop Grindal's Visitation*, 1–88 passim.

189 Williams, ed., *Bishop Redman's Visitation*, 29–70.

190 NRO DN/VIS 2/1, ff. 3v–9v.

191 Williams, ed., *Bishop Redman's Visitation*, 50.

192 NRO ANW/1/17.

193 Sheils, *Archbishop Grindal's Visitation*, 28.

194 BI V.1590-1/CB2, f.25r.

195 *State of the Church in the Reigns of Elizabeth and James I*, 222.

196 Shorrocks, ed., *Bishop Still's Visitation, 1594*, 102.

197 BL Additional MSS 39227, f. 98r.

198 TNA SP 59/31, f. 141r.

199 TNA SP 46/24, f. 229r.

200 Purvis, *Conditions of Yorkshire Church Fabrics*, 17.

201 Even archivally focused historians have fallen into this trap. J.S. Purvis, for example, describes presentments for chancel disrepair as painting "a startling and deplorable picture" of an "evil [which] was widespread" – and on the following page tallies figures indicating dilapidation rates of under 15 per cent (15–16). This cognitive disconnect can also be found in Sheils's edition of Archbishop Grindal's visitation, where he describes "the almost universal negligence of impropriators," followed by a table listing under 12 per cent of chancels as dilapidated (vii).

202 Cross, ed., *Patronage and Recruitment.*

203 Quoted in Sheils, "Rectory Estates of the Archbishopric of York," 100.

204 As in the rectors of Langton, Yorkshire (BI CP.G.1376).
205 *Calendar of Manuscripts*, 163.
206 Most recently Finch, *Church Monuments*; Gaimster and Gilchrest, eds., *The Archaeology of Reformation*; Owen, "The Reformed Elect."
207 Cf., to begin, R.H. Tawney's classic "The Rise of the Gentry" and the controversy it engendered.
208 An important exception can be found in Lowe, *Commonwealth and the English Reformation,* 141–77.
209 Cf. Zell, "Economic Problems" for a discussion of ideals versus reality in regard to the ministry.

Chapter Five

1 Sutton's earnest, sometimes painfully sincere, advice was perhaps delivered to an inapposite target. Four years later, Elizabeth, a lady-in-waiting to the queen, would run off to France with her cousin Robert Dudley – himself a son of the late earl of Leicester – and would convert there to Catholicism. When Sutton republished the book a decade later, Elizabeth's name had been erased, replaced instead with two of her younger, and less startling, sisters.
2 Sutton, *Godly Meditations*, 47.
3 Sutton, *Disce Mori*, iv.
4 A short note about terms. Through this chapter, eucharist, communion, the sacrament, and Lord's Supper are used generally interchangeably. The terms used in the period varied, with different connotations; the "Lord's Supper" was particularly used by the evangelical wing of the church, while "the sacrament" remained a term embraced by most. The term "eucharist" may have had more of a high-church flavour and was used by a number of Catholic authors during the late sixteenth century, but it appeared regularly in defences of the Elizabethan church by staunch (if centrist) authors like Thomas Bilson or John Bridges. (Cf. Bilson, *The Perpetual Governement*; Bridges, *A Defence of the Government.*) Moreover, it was used in translations of Continental evangelical works, such as Bullinger's *Fiftie Godlie and Learned Sermons*, in direct reference to the reformed ceremony (e.g. "He is our Passover, who in steed of the Paschal lamb hath ordained the Eucharist or supper of the Lord," 407). Using all terms here, rather than restricting usage to language more familiar on the Continent, is deliberate and meant at least in part to indicate contemporary English plurality of usage.

5 Russell, *The Causes of the English Civil War*, 93.
6 Hunt, "The Lord's Supper in Early Modern England"; Haigh, "Communion and Community."
7 Bossy, "The Mass as a Social Institution"; Rubin, *Corpus Christi*; Reinburg, "Litugy and the Laity"; Bynum, *Wonderful Blood.*
8 Sabean, *Power in the Blood*, chap. 1; Elwood, *The Body Broken*; Edward Muir, *Ritual in Early Modern Europe*, chap. 5; Wandel, *The Eucharist in the Reformation*; Van Amberg, *A Real Presence*; Burnett, "The Social History of Communion." Sabean's work is particularly important and echoes many of the points made in Hunt's and Haigh's arguments.
9 Bernard, *The King's Reformation*, 228, 237–8.
10 Cox., ed., *Miscellaneous Writings*, 424.
11 Heal, *Reformation in Britain and Ireland*, 161.
12 Martyr, *An Unpublished Letter of Peter Martyr*, 5.
13 *A Briefe Examination for the Tyme*, A2r. This comment was originally made in the context of Cranmer's request that Bucer step into Hooper's vestments debate. The debate was reignited in 1566, when some of Bucer and Peter Martyr's letters were reprinted in *A Brief Examination for the Tyme* in the light of the vestarian controversy (of which the best description can still be found in Collinson, *The Elizabethan Puritan Movement*, Part 2).
14 *The Boke of the Common Praier* (1549), 91v.
15 Haigh, *English Reformations*, 173–9.
16 *A Copye of a Letter*, C2v.
17 *The Boke of Common Praier* (1552), 97r.
18 *The Booke of Common Prayer* (1559), Q6r.
19 Traditionally, such flexibility was seen as a concession to Catholics, but I join with Diarmaid MacCulloch in his appraisal of such a formulation: "This is absurd." As MacCulloch notes, the shape of the new liturgy was unmistakably Protestant; variations would have appeased only traditionalist or Lutheran Protestants, not anyone who wished to return to the Catholic Church. MacCulloch, "Putting the Reformation on the Map," 88.
20 Bossy, "Mass as a Social Institution," 43–53.
21 The *Booke of Common Prayer* (1559), Q8v.
22 Ibid., Q2r.
23 Ibid., Q1r.
24 Ibid., R1r.
25 *Booke of Common Prayer* (1552), 93v–94r.
26 Calvin, *A Faythfull and Moost Godlye Treatyse*, F1r.

27 Calvin, *Institutes*, 4:xvii:38. This pulls on a long doctrinal identification of the sacrament as a feast of reconciliation; as Calvin himself writes, this strand can be found in Augustine, who called communion "the bond of charity."

28 Ibid., 4: xvii:43. Cf. Kingdon, "The Jacques Royer Affair," 180–2, and Wandel, *The Eucharist in the Reformation*, 164–6.

29 Robinson, ed., *Zurich Letters*, 32. For the best description of this legislation, cf. Jones, *Faith by Statute*, especially chapters 4 and 5.

30 Gee, *Elizabethan Prayer Book*, 82.

31 Jones, *Faith by Statute*, 96–7.

32 Robinson, ed., *Zurich Letters*, 1:85.

33 Calvin, *Institutes*, 4:xvii:46. Cf. Rubin, *Corpus Christi*, 147–9.

34 Cf. Neale, "Parliament and the Articles of Religion, 1571"; Neale, *Elizabeth and Her Parliaments*. Vol. 1, 215–17.

35 Neale, *Elizabeth and Her Parliaments*. Vol. 2, 163.

36 *Articles to be enquired in the visitation* (1559), A3r.

37 For more on Elizabethan catechisms, cf. Green, *The Christian's ABC*.

38 *A breefe catechisme*, A5r and A6v.

39 Ibid., A5v.

40 Sutton, *Godly Meditations*, 111.

41 *A Preparation to the Due Consideration*, C8r–v.

42 Cooper, *A Briefe homily*, B1r.

43 Bartimeus Andrews, *A Very Short and Pithie Catechisme*, B5v–B6r. Andrews was named a preacher by the corporation in 1585, the year before this catechism was published; he would go on to write an eight-volume set of catechisms published in 1591. (Palmer, *The History of Great Yarmouth*, 151.)

44 Shute, *The Testimonie of a True Fayth*, B7r.

45 It is worth noting that, while all of these writers operated within the confines of the Church of England, they represented markedly different flavours of Elizabethan preaching. Christopher Sutton's universalism would have sat very awkwardly against Christopher Shute's sharp godliness; Thomas Cooper was a target of Martin Marprelate tracts, while the gloriously (self?) named Bartimeus Andrews was lured away from the notorious region around Dedham, Essex, to preach puritan lectures in Yarmouth. (For the latter, cf. Collinson, *Birthpangs of Protestant England*, 43–4.) Nevertheless, in the public-facing roles, each exhorted their congregations to serious self-examination.

46 Ryrie, *Being Protestant*, especially chapters 9 and 15.

47 Todd, "Puritan Self-Fashioning."

48 Sidney Sussex College Library, Cambridge, MS 45, f. 17v.

49 It should be stressed that I am not arguing here for any form of doctrinal analogue – both late-medieval Catholics and 1590s puritans would be horrified by the idea. The confession was itself a sacrament, of course, and the practice of preparation also relied on an entirely different conception of both the place of the cleric and the very notion of salvation.

50 Dent, *Plain-man's Pathway*, 344.

51 *The Boke of Common Prayer* (1560), P3v.

52 *Articles to be Enquired of within the Dioces of Norwich* (10288), A3v.

53 Note for the reader: pew rents and assignments are covered in previous chapters, particularly chapter 1 and chapter 4.

54 The description of the ceremony that follows is taken from the order of service in the Book of Common Prayer (cf. *The Boke of Common Prayer* [1560], P3v–R1r).

55 This was one of two collects that could be read, and by far the most interesting.

56 Ibid., O1r.

57 Ibid., P3r.

58 Ibid., P3v.

59 Ibid., O2r.

60 Smith, *A Treatise of the Lords Supper*, A2r and C4r. Cf. Livesay, "'Silver-Tongued Smith,'" 13–36.

61 BI, CP.G.824, f.5r.

62 In addition to accusations of nonconformity, Katherine may have been worried that she would be accused of witchcraft. Bread from the sacrament was thought to be of particular spiritual power and was concealed by those who wished to use it for supernatural purposes. There is no evidence in this case, however, that witchcraft was a factor. (Cf. Sharpe, *Instruments of Darkness*, 151–2, for more on sacramental power and witchcraft.)

63 BI CP.G.824, ff. 5r–v.

64 Ibid., f. 5v.

65 Duffy, *Voices of Morebath*, 67.

66 The accounts of St Michael, Cornhill, for instance, reflect a quick Reformation of sacramental materials and a monthly communion by 1563, but no payments for bread or wine. Overall, ed., *St Michael, Cornhill*, 144–92.

67 SWHC Somerset, D/P/yeoj. 4/1/1568; D/P/yeoj/4/2/1587.

68 Hanham, ed., *Churchwardens' Accounts of Ashburton*, 145, 185; Amphlett, ed., *Churchwardens' Accounts of St Michael's in Bedwardine*, 42, 84–5.
69 NRO PD 24/1, ff. 6r–v; 57r–v.
70 OHC PAR 214/4/F1/ff. 32 and 37.
71 CA, KP30/4/1, ff. 129r and 177r.
72 NRO PD52/71/ff.178–180 and 256r.
73 SWHT Devon, 3009A/add99/PW/1, f. 8, 10, 15, 102, 112, 119.
74 SWHT Somerset, D/P/tin4/1/1, ff. 149 and 169.
75 Stallard, ed., *Accounts of the Parish of Tilney All Saints*, 192–3, 241–2.
76 CA KP30/4/1, f. 238r.
77 OHC PAR 214/4/F1/32, /37, and /48.
78 Savage, ed., *Churchwardens Accounts of St Nicholas Warwick*, 28, 71, 111.
79 LMA P69/STE2/B/008, ff. 44r–53r; 69r–74r; 101r–103r.
80 Wrightson, *Earthly Necessities*, 109–10; Wrigley and Schofield, *The Population History of England, 1541–1871*, Appendix 3 (528–9).
81 SWHT Devon, 3009A/add99/PW/1; Hanham, ed., *Churchwardens' Accounts of Ashburton*, 143–66.
82 WSA, 3353/33, ff. 18v–55r.
83 Almost no full sets of accounts exist from the north of England, which is a blind spot in this study. Attempts to address questions of parochial and individual conformity in this famously traditional area of the country will be found later in the chapter.
84 Smith, *A Treatise of the Lords Supper in Two Sermons*, A3v–A4r.
85 *Articles to be Enquired of in the Visitation of the Dioces of London* (1571), A4r.
86 This is a smaller subset of surviving account books, as even those that record annual communion expenditure often do so as annual totals (e.g., "bread and wine for the year") rather than as individual receipts.
87 HRO, 3M32/W/PW1, f. 37v.
88 HRO, 75M/72/PW1, f. 50r.
89 Legge, ed., *Churchwardens' Accounts in the Parish of North Elmham*, 80–2.
90 SWHT Somerset, D/P/tin3/1/1, 175; Savage, ed., *Churchwardens' Accounts of the Parish of St Nicholas Warwick*, 71.
91 Hunt, "Lord's Supper," 45.
92 Boulton, "The Limits of Formal Religion," 179–93; MacCulloch, *The Later Reformation*, 116.
93 NRO PD/52/71/178–80.
94 Overall, ed., *St Michael, Cornhill*, 229–30; Foster, ed., *St Mary the Great, Cambridge*, 161–2.

95 NRO PD 337/85, 143–5.
96 SWHT Somerset, D/P/tin4/1/1, f. 169–71.
97 WSA, 2944/44/49.
98 Analysis comes from Farmiloe and Nixseaman, eds., *Elizabethan Churchwardens' Accounts*, 9–48. The listed examples can be found on 9, 13–14, 25–6, and 47–8.
99 WSA, 2944/44/49; SWHT Somerset, D/P/yat/4/4, f. 6.
100 Cf., e.g., SWHT Somerset D/P/tin4/1/1; HRO, 3M32/W/PW1; OHC PAR 214/4/F1.
101 HRO 75M/72/PW1, f. 50.
102 CA, KP30/4/1 f.173v.
103 Boulton, "Limits of Formal Religion," 143.
104 *Articles to be enquired of in the visitation of … Matthew* (1563), A2r–A4r.
105 *Iniunctions with Certaine Articles* (1569), B1r.
106 *Articles to be enquired of in the visitation of the Dioces of London* (1571), A4r.
107 *Articles to be inquired by the churchwardens … of Peterborough* (1602), 1.
108 Williams, ed., *Bishop Redman's Visitation*, 29–36.
109 Reliable estimates put the population of Norwich at fifteen thousand in 1600, of whom perhaps a quarter were immigrants from the Low Countries. These "Strangers" generally worshipped in their own churches, bringing the potential congregation size for the city down to about 11,250. Assuming roughly two-thirds of the population was over the age of fourteen, I estimate a potential communicant population of seven thousand. Should this estimate be significantly skewed and the communicant population standing at five thousand, the percentage presented would still be a tiny .5 per cent. (Emery, "England circa 1600," 294.)
110 Williams, ed., *Bishop Redman's Visitation*, 32.
111 Shorrocks, ed., *Bishop Still's Visitation, 1594*, 19. One additional parish, Taunton St Mary, seems to have been an unusual hub of nonconformity and, as an utter anomaly, is not included in this count; it seems unique to this parish, as neighbouring Taunton St James has only two people listed for not coming to church. (Ibid., 98–100.)
112 Marchant, *Church under the Law*, 219.
113 BI, V.1590–1/CB.1, V.1595/CB.1, V.1600/CB1. Putting these numbers into any sort of demographic context is nearly impossible, as no reliable data for the population of the archdeaconry itself exist; ten years later, though, there were over two hundred thousand communicants in the diocese of York writ large. (*Diocesan Population Returns*, lxxxiv.)

114 Questier, *Catholicism and Community*; Collinson, *Elizabethan Puritan Movement*, part 8.

115 TNA, SP/12/67, f. 89r.

116 TNA, SP 12/176/1, f. 6r; SP 12/188, f. 38r.

117 TNA, SP 12/193, f. 144r.

118 *Miscellanea II*, 267.

119 *Seconde Parte of a Register*, 1:113–14.

120 Roberts, ed., *Calendar of Manuscripts*, 4:67.

121 Lennam, "Francis Merbury," 217–18.

122 BL, Landsdowne Vol/49 f. 184r–v.

123 Ibid., f. 184v.

124 England was by no means alone in using the sacrament as a test; it was a common procedure across Europe, used by a variety of confessions. It was particularly useful for ecclesiastical tests and Inquisitions, such as the one undergone by a host of English sailors captured in Spain around the time of Drake's departure from Cadiz. There, English Catholic priests in exile attempted to convert them, with reception of the Catholic sacrament as proof of their new faith. The one sailor who refused, a Captain Crosse, "was carried to the Inquisition house, where he still remains prisoner." (TNA SP/262, ff. 148–9.)

125 For a fascinating discussion about the complex ideological battles surrounding 1577, cf. Lake, "A Tale of Two Episcopal Surveys."

126 TNA SP 12/114 f. 39r.

127 Ibid.

128 Ibid.

129 Nor did the attempts by Parliament in 1571, which were passed by both houses but vetoed by the queen.

130 TNA SP 12/116 f. 45.

131 Ryan, "Diocesan Returns for England and Wales," 9.

132 TNA SP 12/117, f. 7r.

133 TNA SP 12/117 f. 7r–60r passim.

134 TNA SP 12/117, f. 29.

135 TNA SP 12/117, ff. 51–54.

136 Ibid., f. 51r.

137 TNA SP 12/117, ff. 32r, 52v; SP 12/118, f. 78r.

138 TNA SP 12/117, f. 32r.

139 TNA SP 12/117, f. 41r.

140 TNA SP 12/118, f. 138r–v.

141 TNA SP 12/117, f. 41r.

142 TNA SP 12/118, f. 149v.
143 TNA SP 12/117, f. 32v.
144 TNA SP 12/119, f. 13v.
145 Ibid., f. 14v.
146 TNA SP 12/117, f. 38.
147 Cf. Neale, *Elizabeth I and Her Parliaments.* Vol. 1, 212–16.
148 Calthorp, ed., *Recusant Roll No. 1*, xvi.
149 Wrigley and Schofield calculate a population in 1591 of 3.899 million people in England, estimating about 60 per cent of the population at an eligible age. This is also roughly in line with the demographics taken from the diocesan population returns discussed later in the chapter. (Wrigley and Schofield, *Population History of England*, 528; Dyer and Palliser, *Diocesan Population Returns*, lxxxv.)
150 TNA SP 12/43, f. 25; BL, Lansdowne Vol/12, f. 190; Collinson, *Elizabethan Puritan Movement*, 122–4.
151 CUL, UA Luard 187. See, e.g., Cap XLI and XLII, ff. 8r–v.
152 Usher, *Rise and Fall of High Commission*, 71.
153 TNA SP 12/190, ff. 99–107.
154 Kaufman, "The Process of Protest."
155 Strype, *Whitgift*, 3:73.
156 Wilkins, *Concilia*, 4:344–5.
157 Ibid., 303.
158 Ibid., 363.
159 Dyer and Palliser, eds., *Diocesan Population Returns*, lvi–lvii. (Hereafter *DPR*.)
160 LPL, Reg. I Whitgift 150v; Wilkins, *Conciliae*, 368–9.
161 There had been diocesan surveys, particularly in the first decades of Elizabeth's reign, but nothing on a national scale. (Cf. *DPR*, liv.)
162 Ibid., lxvi–lxxi.
163 Ibid.
164 Dekker, C3r.
165 In the Harley manuscripts, the number was 8,512, while the Bodleian number was 8,483. These are modern calculations that correct for errors included in the contemporary summaries. (*DPR*, lxxxv.)
166 *DPR*, 310.
167 Ibid., 323.
168 Ibid., 452–3n183.
169 Ibid., 509.
170 Ibid., 334.
171 Ibid., 312.

172 TNA SP 14/3, f. 42.
173 *DPR*, 325.
174 *DPR*, 495; Page, ed., *History of the County of Hampshire*, 3:134–9; *Miscellanea XII*, 39.
175 Page, ed., *History of the County of Hampshire*, 3:144–5; *Miscellanea XII*, 41.
176 *DPR*, 495.
177 Totals were 398 recusants and 230 non-communicants, versus 58,707 communicants, for 1.06 per cent of all adults. (*DPR*, 485.)
178 *Conciliae*, 363.
179 BI, CP.G.2539, f. 4r.
180 Shiels, ed., *Archbishop Grindal's Visitation*, 16.
181 BI V. 1595/CB.1, f. 93r.
182 Williams, ed., *Bishop Redman's Visitation*, 44.
183 BI V.1582/CB.1, f. 227v.
184 BI V.1575/CB.1, f. 28v; cf. also Purvis, ed., *Tudor Parish Documents*, 69.
185 NRO ANW/6/1, f.4v.
186 NRO DN/VIS 2/1, f. 11v.
187 Haigh, "Communion and Community," especially 722–8.
188 Hunt, "The Lord's Supper," 47–9.
189 Sheils, ed., *Archbishop Grindal's Visitations*, 31.
190 For an overview of early modern conceptions of order, cf. Wrightson, *English Society, 1580–1680*, chap. 6.
191 Hunt, "The Lord's Supper," 63.
192 Sabean, *Power in the Blood*, chap. 1.
193 Wrightson, *English Society*, 45–50.
194 Walsham, *Church Papists*, 86.
195 Burton, *A Sermon Preached in the Cathedrall Church in Norwich*, D2r.
196 Brinkworth, *The Archdeacon's Court*, 29. Christopher Boreman of South Newton made similar testimony to the same court, confessing "there was some controversy in law between this respondent and two other of his neighbours, and by that means he was not in perfect love and charity, and did not refuse to receive in contempt of the Queen's laws" (ibid., 122). Also quoted in Hunt, "Lord's Supper," 48.
197 Earle, *Micro-cosmographie*, B7v–B8r. Cf. Hunt, "The Lord's Supper," 48.
198 Walsham, *Church Papists*, 86–9; Hunt, "The Lord's Supper," 40.
199 This was clearly not true in the small minority of parishes with strong bases of recusancy.
200 Cooper, *Certain Sermons*, Fi v.

201 *Book of Common Prayer* (1559), P3v.

202 E.g., *Articles to be enquired of in the visitation of the Dioces of London* (1571), A3r.

203 Haigh, "Communion and Community," 722.

204 *Articles to be enquired of, within the diocesse of Lincolne* (1598), B3r.

205 Thomas, "The Puritans and Adultery," 263–7; Ingram, *Church Courts*, especially chaps. 1 and 11.

206 Emphasis mine. *Articles to be enquired of, within the diocesse of Lincolne* (1598), B3r.

207 *Book of Common Prayer* (1559), P3v.

208 Raine, ed., *The Injunctions of Richard Barnes*, 125.

209 Amongst many others, cf. Wrightson and Levine, *Poverty and Piety*; Wrightson, "The Politics of the Parish"; Ingram, "Reformation of Manners"; Andy Wood, *The Politics of Social Conflict*, esp. chap 1; Hindle, *On the Parish?*; Shepard, *Meanings of Manhood*; Gaskill, "Little Commonwealths II."

210 Williams, ed., *Bishop Redman's Visitation*, 115.

211 Hindle. *On the Parish?* 58–81.

212 Haigh, "Communion and Community," 726.

213 Paul Griffiths, *Youth and Authority*, 86–7.

214 Collinson, Craig, and Usher, eds., *Conferences and Combination Lectures*, 138.

215 *Articles to be Inquired of within the Dioces of London* (1586), A3r; *Articles Ecclesiasticall to be Inquired of … within the Dioces of Hereford* (1586). STC /10215, A3r.

216 Raine, ed., *The Injunctions of Richard Barnes*, 122. Brancepeth was the seat of the Neville family until the Northern Rising of 1569, which was both a Catholic and a dynastic rebellion. Brancepeth was, at this time, confiscated by the crown. (Liddy, *The Bishopric of Durham*, 20.)

217 Raine, ed., *The Injunctions of Richard Barnes*, 122.

218 Haigh, "Communion and Community," 728.

219 Calvin, *The Catechisme*, 141.

220 Hunt, "The Lord's Supper," 65. For more on closed communion, cf. Collinson, *The Elizabethan Puritan Movement*, 348–9.

221 Haigh, "Communion and Community," 736.

222 *Iniunctions given by … Thomas Bishop of Lincolne* (1577), A2v.

223 Ibid. Thomas Cooper, bishop of Lincoln from 1571 to 1584, was a centrist in both doctrine and discipline. Though a reformer, he was criticized by the

more godly for his devotion to the prayer book and the episcopal system; he was also suspicious of lay attendance at exercises and kept a tight lid on dissent in his diocese. (Bowker, "Cooper, Thomas.")

224 Such was the hope of the litigants against Thomas Pestell, who brought him before the High Commission for various charges, including illegal exclusion. While the commission ultimately refused to deprive Pestell of his post, they did admonish him that such actions were "in themselves no way justifiable but worthy of severe punishment" (Haigh, "Parish Squabbles," 415).

225 Williams, ed., *Bishop Redman's Visitation*, 61. Either the pressures of such presentment or a general feeling of insufficiency must have dogged Gibson: shortly after being presented to the Archdeacon's Court, he fled the parish.

226 Haigh, "Communion and Community," 721.

227 Dod, John. *Dods Droppings a few of them as at severall times they have been gathered from his mouth* (Beinecke MSS Osb/b/235), 113; Hunt, "The Lord's Supper," 64.

228 Cf. Wrightson, "Mutualities and Obligations," especially 163–76; Shepard, "Manhood, Credit, and Patriarchy"; Muldrew, *The Economy of Obligation*; Muldrew, "The Culture of Reconciliation"; Withington "Citizens, Community, and Political Culture."

229 Beaver, *Parish Communities and Religious Conflict*, 59.

230 Cf. Muldrew, *The Economy of Obligation*, especially chap. 6.

231 Wrightson, "The Politics of the Parish," 13; Withington and Shepard, "Introduction: Communities in Early Modern England," 5–9.

232 CUL, GBR/0265/UA/Comm.Ct. II.11, f. 27r–v.

233 Ingram, *Church Courts*, 52–3. Ingram notes that there were technically two forms of excommunication, the greater and the lesser; lesser communication is perhaps best described as a court-ordered suspension, with none of the more severe penalties of greater excommunication. By the late-Elizabethan period, however, lesser excommunication was rarely used, and had died out in almost all areas of England by the early seventeenth century.

234 Gibson, *A System of English Ecclesiastical Law*, 405–6.

235 Price, "The Abuses of Excommunication."

236 Bacon, *Certaine Considerations*, E3r.

237 Ingram, *Church Courts*, 351. Ingram has analyzed the adjusted rates of attendance in the Diocese of Ely at 93 per cent (1590/1) and 83 per cent (1619) and in the Archdeaconry of Leicester at 69 per cent (1586) and 73 per cent (1615).

238 Figures taken from Shiels, *Archbishop Grindal's Visitation*, ix–xi. As Sheils notes, Pickering was a strange case, with most presentments coming from

the urban parishes of Scarborough and Bridlington. These towns seem to have been going through a disciplining frenzy, and the court clerk notes that many of the absent were "paupers" (x).

239 Sutton, *Godly Meditations*, 265 (O r).

240 Adair, *Courtship, Illegitimacy, and Marriage*, 157.

241 Williams, ed., *Bishop Redman's Visitation*, 117.

242 Raine, ed., *The Injunctions of Richard Barnes*, 133.

243 While it is certainly possible that such a focus was present before the 1590s, a systematic search of contemporary publications of such Articles reveals no such injunction or question before the Lincoln Articles of 1591. (*Articles to be Enquired of by the Churchwardens … within the Diocesse of Lincoln* [1591], B2v.) The most frequently printed example of the Articles, *Articles to be enquired in the visitation, in the firste yere of the raigne of our moste dread soueraigne lady Elizabeth*, never makes mention of such a question (first printing 1561). Examples of earlier diocesan Articles without such a focus include: *Articles to be enquired of in the visitation of the Dioces of London* (1571); *Articles to be enquired of within the dioces of Winchester* (1575); *Iniunctions given by the reuerende Father in God, Thomas Bishop of Lincolne* (1577); *Articles to be enquired of within the dioces of London* (1577); *Articles to be enquired of by the church-wardens & sworn-men within the dieocsse* [*sic*] *of Lincoln* (1585); *Articles to be enquired of by the churchwardens and swornemen in the Metropoliticall visitation of the … Archbishop of Yorke* (1590).

244 As Martin Ingram has succinctly described, "those who consorted with excommunicates, bought and sold with them, or gave them succour of harbour were themselves subject to excommunication." Ingram, *Church Courts*, 52–3.

245 The 1594 Visitation Articles of the diocese of Peterborough inquired "whether your minister have admitted anie excommunicte person to answere as godfather or godmother at the christening of any childe, or anie that have not before received the holy communion." (*Articles to Bee Enquired of by the Churchwardens … of Peterborough*, 3r.)

246 Beaver, *Parish Communities*, 104.

247 Coster, *Baptism and Spiritual Kinship*, chap. 6.

248 Gibson, *A System of English Ecclesiastical Law*, 401; Ingram, *Church Courts*, 53.

249 Monro, ed., *Acta Cancellariae*, 13, no. VII.

250 Gowing, *Domestic Dangers*, 111–12.

251 *Articles to be Enquired in the Dioces of London* (1598), B4v.

252 Williams, ed., *Bishop Redman's Visitation*, 53.

253 Ibid., 95.
254 Brinkworth, *The Archdeacon's* Court, 25.
255 Williams, ed., *Bishop Redman's Visitation*, 95.
256 Haigh, "Communion and Community," 738.
257 Spurr, *The Post-Reformation*, 285.
258 E.g., *Articles to Bee Enquired of by the Church-wardens and Sworne-men*, A3v.
259 BI CP.G.2603/Haworth.
260 Ingram, *Church Courts, Sex, and Marriage in England, 1570–1640*, 53.
261 *Articles to be inquired of* (1584), A2r.
262 Price, "Abuses of Excommunication," 108.
263 Williams, ed., *Bishop Redman's Visitation*, 107.
264 A full 202 of the 930 people presented to appear at the church courts attended only after they had been excommunicated. Ingram, *Church Courts*, 347.
265 Wrightson and Levine, *Poverty and Piety*, 156.
266 Hindle, *On the Parish*, 146–9.
267 LMA P69/BAT1/B/001/MS04384/001/40.
268 Burne, ed., *Staffordshire Quarter Sessions Rolls*, 3:229.
269 Ibid., 137
270 Kennedy, "Bishop Bickley's Articles for Chichester Diocese, 1586," 218; *Articles ecclesiasticall to be inquired of by the churchwardens and the sworne-men within the dioces of Hereford*, A2v.
271 Williams, ed., *Bishop Redman's Visitation*, 124.
272 Parish boundaries were also being drawn more closely following the implementation of parochial poor relief, compounding the sense of more rigid boundaries to belonging. Slack, *Poverty and Policy*, chap. 5.
273 NRO DN/VIS 2/1, f. 22r.
274 Ingram, *Church Courts, Sex, and Marriage in England*, 354–8, quote 357.
275 *Articles to be Enquired in the Dioces of London* (1598), A4r.

Conclusion

1 WSHC PR207/2944/44, 7–12.
2 Ibid., 14.
3 Ibid., 23.
4 Ibid., 27.
5 Ibid., 33.
6 Ibid., 35.

7 Ibid., 41–8.
8 Ibid., 49.
9 Ibid., 59.
10 Ibid., 79.
11 Ibid., 51, 101, 134.
12 Ibid., 86, 103.
13 Ibid., 96.
14 Ibid., 131–3. The citations that follow will all be from these pages, unless otherwise noted.
15 Ibid.
16 Ibid., 128.

Bibliography

Bibliographical Note

As much as possible, I have tried to draw from primary source material across the country. In addition to material that covers all of England, such as the Queen's Injunctions of 1559 or letters from the Privy Council to all bishops, I have consulted primary sources (printed or archival) that specifically address the historical counties of Berkshire, Buckinghamshire, Cambridgeshire, Cheshire, Cornwall, Cumberland, Derbyshire, Dorset, Durham, Essex, Gloucestershire, Hampshire, Herefordshire, Hertfordshire, Huntingdonshire, Kent, Lancashire, Leicestershire, Lincolnshire, Middlesex, Norfolk, Northumberland, Nottinghamshire, Oxfordshire, Rutland, Shropshire, Somerset, Staffordshire, Suffolk, Sussex, Warwickshire, Wiltshire, Worcestershire, and Yorkshire, as well as the City of London.

Archival Material

Beinecke Library (BeL)
Bodleian Library (BodL)
Borthwick Institute for Archives (BI)
British Library (BL)
Cambridgeshire Archives (CA)
Cambridge University Library, University Archives (CUL)
Canterbury Cathedral Archives (CCA)
Corpus Christi College Archives, University of Oxford (CCC)
Cumbria Archive Centre (CAC)
Devon Heritage Centre, Southwest Heritage Trust (SWHT, Devon)
Durham University Library, Archives and Special Collections (DUL)

Folger Library (FL)
Gloucestershire Archives (GA)
Hampshire Record Office (HRO)
Inner Temple Library (ITL)
London Metropolitan Archives (LMA)
The National Archives, Kew (TNA)
Norfolk Record Office (NRO)
Oxfordshire History Centre (OHC)
Queens' College Archives, University of Cambridge (QCA)
Record Office for Leicestershire, Leicester, and Rutland (ROL)
Shropshire Records Office (SRO)
Somerset Heritage Centre, Southwest Heritage Trust (SWHT, Somerset)
Wiltshire and Swindon History Centre (WSHC)
Worcester College Archives, University of Oxford (WCA)

Printed Materials

Note: All books printed before 1800 are from London, unless otherwise noted. For clarity, the Short Title Catalogue (STC) references have been included.

Acheson, R.J. *Radical Puritans in England, 1550–1660*. London: Longman, 1990.

Adair, Richard. *Courtship, Illegitimacy, and Marriage in Early Modern England*. Manchester: Manchester University Press, 1996.

Addy, John. *The Archdeacon and Ecclesiastical Discipline in Yorkshire, 1598–1714: Clergy and the Churchwardens*. St Anthony's Hall Publications, No. 24. York: St Anthony's Press, 1963.

Amphlett, John, ed. *Churchwardens' Accounts of St Michael's in Bedwardine, Worcester, from 1539 to 1603*. Worcestershire Historical Society. Vol. 8. Oxford: J. Parker and Co., 1896.

Amussen, Susan. *An Ordered Society: Gender and Class in Early Modern England*. New York: Columbia University Press, 1988.

Andrews, Bartimeus. *A Very Short and Pithie Catechisme* (1586). STC (2nd ed.)/586.

Andrews, K.R. "Christopher Newport of Limehouse, Mariner." *William and Mary Quarterly* 11, no. 1 (1954): 28–41.

Archer, Ian, "The Burden of Taxation on Sixteenth-Century London." *Historical Journal* 44, no. 3 (Sept. 2001): 599–627.

– *The Pursuit of Stability: Social Relations in Elizabethan England.* Cambridge: Cambridge University Press, 1991.

Articles ecclesiasticall to be inquired of by the Churchwardens and the sworne-men within the dioces of Hereford in the first visitation of the reuerend father in God, Harbart Bishop of the said dioces (Oxford, 1586). STC (2nd ed.)/10215.

Articles ecclesiasticall to be inquired of by the Churchwardens and the sworne-men within the dioces of Hereforde in … this present yeare MD LXXXXII (Oxford, 1592). STC (2nd ed.)/10215.5.

Articles ministered in the visitation of the right worshipfull maister John King, Archdeacon of Nottingham (Oxford: 1599). STC (2nd ed.)/10304.

Articles to be enquired in the visitation, in the firste yere of the raigne of our moste dread soueraigne lady Elizabeth (1561). STC (2nd ed.)/10119.

Articles to be enquired of by the Church-wardens & sworn-men within the dieocsse (sic) of Lincoln (1585). STC (2nd ed.)/10231.

Articles to be enquired of by the Churchwardens and Sworne men within the deane of Shorham (1597). STC (2nd ed.)/10133.7.

Articles to be enquired of by the Churchwardens and swornemen in the Metropoliticall visitation of the most reuerend father in God, L. Iohn, by the prouidence of almightie God, Archbishop of Yorke (1590). STC (2nd ed.)/10377.

Articles to be enquired of by the Churchwardens and swornmen within the diocesse of Lincoln and the truth thereof to be by them vpon their othes duelie presented unto the Bishop, or his deputies, at his visitation; now to be holden this present yeere of our Lord 1591, with particular answer to euery interrogatorie. (1591). STC (2nd ed.)/10233.

Articles to be enquired of in the visitation of the Dioces of London by the reuerende father in God, Edwyn Bishop of London In the thirtenth yeare of the raigne of our soueraigne ladie Elizabeth, by the grace of God Queene of Englande, Fraunce and Irelande defender of the fayth. &c. (1571). STC (2nd ed.)/10250.

Articles to be enquired of in the visitation of the most Reverend father in God, Matthew … Archebyshop of Canterbury. (1563). STC (2nd ed.)/10152.

Articles to be enquired of within the dioces of London, in the visitation of the Reuerend Father in God, Ihon Bishop of London, 1589. (1589). STC (2nd ed.)/10252.5.

Articles to be enquired of within the dioces of London (1577). STC (2nd ed.)/10251.

Articles to be enquired of within the dioces of London (1598). STC (2nd ed.)/10253.

Articles to be enquired of within the dioces of London (1601). STC (2nd ed.)/10254.

Articles to be enquired of within the dioces of Norwiche … in the yeare of our Lorde God, M.D. LXVII (1567). STC (2nd ed.)/10287.

Articles to be enquired of within the dioces of Norwich (1567). STC (2nd ed.)/10288.

Articles to be enquired of within the dioces of Winchester (1575). STC (2nd ed.)/10352.5.

Articles to be enquired of, within the diocese of Lincolne (1598). STC (2nd ed.)/10235.

Articles to be enquired of, within the province of Canterburie … in the xviij yeare of the reygne of our most gracious sovereygne Ladie Elizabeth (1577). STC (2nd ed.)/10155.3.

Articles to be enquyred in the visitacyon, in the fyrst yeare of the raigne of our most drad (sic) soveraygne Lady (1559). STC (2nd ed.)/ 10118.5

Articles to be inquired of, by the reverende father in God, Richarde by Gods providence Bishop of Elye (1573). STC (2nd ed.)/10194.5.

Articles to be Inquired of, in the Metropolitical Visitation of the Moste Reverende father in God Matthew … Archebyshop of Canterbury … MDLX (1560). STC (2nd ed.)/10151.

Articles to be Inquired of in the Ordinarie Visitation of the Right Reuerende Father in God, William Lorde Bishop of Couentrie and Lichfielde (1584). STC (2nd ed.)/10224.

Articles to Bee Enquired of by the Church-wardens and Sworne-men, in the Oridnary Vistiation of the Lord Bishop of Excester, within the Dioces of Excester (1599). STC (2nd ed.)/10204.

Articles to bee enquired of by the Churchwardens and sworn-men within the diocesse of Peterborough (1594). STC (2nd ed.)/ 10314.

Articles: whereupon it was agreed … in the convocation holden at London. (1563). STC (2nd ed.)/10038.3.

Aston, Margaret. *Broken Idols of the English Reformation.* Cambridge: Cambridge University Press, 2016.

– *England's Iconoclasts.* Oxford: Clarendon Press, 1988.

– *Lollards and Reformers: Images and Literacy in Late Medieval Religion.* London: Hambledon Press, 1984].

Atchley, E.G.C.F. "The Parish Records of All Saints, Bristol," in *Transactions of the Bristol and Gloucestershire Archaeological Society*. 27 (1904): 221–74.

Aveling, J.C.H. *The Handle and the Axe: The Catholic Recusants in England from Reformation to Emancipation*. London: Blond and Briggs, 1976.

Bacon, Francis. *Certaine considerations touching the better pacification, and edification of the Church of England dedicated to His most excellent Maiestie* (1604). STC (2nd ed.)/1120.

Bailey, F.A., ed., *The Churchwardens' Accounts of Prescot, Lancashire, 1523–1607*. Record Society of Lancashire and Cheshire. Vol. 104. Preston: Record Society of Lancashire and Cheshire, 1953.

Baker, T.F.T., ed. *A History of the County of Middlesex*. Vol. 11: *Stepney, Bethnal Green*. London: Victoria County History, 1998.

Baldwin, R.C.D. "Borough, William," *Oxford Dictionary of National Biography*, 2004.

Barmby, James, ed. *Churchwardens' Accounts of Pittington and Other Parishes in the Diocese of Durham from AD 1580 to 1700*. Durham: Surtees Society, 1888.

Barnard, E.A.B., ed. *Churchwardens Accounts of South Littleton*. Worcester: E. Baylis and Son, 1926.

Barratt, Dorothy Mary, ed. *Ecclesiastical Terriers of Warwickshire Parishes*, Vol. 1. Dugdale Society, Vol. 22. Oxford: Dugdale Society at the University Press, 1955.

Beatniffe, John. *A sermon preached at Torceter … at the visitation of the right reverend Father in God, the Bishop of Peeterborow* (1590). STC (2nd ed.)/1662.

Beaver, Daniel C. *Parish Communities and Religious Conflict in the Vale of Gloucester, 1590–1690*. Cambridge, MA: Harvard University Press, 1998.

Becon, Thomas. *The New Pollecye of Warre* [1542]. STC (2nd ed.)/1735.

Beer, Barrett L. *Rebellion and Riot: Popular Disorder in England during the Reign of Edward VI*. Kent, OH: Kent State University Press, 2005.

Beloe, Edward Milligen. *Our Borough: Our Churches*. Cambridge: Macmillan and Bowes, 1899.

Ben-Amos, Ilana Krausman. *The Culture of Giving: Informal Support and Gift-Exchange in Early Modern England*. Cambridge: Cambridge University Press, 2008.

– "'Good Works' and Social Ties: Helping the Migrant Poor in Early Modern England," in *Protestant Identities: Religion, Society, and*

Self-Fashioning in Post-Reformation England, edited by Murial C. McClendon, 125–40. Stanford: Stanford University Press, 1999.

Bennett, J.H.E., and J.C. Dewhurst, eds. *Quarter Sessions Records with Other Records of the Justices of the Peace for the County Palatine of Chester, 1559–1760*. The Record Society for the Publication of Original Documents Relating to Lancashire and Cheshire 94. Chester: Record Society of Lancashire and Cheshire,1940.

Bernard, George. "The Church of England, c. 1529–1642," *History* 75 (1990): 183–206.

Best, G.F.A. *Temporal Pillars: Queen Anne's Bounty, the Ecclesiastical Commissioners, and the Church of England.* Cambridge: Cambridge University Press, 1964.

Bilson, Thomas. *The perpetual governement of Christes Church* (1593). STC (2nd ed.)/3065.

Black, Jeremy. *English Nationalism: A Short History.* London: Hurst, 2018.

Blagg, Thomas M., ed. *A Miscellany of Nottinghamshire Records.* Thoroton Society Record Series 11. Nottingham: Thoroton Society, 1945.

Blair, John. *The Church in Anglo-Saxon Society*. Oxford: Oxford University Press, 2005.

Blickle, Peter, *The Revolution of 1525: The German Peasants' War from a New Perspective.* Baltimore: Johns Hopkins University Press, 1977.

Blomefield, Francis. *An Essay Towards a Topographical History of the County of Norfolk: Volume 9.* London: W. Miller, 1808.

Boettecher, Susan R. "Confessionalization: Reformation, Religion, Absolutism, and Modernity," *History Compass* 2, no. 1 (Jan. 2004): 1–10.

The Boke of Common praier, and Adminstracion of the Sacraments, and Other Rites and Ceremonies in the Churche of Englande (1552). STC (2nd ed.)/16285.

The boke of the Common Praier and Administration of ye Sacramentes (Worcester, 1549). STC (2nd ed)/16276.

The Boke of Common Prayer, and Administration of the Sacramentes, & Other Rites & Ceremonies in the Church of England (1560). STC (2nd ed.)/16294.

The Booke of Common Prayer, and Administracion of the Sacramentes, and Other Rites and Ceremonies in the Church of England (1559). STC (2nd ed.)/16293.3.

Borthwick Institute for Archives. *The Cause Papers in the Diocesan Courts of the Archbishopric of York, 1300–1858.* [Database] https://www.dhi.ac.uk/causepapers/.

Bossy, John. *The English Catholic Community, 1570–1850*. New York: Oxford University Press, 1976.

– "The Mass as a Social Institution, 1200–1700." *Past and Present* 100 (Aug, 1983): 29–61.

– "The Social History of Confession in the Age of Reformation." *Transactions of the Royal Historical Society*, 5th Series, 25 (1975): 21–38.

Boulton, Jeremy. "The Limits of Formal Religion: The Administration of Holy Communion in Late Elizabethan and Early Stuart London." *London Journal* 10 (Winter 1984): 179–93.

– *Neighbourhood and Society: A London Suburb in the Seventeenth Century*. Cambridge: Cambridge University Press, 1987.

Bowden, Peter. "Statistical Appendix." In *The Agrarian History of England and Wales*. Vol. 4: *1500–1640*, edited by Joan Thirsk, 814–70. Cambridge: Cambridge University Press, 1967.

Bowker, Margaret. "Cooper, Thomas (c.1517–1594)," in *Oxford Dictionary of National Biography*. Oxford: Oxford University Press, 2004.

Braddick, Michael. "State Formation and Social Change in Early Modern England: A Problem Stated and Approaches Suggested." *Social History* 16, no. 1 (1991): 1–17.

Braddick, Michael, and John Walter. "Grids of Power: Order, Hierarchy, and Subordination in Early Modern Society." In *Negotiating Power in Early Modern Society: Order, Hierarchy, and Subordination in Britain and Ireland*, edited by Michael Braddick and John Walter, 1–42. Cambridge: Cambridge University Press, 2001.

Bramhall, Eric. "Penitence, Preachers, and Politics, 1533–47: Thomas Cranmer's Influence on Church Teaching on Penance during the Henrician Reformation." *Historical Research* 89, no. 246 (2016): 687–707.

Branch, Laura. *Faith and Fraternity: London Livery Companies and the Reformation, 1510–1603*. Leiden: Brill, 2017.

Bray, Gerald, ed. *The Anglican Canons, 1529–1947*. Church of England Record Society 6. Woodbridge, UK: The Boydell Press, 1998.

– *Tudor Church Reform: The Henrician Canons of 1535 and the Reformatio Legum Ecclesiasticarum*. Church of England Record Society 8. Woodbridge, UK: The Boydell Press, 2000.

A breefe catechisme so necessarie and easie to be learned even of the symple sort that whosoever can not or wyll not attayne to the same, is not to be counted a good Christian, much lesse be admitted to the Supper of the Lorde (1576). STC (2nd ed.)/4798.

Brenner, Robert. *Merchants and Revolution: Commercial Change, Political Conflict, and London's Overseas Traders, 1550–1653*. London: Verso, 2003.

Bridgeman, George. *The History of the Church and Manor of Wigan*. Chetham Society 15. Manchester: Chetham Society, 1888.

Bridges, John. *A defence of the gouernment established in the Church of Englande for ecclesiasticall matters* (1587). STC (2nd ed.)/3734.

A briefe examination for the tyme (1566). STC (2nd ed.)/10387.

Brigden, Susan. *London and the Reformation*. Oxford: Oxford University Press, 1989.

– "Tithe Controversy in Reformation London." *Journal of Ecclesiastical History* 32, no. 3 (1981): 285–301.

Brinkworth, E.R., ed. *The Archdeacon's Court: Liber Actorum, 1584*. Oxford Record Society 24. Oxford: Oxfordshire Record Society, 1942.

– *South Newington Churchwardens' Accounts, 1553–1684*. Banbury Historical Society Series 6. Banbury: Banbury Historical Society, 1964.

Brooks, Christopher W. *Law, Politics, and Society in Early Modern England*. Cambridge: Cambridge University Press, 2008.

– *Lawyers, Litigation, and English Society since 1450*. London: Hambledon Press, 1998.

– *Pettyfoggers and Vipers of the Commonwealth: The "Lower Branch" of the Legal Profession in Early Modern England*. Cambridge: Cambridge University Press, 2004.

"Browne, Henry (CCEd Person ID 115055)." *Clergy of the Church of England Database*, last updated February 2019. https://theclergydatabase.org.uk/.

Brownlee, Victoria. "Imagining the Enemy: Protestant Readings of the Whore of Babylon in Early Modern England, c.1580–1625." In *Biblical Women in Early Modern Literary Culture, 1550–1700*, edited by Victoria Brownlee and Laura Gallagher, 213–33. Manchester: Manchester University Press, 2015.

Buck, Lawrence P. "Opposition to Tithes in the Peasants' Revolt: A Case of Nuremberg in 1524," *Sixteenth Century Journal* 4, no. 2 (Oct. 1973): 11–22.

Bullinger, Heinrich. *Fiftie Godlie and Learned Sermons* (1577). STC (2nd ed)/4056.

Burg, David F. *A World History of Tax Rebellions: An Encyclopedia of Tax Rebels, Revolts, and Riots from Antiquity to the Present*. New York: Routledge, 2004.

Burne, S.A.H., ed. *Staffordshire Quarter Sessions Rolls*. Vol. 3: *1594–1597*. Staffordshire: County Council for the William Salt Archaeological Society, 1933.

Burnett, Amy Nelson. 'The Social History of Communion and the Reformation of the Eucharist." *Past and Present* 211 (May 2011): 77–119.

Burton, William. *A Sermon Preached in the Cathedrall Church in Norwich* (1590). STC (2nd ed.)/ 4178.

Bush, M.L. *Pilgrimage of Grace: A Study of the Rebel Armies of October 1536*. Manchester: Manchester University Press, 1996.

Bynum, Caroline Walker. *Wonderful Blood: Theology and Practice in Late Medieval Northern Germany and Beyond*. Philadelphia: University of Pennsylvania Press, 2007.

Calendar of Manuscripts of the Most Honorable the Marquis of Salisbury. Vol. 4. London: HMSO, 1883.

Calthorp, M.M.C., ed. *Recusant Roll No. 1, 1592–93*. Catholic Record Society 18. London: privately printed by Strowger and Son, 1916.

Calvin, John. *The Catechisme, or Manner to Teache Children the Christian Religion Wherin the Minister Demandeth the Question, and the Childe Maketh Answere* (Geneva, 1556). STC (2nd ed.)/4380.

– *A Faythfull and Moost Godlye Treatyse Concernyng the Most Sacred Sacrament* (1548). STC (2nd ed.)/4411.

– *Institutes of the Christian Religion: Volume 2*. Translated by Henry Beveridge. Edinburgh: T. and T. Clark, 1863.

Campbell, William H. *The Landscape of Pastoral Care in 13th-Century England*. Cambridge: Cambridge University Press, 2018.

Canny, Nicholas P. *Making Ireland British, 1580–1650*. Oxford: Oxford University Press, 2001.

Carlson, Eric. "The Origins, Function, and Status of the Office of Churchwarden, with Particular Reference to the Diocese of Ely." In *The World of Rural Dissenters, 1520–1725*, edited by Margaret Spufford, 164–207. Cambridge: Cambridge University Press, 1995.

Carroll, John. 'The Role of Guilt in the Formation of Modern Society: England, 1350–1800." *British Journal of Sociology* 32, no. 4 (Dec. 1981): 459–503.

Chaucer, Geoffrey. "General Prologue." In *The Riverside Chaucer*, edited by Larry Benson and F.N. Robinson, 23–35. Oxford: Oxford University, 2008.

Cheney, C.R. *Episcopal Visitation of Monasteries in the Thirteenth Century*. Publications of the University of Manchester, Historical Series, 58. Manchester: Manchester University Press, 1931.

Clark, Gregory. "The Price History of English Agriculture, 1209–1914." *Research in Economic History* 22 (2004): 41–124.

Clark, Margaret. "Northern Light? Parochial Life in a 'Dark Corner' of Tudor England." In *The Parish in English Life, 1400–1600*, edited by Katherine French, Gary Gibbs, and Beat A. Kümin, 56–73. Manchester: Manchester University Press, 1997.

Clark, William. *Tithes and Oblations* (1595). STC (2nd ed.)/4323.2.

Clarke, H.W. *History of Tithes from Abraham to Queen Victoria*. London: George Redwary, 1887.

Clarke, Samuel. *A General Martyrologie* (1651). Wing/C4513.

Claydon, Tony. "The Reformation of the Future: Dating English Protestantism in the Late Stuart Era." *Etudes Epistémè* 32 (2017).

Clegg, Cyndia Susan. "The 1559 Books of Common Prayer and the Elizabethan Reformation." *Journal of Ecclesiastical History* 67, no. 1 (2016): 94–121.

Clowes, William L. *The Royal Navy: A History from the Earliest Times to the Present*. Vol. 2. London: Sampson Low, Marston and Company, 1898.

Cohn, H.J. "Anticlericalism in the German Peasants' War, 1525." *Past and Present* 83 (1979): 3–31.

Coke, Edward. *The Reports of Edward Coke, Knt: In Thirteen Parts*. Vol. 3. Edited by J.H. Thomas. London: Joseph Butterworth and Son, 1826.

Collier, Jeremy. *An Ecclesiastical History of Great Britain, Chiefly of England*. Vol. 9. London: William Straker, 1846.

Collins, W.E., ed. *The Canons of 1571 in English and Latin*. The Church Historical Society 40. London: Society for Promoting Christian Knowledge, 1899.

Collinson, Patrick. *Archbishop Grindal, 1519–1583: The Struggle for a Reformed Church*. Berkeley: University of California Press, 1979.

– *Birthpangs of Protestant England: Religious and Cultural Change in the Sixteenth and Seventeenth Centuries*. New York: St Martin's Press, 1988.

– *Elizabethan Puritan Movement*. Berkeley: University of California Press, 1967.

– *Godly People: Essays on English Protestantism and Puritanism*. London: The Hambledon Press, 1983.

– "Protestant Culture and the Cultural Revolution." In *Reformation to Revolution: Politics and Religion in Early Modern England*, edited by Margo Todd, 33–52. London: Routledge, 1995.

– *The Religion of Protestants: The Church in English Society, 1559–1625*. Oxford: Clarendon Press, 1982.

Collinson, Patrick, John Craig, and Brett Usher, eds. *Conferences and Combination Lectures in the Elizabethan Church, 1582–1590*. Church of England Record Society 10. Woodbridge, UK: Boydell and Brewer, 2003.

Connolly, Margaret. *Sixteenth-Century Readers, Fifteenth-Century Books: Continuities of Reading in the English Reformation.* Cambridge, Cambridge University Press, 2019.

Cooper, Thomas. *A Briefe homily wherin the most comfortable and right use of the Lords Supper is very plainly opened and delivered* (1580). STC (2nd ed.)/5684.5.

– *Certain Sermons* (1580). STC (2nd ed)/5685.

A Copye of a letter Contayning Certayne Newes, & the Articles or Requestes of the Devonshyre & Cornyshe Rebelles (1549). STC (2nd ed.)/15109.3.

Cornish, Robert, ed. *Kilmington Church Wardens' Accounts, MDLVV–MDCVIII*. Exeter: William Pollard and Co., 1901.

Corthell, Ronald. *Catholic Culture in Early Modern England.* Notre Dame, IN: University of Notre Dame Press, 2007.

Cox, J.C. *Pulpits, Lecterns, and Organs in English Churches*. Oxford: Humphrey Milford, Oxford University Press, 1915.

Coster, Will. *Baptism and Spiritual Kinship in Early Modern England.* Abington, UK: Ashgate Publishing, 2002.

Cowan, Brian. "Refiguring Revisionisms." *History of European Ideas* 29, no. 4 (Dec 2003): 475–89.

Cox, J. Charles. *Churchwardens Accounts from the Fourteenth Century to the Close of the Seventeenth Century.* London: Methuen and Co., 1913.

– *Pulpits, Lecterns, and Organs in English Churches*. Oxford: Humphrey Milford, Oxford University Press, 1915.

Cox, J.E., ed. *Miscellaneous Writings and Letters of Thomas Cranmer*. Cambridge: Parker Society, 1846.

Craig, John. "Co-operation and Initiatives: Elizabethan Churchwardens and the Parish Accounts of Mildenhall." *Social History* 18, no. 3 (Oct. 1993): 357–80.

– *Reformation, Politics, and Polemics: The Growth of Protestantism in East Anglian Market Towns, 1500–1610*. Aldershot, UK: Ashgate, 2001.

Cressy, David, and Lori Anne Ferrell, eds. *Religion and Society in Early Modern England: A Sourcebook*. New York: Routledge, 2010.

Crittall, Elizabeth, ed. *A History of the County of Wiltshire*. Vol. 8: *Warminster, Westbury, and Whorwellsdown Hundreds*. London: Victoria County History, 1965.

Cross, Claire. *Church and People, 1450–1660: The Triumph of the Laity in the English Church*. Hassocks, UK: Harvester Press, 1976.

– ed. *Patronage and Recruitment in the Tudor and Early Stuart Church*. Borthwick Studies in History 2. York, UK: St Anthony's Press, 1996.

– "Incomes of Provincial Urban Clergy." In *Princes and Paupers in the English Church, 1500–1800*. edited by Rosemary O'Day and Claire Cross, 65–89. Leicester: Leicester University Press, 1961.

Cross, Claire, and Noreen Vickers. *Monks, Friars, and Nuns in Sixteenth Century Yorkshire*. Yorkshire Archaeological Society 150. York, UK: Printed for the Society, 1995.

Cuttica, Cesare. "Popularity in Early Modern England (ca. 1580–1642): Looking Again at Thing and Concept." *Journal of British Studies* 58, no. 1 (2019): 1–27.

Cutts, Edward. *A Dictionary of the Church of England*. London: SPCK, 1887.

D'Ewes, Simonds. *The Journals of All the Parliaments during the Reign of Queen Elizabeth* (1682). Wing/D1250.

Davies, C.S.L. "Popular Religion and the Pilgrimage of Grace." In *Order and Disorder in Early Modern England*, edited by Anthony Fletcher and John Stevenson, 137–65. Cambridge: Cambridge University Press, 1985.

Day, William, ed. *Oswestry Parish Church: The Churchwardens' Accounts for 1579–1613*. Oswestry: Wm. Day, 1970.

Dekker, Thomas. *The Wonderful Year* (1603). STC (2nd ed.)/6535.5.

Dent, Arthur. *Plain-man's Pathway to Heaven* (1601). STC (2nd ed.)/6646.5.

– *The Ruine of Rome* (1603). STC (2nd ed.)/6640.

Dering, Edward. *A Sermon Preached before the Quenes Majestie* (1569). STC (2nd ed)/6699.

Dickens, A.G. *The English Reformation*. London: Collins, 1967.

– "Extent and Character of Recusancy in Yorkshire, 1604." *Yorkshire Archaeological Journal* 37 (1951): 24–48.

Dillon, Anne. *Construction of Martyrdom in the English Catholic Community, 1535–1603*. Aldershot, UK: Ashgate, 2002.

Dipple, Geoffrey. *Antifraternalism and Anticlericalism in the German Reformation: Johann Eberlin von Günzburg and the Campaign against the Friars*. Aldershot, UK: Ashgate, 1996.

Drew, Charles. *Early Parochial Organization in England: The Origins of the Office of the Churchwarden.* St Anthony's Hall Publications 7. York, UK: St Anthony's Press, 1954.

– ed. *Lambeth Churchwardens' Accounts, 1504–1645*. Vol. 1. Surrey Record Society, Vol. 18. London: Butler and Tanner, 1941.

Dropuljic, Stephanie. "The Role of Women in Pursuing Scottish Criminal Actions, 1580–1650." *Edinburgh Law Review* 24, no. 2 (2020): 232–50.

Duffy, Eamon. *Fires of Faith: Catholic England under Mary Tudor*. New Haven: Yale University Press, 2009.

– *Reformation Divided: Catholics, Protestants, and the Conversion of England.* London: Bloomsbury, 2017.

– *The Stripping of the Altars: Traditional Religion in England, c. 1400–1580.* New Haven: Yale University Press, 1992.

– *Voices of Morebath: Reformation and Rebellion in an English Village.* New Haven: Yale University Press, 2001.

Dures, Alan. *English Catholicism, 1558–1642*. Harlow: Longman, 1983.

Dyer, Alan, and D.M. Palliser, eds. *The Diocesan Population Returns for 1563 and 1603*. British Academy Records of Social and Economic History, New Series 31. Oxford: Oxford University Press, 2005.

Dykema, Peter, and Heiko Oberman, eds. *Anticlericalism in Late Medieval and Early Modern Europe*. New York: E.J. Brill, 1993.

Earle, John. *Micro-cosmographie; or, A peece of the world discovered in essayes and characters.* (1628). (STC/7440.2)

Earwaker, J.P. *The History of the Church and Parish of St Mary-on-the-Hill, Chester*. London: Love and Wyman, 1898.

East London History Group. "The Population of Stepney in the Early Seventeenth Century." *Local Population Studies* 3 (1969): 39–52.

Eire, Carlos. *Reformations: The Early Modern World, 1450–1650*. New Haven: Yale University Press, 2016.

– *War Against the Idols: The Reformation of Worship from Erasmus to Calvin.* Cambridge: Cambridge University Press, 1986.

Elton, G.R. *The Parliament of England, 1559–1581*. Cambridge: Cambridge University Press, 1986.

– "Politics and the Pilgrimage of Grace." In *After the Reformation: Essays in Honor of J.H. Hexter*, edited by Barbara C. Malament, 25–56.

Manchester: Manchester University Press, 1980.
– *Tudor Revolution in Government: Administrative Changes in the Reign of Henry VIII.* Cambridge: Cambridge University Press, 1953.

Elwood, Chrisopher. *The Body Broken: The Calvinist Doctrine of the Eucharist and the Symbolization of Power in Sixteenth-Century France.* Oxford: Oxford University Press, 1999.

Emery, F.V. "England circa 1600." In *A New Historical Geography of England before 1600*, edited by H.C. Darby, 248–301. Cambridge: Cambridge University Press: 1976.

Estabrook, Carl B. "Ritual, Space, and Authority in Seventeenth-Century English Cathedral Cities." *Journal of Interdisciplinary History* 32, no. 4, The Productivity of Urban Space in Northern Europe (Spring 2002): 593–620.

The Examination of Master William Thorpe Preste Accused of Heresye (Antwerp, 1530). STC 2nd ed./24045.

Farmiloe, J.E., and Rosita Nixseaman, eds. *Elizabethan Churchwardens' Accounts*. Bedfordshire Historical Record Society 33. Streatley: Bedfordshire Historical Record Society, 1953.

Fenner, Dudley. *A briefe and plaine declaration* (1584). STC (2nd ed.)/10395.

Field, John. *An Admonition to the Parliament* (1572). STC (2nd ed.)/10848.

Finch, Jonathan. *Church Monuments in Norfolk before 1850: An Archaeology of Commemoration*. Oxford: Archaeopress, 2000.

Fincham, Kenneth, ed. *The Early Stuart Church, 1603–1642*. Houndmills, UK: Macmillan, 1993.

Fincham, Kenneth, and Nicholas Tyacke. *Altars Restored: The Changing Face of English Religious Worship, 1547–c.1700.* Oxford: Oxford University Press, 2007.

Fincham, Kenneth, and Peter Lake, eds. *Religious Politics in Post-Reformation England: Essays in Honour of Nicholas Tyacke.* Woodbridge, UK: Boydell and Brewer, 2006.

Flather, Amanda. *Gender and Space in Early Modern England.* Woodbridge, UK: Boydell Press, 2007.
– *Politics of Place: A Study of Church Seating in Essex, c. 1580–1649.* Leicester: Friends of the Department of English Local History, 1999.

Fleming, P.W. "Charity, Faith, and the Gentry of Kent, 1422–1529." In *Property and Politics: Essays in Late Medieval English History*, edited by Tony Pollard, 36–58. Gloucester: A. Sutton, 1984.

Fletcher, Anthony. *Tudor Rebellions.* London: Longman, 1983.

Foster, C.W., ed. *The State of the Church in the Reigns of Elizabeth and James I, as Illustrated by Documents Relating to the Diocese of Lincoln.* Lincoln Record Society 23. Lincoln: Lincoln Record Society,1926.

Foster, J.E., ed. *Churchwardens' Accounts St Mary the Great, Cambridge, from 1504 to 1635.* Cambridge: Cambridge Antiquarian Society, 1905.

Foster, Joseph, ed., *The Visitation of Yorkshire, Made in the Years 1584/5.* London: private publication, 1875.

Freeman, Thomas. "Restoration and Reaction: Reinterpreting the Marian Church." *Journal of Ecclesiastical History* 69, no. 1 (2018): 105–12.

French, Henry. *The Middle Sort of People in Provincial England, 1600–1750.* Oxford: Oxford University Press, 2008.

French, Katherine. *People of the Parish: Community Life in a Late Medieval English Diocese.* Philadelphia: University of Pennsylvania Press, 2001.

Frere, W.H., ed. *Visitation Articles and Injunctions of the Period of the Reformation.* Vol. 1: *Historical Introduction and Index.* London: Longmans, Green and Co., 1910.

Freshfield, Edwin, ed. *Minutes of the Parish of St Christopher le Stocks.* London: Rixon and Arnold, 1886.

– ed. *The Vestry Minute Books of the Parish of St Bartholomew Exchange in the City of London, 1567–1676.* London: privately printed, 1890.

– ed. *The Vestry Minute Book of the Parish of St Margaret Lothbury in the City of London, 1571–1677.* London: privately printed, 1887.

Gaimster, D.R.M., and R. Gilchrest, eds., *The Archaeology of Reformation, 1480–1580.* Leeds: Maney Publications, 2003.

Gallagher, John. *Learning Languages in Early Modern England.* Oxford: Oxford University Press, 2019.

Garry, Francis N.A., and A.G. Garry, eds. *Churchwardens' Accounts of the Parish of St Mary's, Reading, Berks, 1550–1662.* Reading, UK: Edward J. Blackwell, 1893.

Gaskill, Malcolm. "Little Commonwealths II: Communities," in *A Social History of England,* edited by Keith Wrightson, 84–104. Cambridge: Cambridge University Press, 2017.

Gee, Henry. *Elizabethan Prayer Book and Ornaments.* London: Macmillan and Co., 1902.

Gee, Henry, and William John Hardy, eds., *Documents Illustrative of English Church History.* London: Macmillan and Co., 1896.

Gibson, Edmund. *A system of English ecclesiastical law. Extracted from the Codex juris ecclesiastici anglicani of the Right Reverend the Lord Bishop of London.* 1730.

Gilby, Anthony. *A Pleasant dialogue, betweene a souldior of Barwicke, and an English chaplaine* (1581). STC (2nd ed.)/ 11888.

Glasscock, J.L., ed. *The Records of St Michael's Parish Church, Bishop's Stortford.* Bishops Stortford: E. Stock, 1882.

Gomme, George Laurence. *The History of Thomas Hickathrift.* London: The Villon Society, 1885.

Gowing, Laura. *Domestic Dangers: Women, Words, and Sex in Early Modern London.* Oxford: Oxford University Press, 1996.

Grassby, Richard. *Kinship and Capitalism: Marriage, Family, and Business in the English-Speaking World, 1580–1720.* Cambridge: Cambridge University Press, 2001.

Graves, Michael A.R. "Strickland, William (d. 1598)," in *Oxford Dictionary of National Biography.* Oxford: Oxford University Press, 2004.

Green, Ian. *The Christian's ABC: Catechisms and Catechizing in England, c. 1530–1740.* Oxford: Clarendon Press, 1996.

Green, Mary Anne Everett, ed., *Calendar of State Papers Domestic: James I, 1603–1610.* London: HMSO, 1857.

Grierson, Edward. *The Companion Guide to Northumbria.* London: Collins, 1986.

Griffiths, Paul. *Lost Londons: Change, Crime, and Control in the Capital City, 1550–1660.* Cambridge: Cambridge University Press, 2010.

– *Youth and Authority: Formative Experiences in England, 1560–1640.* Oxford: Oxford University Press, 1996.

Hadfield, Andrew. Lying in Early Modern English Culture: From the Oath of Supremacy to the Oath of Allegiance. Oxford: Oxford University Press, 2017.

Haigh, Christopher. "Anticlericalism and the English Reformation." In *The English Reformation Revised*, edited by Christopher Haigh, 56–74. Cambridge: Cambridge University Press, 1987.

– "Communion and Community: Exclusion from Communion in Post-Reformation England," *Journal of Ecclesiastical History* 51, no. 4 (Oct. 2000): 721–40.

– *English Reformations: Religion, Politics, and Society under the Tudors.* Oxford: Clarendon Press, 1993.

– *Plain Man's Pathways to Heaven: Kinds of Christianity in Post-Reformation England, 1570–1640.* Oxford: Oxford University Press, 2007.

– *Reformation and Resistance in Tudor Lancashire.* Cambridge: Cambridge University Press, 1975.

– "Slander and the Church Courts in the Sixteenth Century." *Transactions of the Lancashire and Cheshire Antiquarian Society* 78 (1975): 1–13.

Hall, John. *A History of South Cave and of Other Parishes in the East Riding of the County of York.* Hull: Edwin Ombler, 1892.

Halton, Edward. *A New View of London; or, a Ample Account of that City.* Vol. 1. London: R. Chiswell, 1708.

Hanham, Alison, ed. *Churchwardens' Accounts of Ashburton, 1479–1580.* Devon and Cornwall Record Society, New Series 15. Torquay: Devon and Cornwall Record Society, 1970.

Harding, Vanessa. "City, Capital, and Metropolis: The Changing Shape of Seventeenth Century London." In *Imagining Early Modern London: Perceptions and Portrayals of the City from Stow to Strype, 1598–1720,* edited by J.F. Merritt, 117–43. Cambridge: Cambridge University Press, 2001.

Harkrider, Melissa F. *Women, Reform, and Community in Early Modern England: Katherine Willoughby, Duchess of Suffolk, and Lincolnshire's Godly Aristocracy, 1519–1580.* Woodbridge, UK: The Boydell Press, 2008.

Hartley, T.E., ed. *Proceedings in the Parliaments of Elizabeth I.* Vol. 1: *1558–1581.* Leicester: Leicester University Press, 1981.

Hasler, P.W., ed. *The House of Commons, 1558–1603: Members, M–Z.* London: History of Parliament Trust, 1981.

Hassett, M.K. *Anglican Communion in Crisis: How Episcopal Dissidents and Their African Allies Are Reshaping Anglicanism.* Princeton: Princeton University Press, 2007.

Heal, Felicity. *Hospitality in Early Modern England.* Oxford: Clarendon Press, 1990.

– *Reformation in Britain and Ireland.* Oxford: Oxford University Press, 2003.

Heal, Felicity, and Rosemary O'Day, eds. *Princes and Paupers in the English Church, 1500 to 1800.* Leicester: Leicester University Press, 1981.

Heath, Peter. *The English Parish Clergy on the Eve of the Reformation.* London: Routledge and Kegan Paul, 1969.

Hebditch, M.J. *Yorkshire Deeds.* Vol. 9, 2nd ed. Cambridge: Cambridge University Press, 2013.

Heller, Henry. *Iron and Blood: Civil Wars in Sixteenth Century France.* Montreal: McGill-Queen's University Press, 1991.

Helmholz, R.H. *Marriage Litigation in Medieval England.* Cambridge: Cambridge University Press, 1974.

– *Oxford History of the Laws of England*. Vol. I: *The Canon Law and Ecclesiastical Jurisdiction from 597 to the 1640s*. Oxford: Oxford University Press, 2004.

– *Roman Canon Law in Reformation England.* Cambridge: Cambridge University Press, 2004.

Herrup, Cynthia. *The Common Peace: Participation and the Criminal Law in Seventeenth-Century England.* Cambridge: Cambridge University Press, 1987.

Hill, Christopher. *Economic Problems of the Church, from Archbishop Whitgift to the Long Parliament.* Oxford: Clarendon Press, 1968.

– "From Lollards to Levellers." In *The Collected Essays of Christopher Hill: Religion and Politics in Seventeenth-Century England*, Vol. 2, 89–116. Amherst: University of Massachusetts Press, 1985.

– *Society and Puritanism in Pre-revolutionary England.* New York: Schocken Books, 1964.

Hill, G.W., and W.H. Frere, *Memorials of Stepney Parish.* Guildford: Billing and Sons, 1890–91.

Hindle, Steve. "A Sense of Place? Becoming and Belonging in the Rural Parish, 1550–1650." In *Communities in Early Modern England: Networks, Place, Rhetoric*, edited by Alexandra Shepard and Phil Withington, 96–114. Manchester: Manchester University Press, 2000.

– "Beating the Bounds of the Parish: Order, Memory, and Identity in the English Local Community, c. 1500–1700." In *Defining Community in Early Modern Europe*, edited by Michael J. Halvorson and Karen E. Spierling, 205–28. Abingdon, UK: Ashgate, 2008.

– "Hierarchy and Community in the Elizabethan Parish: The Swallowfield Articles of 1596." *The Historical Journal* 42, no. 3 (Sept. 1999): 835–51.

– *On the Parish? The Micro-Politics of Poor Relief in Rural England, c. 1550–1750.* Oxford: Clarendon Press, 2004.

– *The State and Social Change in Early Modern England, c. 1550–1640.* Houndmills, UK: Palgrave Macmillan, 2000.

Hodgett, G.A.J. "The Unpensioned Ex-religious in Tudor England." *Journal of Ecclesiastical History* 13, no. 2 (Oct. 1962): 195–202.

Holderness, B.A. "The Clergy as Money-Lenders." In *Princes and Paupers in the English Church, 1500–1800*, edited by Rosemary O'Day and Claire Cross, 195–209. Leicester: Leicester University Press, 1961.

Holland, William, ed. *Cratfield: A Transcript of the Parish, from A.D. 1490 to A.D. 1642*. London: Jarrold and Sons, 1895.

Hoskins, W.G. "Harvest Fluctuations and English Economic History, 1480–1619." *Agricultural History Review* 12, no. 1 (1964): 28–46.

Houlbrooke, Ralph. *Church Courts and People during the English Reformation, 1520–1570*. Oxford: Oxford University Press, 1979.

– "The Decline of Ecclesiastical Jurisdiction under the Tudors." In *Continuity and Change: Personnel and Administration of the Church in England, 1500–1642*, edited by Rosemary O'Day and Felicity Heal, 239–57. Leicester: Leicester University Press, 1976.

Houliston, Victor. *Catholic Resistance in Elizabethan England: Robert Persons's Jesuit Polemic, 1580–1610*. Aldershot, UK: Ashgate, 2007.

Howse, Violet M., ed. *Stanford-in-the-Vale Churchwardens' Accounts, 1552–1725*. Faringdon, UK: Rosemary House, 1987.

Hoyle, R.W., ed. *Custom, Improvement, and the Landscape in Early Modern Britain*. Farnham, UK: Ashgate, 2011.

– "Rural Economies under Stress." In *The Elizabethan World*, edited by Susan Doran and Norman Jones, 439–57. London: Routledge, 2011.

Howland, Charles Roscoe. *A Brief Genealogical and Biographical Record of Charles Roscoe Howland*. Rutland, VT: Tuttle Publishing Co., 1946.

Hudson, Winthrop S. *The Cambridge Connection and the Elizabethan Settlement of 1559*. Durham, NC: Duke University Press, 1980.

Hughes, Anne. "Introduction: After Revisionism." In *Conflict in Early Stuart England*, edited by Richard Cust and Anne Hughes, 1–46. London: Longman, 1989.

Hughes, Jonathan. "Rolle, Richard." *Oxford Dictionary of National Biography*. Oxford: Oxford University Press, 2004.

Hull, Helen. "'Lowe and Lay Ministers of the Peace': The Proliferation of Officeholding Manuals in Early Modern England." In *Renaissance Papers 2009*, 37–53.

Hunt, Arnold. *The Art of Hearing: English Preachers and Their Audiences, 1590–1640*. Cambridge: Cambridge University Press, 2010.

– "The Lord's Supper in Early Modern England." *Past and Present* 161 (Nov. 1998): 39–83.

Hutton, Ronald. *The Rise and Fall of Merry England: The Ritual Year, 1400–1700*. Oxford: Oxford University Press, 2001.

Ingram, Martin. *Church Courts, Sex, and Marriage in England, 1570–1640*. Cambridge: Cambridge University Press, 1987.

– "Reformation of Manners in Early Modern England." In *The Experience of Authority in Early Modern England*, edited by Paul Griffiths, Steve Hindle, and Adam Fox, 47–88. London: Macmillan, 1996.

Ingram, Robert G. *Reformation without End: Religion, Politics, and the Past in Post-revolutionary England.* Manchester: Manchester University Press, 2018.

Injunctions exhibited by Iohn by gods sufferance Bishop of Norwich in his first visitacion (1561). STC (2nd ed.) / 10286.

Injunctions geven by the Quenes Majestie anno Domini MD.LIX. (1559). STC (2nd ed.)/10100.3.

Injunctions given by the most reverende father in Christ, Edmonde … Anno do. 1571. (1571). STC (2nd ed.)/10375.

Injunctions given by the reuerende Father in God, Thomas Bishop of Lincolne to be obserued throughout his diocesse (1577). STC (2nd ed.)/10230.

Injunctions given by the Reverend Father in Christ John … Bishop of Sarisburie (sic) (1569). STC (2nd ed.)/10326.5.

Iniunctions with Certaine Articles to be Enquired of in the Visitation of the Reuerend Father in Christ, Iohn (1569). STC (2nd ed.)/10289.

Interrogatories for the doctrine and maners … in the Churche. (1560). STC (2nd ed.)/10133.5.

Interrogatories to bee enquired of by the Churchewardens and swornemenne within the diocesse of Lincoln … 1580. (1580). STC (2nd ed.)/10155.7.

Jakovac, Gašper. "The Catholic Country House in Early Modern England: Motion, Piety, and Hospitality, c. 1580–1640." In *Early Modern Spaces in Motion: Design, Experience, and Rhetoric*, edited by Kimberley Skelton, 81–110. Volume 26 of Visual and Material Culture, 1300–1700, Amsterdam: Amsterdam University Press, 2020.

Jewell, Helen. *Education in Early Modern England.* Houndmills, UK: Macmillan, 1998.

Jones, Jude. "Being, Belief, Comprehension, and Confusion: An Exploration of the Assemblages of English Post-Reformation Parochial Religion." *Cambridge Archaeological Journal* 27, no. 1 (2017): 141–54.

Jones, Norman L. *The English Reformation: Religion and Cultural Adaptation.* Oxford: Blackwell Publishers, 2001.

– *Faith by Statute: Parliament and the Settlement of Religion, 1559.* London: Royal Historical Society, 1982.

Jones, W.J. *Elizabethan Court of Chancery.* Oxford: Clarendon Press, 1967.

Jordan, W.K., *Philanthropy in England, 1480–1660.* London: Allen and Unwin, 1959.

Kain, Roger J.P., and Hugh C. Prince. *The Tithe Surveys of England and Wales.* Cambridge: Cambridge University Press, 1985.

Kamen, Henry. *The Iron Century: Social Change in Europe, 1550–1660*. London: Weidenfeld and Nicolson, 1971.

Karremann, Isabel. "The Inheritance of Loss: Post-Reformation Memory Culture and the Limits of Antiquarian Discourse." In *Remembering the Reformation*, edited by Brian Cummings, Ceri Law, Riley Karis Grace, and Alexandra Walsham, chapter 3. Abingdon: Routledge, 2020.

Kaufman, Lucy. "The Process of Protest: Religious Petitioning and Quiet Dissent in England, 1583–1586." Master's diss., University of Cambridge, 2007.

Kelly, James E. "Counties without Borders? Religious Politics, Kinship Networks, and the Formation of Catholic Communities." *Historical Research* 91, no. 251 (2018): 22–38.

Kennedy, W.P.M., ed. *Elizabethan Episcopal Administration*. Vol. 3: *Visitations Articles and Injunctions, 1583–1603*. London: A.R. Mowbray, 1924.

Kent, Joan. *The English Village Constable, 1580–1642: A Social and Administrative Study*. Oxford: Clarendon Press, 1986.

Kesselring, Krista, *The Northern Rebellion of 1569: Faith, Politics, and Protest in Elizabethan England*. New York: Palgrave Macmillan, 2007.

Kethe, William. *A sermon made at Blanford Forum in the countie of Dorset* (1571). STC (2nd ed.)/14943.

Kingdon, Robert. "The Jacques Royer Affair, 1604–1624: An Argument over Liturgy in Geneva and France," in *Adaptations of Calvinism in Reformation Europe: Essays in Honour of Brian G. Armstrong*, edited by Mack P. Holt, 179–91. Aldershot, UK: Ashgate, 2007.

Kitching, C.J., ed. *The Royal Visitation of 1559: Act Book for the Northern Province*. Surtees Society 187. Gateshead, UK: Northumberland Press, 1975.

Kitto, J.V., ed. *St Martin in the Fields: The Accounts of the Churchwardens, 1525–1603*. London: Dryden Press, 1901.

Koerner, Joseph Leo. *The Reformation of the Image*. Chicago: University of Chicago Press, 2004.

Kümin, Beat. *The Shaping of a Community: The Rise and Reformation of the English Parish, c. 1400–1560*. Aldershot, UK: Ashgate, 1996.

Kunze, Neil L. "The Origins of Modern Social Legislation: The Henrician Poor Law of 1536," *Albion* 3, no. 1 (Spring, 1971): 9–20.

Ladurie, Emmanuel Le Roy. *The French Peasantry, 1540–1600*. Translated by Alan Sheridan. Aldershot, UK: Scolar Press, 1987.

Lake, Peter. *Anglicans and Puritans? Presbyterianism and English Conformist Thought from Whitgift to Hooker*. London: Unwin Hyman, 1988.

– *Moderate Puritans and the Elizabethan Church*. Cambridge: Cambridge University Press, 1982.

– "A Tale of Two Episcopal Surveys: The Strange Fates of Edmund Grindal and Cuthbert Mayne Revisited." *Transactions of the Royal Historical Society* 18 (Dec. 2008), 129–63.

Lake, Peter, and Michael Questier. *The Anti-Christ's Lewd Hat: Protestants, Papists, and Players in Post-Reformation England*. New Haven: Yale University Press, 2002.

Lake, Peter, and Michael Questier, eds. *Conformity and Orthodoxy in the English Church, c. 1560–1660*. Woodbridge, UK: The Boydell Press, 2000.

Lambarde, William. *The Duties of Constables, Borsholders, Tythingmen, and Other Such Lowe Ministers of the Peace*. (1582). STC (2nd ed.)/15146.

Lawson, Peter. "Property Crime and Hard Times in England, 1559–1624." *Law and History Review* 4, no. 1 (Spring, 1986): 95–128.

Legge, A.G., ed. *Ancient Churchwardens' Accounts in the Parish of North Elmham, from A.D. 1559 to A.D. 1577*. Norwich: A.H. Goose, 1891.

Lennam, T.N.S., "Francis Merbury, 1555–1611." *Studies in Philology* 65, no. 2 (Apr. 1968): 207–22.

Liddy, Christian D. *The Bishopric of Durham in the Late Middle Ages: Lordship, Community, and the Cult of St Cuthbert*. Woodbridge, UK: Boydell Press, 2008.

Lindberg, Carter. *European Reformations*. Oxford: Blackwell Publishers, 1996.

Little, A.G. "Personal Tithes." *English Historical Review* 60, no. 236 (Jan. 1945): 67–88.

Litzenberger, Caroline. *English Reformation and the Laity: Gloucestershire, 1540–1580*. Cambridge: Cambridge University Press, 1997.

– ed. *Tewkesbury Churchwardens' Accounts, 1563–1624*. Gloucester: Bristol and Gloucestershire Record Society, 1994.

Livesay, John L. "'Silver-Tongued Smith,' Paragon of Elizabethan Preachers." *Huntington Library Quarterly* 11 (1947–48): 13–36.

Lockwood, Matthew. *The Conquest of Death: Violence and the Birth of the Modern English State*. New Haven: Yale University Press, 2017.

Lowe, Ben. *Commonwealth and the English Reformation: Protestantism and the Politics of Religious Change in the Gloucester Vale, 1483–1560*. New York: Routledge, 2016.

Lowndes, G. Alan. "The History of the Barrington Family," in *Transactions of the Essex Archaeological Society* 1, 251–73. Colchester: W. Wiles, 1884.

MacCulloch, Diarmaid. *The Later Reformation in England, 1547–1603*. New York: Palgrave, 2001.

– "The Myth of the English Reformation." *Journal of British Studies* 30, no. 1 (Jan. 1991): 1–19.

– "Putting the Reformation on the Map." *Transactions of the Royal Historical Society*, Sixth Series 15 (2005): 75–95.

– *Thomas Cranmer: A Life*. New Haven: Yale University Press, 1996.

– *Thomas Cromwell: A Revolutionary Life*. New York: Viking, 2018.

Magagna, Victor V. *Communities of Grain: Rural Rebellion in Comparative Perspective*. Ithaca, NY: Cornell University Press, 1991.

Maltby, Judith. *Prayer Book and People in Elizabethan and Early Stuart England*. Cambridge: Cambridge University Press, 1998.

Marchant, Ronald A. *The Church under the Law: Justice, Administration, and Discipline in the Diocese of York, 1560–1640*. Cambridge: Cambridge University Press, 1969.

Marsh, Christopher. "Common Prayer in England, 1560–1640: The View from the Pew." *Past and Present* 171 (May 2001): 66–94.

– *Family of Love in English Society, 1550–1630*. Cambridge: Cambridge University Press, 1993.

– *Music and Society in Early Modern England*. Cambridge: Cambridge University Press, 2011.

– "Order and Place in England, 1580–1640: The View from the Pew." *Journal of British Studies* 44, no. 1 (January 2005): 3–26.

– *Popular Religion in Sixteenth-Century England: Holding Their Peace*. Cambridge: Cambridge University Press, 1998.

Marshall, Peter. *Beliefs and the Dead in Reformation England*. Oxford: Oxford University Press, 2002.

– *Catholic Priesthood and the English Reformation*. Oxford: Clarendon Press, 1994.

– *The Face of the Pastoral Ministry in the East Riding, 1525–1595*. Borthwick Papers 88. York, UK: University of York, Borthwick Institute of Historical Research, 1995.

– *Heretics and Believers: A History of the English Reformation*. New Haven: Yale University Press, 2017.

– "(Re)defining the English Reformation" *Journal of British Studies* 48, no. 3 (July 2009): 564–86.

Marshall, Peter, and Morgan, John. "Clerical Conformity and the Elizabethan Settlement Revisited." *Historical Journal* 59, no. 1 (2016): 1–22.

Martin, J.W. *Religious Radicals in Tudor England.* London: Hambledon, 1989.

Martyr, Peter. *An Unpublished Letter of Peter Martyr to Henry Bullinger.* Edited by William Goode. London: J. Hatchard and Son, 1850.

McClain, Lisa. *Lest We Be Damned: Practical Innovation and Lived Experience among Catholics in Protestant England, 1559–1642.* New York: Routledge, 2004.

McGrath, Patrick. *Papists and Puritans under Elizabeth I.* London: Blandford Press, 1967.

McIntosh, Marjorie. *Poor Relief in England, 1350–1600.* Cambridge: Cambridge University Press, 2011.

– "Poverty, Charity, and Coercion in Elizabethan England." *Journal of Interdisciplinary History* 35, no. 3 (1985): 143–63.

McRae, Andrew. "Husbandry Manuals and the Language of Agrarian Improvement." In *Culture and Cultivation in Early Modern England: Writing and the Land,* edited by Michael Leslie and Timothy Raylor, 35–62. Leicester: Leicester University Press, 1992.

Mears, Natalie. "Public Worship and Political Participation in Elizabethan England." *Journal of British Studies* 51, no. 1 (January 2012): 4–25.

Merritt, J.F. "Puritans, Laudians, and the Phenomenon of Church-Building in Jacobean London." *Historical Journal* 41, no. 4 (Dec. 1998): 935–60.

Mirehouse, John. *A Practical Treatise on the Law of Tithes.* 2nd ed. London: A. Strahan for J. Butterworth and J. Cooke, 1822.

Miscellanea II. Catholic Record Society Series, Vol 2. London: Privately printed at the Arden Press, 1905.

Monro, Cecil, ed. *Acta Cancellariae, or Selections from the Records of the Court of Chancery: Volume 1.* London: W. Benning, 1847.

Moorman, J.R.H. *Church Life in England in the Thirteenth Century.* Cambridge: Cambridge University Press, 1945.

Morgan, John Emrys. "The Representation and Experience of English Urban Fire Disasters, c.1580–1640." *Historical Research* 89, no. 244 (2016): 268–93.

Morris, Steven. "Church Bill for £230,000 Forces Couple to Sell Farm." *Guardian,* 28 Sept. 2009.

Muir, Edward. *Ritual in Early Modern Europe*. 2nd ed. Cambridge: Cambridge University Press, 2005.

Muldrew, Craig. "The Culture of Reconciliation: Community and the Settlement of Economic Disputes in Early Modern England." *Historical Journal* 39, no. 4 (Dec. 1996): 915–42.

– *Economy of Obligation: Culture of Credit and Social Relations in Early Modern England.* Houndmills, UK: Macmillan, 1998.

– "Interpreting the Market: Ethics of Credit and Community Relations in Early Modern England." *Social History* 18, no. 2 (May 1993): 163–83.

Nadri, Ghulam A. *The Political Economy of Indigo in India, 1580–1930.* European Expansion and Indigenous Response 22. Leiden: Brill, 2016.

Neale, J.E. *Elizabeth I and Her Parliaments.* Vol 1: *1559–1581.* London: Cape, 1953.

– *Elizabeth I and Her Parliaments.* Vol. 2: *1584–1601.* New York: St Martin's Press, 1957.

– "Parliament and the Articles of Religion, 1571." *English Historical Review* 67, no. 265 (Oct. 1952): 510–21.

Newton, Diana. *North-East England, 1569–1625: Governance, Culture, and Identity*. Woodbridge, UK: Boydell, 2006.

Nichols, Ann Eljenholm. "The Etiquette of Pre-Reformation Confession in East Anglia." *Sixteenth Century Journal* 17, no. 2 (Summer 1986): 145–63.

Nichols, J.B., ed. *Depositions and Other Ecclesiastical Proceedings from the Courts of Durham: Extending from 1311 to the Reign of Elizabeth*. Surtees Society 21. London: Surtees Society, 1845.

North, Thomas, ed. *The Accounts of the Churchwardens of S Martin's, Leicester, 1489–1844*. Leicester: S. Clarke, 1884.

O'Day, Rosemary. *Routledge Companion to the Tudor Age.* New York: Routledge, 2010.

Oliver, George. *The History and Antiquities of the Town and Minster of Beverley*. Beverley: M. Turner, 1829.

Oren-Magidor, Daphna. *Infertility in Early Modern England.* Basingstoke, UK: Palgrave Macmillan, 2017.

Orridge, Benjamin. *Some Accounts of the Citizens of London and Their Rulers from 1060 to 1867.* London: Tegg, 1867.

Outhwaite, R.B., *Inflation in Tudor and Early Stuart England.* 2nd ed. London: Macmillan, 1982.

– "Progress and Backwardness in English Agriculture, 1500–1650." *Economic History Review*. 2nd Series, 39 (1986): 1–18.

– *The Rise and Fall of the Ecclesiastical Courts, 1500–1860*. Cambridge: Cambridge University Press, 2006.

Overall, William Henry, ed. *The Accounts of the Churchwardens of the Parish of St Michael, Cornhill, in the City of London, from 1456 to 1608. With Miscellaneous Memoranda Contained in the Great Book of Accounts and Extracts from the Proceedings of the Vestry, from 1563 to 1607*. London: Printed by Alfred James Waterlow for private circulation only, 1871.

Overton, Mark. *Agricultural Revolution in England: The Transformation of the Agrarian Economy, 1500–1850*. Cambridge: Cambridge University Press, 1996.

Owen, Dorothy. *Records of the Established Church in England, Excluding Parochial Records*. British Records Association, Archives and the User 1. London: British Records Association, 1970.

Owen, Gareth. "The Episcopal Visitation: Its Limits and Limitations in Elizabethan London." *Journal of Ecclesiastical History* 11, no. 2 (1960): 179–85.

Owen, Kirsty. "The Reformed Elect: Wealth, Death, and Sanctity in Gloucestershire, 1550–1640." *International Journal of Historical Archaeology* 10, no. 1 (March 2006): 1–34.

Page, William, ed. *Victoria County History of the County of Durham*. Vol. 2. London: Longmans, 1907.

Palliser, David. "Popular Reactions to the Reformation during the Years of Uncertainty, 1530–1570." In *Church and Society in England*, edited by Felicity Heal and Rosemary O'Day, 35–56. London: Palgrave Macmillan, 1977.

– *The Reformation in York, 1534–1553*. Borthwick Papers 40. York, UK: St Antony's Press, 1971.

Palmer, Anthony, ed., *Tudor Churchwardens' Accounts*. Ware: Hertfordshire Record Society, 1985.

Palmer, Charles John. *The History of Great Yarmouth*. Vol. 2. London: Meall, 1856.

Palmer, Robert. *Selling the Church: The English Parish in Law, Commerce, and Religion, 1350–1550*. Chapel Hill: University of North Carolina Press, 2002.

Parliamentary Debates, Commons, 5th series (1909–). October 2012.

Patterson, Catherine. *Urban Patronage in Early Modern England: Corporate Boroughs, the Landed Elite, and the Crown, 1580–1640*. Stanford: Stanford University Press, 1999.

Peachy, Stuart. *Singlewomen, 1580–1660: The Life Styles of Spinsters, Singlewomen, Maid Servants, and Maidens.* Bristol: Stuart Press, 1998.

Peacock, Edward, ed. *English Church Furniture, Ornaments, and Decorations at the Period of the Reformation, as Exhibited in a List of the Goods Destroyed in Certain Lincolnshire Churches, AD 1566.* London: John Camden Hotten, 1866.

– *A List of the Roman Catholics in the County of York in 1604*. London: John Camden Hotten, 1872.

Pearse, Michael. *Between Known Men and Visible Saints: A Study in Sixteenth-Century English Dissent*. Madison, NJ: Fairleigh Dickinson University Press, 1994.

Pearson, A.F. Scott. *Thomas Cartwright and Elizabethan Puritanism, 1535–1603*. Cambridge: Cambridge University Press, 1925.

Peel, Albert, ed. *The Seconde Part of a Register*. Vol. 2. Cambridge: Cambridge University Press, 1914.

Pett, Phineas. *The Autobiography of Phineas Pett*. Edited by W.G. Perrin. London: Navy Records Society, 1918.

Pettegree, Andrew. *Reformation and the Culture of Persuasion.* Cambridge: Cambridge University Press, 2005.

– *Reformation World*. London: Routledge, 2000.

Pitman, Jan. “Tradition and Exclusion: Parochial Officeholding in Early Modern England: A Case Study from North Norfolk.” *Rural History* 15 (2004): 27–45.

Pittman, Susan. “The Social Structure and Parish Community of St Andrew’s Church, Calstock, as Reconstituted from Its Seating Plan, c. 1587–8.” *Southern History* 20–1 (1988–89): 44–67.

Pollard, A.F. *Henry VIII*. New York: Longmans, 1905.

Pollman, Judith. *Memory in Early Modern Europe, 1500–1800*. Oxford: Oxford University Press, 2017.

Porter, Muriel. *New Puritans: The Rise of Fundamentalism in the Anglican Church*. Carlton, Australia: Melbourne University Press, 2006.

Porter, Roy. *London: A Social History*. Cambridge, MA: Harvard University Press, 1995.

Postles, David. “The Market Place as Space in Early Modern England.” *Social History* 29, no. 1 (Feb. 2004): 41–58.

Poulson, George. *Beverlac; or, the Antiquities and History of the Town of Beverley*. London: Printed for S. Scaum, Beverley, 1829.

A Preparation to the Due Consideration and Reverent Comming to the Holy Communion of the Body and Blood of our Lorde (1580). STC (2nd ed.)/20203.

Price, F. Douglas. "The Abuses of Excommunication and the Decline of Ecclesiastical Discipline under Queen Elizabeth." *English Historical Review* 57, no. 225 (Jan. 1942): 106–15.

Pritchard, Arnold. *Catholic Loyalism in Elizabethan England*. London: Scolar Press, 1979.

Pullan, Brian. "Catholics, Protestants, and the Poor in Early Modern Europe." *Journal of Interdisciplinary History* 35, no. 3 (Winter 2005): 441–56.

Purvis, J.S. *The Condition of Yorkshire Church Fabrics, 1300–1800*. St Anthony's Hall Publications 14. London: St Anthony's Press, 1958.

– ed. *Select XVI Century Causes in Tithe*. Yorkshire Archaeological Society 114. York: Yorkshire Archaeological Society, 1949.

– *Tudor Parish Documents of the Province of York*. Cambridge: Cambridge University Press, 1948.

Questier, Michael. *Catholicism and Community in Early Modern England: Politics, Aristocratic Patronage, and Religion, c. 1550–1640* Cambridge: Cambridge University Press, 2006.

– *Conversion, Politics, and Religion in England, 1580–1625*. Cambridge: Cambridge University Press, 1996.

Raine, James, ed. *Depositions and Other Ecclesiastical Proceedings from the Courts of Durham: Extending from 1311 to the Reign of Elizabeth*. Surtees Society 21. London: J.B. Nicholas and Son, 1845.

– ed. *The Injunctions and Other Ecclesiastical Proceedings of Richard Barnes, Bishop of Durham, from 1575 to 1587*. Surtees Society 22. Durham: George Andrews, 1850.

Raines, F.R., ed. "A Description of the State, Civil and Ecclesiastical of the County of Lancaster about the Year 1590 by some of the Clergy of the Diocese of Chester." In *Remains Historical and Literary Connected with the Palatine Counties of Lancaster and Chester*. Chetham Society 96. Manchester: Printed for the Chetham Society, 1875.

Rapport, Steve. *Worlds within Worlds: Structures of Life in Sixteenth-Century London*. Cambridge: Cambridge University Press, 1989.

Reinburg, Virginia. "Liturgy and the Laity in Late Medieval and Reformation France." *Sixteenth Century Journal* 23 (Autumn 1992): 526–47.

Reinhard, Wolfgang. "Reformation, Counter-Reformation, and the Early Modern State: A Reassessment." *Catholic Historical Review* 75, no. 3 (July 1989): 383–404.

Rhodes, Bess. *Riches and Reform: Ecclesiastical Wealth in St Andrews, c. 1520–1580*. St Andrew's Studies in Reformation History 15. Leiden: Brill, 2019.

Richardson, R.C. *Puritanism in North-West England: A Regional Study of the Diocese of Chester to 1642*. Manchester: Manchester University Press, 1972.

Roberts, R.A. *Calendar of the Manuscripts of the Most Hon. The Marquis of Salisbury*. Vol. 4. London: HMSO, 1892.

– *Calendar of the Manuscripts of the Most Hon. The Marquis of Salisbury*. Vol. 11. London: HMSO, 1906.

Robinson, Hastings, ed. *Zurich Letters: Comprising the Correspondence of Several English Bishops and Others, with Some of the Helvetian Reforms, during the Reign of Queen Elizabeth*. Parker Society 35. Cambridge: Cambridge University Press, 1842.

Rolle, Richard. *Here Begynneth a Lytell Boke, that Speketh of Purgatorye* (1534). STC (2nd ed)/3360

Rubin, Miri. *Corpus Christi: The Eucharist in Late Medieval Culture*. Cambridge: Cambridge University Press, 1991.

Russell, Conrad. *The Causes of the English Civil War: The Ford Lectures Delivered in the University of Oxford, 1987–1988*. Oxford: Oxford University Press, 1990.

Ryan, Patrick. "Diocesan Returns for England and Wales." *Miscellanea XII*. Catholic Record Society 22, 1–114. London: Privately printed by J. Whitehead and Son, 1921.

Ryrie, Alec. *The Age of Reformation: The Tudor and Stewart Realms, 1485–1603*. London: Pearson, 2009.

– *Being Protestant in Reformation Britain*. Oxford: Oxford University Press, 2013.

– *The Gospel and Henry VIII: Evangelicals in the Early English Reformation*. Cambridge: Cambridge University Press, 2003.

Sabean, David. *Power in the Blood: Popular Culture and Village Discourse in Early Modern Germany*. Cambridge: Cambridge University Press, 1987.

Sachs, W.L. *Homosexuality and the Crisis of Anglicanism*. Cambridge: Cambridge University Press, 2009.

Savage, Richard, ed., *Churchwardens' Accounts of the Parish of St Nicholas, Warwick, 1547–1621*. Warwick: Henry T. Cook and Son, 1917.

Scargill-Bird, S.R., ed. *Calendar of the Manuscripts of the Most Hon. The Marquis of Salisbury*. Vol. 1: *1306–1571*. London: HMSO, 1883.

Scarisbrick, J.J. *The Reformation and the English People*. Oxford: Blackwell Press, 1984.

Schilling, Thomas. "Confessional Europe." In *Handbook of European History, 1400–1600*. Vol. 2, edited by Thomas Brady, Jr., Heiko Oberman, and James D. Tracy, 641–81. Leiden: E.J. Brill, 1995.

Schwyzer, Philip. "'A Tomb Once Stood in This Room': Memorials to Memorials in Early Modern England." *Journal of Medieval and Early Modern Studies* 48, no. 2 (2018): 365–85.

Scott, James C. *Domination and the Arts of Resistance: Hidden Transcripts*. New Haven, CT: Yale University Press, 1990.

– *Weapons of the Weak: Everyday Forms of Peasant Resistance*. New Haven, CT: Yale University Press, 1985.

Scribner, Robert. *For the Sake of Simple Folk: Popular Propaganda for the German Reformation*. Oxford: Clarendon Press, 1994.

– *Popular Culture and Popular Movements in Reformation Germany*. London: Hambledon Press, 1987.

Sea, Thomas F. "The Swabian League and Peasant Disobedience before the German Peasants' War of 1525." *Sixteenth Century Journal* 30, no. 1 (Spring 1999): 89–111.

Seaver, Paul. *Puritan Lectureships: The Politics of Religious Dissent, 1560–1662*. Stanford: Stanford University Press, 1970.

The Second Tome of Homelyes. (1563) STC (2nd ed.)/13663.3.

Shagan, Ethan, ed. *Catholics and the 'Protestant Nation': Religious Politics and Identity in Early Modern England*. Manchester, UK: Manchester University Press, 2005.

– "Clement Armstrong and the Godly Commonwealth." In *The Beginnings of English Protestantism*, edited by Peter Marshall and Alec Ryrie, 60–83. Cambridge: Cambridge University Press, 2002.

– "The Ecclesiastical Polity." In *The Oxford Handbook of English Law and Literature, 1500–1700*, edited by Lorna Huston, 337–52. Oxford: Oxford University Press, 2017.

– *Popular Politics and the English Reformation*. Cambridge: Cambridge University Press, 2003.

– *The Rule of Moderation: Violence, Religion, and the Politics of Restraint in Early Modern England*. Cambridge: Cambridge University Press, 2011.

Sharp, Buchanan. *In Contempt of All Authority: Rural Artisans and Riot in the West of England, 1586–1660*. Berkeley: University of California Press, 1980.

Sharpe, J.A. *Crime in Early Modern England, 1550–1750*. New York: Longman, 1999.

– *Instruments of Darkness: Witchcraft in Early Modern England*. Philadelphia: University of Pennsylvania Press, 1996.

– "Such Disagreement Betwyx Neighbours": Litigation and Human Relations in Early Modern England." In *Disputes and Settlements: Law and Human Relations in the West*, edited by John Bossy, 167–87. Cambridge: Cambridge University Press, 1983.

Sharpe, Kevin. *The Personal Rule of Charles I*. New Haven: Yale University Press, 1992.

Sheils, W.J., ed. *Archbishop Grindal's Visitation, 1575: Comperta et Detecta Book*. Borthwick Texts and Calendars: Records of the Northern Province 4. York, UK: University of York, 1977.

– *The English Reformation, 1530–1570*. London: Longman, 1989.

– ed. *Papers of the York Court of High Commission, c.1560–1641*. Reading: Research Publications, 1989.

– "Profit, Patronage, or Pastoral Care: The Rectory Estates of the Archbishopric of York, 1540–1640." In *Princes and Paupers in the English Church*, edited by Felicity Heal and Rosemary O'Day, 91–110. Leicester: Leicester University Press, 1961.

– "'The Right of the Church': The Clergy, the Tithe, and the Courts at York." In *Church and Wealth*, edited by W.J. Sheils and Diana Wood, 231–55. Oxford: Ecclesiastical History Society by Blackwell, 1987.

Shepard, Alexandra. *Accounting for Oneself: Worth, Status, and the Social Order in Early Modern England*. Oxford: Oxford University Press, 2015.

– "Manhood, Credit, and Patriarchy in Early Modern England, c. 1580–1640." *Past and Present* 167 (May 2000): 75–106.

– *Meanings of Manhood in Early Modern England*. Oxford: Oxford University Press, 2010.

Shepard, Alexandra, and Phil Withington, eds. *Communities in Early Modern England*. Manchester: Manchester University Press, 2000.

Sherlock, Peter. *Monuments and Memory in Early Modern England*. Aldershot, UK: Ashgate, 2008.

Shorrocks, Derek, ed. *Bishop Still's Visitation 1594 and the 'Smale Book' of the Clerk of the Peace for Somerset*. Somerset Record Society 84. Taunton: Somerset Record Society, 1998.

Shrank, Cathy. *Writing the Nation in Reformation England, 1530–1580*. Oxford: Oxford University Press, 2004.

Shuger, Debora. "The Reformation of Penance." *Huntington Library Quarterly* 71, no. 4 (Dec. 2008): 557–71.

Shute, Christopher. *The testimonie of a true fayth conteyed in a short catechisme necessary to all families* (1577). STC (2nd ed.)/22467.

Slack, Paul. *Poverty and Policy in Tudor and Stuart England.* London: Longman, 1988.

Smith, A. Hassell. *County and Court: Government and Politics in Norfolk, 1558–1603*. Oxford: Clarendon Press, 1974.

Smith, D.M. *Guide to Bishops' Registers of England and Wales: A Survey from the Middle Ages to the Abolition of Episcopacy in 1646*. London: Royal Historical Society, 1981.

Smith, Henry. *A Treatise of the Lords Supper in Two Sermons* (1591). STC (2nd ed)/22705.

Smith, J. Toulmin. *The Parish: Its Powers and Obligations at Law, as Regards the Welfare of Every Neighbourhood.* London: H. Sweet, 1857.

Smith, Thomas. *De Republica Anglorum* (1583). STC (2nd ed.)/22857.

Spufford, Margaret, *Contrasting Communities: English Villagers in the Sixteenth and Seventeenth Centuries.* Cambridge: Cambridge University Press, 1974.

– ed. *World of Rural Dissenters: 1520–1725*. Cambridge: Cambridge University Press, 1995.

Spurr, John. *The Post-Reformation: Religion, Politics, and Society in Britain, 1603–1714*. London: Routledge, 2014.

Stallard, A.D., ed. *The Transcript of the Churchwardens' Accounts of the Parish of Tilney All Saints, Norfolk, 1443–1589*. London: Mitchell, Hughes, and Clark, 1922.

Stevenson, Joseph, ed. *Calendar of State Papers, Foreign, Elizabeth, 1558–1589*. Vol. 4: *1561–1562*. London: HMSO, 1866.

Stewart, Alan. "Letters." In *The Oxford Handbook of English Prose*, edited by Andrew Hadfield, 415–33. Oxford: Oxford University Press, 2013.

Stoughton, William. *An Abstract, of Certain Acts of Parliament* (1583). STC (2nd ed.)/10394.

Stowe, *A Survay of London* (1598). STC (2nd ed.)/23341.

Stretton, Tim. *Women Waging Law in Elizabethan England.* Cambridge: Cambridge University Press, 2005.

Strype, John. *Life and Acts of John Whitgift* (1718).

– *Life and Acts of John Whitgift.* Vol. 3. Oxford: Clarendon Press, 1822.

Stubbes, Phillip. *A Motive to Good Workes, or Rather, to True Christianitie Indeede* (1593). STC (2nd ed.)/23397.

Sutton, Christopher. *Godly meditations vpon the most holy sacrament of the Lordes Supper With manie thinges apperteininge to the highe reuerenee (sic) of soe greate a mysterie* (1601). STC (2nd Edition)/ 23491.

Swanson, R.W. *Church and Society in Late Medieval England.* Oxford: Basil Blackwell, 1989.

Swayne, Henry James Fowler, and Mary Amy Swayne Straton, eds. *Churchwardens' Accounts of S Edmund & S Thomas, Sarum, 1443–1702.* Salisbury: Bennett Bros., 1896.

Tanner, J.R., ed. *Tudor Constitutional Documents, A.D. 1485–1603.* Cambridge: Cambridge University Press, 1951.

Tate, W.E. *Parish Chest: A Study of the Records of Parochial Administration in England.* Cambridge: Cambridge University Press, 1946.

Tawney, R.H. *Religion and the Rise of Capitalism.* New York: Harcourt, Brace, and Co., 1926.

– "The Rise of the Gentry, 1558–1640." *Economic History Review* 11, no. 1 (1941): 1–38.

Thirsk, Joan. *The Rural Economy of England.* London: Hambledon Press, 1984.

Thomas, Keith. "The Puritans and Adultery: The Act of 1650 Reconsidered." In *Puritans and Revolutionaries: Essays in Seventeenth-Century History Presented to Christopher Hill*, edited by Donald Pennington and Keith Thomas, 263–7. Oxford: Clarendon Press, 1978.

– *Religion and the Decline of Magic: Studies in Popular Beliefs in Sixteenth and Seventeenth Century England.* London: Weidenfeld and Nicolson, 1971.

Thompson, A. Hamilton. *The English Clergy and Their Organization in the Later Middle Ages.* Oxford: Clarendon Press, 1947.

Thompson, E.P. "Custom, Law, and Common Right." In *Customs in Common*, 97–184. London: Merlin Press, 1991.

– "Moral Economy of the English Crowd in the Eighteenth Century." *Past and Present* 50 (Feb. 1971): 76–136.

Thomson, J.A.F. "Tithe Disputes in Later Medieval London." *English Historical Review* 78, no. 306 (Jan. 1963): 1–17.

Tittler, Robert. *Early Modern English British Painters, c. 1500–1640.* [Dataset] Unpublished, last revised February 2022. https://spectrum.library.concordia.ca/id/eprint/980096/.

– *The Reformation and the Towns in England.* Oxford: Clarendon Press, 1998.

– "Rural Society and the Painters' Trade in Post-Reformation England." *Rural History* 28, no. 1 (2017): 1–19.

– "Seats of Honor, Seats of Power: The Symbolism of Public Seating in the English Urban Community, c. 1560–1620." *Albion: A Quarterly Journal Concerned with British Studies* 24, no. 2 (Summer 1992): 205–23.

Todd, Margo. "Puritan Self-Fashioning: The Diary of Samuel Ward." *Journal of British Studies* 31 (July 1992): 236–64.

Toller, Samuel. *A Treatise of the Law of Tithes.* London: Joseph Butterworth and Sons, 1808.

Tong, Stephen. "The Doctrine of the Sabbath in the Edwardian Reformation." *Historical Research* 91, no. 254 (2018): 647–61.

Turner, Thomas. *The Second Appendix to Mr Turner's Letter to the Bishop of Manchester.* London: James Ridgway, 1850.

Tutino, Stefania. *Law and Conscience: Catholicism in Early Modern England, 1570–1625.* Aldershot, UK: Ashgate, 2007.

Tyacke, Nicholas. "Anglican Attitudes: Some Recent Writings on English Religious History, from the Reformation to the Civil War." *Journal of British Studies* 35 (1996): 139–67.

– *Calvinists: The Rise of English Arminianism, c. 1590–1640.* Oxford: Clarendon Press, 1987.

– "Puritanism, Arminianism, and Counter-Revolution." In *The Origins of the English Civil War*, edited by Conrad Russell, 119–43. London: Macmillan, 1973.

Underdown, David. *Revel, Riot, and Rebellion: Popular Politics and Culture in England, 1603–1660.* Oxford: Clarendon Press, 1985.

Usher, Roland G. *Presbyterian Movement in the Reign of Queen Elizabeth, as Illustrated by the Minute Book of the Dedham Classis, 1582–1589.* London: Royal Historical Society, 1905.

– *The Rise and Fall of the High Commission.* Oxford: Clarendon Press, 1913.

Van Amberg, Joel. *A Real Presence: Religious and Social Dynamics of the Eucharistic Conflicts in Early Modern Augsburg.* Leiden: Brill, 2012.

Van Engen, John. "Anticlericalism among the Lollards." In *Anticlericalism in Late Medieval and Early Modern Europe,* edited by Peter A. Dykema and Heiko A. Oberman, 53–64. Leiden: Brill, 1993.

Venn, John, and J.A. Venn, eds. *Alumni Cantabrigienses.* Part 1: *From the Earliest Times to 1751.* Volume 2: *Dabbs–Juxton.* Cambridge: Cambridge University Press, 1922.

– *Alumni Cantabrigienses.* Part I: *From the Earliest Times to 1751.* Volume 3: *Kaile–Ryves.* Cambridge: Cambridge University Press, 1924.

Wall, Alison D. "'The Greatest Disgrace': The Making and Unmaking of JPs in Elizabethan and Jacobean England." *English Historical Review* 119, no. 481 (2004): 312–32.

Walsham, Alexandra. *Church Papists: Catholicism, Conformity, and Confessional Polemic in Early Modern England.* Woodbridge, UK: Boydell Press, 1993.

– "Recycling the Sacred: Material Culture and Cultural Memory after the English Reformation." *Church History* 86, no. 4 (2017): 1121–54.

– *The Reformation of the Landscape: Religion, Identity, and Memory in Early Modern Britain.* Oxford: Oxford University Press, 2012.

Walsham, Alexandra, Bronwyn Wallace, Ceri Law, and Brian Cummings, eds. *Memory and the English Reformation.* Cambridge: Cambridge University Press, 2020.

Walter, John. *Crowds and Popular Politics in Early Modern England.* Manchester: Manchester University Press, 2006.

– "Popular Iconoclasm and the Politics of the Parish in Eastern England, 1640–1642." *Historical Journal* 47, no. 2 (June 2004): 261–90.

– "A 'Rising of the People'? The Oxfordshire Rising of 1596." *Past and Present* 107 (May 1985): 90–143.

– "The Social Economy of Dearth in Early Modern England." In *Famine, Disease, and the Social Order in Early Modern Society*, edited by John Walter, 75–128. Cambridge: Cambridge University Press, 1989.

Walter, John, and Keith Wrightson. "Dearth and the Social Order in Early Modern England." *Past and Present* 71 (May 1976): 22–42.

Wandel, Lee Palmer. *The Eucharist in the Reformation.* Cambridge: Cambridge University Press 2006.

– *Voracious Idols and Violent Hands: Iconoclasm in Reformation Zurich, Strasbourg, and Basel.* Cambridge: Cambridge University Press, 1999.

Ware, Sedley Lynch. *The Elizabethan Parish in Its Ecclesiastical and Financial Aspects.* Baltimore: Johns Hopkins University Press, 1908.

Waterson, Edward, and Peter Meadows. *Lost Houses of York and the North Riding.* York: Jill Raines, 1990.

Watt, Tessa. *Cheap Print and Popular Piety, 1550–1640*. Cambridge: Cambridge University Press, 1991.

Webb, Sidney, and Beatrice Webb. *English Local Government from the Revolution to the Municipal Corporations Act: The Parish and the County.* London: Longmans, Green, and Co., 1906.

Wenig, Scott. "The Reformation in the Diocese of Ely during the Episcopate of Richard Cox, 1559–77." *Sixteenth Century Journal* 33, no. 1 (Spring 2002): 151–80.

Weston, F.H. *History of the Ancient Parish of Lastingham*. Leeds: Whitehead, 1914.

White, J.G. *History of the Ward of Walbrook in the City of London*. London: Private circulation, 1904.

White, Peter. *Predestination, Policy, and Polemic: Conflict and Consensus in the English Church from the Reformation to the Civil War*. Cambridge: Cambridge University Press, 1992.

Whiting, Robert. "For the Health of My Soul: Prayers for the Dead in the Tudor South-West." *Southern History* 5 (1983): 68–94.

– *Local Responses to the English Reformation.* Houndmills, UK: Macmillan, 1998.

– *The Reformation of the English Parish Church*. Cambridge: Cambridge University Press, 2010.

Whittle, Jane. *The Development of Agrarian Capitalism: Land and Labour in Norfolk, 1440–1580*. Oxford: Oxford University Press, 2000.

Wilkins, David, ed. *Concilia Magnae Britanniae, Volumen Secundum.* London: R. Gosling, 1737.

Williams, J.F., ed. *Bishop Redman's Visitation, 1597: Presentments in the Archdeaconries of Norwich, Norfolk, and Suffolk*. Norfolk Record Society 13. Norwich: Norfolk Record Society, 1946.

Willis, Jonathan. *Church Music and Protestantism in Post-Reformation England*. New York: Routledge, 2016.

Winship, Michael. *Hot Protestants: A History of Puritanism in England and America.* New Haven: Yale University Press, 2018.

Withington, Phil. "Citizens, Community, and Political Culture in Restoration England." In *Communities in Early Modern England*, edited by Alexandra Shepard and Phil Withington, 134–55. Manchester: Manchester University Press, 2000.

Wood, Andy. *1549 Rebellions and the Making of Early Modern England.* Cambridge: Cambridge University Press, 2007.

– *Riot, Rebellion, and Popular Politics in Early Modern England.* Houndmills, UK: Macmillan, 2002.

Wooding, Lucy. *Rethinking Catholicism in Reformation England.* Oxford: Oxford University Press, 2000.

Woodward, Donald. "The Determination of Wage Rates in the Early Modern North of England." *Economic History Review.* 2nd Series, 47, no. 1 (Feb. 1994): 22–43.

– *Men at Work: Labourers and Building Craftsmen in the Towns of Northern England.* Cambridge: Cambridge University Press, 1995.

Wright, Thomas, ed. *Churchwardens' Accounts of the Town of Ludlow, in Shropshire, from 1540 to the End of the Reign of Queen Elizabeth.* Camden Society First Series 102. London: Camden Society, 1869.

Wrightson, Keith. *Earthly Necessities: Economic Lives in Early Modern Britain.* New Haven: Yale University Press, 2000.

– *English Society, 1580–1680.* 2nd ed. London: Routledge, 2002.

– "Mutualities and Obligations: Changing Social Relationships in Early Modern England." Proceedings of the British Academy 139 (2006): 157–94.

– "The Politics of the Parish." In *The Experience of Authority in Early Modern England*, edited by Paul Griffiths, Adam Fox, and Steve Hindle, 10–46. Basingstoke, UK: Macmillan, 1996.

Wrightson, Keith, and David Levine. *Poverty and Piety in an English Village: Terling, 1525–1700.* Oxford: Clarendon Press, 1995.

Wrigley, E.A., and R.S. Schofield. *The Population History of England, 1541–1871: A Reconstruction.* Cambridge: Cambridge University Press, 1981.

Youings, Joyce. *The Dissolution of the Monasteries.* London: Taylor and Francis, 1971.

Zedeen, Ernst Walter. *Entstehung der Konfessionen: Grundlagen und Formen der Konfessionsbildung im Zeitalter der Glaubenskämpfe.* Munich: R. Oldenbourg, 1965.

Zell, Michael. "Economic Problems of the Parochial Clergy in the Sixteenth Century." In *Princes and Paupers in the English Church, 1500–1800*, edited by Rosemary O'Day and Felicity Heal, 19–44. Leicester: Leicester University Press, 1961.

Index

Abbott, Thomas, 237–8
Acts and Monuments, 100
Admonition to the Parliament, 166, 169, 243
Adwicke le Street (Yorkshire), 172
Aglionby, Edward, 13
agriculture: dearth, 149–50, 152–5; and fundraising, 123–4; grain prices, 135, 149–52, 154; grain riots, 14, 149–50; and tithes, 144
All Hallows Staining (London), 53, 68, 70, 88
All Saints Cawood (Yorkshire), 24–5, 45
altar stones, 97–8, 100, 242
altars: dismantling, 19, 93–5, 98, 104, 245; persistence of, 96–7, 100; replaced by communion tables, 94, 120, 194–5, 201
Apology of the Church of England, 109
apparitors. *See* summoners
Armstrong, Clement, 50
artists, role in church decoration, 99–100
Ashburton (Devon), 95, 202, 204
Ashwell (Hertfordshire), 119, 123
Astonfield (Staffordshire), 176
Atkinson, John, 223
Atlay, Francis, 148
auditors, 4, 73, 76, 85, 246
Awd, Elinor, 228
Axminster (Devon), 203
Aylmer, John, 40, 96–7, 213

Babington Plot, 111, 211
Babworth (Nottinghamshire), 220
Bacon, Francis, 233
Bagbie Chapel (Yorkshire), 113
Bancroft, Richard, 32, 41, 50, 87, 167
Barner, John, 223
Bate, Susan, 234
Batey, Reginald, 147–8
Bath, 55, 57, 92, 122
Bath and Wells, 36
Batley, 238
bawdy courts, 39. *See also* ecclesiastical courts
Beatniffe, John, 32
bells, 17, 62, 110–11, 120, 207, 246
Belton, 97

Bemond, Robert, 53, 68, 70, 88
benefices, 40, 138, 163, 166, 171–2, 175–6, 218
Best, William, 68
Bible: cost of purchase, 106, 108; requirements for parishes, 19, 101, 106, 109, 114; resold to raise funds, 122; vernacular, 4, 7, 106, 246
Bilsdale (Yorkshire), 92, 114
Bilson, Thomas, 109
Black Death, 76, 142. *See also* plagues
Blasie, Alice, 223
Boarhunt (Hampshire), 220
Book of Common Prayer, 13, 41, 46, 51, 95, 105–6, 109, 114, 212, 217, 226, 226–7; of 1549, 7, 108, 184, 184–9; of 1552, 7, 9, 184, 184–7, 189–90; of 1559, 184, 186–91, 210, 227, 242–4
Book of Homilies, 4, 51, 106, 109, 119–20
books: expense of acquiring, 105–6; resold, 122; supplementary, 109. *See also* Book of Common Prayer; Book of Homilies
borders. *See* boundaries
boundaries, 24, 26, 47–9, 52, 62, 64, 68, 153, 239–40; and church attendance, 46, 48, 52; enforcement, 26, 46, 48–9, 52, 102; and excommunication, 240–1; and migration, 26; and visitations, 46–7
Brafferton (Yorkshire), 113
Brancepeth (Durham), 229
Brandesburton (Yorkshire), 153
Brandiston (Norfolk), 174
Brantingham (Yorkshire), 135
Brasse, William, 229
Bridges, John, 168
Browne, Henry, 134–5
Bucer, Martin, 184–5
Bullinger, Heinrich, 185, 189
Burnett, Elizabeth, 161
Burrell family, 83
Burton, William, 166, 225
Bury, Thomas, 70
Bury St Edmunds (Suffolk), 135, 137, 155

Calvin, John, 188–90, 230
Calvinism, 187–8, 191, 199, 207–8, 225, 247
Cambridge, 71, 80, 95, 98, 119–20, 193, 200, 203–4, 206, 209, 216
Canons of 1571, 47, 61, 64, 114; on churchwardens, 62–4, 73
Canterbury, 40, 47, 64, 221
Carrington, William, 153
Cartwright, Thomas, 11, 64, 212, 216
Cassinger, Nicholas, 214
Caston (Norfolk), 181
catechisms, 100, 192, 229–30
Catholic architecture, dismantling of, 58, 75, 98, 100
Catholic implements: eradication, 58, 61, 93–4, 104–5; persistence, 100; reselling, 119–21; vestments, 4, 43, 104–5, 120
Catholicism, 10–11, 22; mass, 184–6; Northern Rebellion, 11; persistence, 11, 15, 113, 225–6; suppression, 10, 43; and visitations, 38

Cecil, William (Baron Burghley), 48, 198
censorship, 28–9, 216
centralization: of the church, 29, 45, 50–2, 57, 63–5; of the economy, 143, 148, of the state, 19–20, 60, 68; and state formation, 18, 72, 87
chalices, 78, 109, 121, 246. *See also* Catholic implements
chancels, 89, 96, 112–14, 172–6, 180, 195, 247
chantries, 50, 58, 77, 79, 125, 184
chapels-of-ease, 27, 113, 132
charity, 50, 129–30, 152, 183, 194–6, 224–8, 230, 239, 243
Cheshire, 95, 174
Chester (Cheshire), 64, 211
Cheswicke, Thomas, 229
Chichester (Sussex), 30
Chudleigh (Devon), 72, 74–5, 203–4
church ales, 17, 56, 75, 111, 116–17, 119, 131, 133, 246–7
church attendance: fines, 47; mandatory, 14, 25, 46, 48, 50–2, 102–3, 117; monitored, 48–9, 53; in one's own parish, 46–7
church courts. *See* ecclesiastical courts
churches: and artists, 99–100; dilapidation, 113–14, 173–4, 176, 178
church fabric: *adiaphora*, 94, 189; expense, 62, 98–9, 104–5, 111, 119, 133; maintenance, 83, 110, 113, 115, 117, 130, 172, 176–7; as measure of conformity, 92–3; repurposing, 121; requirements, 97, 114; reselling, 119, 121–2; wall paintings, 99–100. *See also* altars; communion tables; pews; pulpits; rood screens
church flocks, 3–4, 17, 61, 115, 123–4
church maintenance: assessed by visitations, 104, 112–14; church flock, 61, 115, 123; churchwardens, 55, 57, 131; funding, 111, 115, 133; roof repairs, 111–12; source of employment, 112
church plate, 56, 109–10, 119
church property, 124, 165, 170, 177; lease of, 177, 246
church rates, 116–19, 126, 132, 180
church seating, 127, 247. *See also* pews
churchwardens: in 1571 Canons, 62–4; checks and balances for, 43–4; and church fabric, 61, 92, 94, 98–9, 104–6, 108, 112, 119–20; and clergy, 63–4; and community surveillance, 4, 45–6, 48, 59, 61, 63, 78, 102–3, 226, 235, 240; as disciplinarians, 62–5; duties, 53–7, 60, 65–7, 73, 76, 85, 188, 196–7, 246; electing, 19, 53, 56, 61, 68–73, 81, 88, 105; expanded powers, 65–8; financial role, 74, 89–90, 108, 117–18, 125–6, 201–2; and fundraising, 58, 60, 116, 123, 133; junior, 70, 72; and moral regulation, 58, 60–1; power of, 16, 43–4, 65–6; pre-Reformation, 54–8, 75; reformed, 57–8, 60; social role, 58, 62, 115, 131, 223; training, 72; and visitations, 31–2, 39–43, 60, 87, 194, 227, 231, 245

citations, 32–3; response to, 35–7
civil courts, 157, 194, 222, 236–7; Chancery, 145, 236; Quarter Sessions, 37; Star Chamber, 70, 100, 145, 216–17
clergy: and advowsons, 86, 169; and churchwardens, 63–4; education, 138, 177; expectations for, 42, 162–4; glebe lands, 40, 138; income, 137–8, 155, 162–4, 171, 177; and marriage, 8, 138; mistrust of by church, 41–2; monitored through visitation, 40–1; pensions for, 159–60; and sacramental exclusion, 230–1; and tithes, 158–63
Clifton, Cuthbert, 211–12
Cockell, Joan, 160
coercion, 36, 182, 198, 239
Coke, Edward, 118
common fame. *See* reputation
Commonplaces of Christian Religion, 100, 109
communion: abstention, 195, 199, 215, 220, 223–6; acceptance of, 200–8; in church records, 201–9; as communal act, 61, 117, 187–8, 194, 196, 204, 208, 212–13, 225, 227, 243; and conformity, 181–3, 212–14, 216, 221, 243–4; Easter, 117, 204–6, 224; exclusion from, 222–6, 228–9, 232, 234–8, 240; fines for refusing, 213–14; frequency, 204–7, 247; as loyalty test, 190–1, 211–13, 218; monitored by visitation, 13, 33, 42, 209–12, 229; in one kind, 7, 186; practice, 191–8; preparation for, 192–4; provisioning, 188, 202–4, 208, 243, 247; reformed, 183, 186, 198; requisites for receiving, 192–4, 229–31; resistance to, 59, 126, 198–9, 210–11, 218–20, 223; token books, 183, 208–9; in two kinds, 9, 185, 189, 196, 198, 248
communion bread, 117, 206, 246–7. *See also* holy loaf
communion cups, 109–10, 197. *See also* chalices
communion tables, 92, 94, 96, 103–4, 120, 172, 195, 209, 226, 228
community: and communion, 61, 117, 187–8, 194, 196, 204, 208, 212–13, 225, 227, 243–4; compulsory, 21–2, 51–2, 247–8; construction of, 47–9, 52, 101–2, 163–4, 229–3; and discipline, 24–5, 45–6, 228–9, 231–2; and economy, 122–4, 132–3, 246–7; exclusion from, 227–9, 233–5, 239; governance of, 73–4, 83–4; as a public, 24–5, 50–2; and religious conformity, 23, 224–6
compromises: liturgical, 45, 189–90; political, 20, 90–1, 156, 179–80; and sacrament, 182, 185–6, 188, 208; and tithes, 143–5, 156–8
confession: auricular, 7, 49; public, 25, 52, 196
confessionalization, 18–20
conformity: church attendance, 10, 103; and church fabric, 92, 96, 109; enforcement, 18–19, 26, 32, 39, 45, 59, 61, 63, 66, 92, 132; flexibility, 19–20, 88; pews, 103, 126; public versus private, 5, 13–14, 110; and sacrament, 181–3, 190–1, 197–201, 204–5,

209, 211, 215, 218–20, 222–3, 243; surveillance of, 17, 61, 103
Consensus Tigurinus, 189–90
Continental Europe: models of governance from, 54, 65, 73, 188–9; reform in, 8–9, 182, 185, 189–90; revolt in, 146–7, 156; theological influence of, 184–5, 208, 230, 249n10, 263n63, 280n4
convocation, 11–12, 35–8, 60, 152, 186–7; of 1559, 189; of 1563, 9; of 1571, 60–1
Cooke, John, 214
Cooper, Thomas, 214, 223
Cope, Anthony, 167, 191
copes, 3–5, 93, 104. *See also* vestments
Copley, Edward, 154–5
Cordingley, Elizabeth, 223
Cotton, George, 220
Cotton, Margaret, 51, 232
Cranmer, Thomas, 7–9, 184–6
Cratfield (Suffolk), 95
credit, 14, 50–2, 88, 118, 125–6, 132, 160–1, 183–4, 232, 238. *See also* reputation
Cromwell, Thomas, 7
Crowley, Richard, 232
Cudnor, Robert, 129

Day, John, 64
Dekker, Thomas, 219
demographic expansion, 27, 76, 148, 150, 179, 203
Dent, Arthur, 166, 194
Dering, Edward, 166
Devon, 27, 31, 69, 72, 74, 79–80, 95, 116, 119, 202–3, 219–20
Diocese of Ely, 42, 233
Dod, John, 232
Dorset, 116, 219–20
Durham, 31, 64, 80, 97, 100, 123, 175, 220, 228–9

Easte, Richard, 225
Easter, 33, 42, 47, 95, 117, 186, 198, 204–7, 209, 224, 247
Ecclesiastical Census of 1603, 217–21
ecclesiastical courts: of Arches, 31; bawdy courts, 39; coercion in, 36–7; and excommunication, 231, 233, 235–6, 238, 240; of High Commission, 70, 100–2, 212, 216–17; and penance, 25, 45, 49–51; and recusants, 211, 222–5; versus secular courts, 37; tithe cases, 137–8, 145–6, 148, 156–7; and visitations, 32–3, 35–6, 40, 43–4, 113, 227
Economic Problems of the English Church, 138, 165
economy, 17, 39 49–50; and the church, 143–5, 165–8; growing stratification of, 86, 140, 156, 203–4, 222; medieval, 54–5, 141–2; parochial, 66, 111–12, 122–6, 130–3; policy, 20–1, 76–7, 81–2, 179. *See also* agriculture; credit; impropriation; inflation; tithes
Edington (Wiltshire), 3–4
Edward VI: and canon law, 8, 58; and church ornament, 58, 96, 100, 106, 121; and iconoclasm, 21, 93, 98; and mass, 184–5; and the *Reformatio*, 59–60; and tithes, 139, 143–5, 149, 156
Egerton, Thomas, 167

Elizabeth I: and 1571 Canons, 64; appoints John Whitgift, 10; and Catholicism, 22; and communion, 190; Coronation Day celebrations, 111, 207, 246; excommunicated by Pius V, 11, 46; and the godly, 28–9, 38, 213; Injunctions, 94–6, 100, 105–6, 108, 110, 119–21; loyalty to, 164, 190, 195–6, 242–3; overthrow attempt, 11; and parliament, 13, 167, 191; reforms, 22, 74–5, 79, 82; religious policy of, 42, 94; as Supreme Governor of the church, 9–10, 190, 195, 208
Ellerker, Edward, 134–5
Ellerker, Ralph, 134–7, 148, 153–5
Elwick (Durham), 228
enclosure, 14, 76–7, 144, 147–8
Erasmus, 4, 100, 106, 120, 245
eucharist. *See* communion
excommunication: and citations, 32–3, 35–7, 45; efficacy of, 233–4; and poor relief, 239–40; social consequences, 235–41, 243; spiritual consequences, 234

Farnham (Surrey), 174
Fawtless, Thomas, 240
Felton, John, 215
Fenner, Dudley, 166
Field, John, 166, 169
fixed communities, 46–7, 49, 52, 103; church seating, 21, 78, 101–2
fontwives, 123
Forward, John, 245
Forward, Roger, 245
Fourth Lateran Council, 141
Foxe, John, 100
fundraising, 115–17, 128, 133; agricultural, 123–4; and churchwardens, 58, 60, 75; rental of church property, 124–5; through gifts, 128–9; through sale of confiscated items, 4

Gate Helmsley (Yorkshire), 108
Gawtree, John, 161
Gayton, James, 134–7, 148, 154–5
Gibson, John, 231
Gilby, Anthony, 166
Ginacre, Katherine, 225
Gisbrough Priory (Yorkshire), 161
Glastonbury St John (Somerset), 55
Gloucester, 214, 217, 220
godliness, 11, 61, 65, 114–15, 131, 181, 194, 230
godly, the: and church government, 32, 35–6, 62, 75; clergy, 9–10, 28–9, 86–7, 134–5, 152; complaints of, 43, 74–5, 91, 97, 162–6, 174, 177; lay members, 88, 105, 116–17, 129–30, 153–5, 176; and parliament, 13–14, 139, 167–70; regulation of, 38, 213, 216–17; and the sacrament, 184, 186–9, 191, 198, 204–5, 225–6
Godly Meditations, 181
godparentage, 236, 238
Goldworth, John, 223
Gorleston (Norfolk), 240
Goudhurst (Kent), 220
grain: prices, 135, 149–52, 154; riots, 14, 149–50
Great Ellingham (Norfolk), 237
Greenham, Richard, 152
Grindal, Edmund, 172

Hach, William, 215
Hailsham (Sussex), 118
Hall, Robert, 160
Halye, Alice, 55
Hampshire, 220
Hastings, Henry, 135, 176
Hastings, Winifred, 135
Hatton, Christopher, 167–9
Haverland (Norfolk), 42
Haworth, Joseph, 238
Haydon Bridge (Northumberland), 97–8
Hayward, Jane, 237
Helmsley (Yorkshire), 92, 128
Henry VIII: devotion to mass, 184; reforms, 4, 7, 54, 74, 94, 143, 170; seizes monastic plate, 109; and tithes, 139, 143; and vernacular texts, 7
Henslowe, Ralph, 220
Hertfordshire, 71, 105, 119, 122–3
Hickathrift, Tom, 89
Holderness (Yorkshire), 96
holy loaf, 117, 186, 246. *See also* communion bread
homilies, 51, 109, 246; against disobedience, 114; books of, 4, 64, 100–1, 119–20, 131–2
Hooker, Richard, 181

iconoclasm, 7–8, 21, 58, 91, 93–4, 110, 119, 121, 144, 178
Ilchester (Somerset), 30
illegal items, 3–4, 28, 93–4; compliance in removing, 95–7; persistence, 120; sold to fund churches, 4
impropriation, 177–8; critique of, 165–6; reform, 166–70
impropriators, 139, 143, 146, 152–3, 156, 162, 164–5, 174–6, 178–9; and parish maintenance, 172–6
inflation, 139, 148–9, 156, 171, 203–4
Injunctions of 1559, 93–6, 100, 105–6, 108, 110, 119–21
investments, 98, 124–6, 138, 177
Ireland, 111, 247

Jackson, John, 70
James I, 89
Jeffrey, William, 118
Jewel, John, 109, 189

Kaye, Robert, 102
Keble, William, 116
Kelbie Chapel (Northumberland), 97–8
Kendall, Richard, 247
Kenton, Francis, 241
Kilmington (Devon), 119, 203
Kirkby Moorside (Yorkshire), 172
Kirkham Priory, 161
kneeling, during sacrament, 186, 189, 196, 208
Knox, John, 186
Konfessionsbildung. *See* confessionalization

Lacy, Katherine, 198–200
laity: instrumental to Reformation, 17–18, 45; involvement in church, 17–18, 60, 62, 79, 83, 87, 91, 114, 179–80, 188, 240; power of, 26, 44–5, 65; and tithes, 138–9, 152, 155, 157–8, 161–2, 165–6, 171, 177–8
Lambarde, William, 72
Lancashire, 27, 108–9, 112, 224

Langley Chapel (Shropshire), 102
legibility, 12–13, 16, 26–8, 45–7, 103, 246
Leicester, 95, 106, 112, 233
levies, 14, 103, 117–19, 127, 132
Lincoln, 41, 47, 96–7, 119, 175, 193, 212, 214, 226–7, 231
Little Bytham (Lincolnshire), 174
Little Ouseburn (Yorkshire), 147–8
liturgy, 184–5, 187–90, 196, 208, 243, 281n19
Lockey, James, 147–8
Lord's Supper. *See* communion
Ludlow (Norfolk), 95, 99
Ludlow (Shropshire), 95, 108
Lutheranism, 7
Lydford (Devon), 27
Lyme Regis (Dorset), 219

Marbury, Francis, 212
Marianism, 44, 64, 74–5, 93, 106, 108
Marsh, Edmund, 151–2
Marshall, Godfrey, 53
Martyr, Peter (Vermigli), 184–5, 189
Mary I: execution, 169, 245; and monastic property, 167; Northern Rebellion, 11; reforms, 60, 67, 98, 115; restoration of Catholicism, 8, 21, 109, 121
mass (Catholic), 7–8, 78, 109, 182, 184–5, 187, 242
Maunswell, Elizabeth, 36–7
memory, 20–1, 74, 137–8, 157–61; and custom, 57–8, 71–2, 82, 143–5, 158; fading, 159–61
Mere (Wiltshire), 3, 69, 95, 116, 245–6
migration, and church attendance, 48–9, 103
Mildmay, Anthony, 167, 169–70
Minnell, William, 56
Mitchell, Jane, 223
mobility. *See* migration, and church attendance
monasteries, dissolution of, 7, 27, 77, 80, 125, 141–4, 147, 157, 159–61, 165, 167–70
monastic land: sale of, 77, 177; and tithes, 141, 143–5, 157–61, 167, 179
moneylending, 125–6
Montgomery, John, 53, 68, 70, 88
morality, regulation of, 39–40, 51–2, 59–62, 63–6, 125–6, 223–4, 227–9
More, John (Gorleston), 240
More, John (Great Ellingham), 237
More, William, 68
Morebath (Devon), 79
Morris, Francis, 215
Moxby Priory, 161
Musculus, Andreas, 100, 109

neighbourliness, 183, 194, 224, 226, 235, 238
New Buckenham (Norfolk), 237
non-communication. *See* communion: resistance to
nonconformity, 5, 38, 46–8, 148, 191, 200, 209–12, 220, 228, 241
Norfolk, 36, 42–3, 95, 99, 108–9, 112, 121, 123, 172, 174–5, 181, 202, 205–6
North Elmham (Norfolk), 109, 112, 125, 130, 205, 237
Northill (Bedfordshire), 81
Northill (Lincoln), 119

North Newton (Wiltshire), 69
North Riding, 92, 113, 117, 132, 210, 221, 223
Northumbria, 31
Norwich, 30, 38, 40, 93, 95, 98, 171, 173, 209–10, 219, 221
Nottinghamshire, 220
novalia, 144

Oath of Supremacy, 212
Old Byland (Yorkshire), 108
oligarchy, 69, 76–7, 80–5, 131
Orston (Nottinghamshire), 118
orthodoxy, 5, 9, 11, 14, 16, 42, 46, 49, 51, 181, 184, 191, 198; social, 184, 243–4
orthopraxy, 14, 191, 213
Osgathorpe (Leicestershire), 20
Oswaldkirk (Yorkshire), 113
Oswestry (Shropshire), 69, 121
Over Silton (Yorkshire), 114
Oxford, 20, 28, 42, 56, 181, 184–5, 203
Oxfordshire, 19, 215, 225, 232, 237–8
Oxford St Martin, 95, 98

Paraphrases, 4, 100, 106, 108, 120, 245
parish boundaries. *See* boundaries
parishes: centralization of, 28–9; diversity in size, 27; as employer, 126, 130–1; finances, 133, 138–9; as fixed communities, 47; hierarchies in, 28; reliance on by church, 45
Parker, Matthew, 38, 40–1, 95
Parkhurst, John, 40, 95
Parkin, Charles, 89
parliament, 7–13, 37, 66–8, 139–41, 143–4, 191; "bill and book" campaign in, 167, 170, 191; and debates, 162–3, 178–9
Parliamentary Acts: for the Dissolution of Monasteries and Abbeys, 143; for the Payment of Tithes, 143–5; for the Relief of the Poor, 152; of the Six Articles, 7; of Supremacy, 7, 9, 38, 93; of Uniformity, 9, 38, 46, 94, 100, 106, 181, 190, 204–6, 208
parochial economies, 58, 78–9, 83–4, 115–28, 131, 205–6
paschal sacrament. *See* communion: Easter
penance: certification, 25–6, 33, 45; as communal act, 50–2; pre-Reformation, 49–50, 194; public, 24–5, 35, 45, 49, 49–52, 227, 237–9, 247; reformed, 50; as sacrament, 49–50
Permans, Ralph, 245
pews: construction, 101; disputes over, 101–2; enforcement of social hierarchy, 101; fixed, 78, 101, 195; to monitor attendance, 102–3; repairs, 131; rents, 103, 121, 126–8, 133, 139
Picard, Henry, 137
piety: medieval, 55–6, 74; politics of, 16, 21–2; and poor relief, 128–30, 239–40; reformed, 61, 65, 115, 122–3, 133, 187, 200–1; regulation of, 59–60, 229–32
pilgrimages: as form of penance, 50; halted, 125
pilgrimage sites, 27–8

Pittington (Durham), 31, 80–1, 100, 104, 123–4
plagues, 31, 219, 221. *See also* Black Death
Pole, Margaret, 220
poor relief, 49, 54, 84, 119, 129–30, 246; and excommunication, 239–40
popular politics: and churchwardens, 58–9, 65–8, 70–1, 79–82, 126; and custom, 156–7; defining, 15–16, 18–19, 70–1; participation in, 25–6, 84–5, 243; and the sacrament, 190, 198, 213, 222, 225–8. *See also* conformity; poor relief; rebellions; social hierarchy; surveillance; vestries
prayer, 24–5, 38, 48, 51–2, 106, 194–7, 212
Prentice, Robert, 31
presbyterianism, 10–11, 32, 64, 162, 169, 212
Prescot (Lancashire), 108–9, 112
Privy Council, 28–9, 42, 48, 97, 211, 213–17
pulpits, 6, 17, 28, 75, 101, 103–4, 135

real presence. *See* transubstantiation
rebellions: German Peasants' (1525), 146; Kett's (1549), 146–7; Pilgrimage of Grace (1536), 146–7, 268n3; Prayer Book (1549), 7, 185–6; Northern (1569), 11, 38, 46, 64, 97, 100, 134, 199
rectors, 134, 137, 140–3, 153–4, 156, 162, 172, 174–9, 224, 235
recusancy: and communion, 191, 195, 199, 210, 215, 223, 225–6; and ecclesiastical courts, 31, 33, 36–7, 39–40, 48; and Jesuits, 11, 47; persistence of, 10, 15, 46, 64, 88, 97, 221; surveillance of, 213–14, 216, 218–20; and tithe cases, 158, 167; women, 81, 214, 220
Recusancy Rolls, 216
Reedham (Norfolk), 223
Reformatio Legum Ecclesiasticarum, 58–61, 63
Regnans in Excelsis, 11, 46, 215
religious orders, 29, 104, 141–2, 144, 157–9, 166, 170, 179, 234
repentance, 193, 196, 211
reputation: and communion, 228, 231–2; and excommunication, 238–9; importance of, 40, 50–2
Riccall (Yorkshire), 114
Richardson, Edward, 148
Rievaulx Abbey, 108
Ripon (Yorkshire), 55
rood lofts, 56, 96, 98–9, 119–20, 245–6
rood screens, 75, 93, 96, 99, 245
Roome, Henry, 44
Rowley (Yorkshire), 134–5, 153
Royal Visitation of 1559, 106
Ryedall, Thomas, 224

sacraments: Catholic, 4, 49, 182; kneeling during, 186, 189, 196, 208; penance, 49–50; reception, 19, 183, 186, 190, 192, 201, 212, 218, 230; reformed, 9, 94, 98, 182–3, 189, 199, 204, 206–7, 211
St Bartholomew by the Exchange (London), 82, 85
St Botolph (London), 3, 117, 209–10
St Christopher le Stocks (London), 78–9, 129

St Clement (Norwich), 210
St Dunstan (Stepney, Middlesex), 82–5
St Edmund (Salisbury), 56, 108, 119–20
St Giles (Durham), 97
St Hilda (Sherborn, Dorset), 198–9
St James (Yorkshire), 55
St Margaret (Durham), 97, 100
St Martin (Beverley, Yorkshire), 163
St Martin (Leicester), 95, 106, 112
St Martin (Salisbury), 69
St Martin-in-the-Fields (London), 31, 81, 95
St Mary (Beverley, Yorkshire), 70, 163–4
St Mary (Bridgewater, Somerset), 55
St Mary (Reading), 69, 90, 95
St Mary (Yatton, Somerset), 95
St Mary-at-Hill (London), 79
St Mary-on-the-Hill (Cheshire), 95
St Mary the Great (Cambridge), 57, 71, 80, 95, 98, 119–21, 200, 203–4, 206, 209
St Mary Woolnoth (London), 72
St Matthew Friday Street (London), 100
St Michael (Bath), 122
St Michael (South Littleton, Worcestershire), 206
St Michael Cornhill (London), 56, 79, 86, 95, 101, 103, 119, 206
St Michael in Bedwardine (Worcestershire), 101, 103, 109, 111, 118, 122, 124–5, 202
St Michael-le-Querne (London), 69
St Nicholas (King's Lynn, Norfolk), 27
St Nicholas (Warwick), 203, 205
St Olave Jewry (London), 69
St Oswald (Durham), 100
St Peter (Hertfordshire), 105
St Peter (Marlborough, Wiltshire), 69
St Peter (Rowley, Yorkshire), 134
St Peter (St Albans, Hertfordshire), 122
St Peter Cheesehill (Winchester), 205
St Peter-le-Bailey (Oxford), 203
St Stephen Walbrook (London), 69, 95, 203
Salisbury, 56, 69, 108, 119, 168, 245, 247
salvation: personal, 132, 164, 183; theology of, 9, 12, 115–16, 128, 283n49
Salway, Thomas, 124–5
Sampson, Thomas, 189
Saundar, Nicholas, 215
Sedgefield (Durham), 100
separatism, 11, 15, 36, 210, 217, 222, 241
sermons, 29, 41–2, 100, 102–3, 132, 135, 138, 164, 166, 189, 195; during visitations, 32
service, reformed, 95, 122, 148, 172, 195, 195–7
shame, 25–6, 45, 50–2, 232, 238–43
Shepherd's Calendar, The, 141
Sherburn in Elmet (Yorkshire), 151–2
Shillington (Bedfordshire), 128
Shipdham (Norfolk), 95, 98, 108, 121, 123, 206
Shobrooke (Devon), 31
Shrewsbury Abbey, 54
sidemen, 4, 19, 31–2, 73, 76, 118

sin: communion and, 194–6, 209, 227, 232–3; penance and, 24–5, 50–1; regulation of, 39
Smith, Henry, 198, 204, 207
Snettisham (Norfolk), 202
social hierarchy, 22, 103, 130, 132–3; chief inhabitants, 79, 131; elite, 7, 77, 99, 177; and pews, 101; wealth gap, 76, 76–7, 103. *See also* oligarchy
social history, 15, 76
Somerset, 30, 37, 55, 73, 173, 203, 205, 207, 210
Somerton (Somerset), 30
South Littleton (Worcestershire), 206
South Newington (Oxfordshire), 69
South Tawton (Devon), 95, 116
Southwark (Surrey), 209, 214, 221
Southwell, Elizabeth, 181
Spanish Armada, 111
Staffordshire, 176
Staines, John, 161
Stanford-in-the-Vale (Norfolk), 95, 116, 123
Stansby, Thomas, 215, 218
state formation. *See* centralization
Statute of Mortmain, 142, 144
statutory law, 8–9, 66–7, 142–3, 215; based on customs, 157; on tithes, 139; versus visitation articles, 37. *See also* Parliamentary Acts
Steeple Ashton (Wiltshire), 95, 98
Strangemen, John, 215
Strickland, Walter, 153
Stroud, John, 212
Stubbes, Philip, 91
Stubbs, John, 28
Suffolk, 95, 210, 215, 228, 235, 240
summoners, 32, 35, 37
Suncombe (Oxfordshire), 225
surplices, 38, 43, 89, 104, 195, 208. *See also* vestments
surveillance, 26, 53, 59, 73, 103, 210–11, 213–14, 217, 221, 241–2; role of churchwardens, 63, 65
Sutton, Christopher, 181, 184, 193, 234
Sutton, John, 240
Swaffham (Norfolk), 95, 99, 121, 203, 206

Taylor, Thomas, 151–2
Terrington St John (Norfolk), 231
Tewkesbury (Gloucestershire), 111, 122, 127–8
Thetford (Norfolk), 241
Thirty-Nine Articles, 9, 51
Thornton, Percival, 153–4
Tilney All Saints (Norfolk), 89, 101, 110, 203
Tintinhull (Somerset), 30, 203, 205–6
tithe cases, 17, 145–53, 155–62, 164, 179; and religious orders, 158–62; role of laity, 161–4. *See also* tithe disputes
tithe collectors, 149, 152, 156, 248
tithe disputes, 21, 137–8, 148, 151, 160, 162. *See also* tithe cases
tithe payments, 139, 141, 143, 145–7, 149, 157–60, 162, 164, 180; cash, 21, 154, 154–6
tithe reform, 137–8, 143, 147, 165, 169
tithes, 130, 138–42, 145–8, 153–5, 157–65, 167; barns, 113, 147, 149;

exemptions, 142–3, 148–9, 152, 157–9; farmers, 113, 146, 153, 162, 167; great, 140, 142, 153, 170, 172; legislation, 21, 139, 158; lesser, 140; mixed, 139–40; personal, 139–40; predial, 139–40; pre-Reformation, 140–1, 143, 157–61; prosecution, 149–50, 153; rectorial, 165, 168, 176; resistance to, 146–7, 149; small, 140, 142, 146, 153
Townson, Thomas, 70
transubstantiation, 7, 184–7, 189, 198
Tunbridge Wells (Kent), 220

Uffculme (Devon), 219
unchurched women, 195, 199
Utie, Thomas, 163–4

Valor Ecclesiasticus, 170–1
vernacular, 9, 54, 122, 184–5, 189, 198, 242
vestments: Catholic, 4–5, 93, 104–5; controversy over, 38; reformed, 10, 105; repurposed, 104; sold, 120; visitation articles on, 38
vestries: development, 76–9; levies, 103, 117; and oligarchy, 77, 80–1, 83–6; power of, 16, 86–7; pre-Reformation, 77–9; select, 79–81, 83–4; and visitations, 87
via media, 20, 64, 74, 188, 208
via sola, 20, 93, 208
visitation articles: on boundaries, 46–7; and Catholic suppression, 38, 47, 104; on charity, 152; checks and balances, 44; on church ales, 116–17; on church attendance, 46, 48; on church fabric, 93, 104; on churchwardens, 64, 73; on communion, 209–10, 227; early, 31, 38; on excommunication, 235, 241; flexibility, 38–9, 46; on illegal items, 93–4; on morality, 39–40, 194; versus statutory law, 37–8; on vestments, 38; on vestries, 87
visitations: and Catholic suppression, 94, 104; and church maintenance, 112–14; clergy as main targets, 40–1; development, 13, 29, 40; expanded, 16, 40, 48, 65, 176; flexibility, 38, 46; frequency, 29–31, 35, 96; length of, 37, 40; to monitor clergy, 40–1; and morality, 39–40, 44; preliminaries, 31–2; process, 31–3, 36; records of, 30–1; response to, 35–6; role of churchwardens, 42, 59, 87–8; as system of justice, 26, 29, 35, 37, 63

Walsingham, Francis, 213
Warblington (Hampshire), 220
Ward, Samuel, 193, 200
wardens. *See* churchwardens
Wardon, Isabell, 228
Wardon, William, 228
Warthill (Yorkshire), 113
Wary, John, 53
Waterhouse, Gregory, 159
Watson, Elizabeth, 24–6, 45, 49–50, 52
wealth gap, 76, 76–7, 103
Webb, John, 68
Webster, Walter, 24, 45
Wensley, John, 153
West Country, 30, 185, 198, 221

West Riding, 24, 153, 238
West Sussex, 30
Whalley (Lancashire), 27
Wheldrake (Yorkshire), 223
Whitacre, Edward, 154–5
Whitaker, Jeffrey, 3–4
Whitby (Yorkshire), 176
Whitgift, John, 10–11, 13, 29, 35, 53, 168–70, 191, 216–18, 221
Wigan, Agnes, 214
Williams, Thomas, 166
Wiltshire, 3–4, 68–9, 95, 116–17, 206–7, 245
Winchester, 44, 205, 220
Winterslow (Wiltshire), 68, 204
Wolsey, Thomas, 24
women: as church workers, 53, 131, 247; and penance, 52; recusants, 81, 214, 220; unchurched, 195, 199
Woodbury (Devon), 69, 95
Woolton, John, 28–9
Wootton St Lawrence (Hampshire), 205, 207
Worcester, 109, 124, 202
Worcestershire, 206
Worthington, William, 215, 218
Wykeham (Yorkshire), 47

Yarm (Yorkshire), 223
Yatton (Somerset), 96
Yeovil (Somerset), 202
York, 24, 30, 33, 45, 108, 113, 151, 156, 161, 163, 168, 173, 214
Yorkshire, 96, 106, 114, 117, 153, 158–9, 161, 172–3, 193, 199, 224